WHY WOULD I BE
MARRIED HERE?

WHY WOULD I BE MARRIED HERE?

Marriage Migration and Dispossession in Neoliberal India

Reena Kukreja

CORNELL UNIVERSITY PRESS   ITHACA AND LONDON

First published 2022 by Cornell University Press

Library of Congress Cataloging-in-Publication Data

Names: Kukreja, Reena, author.
Title: Why would I be married here? : marriage migration and dispossession
    in neoliberal India / Reena Kukreja.
Description: Ithaca [New York] : Cornell University Press, 2022. |
    Includes bibliographical references and index.
Identifiers: LCCN 2021047842 (print) | LCCN 2021047843 (ebook) |
    ISBN 9781501762550 (hardcover) | ISBN 9781501764134 (paperback) |
    ISBN 9781501762567 (pdf) | ISBN 9781501762574 (epub)
Subjects: LCSH: Intermarriage—India, North. | Married women—India,
    North—Social conditions—21st century. | Migration, Internal—Social
    aspects—India. | Caste—India, North. | India, North—Social conditions—
    21st century.
Classification: LCC HQ1031 .K834 2022 (print) | LCC HQ1031 (ebook) |
    DDC 306.809541—dc23/eng/20211013
LC record available at https://lccn.loc.gov/2021047842
LC ebook record available at https://lccn.loc.gov/2021047843

In loving memory of my dear mother, Urmila Kukreja, strong, gentle, nurturing, and fun-loving. I have so much to learn from you.

This book is a response to and a fulfilment of a promise made in answer to the pointed query of a cross-region bride, Kaushalya. She felt that her voice would gather dust in a notebook on my bookshelf and that nothing would ever change, either for her or for other cross-region brides, who, she was sure, would continue to come to Haryana for reasons similar to hers.

Tell me, what will I gain from this furious writing you are doing in your notebook? Will my reality change? Will I wake up tomorrow morning and find that everyone treats me nicely? Tell me, what is the point of doing all this?

Contents

Preface

"My family is considering 'buying' a bride for my elder brother (*bahar se khar-idne ki sooch rahe hain*). He is thirty-five years old." Pradeep, looking through the rearview mirror at me, smiled as he casually spoke these words.[1] His words jolted me out of my preoccupation with finding a comfortable position in the back of his cab. It was April 2011, and he was taking me on a two-hour ride to a small town about 90 kilometers away from the Indian capital city of New Delhi. I had hired his cab from a neighborhood "taxi station" near my parents' place in New Delhi to go to the Rohtak district, a region in the North Indian state of Haryana.

Pradeep had appeared easygoing, with a curiosity about the world. I was not surprised then that, barely three minutes into my trip, he questioned me about why I wanted to go to a nondescript place in Haryana when cities like Agra and Jaipur, with their touristy attractions of the Taj Mahal, Mughal palaces, and hotels catering to all the comforts desired by tourists, were within a few hours' drive of Delhi.

I was traveling to the rural hinterlands of Haryana to learn more about a crisis that had gradually been unfolding in Haryana's countryside since the mid-1990s: a shortage of women of marriageable age, resulting in almost every village having a sizable number of unmarried adult men. The bride deficit in local marriage pools had led many rural men to disregard taboos on intercaste marriages and instead travel across India in search of wives from distant and economically marginalized states such as West Bengal, Odisha, Assam, Tripura, or Jharkhand. Having grabbed my attention, Pradeep continued, "My brother is a simpleton (*bhola*) and childlike in his behavior, with no steady source of income. No one in our caste (*jaat biradari*) wants to have him as a son-in-law. We have spoken to a couple of agents to find him a suitable wife. There are many people there who have bought brides for their sons. You will find enough people to talk to. So, come to my village, instead, for research."

Given my research preoccupation, I seized the serendipitous encounter with Pradeep to ply him with a series of questions. How common was the practice of "buying" brides in Rajasthan, the region from which Pradeep hailed? Why could his brother not marry locally? Who were the agents or commission-based marriage mediators who had ostensibly just appeared to trade women as a commodity with a "negotiable" price tag? And what about the women's parents? Did the

men and their families ever get to meet the women and learn about their com-
pelling reasons for accepting such marriages? How were the violations of caste
endogamy received by the men's families and kin groups? I was as anxious to
learn how everyone—the women's new husbands, the men's family members,
and the villagers—treated these so-called bought (*kharidi hui*) and other-caste
women (*doosri jaati ki auratein*); I was interested in finding out how the strict
rules of caste behavior and interactions governing daily life between different
castes in the village shaped these women's lives. Was there a difference in their
status and treatment compared with local brides?

Though Pradeep supported the family decision to marry off his elder brother
through this unconventional method, he appeared concerned about the fallout
of this union for future kin relations and for the status of the family.

> It is only because of our inability (*majboori*) to marry locally that we
> are doing this. The household has to run (*ghar to chalana hai*) and
> only a woman can ensure that. However, families that bring in brides
> this way are regarded as a notch below others (*neech nazar se dekhte
> hain*). Behind their back, they are ridiculed. Social relations get strained
> because of this.
>
> My wife and I have had many fights about getting a bride, from "god
> knows what caste," for my elder brother. I am worried too as I have two
> small daughters. This will impact their marriage prospects in our com-
> munity (*biradari*).

Conversing with Pradeep about his family and rearranging my itinerary to
visit his village made the two-hour journey that morning pass quickly, and before
I knew it, we had arrived at Sampla. A small town in the Rohtak district of Haryana, Sampla, with a population of more than 21,000, was dusty and hot. Vast
stretches of fertile agricultural land on either side of national highway NH 10,
which connects the Indian capital of New Delhi to Rohtak and beyond, had been
dug up—a new dual-lane highway was under construction. Signs of feverish construction were everywhere, as people sought to tap into a real estate boom. Property agents had set up business in small one-room shacks by the edge of the
highway. Using catchy hooks such as "throwaway prices" and "affordable dream
villas," they hoped to incite people to invest in offers from newly emerging realty
companies. These gated communities were being constructed on fertile agricultural land that, until a few months ago, had been growing crops of wheat, rice, or
sugarcane. Huge billboards for proposed shopping malls in the area promised
villagers air-conditioned comfort while shopping for branded luxury items.

I had come to Sampla to meet two fieldworkers from a local nongovernmen-
tal organization (NGO), SAHYOG, and to do preliminary fieldwork with a small

sample of cross-region brides. They were also to assist me in conducting a survey of cross-region brides and to set up interviews for the qualitative phase of my research. Santosh, a middle-aged woman from the Jat caste, had been working for the NGO for a couple of years, whereas Sandeep, a young Dalit man, had just been hired a few days before.[2] Given the caste polarization between Jats and Dalits in Haryana, the contradictions inherent in these two working as a team were not lost on me. Both were locals, lived in villages near Sampla, and were familiar with this new form of tradition-bending matrimony occurring in their region.

Fresh from my encounter with Pradeep and his narrative of bride buying, I anxiously plied Santosh and Sandeep with countless questions in the small office of the NGO. Santosh, wiping the sweat off her face with one end of her *dupatta*, dismissed all my concerns and worries with just one sentence: "They are living a life of comfort here, they face no difficulties" (*ji, bahut mauj mein raven hain sab, taqleef koi na se*). I prodded her to elaborate. It came out that, while Santosh had met some cross-region brides during the course of her NGO work, either at meetings or at social functions such as *kirtans* (religious congregations accompanied with devotional songs), she had never really had a one-on-one conversation with any of them: "They do not interact much with local women. They keep to themselves."

Sandeep also knew of several families in his village with cross-region brides. According to him, the women were all Biharan or Bangalan (colloquial terms used to refer to women from the East Indian states of Bihar and West Bengal). He elaborated: "They are all dark-skinned and from low castes. They do not look like us. We know people from Bihar or Bangal are poor. Only *they* would sell their daughters to agents." Sandeep's assertion was based on the presence of migrant workers from Bihar in Haryana. Following the Green Revolution—a World Bank–funded strategy introduced in India in the mid-1960s to improve agricultural production through the use of hybrid, high-yielding varieties of seeds— the labor flow of landless Biharis to Haryana and Punjab has played a key role in constructing the stereotype of poverty-stricken Biharis.

That morning, I had more to dwell on than I had anticipated. However, my ruminations on colorism and ethnocentrism were cut short by Santosh briskly putting an end to any further conversation with "*Chaloji,* we can continue discussing this until night time. We have given a time to the brides and they will be expecting us."

Santosh and I walked a couple of kilometers to nearby Khurdpur, a village where, according to her, four Biharans were married to local men. One bride had gone home with her husband to visit her parents, so we were hoping to meet the other three brides that day. The village appeared deserted, as most people were in the fields harvesting the winter crop of wheat. Santosh and I walked in the hot sun along a wide brick-paved road in the village to reach a two-room, single-story house. The bride, Veena, was not at home, but her thirty-five-year-old husband, Devesh, welcomed us inside. He had taken a day off from his farm work to meet with us. He had been unable to marry locally as he did not have a government job or own land, the two most desired traits for grooms from his Jat caste. A distant relative suggested that he should bring in a wife from another region, just like a man from his village had done. Intrigued, Devesh got in touch with that man and requested that he find him a wife "just like his." The sum of Rs 30,000 (approximately US$435) that he paid the man included the cost of the travel, lodging, and bridal clothes, and all expenses related to the marriage ceremony. He acknowledged that, "there was a bit of fluffing up about my earning capacity. Not huge lies but small ones, such as I owned ten buffalos instead of the four, and that I owned land instead of the fact that I was a tenant farmer."

At the back of the house, a long thin section of the courtyard was thatch-covered and housed the family's prized possessions: four buffalos. While we were talking to Devesh, his wife, Veena, came in carrying a headload of freshly cut hay and grass. Apologizing for making us wait, she proceeded to light a fire in a small hearth and insisted that Santosh and I have tea and freshly made rotis with her.

After my conversation with Pradeep about bride buying, I was anxious to learn how Veena had become married to Devesh, and whether the agent had paid her parents money for the marriage. Veena answered, "My parents have not sold me, they married me off" (*becha naa hai, byaah kiya hai mera*). She told us the story, which began with a woman from a neighboring village, married to a man from Haryana, who had approached her landless father with the proposal. At first, her father, who worked as a casual wage laborer, refused, as he did not want to marry his daughter off to a man far from his region. But, in the end, the "no dowry and all wedding expenses paid" marriage offer was too appealing to turn down. Her wedding had taken place in a village temple, with just a handful of close family members in attendance. Veena recounted, "My father and two paternal cousins (*chachera bhai*) accompanied me here after my wedding. They stayed here for ten days to verify whether the agent had been lying or not. They checked facts about my husband from the neighbors here. Once they were reassured that all was okay, they left for the village."

She clarified that she was not Biharan. Instead, her family was from Uttar Pradesh, a state neighboring Haryana. She commented that everyone in the village called her Biharan, so much so that even she, at times, would forget that she was from Uttar Pradesh: "I am regarded as a Biharan by everyone. Even my husband's family members, who know better, call me Biharan." She appeared both resentful of and resigned to this label.

Our next stop in the village was a long rectangular room that appeared to have been built as an afterthought on the roof of a house. The exposed brick dwelling could be reached only by climbing a metal ladder. This was the home of Ashok and Nitu. According to Santosh, Ashok had married his cross-region bride a few months ago, after years of trying to find a wife locally from his caste pool. Santosh assured me that Ashok's wife, Nitu, was definitely a Biharan: "She is pitch black in her complexion—looks like a Biharan." When we arrived, Nitu was at home watching a reality show on a small television.

Like Veena, Nitu also clarified that she was not from Bihar. She had come from the Central Indian state of Maharashtra. When I asked her why people in her husband's village thought that she was a Biharan, she simply shrugged her shoulders and said, "No idea why." She belonged to a Dalit caste. Her parents were landless, and the entire family worked as seasonal wage laborers on rich farmers' land to survive. Nitu spoke of her experiences back home:

> The farmers would make advances at my sister and I, but we would re-
> main silent, as we needed to be paid our wages. Because I am dark-
> complexioned, local men demanded a higher dowry in order to marry
> me. In desperation, my father approached a village woman, married to
> a Haryanvi man, to find a Haryanvi husband for me. We had heard that
> they did not take any dowry. Life is so unfair. My younger sister, slightly
> less dark than myself, has got married near our village, while fate has
> tossed me here, away from my family, my village, and my region (*desh*).

Ashok and the other woman's husband worked together in a small factory producing ancillary automotive parts, and so the matchmaking was easy. Nitu's father felt reassured that, as the bride-turned-matchmaker was a "daughter of the village" (*gaon ki beti*), he could put community pressure on her if the marriage did not turn out right. Nitu was quick to offer that, although her husband Ashok was caring, the same could not be said about his family, who treated her as an outcaste. Ashok belonged to the dominant peasant caste of Jats. In this context, Nitu's Dalit caste was viewed as a disgrace by his parents and siblings, and so they stigmatized her constantly in everyday interactions. Things had come to such a head that Ashok, at Nita's urging, had broken away from the joint family setup and had taken this room as a rental in the same village. The continual humiliation that Nitu faced because of the tag of *neech jaat* (low caste) had made her both withdrawn and rebellious. She now refused to interact with anyone in the village; instead she chose to keep to herself in the room and whiled away her time watching television. She summed this up with a defiant expression, "I can choose to do what I wish."

Our last stop was Geeta's house. We were met at the door by her mother-in-law and her husband's sister (*nanad*), while Geeta stood nervously behind them.

Acting as her gatekeepers, they quizzed both Santosh and me about my research motives before allowing me to speak to her separately. Her mother-in-law said that the family had paid an agent an all-inclusive sum of Rs 80,000 for her son's marriage. The agent, married to a woman from Odisha, had vouched that he could set up a marriage to a woman from his wife's village. True to the agent's words, Prem, the forty-year-old who worked as part-time help in a small sweet-meat shop (*halwai dukaan*), and who had been rejected by local families because of his precarious employment, and old age, was soon married to the twenty-year-old Geeta. I spoke with Geeta alone in a small dark anteroom, where an oversized bed took up most of the space already crowded with large aluminum trunks placed one on top of another on one side of the room. This was where she spent almost all of her free time when she was not doing household chores. Geeta spoke in a low voice that was sometimes hard to hear. She was angry with the agent and his wife, who had lied about Prem. According to Geeta,

> The mediating couple had said to my father that not only did Prem run his own sweetmeat shop and have five buffalos, he also owned two acres of land. You have no idea how poor my family is. There have been many nights when the entire family has gone to bed hungry. My father thought that at least one child of his would not have to suffer want. I was re-pulsed by Prem's appearance when I first saw him. He was old, bald-ing, and had a potbelly. I had different hopes for my marriage—to get married to a man my age. What other option did I have? An adult woman has to get married, doesn't she?

After arriving in Khurdpur, Geeta had soon realized that her marriage was based on lies. Prem did not own a sweetshop or the two acres of land. Prem and his family, fearful that Geeta might leave him to return home, monitored her each and every move and did not allow her to step out of the house alone. At times, she felt like a prisoner. Despite this, she had decided to continue on in the marriage, as she felt that it was "written in her fate" (*kismet*). However, she did call her parents to "tell them about the bride mediator's lies. Her matchmak-ing career has come to a halt, as villagers now know that she takes money from men's families and lies to people back home."

In just a few hours, my varied encounters had made it abundantly clear to me that no single truth claim could be simplistically made about these marriages or the way these women had ended up as brides of Haryanvi men. Each com-monly held notion about cross-region marriages, the brides, their parents, the mediators, or even whether these alliances constitute societally approved mar-riages or instances of bride selling and coerced marriages had been contested and turned on its head. The narratives of the brides challenged and disputed assumptions of the homogeneity of the modes through which these marriages were arranged; instead, the processes of mediation, motives, and strategies were replete with contradictions and ambiguities.

I ended up taking Pradeep up on his offer and going to his village several times during the course of my four-year-long research study, staying with either his mother or his elder sister. The family, which was warm and loving, embraced me as a sister (*behen*) and took me into their fold, and also welcomed my then three-year-old daughter as another grandchild, who played in the sand with other village kids and who they called out to return home as the sun set. Through them and other families, I obtained a close look at the world of dubious marriage agents, traffickers, and trafficked women. I also was able to grasp the contradictions and paradoxes of paying money to an agent to get a *bahu* (daughter-in-law), just as much as I observed the discrimination faced by the brides on account of their low or suspect caste status within the intimate sphere of family relations.

Practically, in the field, my own "intercaste" marriage to a man from Bihar—a region much maligned in Haryana and Rajasthan, where Biharis are the butt of ethnocultural chauvinism—and the accompaniment of my "dark-complexioned" young daughter during my fieldwork unexpectedly opened new areas of inquiry. It led the brides to interrogate me about my experience and simultaneously share theirs. While viewing me as an outsider precisely because of my multiple privileges of class, caste, education, and location, at the same time, their assumptions about my shared experience enabled the brides to speak, in great detail, about the workings of caste discrimination, colorism, and ethnocentrism in their daily existence. They shared stories not only of unfulfilled desires and broken wishes, but also of their rebellions and resistances. Many of my unplanned and long discussions gave me deep insights into the multifaceted dimensions of their marriages and a privileged view of their everyday lived experience as multiply-othered migrant brides in North India.

Acknowledgments

This book would not have been possible without the cross-region brides who reposed trust in me, took time out of their busy daily routines, and made me privy to their intimate thoughts, feelings, anxieties, and anguish. Their active and enthusiastic participation in the fieldwork, whether it related to locating other cross-region brides in conjugal villages, organizing focus groups, connecting me to their natal families, or phoning their parents to ensure they "found time" for me during my fieldwork in the natal regions, all stemmed from their desire to have their experiences validated and their "voices heard." I am indebted to them for trusting me.

At Cornell University Press, I thank the individuals whose faith in this book helped bring it to light. To Jim Lance, my commissioning editor, a deep gratitude for your continual encouragement and support in shepherding this book to completion and for pushing me to hone my argument. You asked tough but very welcome questions about whom this book was for and what I wanted to narrate in it. Truly, I could not have asked for a better editor. Thanks to the two anonymous reviewers for your generous and useful comments.

To Awet Weldemichael, my dear friend and colleague, who I now call my brother in Kingston, I have no words to express my gratitude for your unstinting encouragement and advice in helping me navigate the publishing world. You have always been there for me whenever I sought assistance or a pep talk. A big thank you also to your partner, Miriam, and the two darlings, Farris and Zoskales, who bring such joy in my life.

I am most thankful to Renu Wadehra, then senior advisor, development, the Royal Norwegian Embassy at New Delhi, India; and Bodil Maal, senior advisor, Department of Economic Development, Gender and Governance, Norwegian Aid, who saw the need for this study and wholeheartedly supported the initial funding from the Royal Norwegian Embassy, New Delhi. Support was also provided by a Social Science and Humanities Research Council of Canada doctoral grant and the Graduate Dean's Grant for Doctoral Field Research.

A heartfelt thanks to Abigail Bakan, who took on the task of being an exemplary intellectual mentor to me. Thanks also to Magda Lewis for her discussions about ethnographic refusals and ethics, and to Margaret Little for her tireless engagement with my work. Prem Chowdhry's writings on rural Haryanvi society have been a continual source of intellectual inspiration for me. I value her discussions on caste contestations in Haryana. I am grateful to Allison Goebel, who read the rough manuscript and encouraged me to publish it as a book. I am appreciative of the hawk-eyed Angela Pietrobon's work in copyediting my manuscript. Her pointed questions and clarifications through the various drafts have helped make the manuscript shine. Thanks also to Brigid Goulem for taking on the thankless chore of cross-checking references.

From the bottom of my heart (and my stomach too), I thank the many people in the villages for their warm hospitality, endless rounds of milky tea, hot meals provided to sustain me and my research assistants, and for the love and care they gave to my daughter Ambalika. I also want to acknowledge Pradeep and his entire family, who accepted me as one of their own and allowed me to witness their negotiations with marriage agents to secure a cross-region bride for one of their sons. I acknowledge the unstinting hard work of my research assistants, translators, and interpreters in ensuring the accuracy of this research. Two of my research assistants, Santosh and Sandeep from Haryana, merit special mention, as they became good friends and allies during the long research process. Their efforts in tracing marriage agents, husband brokers, bride brokers, and families on the cusp of getting cross-region brides were invaluable.

A heartfelt thanks to Sunder Lal ji for facilitating my initial forays into this subject in the Rewari region. I owe a big thanks to the late Dr. Abdul Aziz for encouraging me to research marriage migration among the Meo and for providing support, guidance, and keen insights during fieldwork. Thanks also to his wife, Naseem Apa, for making my stay comfortable in Beesru. The support of Rajib Haldar from CINI was valuable for my research in Cooch Behar. I am grateful to Ananya Bhattacharya and, in particular, Manas Acharya from Banglanatak.com for connecting me with artists Laxmi Devi and Swarna "Rupban" Chitrakar. To Swarna ji and Laxmi ji, I am humbled by your artistic interpretations of cross-region matrimonies.

I am grateful to Kuntala and R. K. Ray for being gracious hosts in Balasore, Odisha; Partha Sarkar and Martin Pinto, for coming up with answers and solutions to any and all of the oddest of my queries and requests; and Rajiv Pratap Singh "Rudy," Ranjanesh Sahai, and Manjula Singh for helping out with travel and accommodation during my fieldwork. Thanks also to Ujjwal Singh and Anupama Roy for always being there when I needed support.

I value the friendship of Reem Khan, Meri and Greg Mcleod, Cindy McQueen, Joy McBride, Mikaela Hughes, Margaret and Ian Hughes, Ramneek Pooni, Anne Marie Murphy, Saraswathi Basappa, Rene Unger, Kiran Basappa-Unger, Ena Dua, Kiran Mirchandani, Kim Rygiel, Martine Bresson, Lorraine Poitras, Margaret Little, Marc Epprecht, Susan Lord, and Clarke Mackey. They have helped me keep my sanity intact and encouraged and nourished my intellectual journey.

Parts of the manuscript were published as articles, as "Caste and Cross-Region Marriages in Haryana, India: Experience of Dalit Cross-Region Brides in Jat Households," in *Modern Asian Studies* 52 (2): 492–531; "An Unwanted Weed: Children of Cross-Region Unions Confront Intergenerational Stigma of Caste, Ethnicity and Religion," in *Journal of Intercultural Studies* 39 (4): 382–398; and "Colorism as Marriage Capital: Cross-Region Marriage Migration in India and Dark-Skinned Migrant Brides," in *Gender & Society* 35 (1): 85–109. I am grateful to the publishers for permission to reprint later versions of these articles.

The unstinting support and encouragement from my parents, Urmila and Krishan, and my in-laws, Shashi Rani and Ishwari Prasad, has nurtured my intellectual journey. Completing this manuscript has been bittersweet, as two of my staunchest supporters—my mother, Urmila, and my mother-in-law, Shashi Rani—both passed away before seeing it come to light. My father, Krishan, who now lives with me in Canada, has borne my absentmindedness with boundless affection and patience. Thank you, Dad, for your loving tolerance of everything, including having to eat bean soup as a quick meal between my stints of writing.

Ambalika, our daughter, has grown up with this book and has suffered from my long absences from home for fieldwork and my distractedness while writing. I am appreciative of her company on field trips and for her lack of complaints about the long hours of work, missed and late meals, and my neglect of her during the interviews. Amba, I look forward to many field trips with you in the future.

I cannot find adequate words to talk about my soul mate and partner, Paritosh Kumar, who has been my pillar of strength and guiding star. He is my friend, mentor, critic, sounding board, and always the first reader of my works. His encouragement of all my ventures, in both documentary film and research, has allowed me to leave home for protracted periods of fieldwork without guilt of familial abandonment. He has supported me during moments of self-doubt, and intellectually challenged me, at every step of the writing process, to think more critically about the interconnections among neoliberalism, class, caste, and gender. His patience and easy laughter keep me grounded, always. Paritosh, I really cannot imagine a life without you.

I reserve the last thanks, the deepest of all, to my late mother, Urmila, for encouraging me to undertake doctoral studies in midlife and for being my emotional anchor. She had hoped that we could have "her and me" time undivided by field trips and my preoccupation with research, data, and manuscript writing. I failed in not being able to finish this one faster. You also cheated me by leaving a bit too early. Perhaps, in the afterlife, we can have chai and uninterrupted long conversations. Mamma, this book is for you. I hope you like it.

WHY WOULD I BE
MARRIED HERE?

MAP 1. Map of India with conjugal and natal research states. Map designed by Aarti for the author.

INTRODUCTION
Few Wives Available Locally

During the run-up to the Indian parliamentary election in spring 2014, the slogan *Bahu Dilao, Vote Pao* (Get me a bride, take my vote), a unique electoral demand for wives in exchange for votes, was raised by an organized group of unmarried men from a village in Haryana, India, called Avivahit Purush Sangathan, or Unmarried Men's Collective.[1] Soon after, during the October 2014 assembly elections for Haryana, one politician went to the extent of promising that, if elected, he would bring brides from Bihar for unmarried Haryanvi men.[2] Never before in the history of Indian elections had aspiring lawmakers used the pawn of "wives" to lure voters. Usually, election demands from the populace and promises by candidates revolved around employment, health care, or infrastructure provisions like electricity, water, and better roads. To this list, for the first time, the new scarce commodity of "women" was added as yet another item that could be bartered for votes.

This marriage crisis, apparently brought on by a bride deficit, it appeared, had been foretold. From 1991 onward, India's decennial censuses had begun flagging the lessening number of women in northern India, in regions such as Punjab, Haryana, Rajasthan, and Western Uttar Pradesh. By 2011 in India, the numbers of "missing women"—a term first used by economist Amartaya Sen (1990) to refer to a shortage of women in relation to men in the adult population—stood at a staggering 37.7 million (Census of India 2011a). The child sex ratio, or CSR, a benchmark of the ratio of females in the population to 1,000 males in the same age group, had declined from 927 females per 1,000 males in 2001 to 914 in 2011, with the biggest drops concentrated in North India and northwest India (Census

of India 2011a). It appeared that the Indian government's family planning policies, put in place to limit family size, had intersected with the proliferation of
new reproductive technologies that enable the detection and elimination of female fetuses, resulting in substantially fewer numbers of girls being born (Jha
et al. 2011). A combination of sex-selective abortions, infanticide, and neglect of
the girl child by discrimination in health care and nutrition, resulting in higher
female infant and child mortality, was also attributed to this crisis of missing
women.

Closely linked with this skewed sex ratio was the emerging evidence about a
new tradition-breaking form of marriage-making in rural North India that began in the late 1990s. A significant bride deficit within the local marriage pool in
almost every village in states such as Haryana and Rajasthan had created a male
marriage squeeze for poor rural men. This led many lower-class rural bachelors—
in particular the Meo Muslim and dominant peasant-caste Hindu groups of Jats,
Yadavs, and Ahirs—to incur huge expenses to travel long distances across India,
oftentimes involving days of travel, to distant states such as Assam, West Bengal,
Jharkhand, Tripura, Odisha, and Maharashtra in search of brides.[3] What marked
these marriages as distinctly different was not only that this set of brides lack
shared cultural markers with their North Indian husbands and conjugal communities, such as language, customs, and food habits, but also that they belonged
to a different caste, ethnicity, region, and sometimes even religion than their husbands. These matrimonies clearly transgressed customary marriage norms, which
regulate matrimonies within one's caste group and/or religion.

This book presents a study of this new form of noncustomary marriage-
making that emerged among both Hindus and Muslims in rural North India in
the late 1990s and increased exponentially within a few short years. In popular
discourse, these matrimonies are overwhelmingly framed and understood
within a discourse of bridal slavery, bride trafficking, and the low societal worth
accorded to Indian women. They are also analyzed as a tragic outcome of skewed
sex ratios and girl dis-preference. Instead of taking either discourse as a foundation for analysis, this book begins with a simple query that has long-term gendered implications: What makes these contemporary cross-region marriages,
conducted "across regions" of India and involving migration of the brides, any
different than other marriages? After all, migration for marriage is not a new
phenomenon in India. Over 80 percent of "lifetime migrants" in India are women
who cite marriage as the main reason for migration from their place of birth
(Rosenzweig and Stark 1989, 906). One study estimates that twenty million Indian women undertake marriage migration each year (Fulford 2013, 2), with a
significant proportion of such marriages being rural-to-rural in nature.

Contemporary cross-region marriages can be considered to have begun occurring in North India in roughly two phases. In the first phase, lasting roughly until the mid- to late 1990s, these occurred sporadically and were not specifically aimed at filling a female deficit in these communities. Livelihood strategies took Haryanvi or Rajasthani men to distant regions of India, where their contact with local communities eventually resulted in marriages with local women. These one-off weddings rarely led to more marriages between the two communities. However, this trend had drastically changed by the late 1990s as the female deficit increased in the men's regions. In this second and current phase, increasing numbers of locally rejected North Indian rural men began deliberately traveling to the so-called female-rich regions of India in a bid to obtain wives. Tapping in to this desperation, a new breed of commercial marriage facilitators emerged to mediate marriages, for a fee, between strangers from different parts of India.

In this book I situate Indian cross-region marriages within the larger, global contexts of marriage-related migratory flows of brides within Southeast and East Asia, while underscoring the distinctly different nature of the marriage migration undertaken in contemporary India. I interrogate whether these marriages should be considered a consequence of the skewed sex ratio or whether other, more complex, reasons are precipitating such alliances. Are the women trafficked, or are these marriages a carefully considered strategic migration strategy? What are these migrant women's lived realities as brides in rural North India, where deeply entrenched ideologies of caste, colorism, and ethnocentrism shape the everyday dynamics of social relations and access to resources and power?

Answering these questions has now become urgent, as the female deficit is expected to widen significantly in India in the coming years. It is estimated that, by the mid-twenty-first century, the number of eligible grooms in the country will exceed eligible brides by more than 50 percent (Guilmoto 2012, 92). In fact, one annual economic report from the government of India starkly stated that, by 2014, the numbers of missing women in India had reached nearly sixty-three million; moreover, for each year, more than two million women had gone missing across a range of age groups because of sex-selective abortions, disease, neglect, and inadequate nutrition (Government of India n.d., 112). A 2017 report reiterates the World Bank projection that, by 2031, the sex ratio will have fallen to 898 girls for 1,000 boys (Government of India 2017, 10). India's decennial census, last undertaken in 2011, also revealed that the skewed child sex ratio is not confined to North Indian states such as Haryana, Punjab, and Rajasthan; other parts of India have also begun displaying a skewed sex ratio at birth, attributable to sex-selective abortion and the preference for male children (Census of

India, 2011b). It is assumed that the resulting male marriage squeeze within India will lead to increased movement of women around the country and to higher numbers of noncustomary marriages, as desperate bachelors seek brides from outside their local marriage pools (Guilmoto 2012). This prediction raises valid concerns about the erosion of gender rights, not only for the migrating brides, but for all women in India.

Using ethnographic evidence and adopting an intersectional theoretical synthesis of feminist political economy and Dalit feminism, in this book I offer an intimate account of the lived experience of cross-region brides within the Meo and Hindu communities in rural North India. I borrow from David Harvey's (2005) theorization of "accumulation by dispossession," extending it to an analysis of cross-region marriages in India. Harvey describes the current neoliberal moment as a set of contemporary processes of dispossession that capital uses in its quest for expansion. This conceptualization is critical in furthering our understanding of the distinctive gendered consequence of the expansion of neoliberal capitalism (Harvey 2005).

Most discussions of contemporary accumulation by dispossession in India focus on the question of land grabs or state-sponsored violence as the state acts as an agent for capital against its own poor citizenry (Levein 2018). In this study I urge readers to shift attention to a significant but ignored aspect of a particular type of contemporary dispossession that has been unfolding silently, yet quite violently, within the intimate sphere of marriage and family life for lower-class rural women. It foregrounds the intimate, daily, and gendered reverberations of the structural violence of neoliberal accumulation by dispossession, revealing how it preys on preexisting discriminations and inequalities to constrict marriage options and reshape social relations for poor women from socioeconomically marginalized groups in India's development peripheries.

This conceptual framework of gendered matrimonial dispossession challenges us to think beyond the blunt categories of caste assimilation, sex deficit, or bridal trafficking in studying these multiply transgressive matrimonies. Instead, the book traces the migrant brides' marriage choices and everyday lives as married women within the intermeshed structural violence of capital accumulation, caste discrimination, religious fundamentalism, and ethnocentrism within India. This micro-study proves that these multiple oppressions have hyper-commodified the female body, particularly of women from historically depressed communities; intensified gender subordination; eroded women's bargaining ability around both their labor and bodies; and increased their vulnerability to new forms of gender-based violence. On a broader level, it offers a macro-analytical framework through which feminists everywhere can acquire a better understanding about the reshaping of structural oppressions due to contemporary forces of neoliberalism, which force poor women from marginalized communities worldwide into making compromised choices about their bodies, their labor, and their lives.

Marriage Migration

Within Asia, migration for marriage is not new. From the mid-1950s onward, as South Asian and East Asian men migrated for better economic opportunities, they sought to maintain connections with their homelands, communities, and families through remittances and arranged marriages with women from their home countries (Ballard 1990; Charsley 2013; Maunaguru 2019; Palriwala and Uberoi 2008; Sabur 2014; Thai 2008). However, since the late 1980s, within Southeast and East Asia, non-mono-ethnic, or non-mono-racial marriage migration has emerged, with a migratory flow of women going from lower-income countries such as Vietnam, China, Indonesia, Thailand, and the Philippines to Taiwan, Japan, and South Korea (Faier 2009; Nyugen and Tran 2010; Suzuki 2005). Such marriage flows are propelled by the rejection of rural men in their local marriage market for reasons that include poverty or low earning capacity, physical handicap, older age, divorce, lower education achievement, and local women's rejection of the traditional marriage package, which means living in rural, extended-family households and caring for elderly in-laws (Cheng 2013; Freeman 2011; Nakamatsu 2005). These men thus look to lower-income countries to find women to marry.

The rich vein of scholarly work on cross-border marriage migration discusses a wide range of topics, including what motivates women to become marriage migrants (Nyugen and Tran 2010); routes and modes of marriage matchmaking, including the role of commercial brokers, bride mediators, and traffickers (Duong, Bélanger, and Hong 2007; Wang and Chang 2002); citizenship rights of marriage migrants (Hwang 2015; Toyota 2008); adjustment problems of marriage migrants (Cheng 2013; Freeman 2011); and questions of racial or social "othering" and assimilation within receiving societies (Lee, Seol, and Cho 2006; Nakamatsu 2005), among others. These works reveal that the reasons for such marriage migration are complex and fluid and need to be understood as part of people's coping strategies in the larger contexts of globalization and structural adjustment programs in sending countries (Hsia 2004; Hsia 2008), and citizenship regimes in receiving countries (Chao 2004; Freeman 2011).

India and the countries in Southeast and East Asia, where cross-border marriage migration is taking place on a large scale, are marked by many socioeconomic and political commonalities. First, these countries are confronted with a male marriage squeeze. Second, all the source countries, also like India, underwent a drastic makeover of their economy around the same time period, from the mid- to late 1980s to the early 1990s, with the adoption of structural adjustment programs at the behest of the World Bank and the International Monetary Fund. Third, these marriages are undertaken almost entirely by rural "farm bachelors." Finally, discourses of racial and ethnic purity, central in matrimonial alliances undertaken locally, are often breached in cross-border weddings in these countries. Despite these similarities, one single difference makes marriage migration in India distinct from intra-Asia marriages, and that is caste.

Situating Caste in Marriage-Making in India

The singular and most significant distinction of Indian cross-region matrimonies rests on the fact that these matrimonies breach customary marriage rules of endogamy followed by both Hindus and Meo Muslims in North India. This transgression can be understood only by recognizing the centrality of caste and religion in governing people's lives and the key role of marriage as a social institution in upholding caste hierarchies in present-day India.

Caste is commonly understood as both an ideology and a rigid hierarchical descent-based kinship system among the Hindus, in which four castes, or *varnas*, are arranged in a pyramid-like structure with Brahmans (priests) at the top, followed by Kshatriyas (warriors), then Vaishyas (merchants and traders), and Shudras (peasants and artisans) at the bottom. Apart from these four castes considered as *savarna*, or pure within the *varna* ideology, a large number of people known as *Avarna*, or "without varna," remain "outside" of the caste system as "outcastes" or "untouchables," as their "touch" or even their shadow is considered ritually polluting to other caste groups. Adivasis,[4] or India's tribal population, similarly remains outside this caste system. In Haryana and Rajasthan, among the Hindus, an overwhelming majority of the bride seekers are Jats, Yadav, and Ahirs, groups that have acquired a dominant caste status in the region because of their dominance in landownership. Ritually, these three castes are located in the bottommost Shudra *varna*, that is, just above the Dalits in the Brahmanical caste hierarchy. The Shudra *varna*, though not deemed "untouchable," forms the peasant proprietary and artisan classes, with tremendous socioeconomic variations occurring among its constituent subcastes. The elites from these three groups, because of their dominance over landholdings in these states, wield considerable sociopolitical clout within this region.

Suvira Jaiswal points to the material basis of caste, with its dependence on land and landownership, as a determinant for caste status and hierarchy in the *varna* order. She argues that caste and class are synonymous, and that caste is a "system . . . in which differences in the distribution of economic and political power are expressed through . . . restrictions" (2000, 34). Jodhka similarly argues that, in relation to rural society and agrarian relations, caste is "conceptualized as a material reality, shaping the economics of inequality and exploitation in the countryside" (2016, 232). This edifice of caste stratifications is asserted through closed and ranked social groups called *jatis* within each *varna*. Usually territorially bound to a specific geographical space, *jatis*, or subcaste groups, are further subdivided into exogamous patrilineal clan groups called *got* or *gotra*. In India, "caste" is used interchangeably with *varna* or *jati*; however, in reality, it is the *jati* or subcaste that determines everyday rules and regulations of behavior and interaction among various caste subgroups.

When one speaks of intercaste marriage in India, then, one refers to taboo marriages, either between different *varnas* or between different *jatis* within the same *varna*. Individual autonomy in mate selection is usually overridden in favor of pragmatic matrimonial choices to ensure that caste hierarchies that otherwise might get eroded are maintained. According to Uberoi, arranged marriages account for over 90 percent of marriages and are not limited to rural society alone (2006, 24). Though hypergamous alliances, or those where the women marry up the socioeconomic ladder, oftentimes involve different regions, there usually is a geographical boundary marking the imaginary cutoff for such unions. Spatial limits are created naturally, as the desired clan groups (*gotras* or *gots*) for marriage alliances are normally concentrated in one particular region and not found elsewhere.

Norms for social behavior and interactions are often dictated by dominant caste groups. In Haryana, it is the Jats, while in Rajasthan, both the Jats and the Rajputs among the Hindus have shaped the trajectory of social relations mimicked by other caste groups. In these two regions, marriage rules on caste endogamy include three- or four-*got* exogamy, namely that of the father's, mother's, and paternal grandmother's *gots*. This prohibition extends to all *gots* and *jatis* within the same village, as people falling under this exclusion are considered brothers and sisters, thus making relationships and marriages taboo between them, as they are considered incestuous (Chowdhry 2007). Historically, intercaste marriages, or those between high-caste men and low-caste women, did take place, but primarily as secondary alliances. This practice, followed mainly by agriculturalist caste groups such as the Jats, Yadavs, and Ahirs in this region, allowed widowed men from these groups to enter into secondary unions with low-caste women as a way to access their productive and reproductive labor (Chowdhry 2007, 46–49). The practice also extended to caste-endogamous re-marriages, specifically between deserted, widowed, or divorced women and their brother-in-law or with another man within the clan.

The patriarchal institution of marriage and endogamy, or marriage within the same *jati*, is pivotal in facilitating the perpetuation of unequal caste hierar-chies (Chakravarti 2003, 27). *Jati* operates as a closed rank within which mar-riage can occur only between its members while following the rules of village exogamy and caste endogamy. With women considered as "gateways . . . to [the] caste system" (Chakravarti 2003, 67), gender subordination by control of female sexuality through arranged marriage is vital to ensuring the reproduction of caste-based stratification and economic hierarchies. Jaiswal argues that patri-archy is "intrinsic to the process of stratification" of the *varna*-based class struc-ture and that endogamy is an "effort to regulate and reproduce patriarchy as well as hierarchy of social groups" (Jaiswal 2000, 9). She contends that endog-amy is, at present, more important for the elites for the maintenance of the caste system, which is faced with threats from globalization and capitalist modes of production (Jaiswal 2000).

The Indian Muslims, despite Islam's emphasis on an egalitarian society, echo the social stratification of Hindus based on occupation and birth. Sectarian iden-tity based on Shia or Sunni beliefs and people's ancestry also creates differences between groups of Indian Muslims (Bhatty 1996). Very much like with the caste Hindus, North Indian Muslims, including the Meo, follow the Hindu marriage customs of caste endogamy, territorial exogamy, and patri(viri)local residence for newlywed women. Among the Meo, marriage with other Indian Muslims is frowned on and invites clan censure (Jamous 2003, 11). The Meo marry within the fifty-two *gotras* comprising Meos while maintaining village and *gotra* exog-amy (Chauhan 2003). Instances where customary marriage boundaries were overstepped were strictly dealt with by Meo caste councils through the social boycott of erring families (Chauhan 2004). Furthermore, despite being Muslim and allowed to marry up to four wives, the men usually do not opt for secondary unions, and if they do, approval has to be obtained from the first wife (Chauhan 2004).

Despite claims of a modernizing impulse of Indians attributed to India's in-tegration into the global capitalist market, increased rural–urban migration, the unquestioning embrace of Western cultural values by most urban elites, and the supposed irrelevance of caste in everyday encounters in many urban areas, reli-gion and caste still play a determining role in marriages among Hindus and Mus-lims. In contemporary India, contrary to the belief that caste would wither to give way to individual merit, its influence has become stronger as it "shapes opportunity structures, status differences, and cultural values" (Jodhka 2016, 229). Marriage is considered a social obligation that not only brings two people together, but also cements a union between families of equal caste and class status, with isogamous (status equal) or hypergamous alliances preferred by the women's families. Prem Chowdhry, in her discussion of marriage-making in rural Haryana, blandly states that "desire, choice, and love are . . . separated from the institution of marriage, which is about social reproduction" (2007, 2). Studies on intercaste marriage in urban India reveal a strong preference for same-caste marriages (Ahuja and Ostermann 2016), with one survey from 2014 revealing that intercaste marriages in both rural and urban India make up a mere 5.4 percent of marriages, a figure unchanged from a previous survey done in 2004–2005.[5]

A number of recent sociological and anthropological works have sought to explore the contradictions of the enduring linkages between marriage, caste, and kinship structures within India, as well as foreground contestations between customary marriage traditions and the aspirations of North Indian youth, both rural and urban, to seek romantic partners (Chowdhry 2007; Grover 2009; Mody 2008; Uberoi 2006). One of the earliest, *Don't Marry Me to a Plowman*, situated the lived experience of Hindu and Muslim married women in rural Uttar Pradesh within prevailing gendered structural and ideological constraints of patriarchy and kinship rules. It was one of the first works to note the localized practice of rural men "buying" brides from neighboring regions (Jeffery and Jeffery 1996). Pervez Mody's *The Intimate State* (2008), an ethnographic study of love marriages that breach boundaries of caste or religion in the urban setting of Delhi, uncovered the role of the state in upholding separate caste and religious identities through the concept of "sexual governance." Shalini Grover's *Marriage, Love, Caste, and Kinship Support* (2009) examined urban poor lower-caste women's experience of love and intimacy brought on through their encounters with urbanism and the consequent loosening of caste rules on marriage. Patricia Uberoi's *Freedom and Destiny* (2006) used the lens of popular Indian culture to interrogate the contradictions and tensions between individual romantic desire, duty toward family in the selection of marriage partners, and resistance against expected gendered roles in urban India. Prem Chowdhry's *Contentious Marriages, Eloping Couples* (2007) drew on her decades-long research in rural Haryana to trace societal tensions to "contentious" alliances that violated marriage rules prohibiting intercaste, inter-*varna*, or intracaste rules of *got*, village, or territorial exogamy.

Other scholars have sought to interrogate changing patterns of marriage-making in relation to migration, transnational desire, and diasporic family formation (Charsley 2013; Maunaguru 2019; Palriwala and Uberoi 2008). Sidharthan

Maunaguru's *Marrying for a Future* (2019) looks at transnational marriage-making strategies emerging between diasporic Sri Lankan Tamils and locally situated Tamils because of the Sri Lankan civil war. While detailing the emergence of a new marriage brokerage industry and marriage facilitators, and the marriage process itself as an in-between space fraught with insecurities, Maunaguru's study emphasizes the enduring nature of kinship ties that are maintained through marriage. Likewise, *Transnational Pakistani Connections: Marrying "Back Home"* by Katherine Charsley (2013), examining the Pakistani diaspora's practice of marrying their daughters "back home" with close kin members as a way to maintain transnational ties, details the cultural challenges and struggles with masculinity and patriarchal roles that "imported" Pakistani husbands face after their transnational relocation to Britain.

In relation to cross-region marriages in India, one cluster of work emerging from anti-trafficking NGOs asserts that all women involved in cross-region marriages to men in rural North India are trafficked (Blanchett 2003; Pandey and Kant 2003; Rahman 2009). These works singularly portray these marriages as trafficking by arguing that the alliances are involuntary, coerced, or forced on the women, and that the strategies used by both traffickers and marriage agents to net their female "victims" involve deception and commodification. This discourse, picked up by national and international media, contends that the bride-victims are trapped in hyper-exploitative "slave-like" conditions and endure gross human rights abuses from their so-called husbands and conjugal families.[6] The women are presented as victims who are sold and resold from one exploitative male to another, with the mediators cum traffickers profiting from their commoditization, while their destitute parents are depicted as "sellers" of their daughters to the highest bidder. While the media disseminates a picture of large-scale cross-border trafficking of women from Bangladesh for coerced marriage,[7] only one report, so far, has detailed the trafficking of Bangladeshi women for marriage to rural North Indian men (Blanchett 2003). Migration or trafficking of Nepali women for marriage to Indian men does not appear to be a trend, unlike their marriage migratory flows to South Korea.[8]

On the other hand, a small but significant body of scholarly work, beginning with Ravinder Kaur in 2004, has largely focused on the Hindus in rural Haryana and the adjoining state of Uttar Pradesh. While effectively countering the "all brides as trafficked" paradigm, these works reveal that the increased dowry demands of local grooms and the prevalence of hypergamy in marriage practice act as contributory push factors for such noncustomary marriage migration from East India (Chaudhry and Mohan 2011; Mukherjee 2015). These works attribute the emergence of cross-region marriages to the female deficit in North India caused by the sex-selective abortions of female fetuses (Ahlawat 2009; John et al. 2009; Mishra 2013), or as an innovative consumption smoothing strategy of poor natal families from East India (Kaur 2012). Two recent edited volumes, *Scarce Women and Surplus Men in China and India* (Srinivasan and Li 2018) and *Too Many Men Too Few Women* (Kaur 2016), undertake a similar comparative analysis of societal changes caused by gender imbalance in China and India. Essays contained in these volumes provide thick descriptive accounts of domestic violence experienced by cross-region brides (Ahlawat 2016), and of the caste-specific adjustments that this set of migrant brides have to make (Mishra 2016).

Evident from scholarly works on caste, kinship, and marriage is the undeniable, enduring salience of caste in regulating marriages and in ensuring homogeneity of kinship ties through arranged same-caste matrimonies. What appears from these works is also the disquieting fact that challenges to caste hierarchies posed by love marriages or by encounters of the younger generation with urbanism or forces of globalization appear to leave the protagonists more bruised, instead adding strength to the violent caste-enforced sexual governance of youth. Similarly, works on cross-region marriages in India detail the conjugal life of migrant brides as they adjust to the differing customs and language of North India (Chaudhry 2018; Kaur 2004; Kaur 2008). Very much along the lines of other works on marriage and kinship in India, these studies conclude that the wives' caste difference creates an uneasy scenario for their acceptance in rural communities (Chaudhry 2018).

However, these works, important as they are in furthering our knowledge about cross-region marriages, also leave some weighty questions unanswered about the emergence and spread of noncustomary cross-region matrimonies in India at this particular neoliberal juncture. First, it would be erroneous to assume that these transgressive matrimonies are a continuum of a similar practice historically undertaken by rural men from the Jat caste group. Then, such marriages were fairly localized to a small region of Haryana; limited to a few landed, rich, and usually widowed men from the dominant-peasant caste of Jats; and involved marrying women either from local Dalit castes or other low-caste groups from neighboring regions. That said, contemporary noncustomary marriages are large-scale in number, and in any medium-sized village, it is easy to find ten to fifteen cross-region brides. Second, instead of trying to source brides from neighboring regions, the men invest a significant amount of money, paid as a commission to a range of marriage brokers to facilitate marriages with poor women from distant parts of India.

If one accepts, prima facie, that skewed sex ratio is the most significant factor causing marriage migration among the Hindus, how then can the prevalence of this practice among the Meo in the same region be explained? The Meo community boasts one of the best CSRs in various censuses and does not appear to suffer from a bride deficit. Such long-distance marriages within this community, wherein Meo men have begun seeking matrimony with Muslim women from other parts of India, are thus an intriguing development. However, extant scholarship on cross-region matrimonies reveals that the caste difference of migrant brides is a continuing concern for the caste-conscious rural communities into which they marry (Chaudhry 2018). Given the continued relevance of caste in regulating social relations, this begets an important question: Why do rural North Indian bachelors continue to seek caste-transgressive alliances from other regions, despite such a prickly and hostile reception to such matrimonies from conjugal communities? If female shortage is indeed a precipitator for some caste groups more than others, why then are wives not obtained from local Dalit caste groups, among whom this female shortage appears to be far less an issue? If caste endogamy is to be violated, why not do it in a more cash-efficient manner, by "sourcing" locally and doing away with expensive marriage brokerage fees? After all, the historicity of this tradition among the Jats, who enter these cross-region marriages more than other caste groups, is well proven (Chowdhry 2011; Darling [1925] 1977).

Reframing Marriage Migration

Putting aside the acerbity of David Harvey's comment, that "anyone who in these times fails to situate themselves inside of the capitalist relations of domination is . . . simply fooling themselves" (1992, 305), in this book I take as a starting point the refocusing of cross-region marriage migration in India. Thus, this work departs significantly from extant works on Indian marriage migration by reconceptualizing these noncustomary cross-region matrimonies as a web of layered, intimate dispossessions that are firmly rooted in the material reality of the violent neoliberal accumulative process that began unfolding in India in 1991. In doing so, I foreground the novel articulation of the exploitative gendered nature of capitalist social relations through the rise in cross-region marriages within India.

David Harvey's formulation of accumulation by dispossession (2005), a term he uses to describe the contemporary accumulation process, which is based on a series of dispossessions, is particularly useful in revealing how these reshape intimate social relations with deleterious gendered outcomes. Karl Marx (2011) first articulated the concept of primitive accumulation to describe a set of processes within England that allowed the separation of producers from means of production and the seizure and conversion of assets into capital. These processes included the expulsion of peasants from their lands and their transformation into wage laborers, the concentration of capital and assets into the hands of a few, and the privatization of the commons, to list a few. However, Harvey contends that within contemporary capitalism, accumulation occurs "without production" (2005, 162)—that is, the freed-up labor is not harnessed as wage labor to create more capital through expanded reproduction. Instead, according to Harvey, the various processes constitutive of accumulation by dispossession include

> commodification and privatization of land and the forceful expulsion of peasant populations; . . . conversion of various forms of property rights (common, collective, state, etc.) into exclusive private property rights; . . . suppression of rights to the commons; commodification of labor power and the suppression of alternative (indigenous) forms of production and consumption; colonial, neocolonial, and imperial processes of appropriation of assets (including natural resources); monetization of exchange and taxation, particularly of land; the slave trade (which continues particularly in the sex industry); and usury, the national debt and, most devastating of all the use of the credit system. (2005, 159)

I broaden the conceptualization of dispossession beyond the spectacular instances of land grabs to one that encompasses a violence occurring silently on a mundane, everyday, and ongoing basis for lower-class, low-caste women from India's peripheries in their marriages with rural men from North India. Being attendant to material reality, I reveal that the existing structural and systemic discriminations that make certain historically marginalized communities within India's development peripheries, such as the Dalits and Muslims, more vulnerable to a series of dispossessions of land, labor, and livelihood also extend to matrimonial options. The burden of capitalist accumulation has been disproportionately borne by these groups, in that the structural and systemic violence of discriminations of caste and religion have translated to their limited to zero access to productive resources, land, and capital (D'Costa and Chakraborty 2017; Levein 2018). I connect the dots between this harsh neoliberal material reality and the intimate gendered nature of dispossessions faced by cross-region brides. These occur both in the constriction of marriage choices locally in their home communities and in their compromised ability to negotiate advantageous bargains, for example, over their labor and/or freedom of movement, with conjugal families in North India. In doing so, I demonstrate how this dispossession is a new manifestation of accumulation that efficiently and effectively harnesses oppressive and exploitative ideologies to reshape social relations—in particular, that of marriage and the practice of dowry—for the efficient extraction of value, and, in turn, create a new neoliberal avatar of gender subordination and oppression.

In undertaking this framing, I draw from feminist political economists who urge there is a necessity to examine how "new mechanisms" are deployed in this dispossession (Hartsock 2006), and how the subordination and exploitation of women's labor is central to this contemporary phase of accumulation (Hartsock 2006; Mies 1998). They argue for attending to "historical and local configurations of power relations in order to understand why certain racialized or ethnicized populations are more vulnerable than others to dispossessions" (Whitehead 2016, 14). Nira Yuval-Davis, in *Gender and Nation*, states that "women's oppression is intermeshed in and articulated by other forms of social oppression and social division," and that these oppressions, linked to women's access to material resources and power, cannot be compartmentalized (1997, 7–8). It appears that the reconfiguration of social relations through commoditization and the harnessing of patriarchal ideology about gender discourses has facilitated capital in gaining unfettered access to gendered labor power (Bannerji 2016; Mies 1998). In the instance of India, this capitalist expansion has exacerbated the structural violence of caste and ethnicity (Teltumbde 2018).

Thus, instead of a perfunctory nod to the role of neoliberal economy in pauperizing certain communities in India more than others, in this book I firmly embed a nuanced discussion of dispossessions within the global and locally specific structural and systemic inequalities that confront the poor, both women and men. I extend Mohanty's argument for an "anti-capitalist feminist critique" that examines hierarchies of privilege and power based on "particular historical, material and ideological power structures" (2003, 28). I contend that the study of marriage migration as a social phenomenon "outside the realm of political economy and the operation of modern market forces" (Palriwala and Uberoi 2008, vii), or as unaffected by caste, patriarchy, religion, and ethnocentrism or ethnocultural chauvinism, fails to acknowledge how these multiple and intersecting oppressions and attendant dispossessions shape unmarried women's options for marriage—just as much as they shape their future lives as brides within the intimacy of their marriages, households, and conjugal communities.

This book therefore connects the macro-political process of neoliberalism to the micro-personal level of marriage and intimate gender relations. It reveals that a shortage of brides caused by the extensive use of sex-selective abortions to eliminate female fetuses while being a precipitator, is not the only causal factor for marriage migration within North India. Instead, as revealed in chapter 2, these transgressive marriages are reframed within the unfolding of neoliberalism-induced agrarian distress and the increased feminization of agriculture in these areas, and linked to the related urgency of rural impoverished North Indian bachelors to secure, through marriage migration, the labor of their cross-region brides. The legitimacy accorded by patriarchal ideology to the transference of women's labor from natal families to that of the bridegrooms acts as a major driver. Although the routes to the bride deficit, or male marriage squeeze, as a societal crisis are different for the Meo and the dominant-peasant castes of the Jats, Yadavs, and Ahirs, they share one striking similarity: not all males from these two groups are rejected in the local marriage market. Instead, those rejected are predominantly men from the lower classes of these two groups, such as landless laborers and marginal landowning peasants, for whom the harnessing of this unpaid gendered labor has become crucial for survival. In India, poor households have reconfigured the use of available family labor to adapt to the agrarian crisis and neoliberal demands for cheap disposable labor by channeling female family labor into paid agricultural work (Pattnaik et al. 2018).

The increased postneoliberal commoditization of marriage, through dowry, unleashes its own violence on poor marriageable-age women from India's marginalized groups, who are then "voluntarily coerced" into setting themselves up for a series of gendered dispossessions that haunt them and their children in rural conjugal communities. As I reveal in chapter 5, these include cultural alienation from their land, language, food habits, and customs; forcible assimilation into local culture through the adoption of local social mores of food, language, and traditions; and cultural othering due to the prevalent ethnocentric discourse about people from East India, such as those from Bihar or Bangal (West Bengal). This cultural othering extends intergenerationally to their children, too.

Thus, through this case study I underline how neoliberalism has not only restructured poor people's daily lives but has also permeated into the most intimate and sacrosanct of social relations—marriage—to reformulate the way it is arranged and negotiated on a personal basis, with differential gendered outcomes. At a macro level, it examines how marriage, as a patriarchal institution, intersects with caste, religion, ethnocultural chauvinism, colorism, and a neoliberal economy to reshape marriage strategies, gender rights, and gender relations for poor women from marginalized groups. At a micro level, it offers an intimate glimpse into the lives of the migrant brides, whose daily existence within their conjugal homes and communities is undergirded by these oppressive ideologies.

Understanding these marriages at the intersections of caste, class, ethnicity, religion, location, and color within the constructed category of cross-region brides, and how these significantly alter the women's status and lived experience in their conjugal homes and communities illuminates a more complex view, one that scholars and activists can employ to gain a nuanced understanding about these marriages and the rights and status of cross-region brides, shape their strategies for engagement, and design policies and programs that are sensitive to the specific needs of the brides. On a broader global level, this micro case study offers a macro analytical framework through which to better understand the workings of neoliberalism, ethnocultural chauvinism, classism, and other social oppressions that shape the choices and vulnerabilities of poor and marginalized women worldwide.

Neoliberal Culture and Marriage

In India, the accumulative process got a fillip from the early 1990s when it wholeheartedly embraced the neoliberal project through the adoption of structural adjustment programs. This resulted in the alienation of producers from means of production and the creation of a reserve army of dispossessed and landless people who could provide cheap, flexible, and disposable labor for the accumulative process; the transformation of the Indian state into a broker for global capital, in its coercive appropriation of land through state-managed acquisitions and corporate land grabs; the large-scale privatization of public services, including the imposition of user fees and removal of subsidies and tariffs, as part of the commoditization and financialization process, exacerbating structural and systemic inequalities for socioeconomically marginalized sections of the Indian population, such as its women and the Dalits, Adivasis, and Muslims; and the reinforcement of class power, by putting wealth and political and economic power into the hands of a thin slice of rural and urban elites. By tapping into preexisting unequal gender norms and relations, predatory accumulative policies extend beyond mere dispossessions of land, livelihoods, and resources. Harvey argues that this contemporary process of capital accumulation "typically undermines whatever powers women may have had within household production/marketing systems and within traditional social structures [by] relocat[ing] everything in male-dominated commodity and credit markets" (2005, 170).

Significantly, the distinctiveness of this phase of capitalist accumulation also lies in the destruction of social relations through commoditization. It commoditizes everything, not even sparing daily life, whereby everything and everyone is treated as a tradeable commodity. Harvey terms this marketized mindset as "neoliberal culture" (2020), in which neoliberalism brings about a cultural transformation in the way we think about ourselves and our relations to each other. Such cultural transformations, notably based on the abandonment of values and established moral order, are locally specific, change the soul of any given society, and have economic implications that are necessary to support the neoliberal order (Harvey 2020). Similarly, Tania Li, in her account of capitalist agricultural penetration among the highlanders of Sulawesi, Indonesia, uses the term "capitalist relations" to describe a set of "relations characterized by private and unequal ownership of the means of production (land, capital)" (2014, 8). For her, capitalist relations are derived from the transformation of labor and land as freely transactable commodities (Li 2014, 8). These conceptualizations about the neoliberal commoditization of social relations are transportable to my theorization about cross-region marriages and the everyday negotiations over incoming brides' labor.

The hyper-commercialization of marriage in general within India, through the spread of the practice of dowry, has occurred in large part through a demand for cash to act as seed capital for small business ventures or to satisfy demands for consumer goods. In rural areas, this crisis is exacerbated as the grooms' families, in light of diminishing returns from agriculture, seek to maximize their profits from marriages, thus forcing the women's families to sell their meagre landholdings or become indebted to meet the dowry demand. Marxian feminist scholar Himani Bannerji positions patriarchy as a social force that enables the appropriation of female family labor for social reproduction, arguing that "patriarchy has been violently activated through the loss of livelihood and the ferocity of the market" (2016, 16). It should be recognized that households do not lie outside of the capitalist economy, and that, with neoliberalism, they get integrated more deeply into it. Households absorb the brunt of the removal of social entitlements by way of female family labor picking up this tab through increased use of their unpaid care work and entry into the wage labor market. With unequal gender relations of power legitimized by patriarchal ideology, marriage marks a key moment in the transference of female labor to conjugal households, which is then used to offset the deleterious impacts of neoliberal agrarian reforms. In the instance of North India, it is most evident in the increased entry of rural women in the agricultural wage market. Marriage, through the use of this labor as a cushioning effect, also enables the neoliberal agenda to continue making inroads within the agrarian economy, thus exacerbating the agrarian crisis.

The spread of the market economy has also paved the way for a mindset that internalizes the capitalist market credo. As I discuss in chapter 2, this neoliberal culture, with its commoditization of social relations, is evident in the "have money, can source a bride" logic expressed by men and their families when faced with rejection in their local marriage markets. This neoliberal cultural transformation coupled with the patriarchally approved appropriation of married women's labor by their husband's families appears to drive more and more cross-region marriages. It fuels marriage rejects from Haryana and Rajasthan to overlook taboos on caste endogamy and instead pay marriage mediators to broker alliances with impoverished women from distant parts of India.

In chapter 3, however, I show that, for lower-class women of marriageable age from parts of eastern India, the inability to marry locally due to increased dowry demands is linked to the monetization of social relations with the spread of neo-liberal culture among communities that would not otherwise exhibit this monetization. They are simultaneously faced with regressive patriarchal gender norms governing marriage and female sexuality and a lack of access to economic resources. The combination forecloses other life options for them. Feminist scholarly works on international marriage migration recognize that "marriage-scapes . . . are shaped and limited by existing and emerging cultural, social, historical, and political-economic factors" (Constable 2005a, 4). The conceptual model of "gendered geographies of power" advanced by Mahler and Pessar (2001, 445) emphasizes that gender operates on multiple intersecting social and spatial levels—or at scales of the body, the family, and the state—to reconfigure or reaffirm gender ideologies and relations. "Hierarchies of class, race, sexuality, ethnicity, nationality and, of course, gender operate at various levels" (Pessar and Mahler 2003, 816), in creating and reinforcing systemic and structural inequalities, and thus in influencing migratory flows of women for marriage or labor transnationally.

It may be argued that the women, ordinarily, do not have much choice in the selection of their marriage partners within the constraints of patriarchal and caste ideologies, but it needs to be emphasized that, in contemporary India, poor women's matrimonial choices have become acutely constrained. The failure to acknowledge the intersectionality of the multiple intersecting oppressions along the axes of gender, caste, patriarchy, and class can lead to weak conceptual architecture in terms of being able to grasp the complex, lived realities of cross-region brides. In this context, I quote Harvey, who states that, "the single-minded pursuit of class questions does not allow of a proper consideration of other important historical oppressions on the basis of gender, sexual preference, lifestyle, racial, ethnic or religious identities or affiliations, geographical region, cultural configuration and the like. . . . The intertwining of, say, racial, gender, geographical and class issues creates all sorts of complexities that make it imperative for several sets of oppressions to be addressed" (1996, 108). Thus, in this study I mesh feminist political economy with Dalit feminism to enable a rethinking about these marriages and the gender relations of the migrant brides, a majority of whom belong to the historically socioeconomic marginalized groups of Dalits and Muslims.

Dalit feminism emerged in the mid-1990s with the founding of the National Dalit Women's Federation, the All India Dalit Women's Forum, and with Dalit feminist scholars' writing on caste and gender. It forced a radical shift in feminist discourse in India by contending that the concerns of India's historically oppressed Dalit women, totaling over 16 percent of India's female population, had been either ignored or silenced by the upper-class/caste women dominating the feminist movement in India. Dalit feminism asserted that hegemonic Indian feminism should be labeled Brahmani or upper-caste feminism (Rege 2006) for giving primacy to patriarchy while questioning women's subordination, for homogenizing Indian women and their experiences without taking their location in the caste hierarchy and attendant (dis)privilege into account, and for failing to interrogate interconnections of caste, class, ethnicity, and gender oppression (Guru 1995; Rege 1995; Rege 2006). In my work, Dalit feminism provides tools to oppose the "manufacture of ignorance" (Rege 2013, 1) in order to excavate the "hierarchical, multiple, changing structural power relations of caste, class and ethnicity" (Rege 1998, 45) that shape the trajectory of the individual and collective "lived experience" (Rege 2006) of low-caste cross-region brides.

This theoretical synthesis allows me to demonstrate how the preexisting oppressive ideologies of patriarchal gender relations and social reproduction, caste hierarchies, and religious identity conjoin with predatory capitalism to result in the "dispossession of matrimonial choice" for poor marriageable-age Dalit and Muslim women. As I show in chapter 3, this shrinks marital choices for such women and reduces their ability to marry locally. At a base level, this dispossession results in the cultural alienation of the women from their homelands and family members as they head off to lead their married lives in distant North India. If not for the increased commoditization of marriage relations coupled with the heightened pauperization of already impoverished communities in the contemporary accumulative phase, a majority of the women would not be voluntarily coerced into making such compromised matrimonial choices. Within the context of the increasing spread of capitalist relations, these women's pragmatic marriage choice needs to be reframed as the exercise of their fractured agency. Although their agency to exercise choice about matrimony is circumscribed by the harsh reality of a limited range of life options, the majority appear to enter into these cross-region matrimonies willingly and with an acute understanding of the reduced or complete lack of bargaining power they face because of a lack of fallback options.

Here, these women's marriage strategies are best understood using the concept of paradoxical hypergamy (Constable 2005b, 167). Though these brides marry up and obtain a slightly better economic status than that of their natal families, they are disadvantaged on two counts: one, by their marriage to economic and "social losers" in Haryana and Rajasthan; and two, by their supposedly undesired caste and/or ethnicity. Because of the latter, they strike strategic patriarchal bargains with North Indian men who were rejected within their own marriage markets for their various shortcomings and flaws. In doing so, these women clearly appear to operate within the gendered geographies of power (Mahler and Pessar 2001) to exercise their circumscribed subjectivity.

Securing Unpaid Female Family Labor

Here, it behooves us to tease out the critical tipping point that makes male "marriage rejects" turn away from their futile search within their local caste-endogamous marriage pools and instead consider endogamy-transgressive marriage migration as a viable marriage option. A clue can be found in looking at the local intercaste marriages that took place among the Hindus in Haryana as early as the nineteenth and early twentieth centuries (Darling [1925] 1977). Such alliances were limited to a few within certain caste groups, such as the moneyed Jats among the Hindus, who had the financial means to pay a bride price. The women usually belonged to local low-caste groups from within the region or adjoining areas. These intercaste alliances, often secondary for the men because of their widower status, were typically driven by a need to fill a labor shortage in families. This, I argue, still holds true today and has acquired even greater urgency within the context of the agrarian distress that besieges rural India.

Unlike in the historical past, during which only a small handful of moneyed Jat men sought such alliances, contemporary bachelors are seeking these marriages in much larger numbers and are, overwhelmingly, from the lowest sections of the dominant-peasant Hindu caste groups and the Meo. As detailed in chapter 2, the centrality of women's free family labor in North India's rural economy is the biggest motive propelling these noncustomary and multiply transgressive alliances. For both sets of men, Hindu and Meo Muslim, their rejection as "husband material" by local women creates a "shortage-of-labor" crisis within rural households. The increasing reliance on female family labor by rural households is revealed in a recent study that shows the percentage of adult women in unpaid work, from 1999 to 2011–2012, increased from 54 percent to 60 percent, with the highest jump for rural women (Mondal et al. 2018). In this context, the need to secure this patriarchally beholden free female labor through marriage is often expressed with such comments from the men and their family members as, "My mother was no longer able to provide for our needs," "I could no longer work in the fields. I needed a hard-working daughter-in-law who could take my place," and "Without a wife, it was proving difficult to take care of the house or the fields" (*ghar aur khet dono se majboor the*).

In rural Haryana and Rajasthan, women's labor accounts for over 80 percent of the agrarian economy, including that of animal husbandry. The inability to replace this unpaid family labor creates a crisis for low-class peasant households. They *need* the free and unpaid female family labor to offset rising agricultural costs, as they can ill afford to hire wage labor to work on their small patches of land. After 1991, in the agricultural sector, under the drive for fiscal austerity, the Indian state reduced or totally withdrew institutional support, including subsides for water, power, fertilizers, and seeds, irrigation infrastructure development, research and development, and institutional access to credit facilities. This withdrawal of support was a shock for small and marginal landholding peasant families.

For small and marginal farmers who eke out a subsistence living, hiring wage laborers is unsustainable and unrealistic, as it would eat away at all their earnings. In the instance of rural North India, Dalit assertion against the exploitation of their wage labor by the dominant peasant castes, done under the guise of customary caste obligations, has eroded the ready availability of this large pool of customarily depressed wage labor. Acquiring wives through marriage migration who are patriarchally beholden to provide free labor for the family should thus be understood as a labor-replenishing or labor-replacement strategy. The mechanism also sets the stage for a greater extraction of labor value from the migrant brides, who, because of the long distance from their families, the lack of fallback options, and the nonpayment of dowry, lack the ability to strike advantageous patriarchal bargains about the use of their labor by conjugal families. Here, the high costs involved in undertaking such marriages, through paying a commission to the marriage broker and absorbing all expenses related to travel and the marriage, should be interpreted as an initial investment by the men—an investment that they hope ensures the future constancy of the reproductive and productive labor of the incoming migrant brides. This neoliberal transformation of marriage into an alliance governed by capitalist relations, and in which the commoditization of brides' labor is paramount, is evident from families stating that they demand a "work horse" (*ghano kaam karne wali ho*)—meaning one who can carry out the labor demands placed on her. One recent work that resonates on the subject of structural constraints that shape women's control over their labor and the remapping of their everyday life and desires is Mythri Jegathesan's *Tea and Solidarity* (2019). An ethnographic account of Tamil women tea plantation workers in Sri Lanka, the book traces their constricted existence as workers and as family women to a series of dispossessions that are explained by structural and historically embedded inequalities and gendered patriarchal expectations about the use of incoming wives' labor (Jegathesan 2019). Jegathesan argues that the Sri Lankan agro-industrial tea plantations utilize the intersections of caste, gender, class, and patriarchal ideology to create a unique set of neocolonial labor relations that serve to further marginalize women workers for greater capital accumulation (Jegathesan 2019, 20–23). In this context, cross-region marriages need to be reconceptualized as a new form of gendered labor migration that gets disguised under the patriarchal gender norms governing female sexuality and marriage.

Caste Fabrications and Multiple "Othering"

This then brings me to another central question of my interrogation: Why do Hindu men not seek wives locally from female-rich Dalit communities, as was done historically, or travel to areas closer to Haryana or Rajasthan that bear more cultural affinity with their communities? This would save on marriage-related costs and on the investment of time and energy required to teach local customs and work habits to culturally alien migrant brides from afar. Here, I argue that these marriages have to be situated within the charged sociopolitical landscape of rural North India, which is marked by increased caste polarization and caste contestations between dominant-peasant castes such as the Jats, Yadavs, and Ahirs, who own the majority of the land, and the assertive Dalits, who have traditionally supplied the bulk of cheap labor to these caste groups but are no longer willing to do so on exploitative terms. Couples that dare to take part in local intercaste or inter-*varna* marriages face social ostracism and violence,[9] including caste-council-sanctioned "honor" killings. The greatest community ire is directed toward Dalit-dominant-peasant caste relationships. Significantly, the state of Haryana has consistently been in the limelight for the gender-regressive stance of its caste councils, or *khap panchayats*.[10]

Within this polarized social landscape, marrying Dalit brides locally, as I show in chapter 5, could result in caste sanctions for the men, and for the couple, as the "truth would be out in a moment" about the infraction of marriage rules on caste endogamy. Instead, "taboo" non-caste-endogamous matrimonies are strategically sought *only* from the distant and remote parts of India. The long distance inhibits inquiries about the brides' caste and/or religion, allows fabrications about their caste to occur with ease, and thwarts challenges posed to the caste system through local intercaste matrimonies. Cross-region marriages also work to defuse class tensions—already aggravated by neoliberalism—within same-caste groups, caused by poor men being forced to remain lifelong bachelors because of the tradition of hypergamy.

In this context, while the integration of women into the labor market as devalued workers and the increased gendered burden of social reproduction have been exhaustively documented by feminist scholars (Dalkuar 2007), there is a pressing need to recognize the emergence of new forms of gendered violence as neoliberalism deepens its stranglehold on societies and as neoliberal culture becomes normalized. Greater synergy between the structural and systemic violence is experienced by lower-class migrant brides. This violence is experienced on a daily basis by the migrant brides as they contend, on one hand, with cultural alienation, forcible cultural assimilation, caste discrimination, and ethnoracist and religious prejudice; on the other hand, they deal with lowered bargaining ability.

These marriages symbolize transgressions of "borders" (Yuval-Davis 1997, 64) that mark the restrictions and limits of caste and ethnicity, thus forcing us to rethink notions of community and its meaning for those who either cannot become full members or are allowed only conditional entry (Yuval-Davis 1997, 71). In addition to the cross-region brides' bodies being desired for their free productive and reproductive labor, they are treated as "internal others" or "cultural others" by their conjugal families and communities. These women emerge as threats to the cultural integrity of an imagined Haryanvi or Meo culture, in particular, because they also constitute harbingers of a future generation that can potentially challenge and erode cultural and caste boundaries that are based on unequal power relations. The inroads of this newer form of gendered violence through marriage migration, within the intimate realm of marriage and domesticity and with spillovers into the conjugal communities, offer a sobering example of how the accumulative process taps into preexisting gender-oppressive ideologies. Examining this process also provides a better understanding about the evolving gendered nature of neoliberal violence.

While presenting this analysis, I am also cognizant of the danger in reproducing the mute bridal slave-victim scenario that is circulated by anti-trafficking activists. The depiction of these women as a homogeneous mass of abject victims assumes the sameness of their oppression, their inability to negotiate and/or resist their victimhood, and their everyday strategies within the intimacy of their marriages to push the boundaries of the intersecting oppressions of patriarchy, caste, and gender. These marriages also allow women who ordinarily might not have been able to (re)marry in their regions, such as widows, deserted women, those who have left their first husband to return to their parents, and those whose "reputation has been tarnished" (*daag*) by failed sexual relationships, the opportunity to (re)enter the heteropatriarchal institution of marriage. I also argue over the course of the book that these cross-region brides occupy a contradictory space, as these marriages foreclose their agency, yet provide them with some limited space within which to challenge established patriarchal norms and power structures through strategies of refusal and resistance, which they carry out within the intimacy of marriage and in relations within their conjugal families and communities.

Setting the Field: Research Methods

My research methods were shaped by epistemological concerns such as the nature of knowledge formation about cross-region marriages and migrant brides in India. To this end, I employed a feminist methodological perspective with an emphasis on social change and social justice (Reinharz 1992). Doing so allowed me to incorporate multiple subjectivities, to recognize manifold forms of women's agency and resistance, and to deconstruct dominant representational strategies and knowledge formation around cross-region brides and their experiences. The widespread public perception that these marriages constitute egregious cases of bride trafficking undertaken by North Indian men led me to consciously use a vast sample pool and diverse research methods. My impulse was driven, in large part, by cautionary notes struck by anti-trafficking scholars on methodology, who advocate adopting multiple methodological approaches and situating individual narratives within broader socioeconomic and political contexts to avoid misgeneralizations (Brunovskis and Surtees 2010).

Thus, I tailored my research tools to include triangulated research methods such as surveys, one-on-one interviews, focus groups, participant observation, and note taking. Ethics approval for this work was obtained by the General Research Ethics Board (GREB) at Queen's University in Kingston, Canada, in accordance with the Tri-Council Guidelines (TCPS) and Queen's University ethics policies. Interviews and focus groups included a wide range of people such as the migrant brides, their parents and siblings, the women's husbands, the men's family members, caste and religious elders, caste council members, and villagers from the natal and conjugal regions. I also conducted interviews with district- and national-level administrators, representatives from law enforcement agencies, anti-trafficking activists, scholars, and a range of people involved in matchmaking, including marriage brokers, human traffickers, bride locators, and altruistic marriage mediators.

The research occurred in four phases spread over four years, from 2011 to 2014, in a total of 246 villages, 226 of which were from the bride-receiving regions of Haryana and Rajasthan in North India, and ten from each of the two sending regions of Odisha and West Bengal in East India. The choice of the North Indian state of Haryana as one of the two conjugal regions was predicated by the fact that cross-region marriages have been occurring there since the early 1990s and the state has had the lowest CSR in the country in recent decennial censuses of India. In contrast, cross-region matrimonies have emerged in the second conjugal region of Rajasthan only since the mid 2000s. I hoped that a comparative analysis of the older and newer sites of these noncustomary marriages could help reveal whether there were any differences in marriage patterns, modes of marriage making, and the treatment of cross-region brides.

With the exception of Jhunjhunu, all the other selected districts of Rohtak, Rewari, and Nuh and Alwar within the two states surround the National Capital Territory of Delhi (commonly referred to as NCT), and are part of the greater Na-

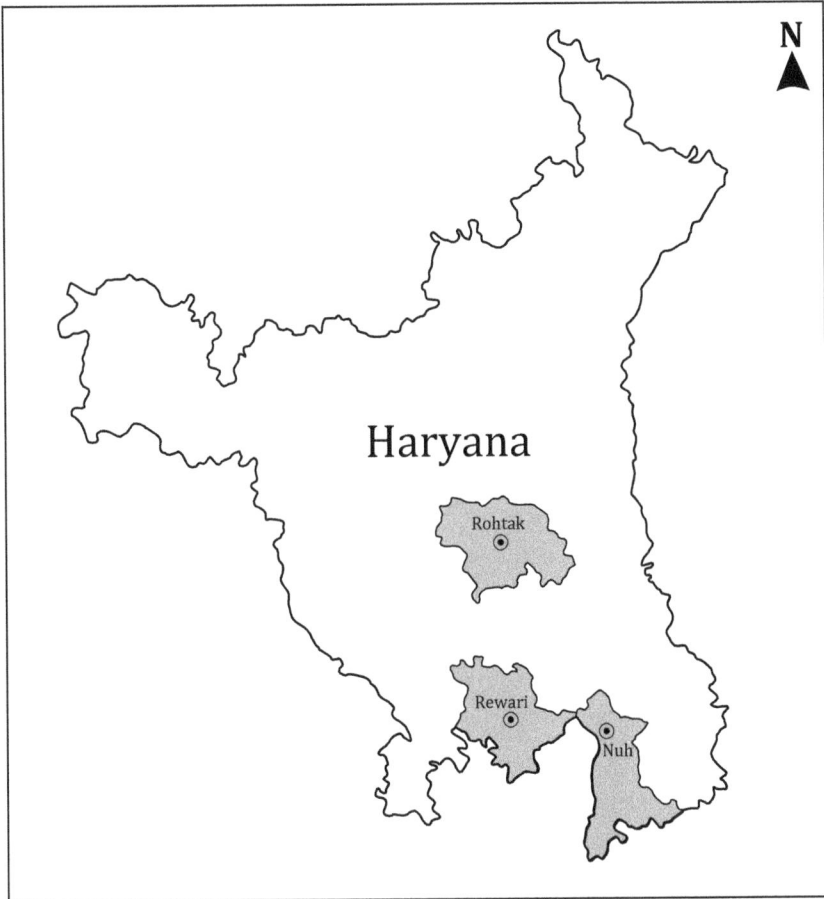

MAP 2. Haryana with research districts of Rohtak, Rewari, and Nuh. Map designed by Aarti for the author.

tional Capital Region (NCR) of Delhi.[11] With the exception of Nuh, since India embraced neoliberal reforms in 1991, all the other regions have witnessed tremendous shifts in their agrarian economies, including increased urbanization, industrialization, and real estate speculation, that have benefited the landowning elites. The study's focus on a select few administrative units, or blocks, within each of the districts was largely determined by the reach of participating local NGOs.

In these two conjugal states, I compared the Hindus and the Meo Muslims to investigate whether there were any variances between these two distinct religious groups; uncover the causes of marriage alliances; examine marriage strategies; determine gender relations and gender power dynamics within such matrimonies; and learn about the lives of the two sets of cross-region brides. A

MAP 3. Rajasthan with research districts of Jhunjhunu and Alwar. Map designed by Aarti for the author.

comparative analysis of the gender relations and gender rights of the local Hindu and Meo brides in these two states in relation to the cross-region brides was continually undertaken. This focus enabled the excavation of commonalities and differences in their lived experiences as brides; their ability to bargain, negotiate, or resist the demands, excessive or not, made on their labor; and the regulatory mechanisms of control exercised over them, among other issues. This allows us to understand how the institutions of marriage, patriarchy, religion, and caste are being reformulated to assert new forms of patriarchal control over both sets of brides.

The selection of the two natal, or source, states of Odisha and West Bengal in East India was done by examining the pattern of data repetition from the survey conducted with cross-region brides in the conjugal areas. For the purposes of maintaining research integrity, clusters of ten villages each from the Tufanganj I, Tufanganj II, and Dinhata II blocks in the Cooch Behar district in West

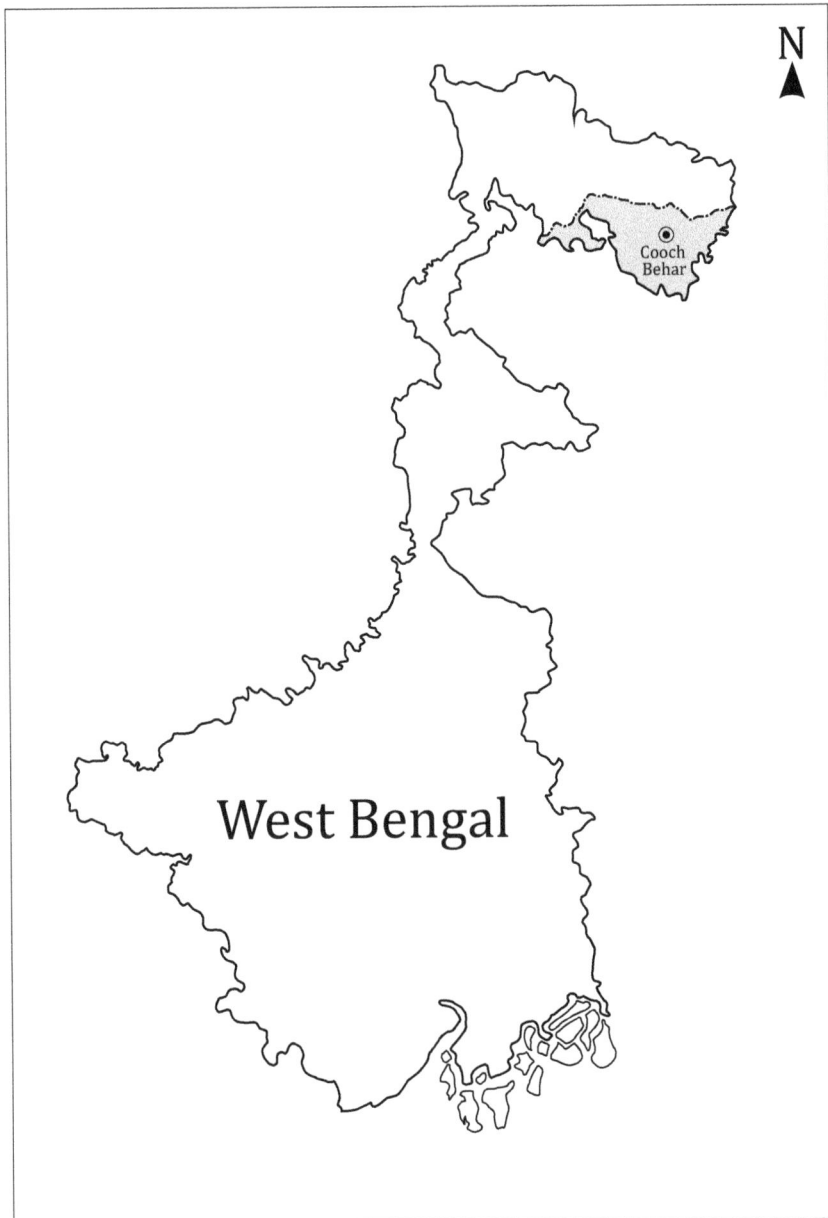

MAP 4. West Bengal with research district of Cooch Behar. Map designed by Aarti for the author.

MAP 5.   Odisha with research district of Baleshwar. Map designed by Aarti for the author.

Bengal, and from the Bhograi and Jaleswar blocks of the Balasore district in Odisha were selected for quantitative and qualitative research. Many marriages in these clusters had been arranged by a couple of brides-turned-mediators or their husbands. Focusing on these villages not only allowed the role of marriage agents to be examined in depth, but also provided an understanding of why some regions within India had emerged as "popular marriage destinations."

The willingness of grassroots NGOs working on issues of gender justice and caste oppression to collaborate in each of the chosen research areas was crucial to the success of the research process and outcomes. The sensitivity of the subject required trust-building and local allies to allay villagers' fears about my motives. I recognized that my positionality as a diasporic Punjabi woman would render me immediately suspect in the eyes of the migrant brides and rural communities. Having my entry into the community mediated by local fieldworkers from collaborating NGOs, who used my history of filmmaking and activism with rural women to introduce both me and my work, including giving screenings of my documentaries, worked to assuage the fears of the brides and the men's families about my research motives. Seven local NGOs and one women's advocacy group came on board for this study. Apart from Shakti Parishad, a rural women's legal advocacy group in Rewari, the collaborating NGOs were SAHYOG and Gramin Mahila Avm Yuvak Vikas Sansthan (Rohtak), Mewat Social and Educational Development Society (Nuh), Shikshit Rojgar Kendra Prabandhak Samiti (Jhunjhunu), Matsya Mewat Shiksha Evam Vikas Sansthan (Alwar), Professional Assistance for Voluntary Action (PRAVA) (Baleshwar), and the Child in Need Institute (CINI) (Cooch Behar).

This research collaboration not only allowed greater transparency and accuracy in data collection, but also enabled the integration of local knowledge about changes in agriculture, gender relations, and social norms about caste, marriage, and dowry. The thirty-one locally situated male and female fieldworkers working with these groups and nominated for the study were trained to conduct close-ended surveys and adhere to a rigorous recruitment strategy that included a diverse set of locators. They proved valuable during the interview phase to fill in background details about local communities, give suggestions about alternate locations for speaking privately with participants, act as foils to deflect prying and inquisitive family members, and step in to act as translators when needed.

A total of 1,546 self-identifying cross-region brides were surveyed through purposive sampling in 226 villages from the districts of Rewari, Rohtak, and Mewat in Haryana and Alwar in Rajasthan. Data collection for the first phase occurred in two rounds: the first round, lasting from April to July 2011, covered Rohtak and Mewat in Haryana, while the second round, in Alwar, Jhunjhunu, and Rewari, was done in October and November 2011. The second phase of the survey was undertaken from April to September 2014. It focused on only the three administrative blocks of the Rohtak district in Haryana that had been surveyed in the first phase in 2011, to assess the change in numbers. Here, all the villages in the three selected blocks were revisited, and a total of 584 cross-region brides participated.

In the selected sending regions of Odisha, fifty families were surveyed in November 2011, while in West Bengal, ninety-one families were surveyed during the period of September to October 2014, with the total reaching 141. The survey model is often derided for its tendency to bring out generalizations without enabling the researcher to look "more closely at the complex, differentiated underlying social reality" (Cilliers 1998, cited in Olsen 2004, 5). However, the paucity of data, about either the exact numbers of cross-region marriages or the socioeconomic background of the grooms and brides, made a close-ended survey a vital research instrument.

In 226 conjugal villages, the entire cohort of brides who fell into the category of being married outside of the customary marriage region—that is, who self-identified as non-Haryanvi or non-Rajasthani by birth—were considered part of the sample group. This exercise was repeated in two clusters in Cooch Behar and Baleshwar, where all the families with a daughter who had married out of their own community were surveyed. The survey also gathered data about livelihood, landholdings, caste, reasons for marriage, and birth order of the bride, among other aspects, to get a clear picture of the socioeconomic status of the families under study. Given the specific sets of people required for the survey, targeted or stratified sampling was adopted as the sample groups were identifiable, small in number, and could not be overlapped with other participant categories. Fieldworkers contacted survey participants and filled in their replies on the survey sheet, to ensure a high response rate and to overcome illiteracy and comprehension concerns. The survey timing was also staggered in each area to avoid times of peak agricultural activity.

The qualitative phase of the research involved visits to fifty-seven villages, of which twelve were in the natal regions of Odisha and West Bengal. A total of twenty-one focus groups and 329 one-on-one interviews, including 116 with cross-region brides from the Hindu and Meo communities, were conducted over the four-year research period. My original plan was to interview only twenty brides from the conjugal regions, but this number had expanded to 116 by the end of the study. Leaving out some brides became ethically problematic, as many women viewed the interview as a process that legitimized their experiences. Consequently, in each selected village, all cross-region brides who had expressed their willingness to be interviewed were contacted.

In the natal communities, six villages were randomly selected in each of the two clusters. Interviews were conducted both individually and in focus groups with available family members, including the bride's father, mother, or both parents, and/or brother or sister. I also spoke with brides who had returned home for good, and to others who were visiting their natal families. As well, apart from speaking with villagers, including neighbors and community leaders, to assess community reactions to the men from other parts of India who were seeking brides from within their community, I also interviewed local marriage agents who had liaised with marriage agents from North India.

All interviews were conducted as open-ended, semi-structured dialogues, in which the spontaneity in conversation allowed interviewees to bring up themes that were not originally planned for. The conjugal communities in Haryana and Rajasthan spoke Hindi or dialects derived from Hindi, my mother tongue, such as Mewati or Bagri. Since people understood Hindi and could choose to reply in their dialect, I did not use any interpreters there. In West Bengal, while I could speak Bengali, I felt the need at times to rely on the interpreters, as the villagers in Cooch Behar spoke a regional dialect of Bengali that was difficult to follow. In Odisha, I relied on my research assistants to step in as interpreters for the Odiya language.

To conclude this chapter, I want to recognize all the participating brides as active collaborators in this study. Snowball sampling of the exact number of cross-region brides in each area was taken with a greater degree of accuracy precisely because many of the brides voluntarily acted as locators and referred other brides to the fieldworkers. This chain referral or snowball sampling method allowed fieldworkers to gain immediate access to additional women without the accompanying distrust. Some of the women also took it upon themselves to facilitate the interviews of other brides, while still others chose to phone their natal families to request that they too participate in the research, be forthright in answering intensely personal questions, and introduce local marriage locators. Without the women's active involvement, at times taken at great risk of violence to themselves from either their husbands or conjugal family members, this study would have simply ended at the survey level.

A SOCIETY IN FLUX

Pradeep sat with his sixty-five-year-old widowed mother, Phoola Devi, on a rope-strung charpoy in the courtyard of their house in Ramsar village. Taking a break from conducting repairs to the crumbling boundary wall of their homestead, Pradeep, along with his mother, reminisced about the family's unsuccessful attempts to get his eldest brother, thirty-eight-year-old Bijai, married within their Jat caste. Bijai was gaunt in frame and walked with a slight stoop. Uneducated and labelled a *bhola*, or simpleton, he was soft-spoken and rarely expressed what was on his mind.

Pradeep's family home sat on slightly more elevated ground than the rest of the village and looked out over the village spread below. As dusk fell, small spirals of smoke rose from various houses, signaling the readying of outdoor kitchen hearths for the evening meal. A group of young boys played an improvised game of cricket in one dusty lane, while another lane appeared blocked by a tractor, from which a family unloaded slabs of red sandstone and bags of cement with which to add an extension to their house. Pradeep's wife, Rajjo, was getting ready to prepare the evening meal, and her elder sister, Sadhana, married to Pradeep's elder brother Rajdeep, fed freshly cut fodder to the two buffalos in one corner of their home.

Phoola Devi felt the need to clarify the family's decision to try to obtain a bride from "outside" (*bahar se*) the caste pool and the region for her eldest son. "People do not view this practice in a bad light. There is a shortage of women in our community (*lardkiyon ki kami chal rahi hain*). Already, we have had ten to twelve such brides get married in our village. More will follow as there are many bachelors here. . . . We need a 'girl' from a *poor* family who can take good care of the household and work in our fields along with us."

In village after village in the conjugal regions of Haryana and Rajasthan, the centrality of unpaid female family labor in the agrarian economy and in animal husbandry is pithily summed up by an oft-repeated refrain, "*lugai ke bina na ghar ka, na khet ka kaam chaale*" (without a wife, both the home and the field go to ruin). Excluding the ploughing, done exclusively by the men, women perform the bulk of agriculture-related activities on their family farmlands, including sowing, weeding, irrigating, spreading fertilizer, harvesting crops, processing harvested crops, and storing food. Women's labor contributions reportedly account for 80 to 90 percent of the work done in the agricultural arena (Chowdhry 2011, 172). Since the Green Revolution, there has been an exponential jump in the "per hectare utilization of female family labour . . . by 22.52 percent between 1971–2 and 1980–1" (Chowdhry 2011, 166). The mechanization of farming that accompanied the Green Revolution, while leading to an increase in production, eased the male side of the gender division of labor; in contrast, however, the women, who were still doing work the old way, witnessed a considerable increase in their work. The resulting upsurge in women's participation in agricultural work and the higher incidence of women agricultural workers and women cultivators, who worked to supplement family incomes, has transformed women into "economic assets" (Sethi 2009, 43).

After agriculture, animal husbandry ranks second in the rural economy in these regions, with the burden of taking care of the cattle (*maveshi*), a labor-intensive activity, being borne entirely by household women. All cattle-related activities—from collecting green fodder to preparing the nutrient-rich feed for the cattle to milking to handling the dung used to make dried cakes for cooking fuel—are done by the women. Rural diets are simple, consisting of wheat as a staple, with milk and dairy products like curds, butter, and *ghee* (clarified butter) used traditionally as the main supplement; owning cattle has thus become not just a matter of family pride but also a necessity for providing high-energy and protein-rich food to these rural families. However, since the White Revolution of the early 1970s, an aggressive state initiative for dairy development has emerged as a steady source of supplemental income for already stretched households. This has also increased the burden of work for rural women such as the two sisters in Pradeep's household, Rajjo and Sadhana.

When I met them, Pradeep and his two elder brothers, Rajdeep and Bijai, had struggled hard as small landholding farmers on the six acres of land that their late father had bought in his ancestral village with his saved-up Indian Army pension money. With each passing year, the family had found it increasingly hard to make ends meet from agriculture alone, because the rising costs of agricultural inputs ate up all their earnings even before they had harvested the crops. Bijai had taken to doing odd jobs in the village, such as in construction and farming, while the two other brothers had learned how to drive and taken up "*dravery*" (driving) with a local man who had a small fleet of passenger vans that plied between villages in Jhunjhunu. Pradeep bitterly recounted, "There was no future left for us anymore in agriculture."

Agrarian Reforms and Rural Distress

In 1991, India voluntarily introduced radical economic reforms through a set of policy packages introduced by the International Monetary Fund and World Bank in many countries of the Global South that, in one fell swoop, irrevocably changed the lives of those, like Pradeep and his brothers, engaged in the subsistence economy. These economic reforms, known by names such as "Washington Consensus," "structural adjustment programs," and "neoliberal reforms," were advocated as a panacea for generating economic growth, increasing efficiency in production and manufacturing, creating additional employment, and reducing poverty. Key features of India's New Economic Policy (NEP) included trade liberalization; deregulation of private business; privatization and sale of public assets and services; 100 percent foreign direct investment in certain sectors of the economy; withdrawal of pro-poor state subsidies and benefits; and incentivization of the private sector through tax breaks, subsidies, infrastructure provisions at throwaway prices, and the creation of SEZs (special economic zones), among other features (for details, see Chandrasekhar and Ghosh 2002).

In the agricultural sector, in the drive for fiscal austerity, the state reduced or totally withdrew institutional support, including subsides for water, power, fertilizers, and seeds, irrigation infrastructure development, research and development, and institutional access to credit facilities. By the mid-1990s, policy reforms in this sector were driven by the World Trade Organization (WTO). Trade liberalization led to a collapse in the state-regulated prices of agricultural commodities: the once heavily protected agricultural sector now had to compete with heavily subsidized agricultural commodities from Western countries (Reddy and Mishra 2009, 10–21). In many cases, crop prices plummeted to as low as 40 to 60 percent of their pre-1996 prices, the year that agrarian reforms started affecting the peasantry in a big way (Walker 2008, 574). The state's withdrawal from providing public services to ostensibly manage the "fiscal deficit" has reverberated through whole communities of marginal and small landholding peasant families and tenant farmers.

The situation of Pradeep's family emblemizes the human cost of integrating rural India into the market economy. The prices they had been procuring for what they grew on the land had made agriculture simply unsustainable in the last decade. Pradeep cited one example: "We had grown onions last year as we had hoped of getting a better price for it in the market (*mandi*). We took a loan from the local grocer to buy seeds and fertilizer. When it came to selling onions in the *mandi*, we were offered only 50 paise per kilo. We cannot even buy onion seed at that price. We cannot store onion like we do with sorghum (*jowar*) or wheat. The government is doing an injustice to us all. It is like a parasite sucking our very life blood."

A vast majority of the rural small and marginal landowning families like Pradeep's live a precarious existence from one agricultural season to another. With no financial savings, the future of the family, and oftentimes the ownership of their land, has always been dependent on a good rainfall and procuring a fair price for their harvest. But cutbacks in subsidies for agriculture, along with an "open" or "free" market determining prices, has led rural families into deeper distress as they have increasingly lost their land to the informal moneylenders. Across India, farm size shrunk from an average of 2.8 acres in 1976 to just over 2.6 acres by 2015.[1] Depeasantization in the agrarian sector, whereby small and marginal farmers are forced to sell their land and are reduced to working as landless agricultural wage laborers or migrating to urban centers for alternative livelihoods, like Pradeep and Rajdeep were eventually forced to do, is directly linked to market-determined state policy interventions (Reddy and Mishra 2009). Another distressing outcome, widely reported in the media, has been that of farmer suicides. By the early 2000s, peasant indebtedness had shot up to nearly 49 percent (NSSO 2005), with peasant suicides numbering a staggering 256,913 during the period of 1995 to 2010 (NCRB 2011). Peasant suicides yearly averaged 16,743 in the eleven years between 2001 and 2011. According to P. Sainath, who has spent years chronicling changes in Indian agriculture, agrarian reforms can be termed a form of "neoliberal terrorism" that results in "around 46 farmers' suicides each day . . . or nearly one every half-hour since 2001."[2]

The agrarian crisis in the two receiving states of Haryana and Rajasthan, as evidenced by the experience of Pradeep's family, has been marked by the "declining profitability of agriculture, increasing risks, degradation of natural resources, steep fall in technological innovations in agriculture, and collapsing agricultural extension" (Radhakrishna and Chandrasekhar 2008, 12), on one hand, and the subsumption of a once relatively autonomous agricultural sector by industrial and speculative capital on the other. The rising costs of agricultural inputs, withdrawal of institutional credit support, and increased reliance on informal moneylenders have dispossessed small and marginal peasantry from their lands, forcing them to seek employment as casual farm laborers or in the tertiary sector in urban centers (Bhalla 1999). To give an example, in Haryana, the number of peasants with marginal landholdings having to rely on wage work in the agricultural sector, or on nonfarm work outside the agricultural season, to supplement their income has increased since 1991 (Bhalla 1999). The period following the agrarian restructuring also witnessed the entry into the workforce of family members from marginal or small landowning peasantry as agricultural wageworkers, yet another indicator of agrarian distress, income depression, and economic unsustainability in agriculture (Bhalla 1999, 47).

Across the villages that I traversed in rural Rajasthan and Haryana, I found that the productive labor of female family members had not only been harnessed for use on the family's own farm holding or in monetized dairy farming, but had also been contracted out to other farmers for earning a wage income. Studies reveal that the restructuring of the agrarian economy caused by neoliberal agrarian distress has drastically shifted women's role in agriculture (Pattnaik et al. 2018; Srivastava 2011). A study of census data for the decades following neoliberal reforms in India reveals that the rise of women in the agricultural workforce was double that of the population increase during the same time frame (Pattnaik et al. 2018). Srivastava and Srivastava (2010) describe this growth in women's participation in smallholder farming, or as wage workers—notably without any concomitant increase in wages or in ownership of productive assets—as the "creeping feminization" of agriculture, but Pattnaik et al. (2018) argue that a more accurate label for this restructuring is feminization of agrarian distress.

Once again, the situation in Pradeep's extended family was a microcosm of these changes transforming the rural landscape of India. Pradeep's elder sister, Kamlesh, who lived thirty kilometers away, had entered the casual wage market in agriculture when her husband, Mohan, migrated to Iraq as a construction worker. Tall, lean, and with an easy smile and gait, Kamlesh recounted that, prior to this, the couple had struggled hard to sustain their family and educate their three children by cultivating onions, mustard seed, and wheat grown on their three acres of land. While the children studied in a government school that provided free education, the family had to meet continual demands for buying uniforms, notebooks, and textbooks, caused in large part by the gradual divestment of the government from the education sector. Having taken a loan from a wealthy landowning farmer at an exorbitant 30 percent monthly rate of interest to pay the commission to the labor agent who secured Mohan's job in Iraq, the couple did not want to lose their portion of land or get into debt peonage, as had some other families in their village.

Countering the harsh lived reality of rural folks like Kamlesh and Pradeep, neoliberal advocates are quick to point out that, since neoliberal reforms began in 1991, India has witnessed a spectacular annual growth rate of 7 to 8 percent, compared with the modest 3 to 4 percent of earlier periods. However, this growth has not generated many jobs, as regular employment has seen a mere 1 percent increase (Bhaduri 2008, 11), while growth in agriculture has been reduced to nearly zero percent (Research Unit in Political Economy 2005). Instead, productivity growth has been largely information-technology (IT) and service-sector driven, while, in the manufacturing sector, it has occurred through mechanization, longer hours of formal work, and casualization and informalization of work (Bhaduri 2008, 11; Sapkal and Chhetri 2019). In the period since 1991, in India, the process of class power restoration has been marked by an intensification of social inequalities. In a study done by Oxfam, the top 1 percent of households owned 73 percent of the country's assets in 2018, indicating a rise of 15 percent in asset ownership from a similar survey done in 2017.[3]

Real Estate Speculation and Rising Rural Inequities

There has also been a gradual decline in the size of landholdings in Haryana and Rajasthan since the advent of neoliberal economic reforms. The number of peasants owning marginal landholdings has increased in both states, very much in line with the All-India figure of 83 percent in 2005–2006 (Chand, Prasanna, and Singh 2011, 7). In Haryana, small and marginal peasants who owned less than six acres constituted 77 percent of rural households in that period (Basole 2010). In Rajasthan, the figure came in at 55 percent in 2012, with the state itself acknowledging that the number might be much higher (Department of Agriculture 2012). There, 43 percent of land was now held by 9 percent of farmers, with only 11 percent of farmland held by over 50 percent of landholders (Department of Agriculture 2012, 54). Tenant farming to supplement income also increased, with the landless, marginal, and small peasantry owning fewer than five acres of land and making up 42.88 percent of lessees in Haryana and 43.92 percent in Rajasthan (Haque nd, 15).

Rural unemployment has also increased, as vast tracts of fertile agricultural land have either been converted for urban planning or rezoned for urban industrial complexes through state-managed land grabs. A study undertaken in one village of the Rohtak district shows that marginal farmers whose land was acquired were forced to take up precarious tenancy farming (Punam 2015). A study on land acquisition in Haryana reveals that Dalits, who constitute the largest group of landless agricultural laborers in the state, have fared the worst (Kennedy 2019). They have been able neither to benefit from the land-change policies nor to derive a livelihood from agricultural labor or tenancy farming. The story is repeated in Rajasthan, where Dalits who do possess land are paid much less compensation than are caste Hindus (Levein 2018).

State-driven expropriation of productive agricultural land—for mining, industries, Special Economic Zones (SEZ), real estate development, dams, and commercial farming, through laws that legitimize acquisitions and evictions—has also led to large-scale evictions and dispossession and displacement for rural families. Since 2005, when the Land Acquisition Bill was passed by the Indian parliament, a total of 581 zones, spread over 149,190 acres or 60,375 hectares of land across the country, has been approved for SEZs alone. Of these, only 232 had become operational by 2019 (Misra 2019, 7). SEZs, in total, have generated a mere 0.2 million jobs instead of the projected 3.9 million, thus falling short on the employment promise by an overwhelming 93 percent.[4]

The research regions of Rohtak and Rewari in Haryana have also witnessed massive land acquisition by the state government for new industrial model townships, expressways, dedicated SEZs, and luxury residential colonies being developed by private estate promoters.[5] There has also been increasing pressure on landowners to sell their land, and oftentimes caste elites are roped in to ensure favorable deals (Kennedy 2019, 4). Within the short period of four years between 2011 and 2014, I saw large tracts of agricultural land in this region gradually fenced off with naked brick boundary walls, parceled into "plots for sale" marked by white-painted cement posts. Signage with bold flourish-filled lettering in expensive granite, using terms such as "dream villa," "landmark," "harmony," and "luxury abode" to lure India's aspirational middle class into investing in the dream of owning a home, often marked the entrances to these future gated communities.

The district of Rohtak witnessed the biggest real estate boom, with land prices surging fivefold in two years. In 2008, one acre of land cost Rs 2.5 million, whereas by early 2015, the price had shot up to anywhere from Rs 10 million to 15 million—an increase of 300 percent to 500 percent within seven years.[6] This escalation in property values was corroborated by the locals several times over the course of my research through comments like those of one focus group of Jat men from Haryana: "Earlier, the rate of one acre of land was between one hundred and fifty to two hundred thousand Rupees. But today, it is as high as five to six million Rupees." Villagers were quick to point out that such high rates were usually evident in transactions undertaken by private developers with individual landowners. Most land acquisitions have been state-driven, at rates much below the prevailing market rates, and with terms and conditions that help investors eventually set up industrial estates or gated communities (Kennedy 2019). Real estate developers have reaped huge profits of 400 to 600 percent through such state-approved land grabs. The cost of acquiring one acre of land for Rs 2.5 million is offset by selling twenty developed plots for more than Rs 100 million. A focus group of members from the Dahiya Khap Panchayat was quite articulate in expressing their discontent:

> The government acquires land from us. It says that it will create an educational hub for the community. But it goes ahead and sells it to the corporate world instead. This way, the land goes away from the landowners. We are not trained to do anything else, so we are rendered useless and without any employment [once the land is taken away]. The money given as compensation—whatever amount—we are unable to put to good use. It finishes up within five to ten years as we lack guidance about setting up a business with that money. So, what happens is that the land goes into the hands of the corporate world, industries, or private educational institutions and we are left with nothing.

Dahiya Khap is part of the larger Jat caste group, which, as the biggest landowner in Haryana, owns over half of the state's arable land (Jodhka 1999, 2218). Kennedy points to the contradictions of anti-acquisition or anti-SEZ movements being spearheaded by *khap panchayats* or the traditional caste councils of the Jats and totally ignoring the concerns of the worst-affected tenant farmers and landless agricultural workers. Within rural areas, existing caste and class inequalities have widened, with the land-rich dominant caste groups such as the Jats overwhelmingly raking in profits from real estate speculation and land deals (Kennedy 2019; Levein 2012, 942). In fact, government compensation for state acquisition of land has excluded agricultural laborers, who are mainly drawn from the Dalit caste (Kennedy 2019, 2). Market reforms have also hastened the transformation of rural rich peasant castes into a "provincial proprietary class" (Balagopal 1987, 1545) in most states in India, including rural North India, dramatically increasing their economic power and assets and also their political control over provincial politics. For example, one news report estimates that 23 percent of Jats control 62.5 of the caste group's income.[7] In Haryana and Rajasthan, the interests of the provincial proprietary class of the Jats and the Yadavs are no longer confined to agriculture. Those of this class continue to farm on their land, largely through sharecropping, tenant farming, and the use of permanent and debt-contract labor; however, they use the surplus profits from agriculture to branch off into urban enterprises (e.g., trade, entertainment, real estate, and, more recently, information and software technology and infrastructure development).

This provincial proprietary class is the biggest supporter of neoliberal reforms, as they are able to benefit the most from economic restructuring, whether from the setting up of Special Economic Zones (SEZs), rezoning of agricultural land for commercial or residential use, or growing of nontraditional, high value gourmet crops for niche markets. They have both land and disposable capital to invest in such ventures. Their actions have also been paralleled by the ultra-coercive management of labor for these enterprises—in construction, in agriculture, and in SEZs.

The Indian state and its role in all of this cannot be absolved from aggressively dispossessing its own poor and marginalized citizenry from their rural livelihoods, land, and resources, and from increasing their vulnerability to new forms of exploitation. With the Indian state acting as "agents for the transfer of seized land to corporate capital, both domestic and foreign" (Walker 2008, 580), the dispossessed and unemployed peasantry, including the Dalits, have no other option but to join the reserve army of labor in the rural areas, thus setting the scene for their further exploitation through growing indebtedness, low wages, or economic-bondage-like situations. The inability of dispossessed families to find alternative land or a new livelihood caused unemployment among agricultural households to increase from 9.5 percent in 1993–1994 to 15.3 percent in 2004–2005 (Sarker 2009, 46).

Tenant and sharecropping farming have emerged as a household survival strategy: 85 percent of those leasing land for farming are either landless or are marginal and small farmers owning less than five acres of land (Department of Agriculture, Cooperation & Farmers Welfare 2020). It is estimated that this number will increase to 91 percent by 2030. In the natal states of Odisha and West Bengal, the figures for marginal and small farmers was already as high as 96.47 and 97.99 percent, respectively (Department of Agriculture, Cooperation & Farmers Welfare 2020). Sharecropping or tenancy to undertake input-intensive farming, especially among the Dalits, has also increased. Aiyar discusses how, during the two decades of reforms, the rise in tenancy and sharecropping among Dalits has risen from 4.9 percent to 11.4 percent in West India and from 16.7 percent to 31.4 percent in East India (2015, 8). In fact, Odisha has the highest rate of tenancy farming in the country, with sharecropping as the main mode of tenancy contract. On the other hand, West Bengal shows a declining trend of tenancy holdings and leased-in areas; instead, casual wage income has emerged as the biggest source of income for its marginal and landless. In Cooch Behar, 57.2 percent of the rural population depends on casual wage labor for primary income, and in Baleshwar that number stands at 51.2 percent (Socio Economic Caste Census 2011b, 2011c). The high numbers of rural agricultural laborers and rural indebtedness are indicative of the increased pauperization of rural households.

Coping Strategies for the Rural Poor

Everywhere in India, it appears that the marginal landholders and landless agricultural wage laborers have been hit the hardest by dispossession. They have lost not only avenues of traditional livelihood but also compensation because of their lack of land ownership (Kennedy 2019, 2). The removal of subsidies for food staples has led to chronic food hunger and food insecurity for many rural folks, like Janaki from Palasa Gandia village in Odisha, whose daughter, Jhimpi, was in a cross-region marriage in the Rewari district of Haryana.

Landless and widowed, Janaki worked as a cook at a roadside eatery (*dhaba*) in the Bhograi block of the Baleshwar district, where entry to the kitchen, located at the back of the *dhaba*, was gained by passing through the small dimly lit dining hall housing six dining tables and two small ceiling fans. Janaki, a slim and slight woman, wore a support brace around her waist for her chronic back pain that was only made worse by the constant bending and lifting of heavy cauldrons of vegetables, dals, and rice. Even at 10:00 in the morning, a roaring wood fire was on in the *chulha*. The thatched kitchen roof was partly open to allow smoke and steam to escape. A rickety pedestal fan on one side was set up to draw away the smoke, to prevent it escaping into the dining area. The high heat and humidity coupled with the noise in the kitchen made it a difficult place to work.

Janaki stated that, with "no other option but to eat food just once at noon and then remain hungry till the next day," this was the only job that she could find that was steady and where she could get to eat a free meal once a day. "You will not know how deep the pain of hunger is," she said as she took me up on my offer to stir the *karahi* of *maacha jhola* (fish curry). Since the *dhaba*'s lunch hour would begin anywhere from noon onward, Janaki did not want to lose a single moment away from her work. So, she continued cutting *patol* (small pointed gourd) and potatoes for making *patol aloo tarkari* as she spoke about her life: "I have no land whatsoever. My husband died when my children were quite young. I would work in other people's fields, transplanting rice, or carrying headloads of harvest. I would beg for food with a bowl in my hand. I could not even arrange for clothes for my children. I have always faced abject poverty."

As landless agricultural wage laborers, she and her late husband had led a hand-to-mouth existence by working in people's fields. With no savings whatsoever, they were extremely vulnerable to vicissitudes beyond their control. The sudden ill health of her husband, and his subsequent death, had in one fell swoop transformed Janaki's and her children's lives. She had returned to her parents' place with her two small daughters and son, where she set up a small one-room mud hut on one side of their dwelling.[8] Janaki's precarious socioeconomic status was unsurprising, given that Odisha has 37 percent of its population below the government benchmark of poverty threshold. Her parents were equally poor and could not help her in any way. So, she struggled as a casual agricultural wage laborer, picking up any job she could get. The children stopped going to the government primary school and became also casual wage laborers, just like her.

In contrast, West Bengal, with 26.7 percent of its population falling below the poverty threshold, appeared far more well off. Notwithstanding the figures, Ahmeduddin's story from Cooch Behar in West Bengal paints a picture not much different than that of Janaki. He had no land to call his own except the 240-square-meter family plot on which stood his single-room tenement with brick walls and a palm-leaf thatch roof. To one side and separate from the house was another smaller room, crudely constructed with naked bricks cemented with clay. Lacking a door, it had two thin slats of wood affixed to one side of the wall that served as makeshift shelves for a meagre assortment of spices and mustard oil. I met Ahmeduddin one October morning at his place in Dakhin Nuapur village where he lived with his wife, Aliya Begum, and a teenage son, Majrul. He looked tense and worried, as he was in the process of finalizing details about his impending seasonal migration with a labor recruiting agent. He recollected, "eight years ago, I contacted a local agent (*thekedar*) who I had heard offered work on construction sites in [the neighboring state of] Bihar. I could not find work here as a mason (*rajmistry*) or as a labourer (*beldar*)."

Since then, Ahmeduddin had begun seasonally migrating to Bihar to work on construction projects. Seasonal and circular intrastate or interstate migration have emerged as the main livelihood option for the rural landless and marginal landowners from Odisha and West Bengal, with households engaging in agricultural wage labor and other nonfarm labor showing the highest rates for seasonal and distress short-term migration. Such migration, undertaken by people like Ahmeduddin, is done through *dadan*, a system of contracting labor for an entire season for a variety of labor sectors. Contractors or middlemen, hired primarily by brick kiln owners, provide a lump sum advance of money, or *dadan*, to people for securing their contract labor and, by default, that of their family, in the brick kilns of Bihar. Construction contractors also employ this strategy to secure workers to work on building sites. This offer of *dadan* is usually made to the male head of the family, and only when the rural labor force is faced with a lack of seasonal employment locally. According to the locals, mass migration from this region occurs during the *dadan* season, from November onward, and "it is not uncommon to see entire rows of houses in a village totally vacant as all people seasonally migrate."[9] *Dadan* has also created a debt-bondage-like situation, as the advance payment ensures the captivity of the labor force, including that of family members such as children. A similar trend of advance payment and bonded labor is visible in Odisha, where the landless Dalits migrate to the brick kilns in the neighboring state of Andhra Pradesh.[10]

With no days off, Ahmeduddin's labor was essentially "held captive" in the hands of his agent and the employer. The knowledge that the rural labor market was constricted played a central role in his passivity toward the exploitative and harsh extraction of his labor. The same knowledge also gave his employer in Bihar the boldness to make his construction workers undertake physically arduous and oftentimes risky work. Ahmeduddin justified it by saying, "at least it (construction labour) is better than working in a brick kiln (*bhatti*)." *Bhatti* or brick-kiln work is the most despised work because of its harsh working conditions, long and backbreaking hours of physically arduous work, pittance piece-rate wages, and slave-like conditions (Anti-slavery International 2017).

Household coping strategies have also led to a higher incidence of the short-term seasonal migration of entire households, particularly from Jharkhand, Odisha, and West Bengal, to work as "bonded" or unfree labor in brick kilns in the neighboring states.[11] The recruitment strategy for this short-term survival migration involves advance payments to male heads of households for a guaranteed captive labor force. As a result, female family members are denied their share of labor compensation, as the monetary payment that they would have otherwise independently earned gets diverted through such gender-biased contracts with the male heads of households.

The agrarian crisis in India has also resulted in rural men migrating, both short and long term, to work in urban centers in the informal economy or in seasonal industries, and in certain sectors such as construction, textiles, and diamond polishing. Men from eastern India also migrate to the National Capital Region of Delhi and to the South Indian state of Kerala for work in the construction industry, service sector, and agriculture.[12] Additionally, an internal migration stream of Odiya men takes them to Goa for work in the fishing industry, while men from Cooch Behar migrate to the neighboring northeastern states of Assam, Tripura, or Mizoram for casual wage labor. Very much like Ahmeduddin in West Bengal, Pradeep and his second eldest brother, located at the other end of India in Rajasthan, had also made the decision to migrate and try earning more than what they could locally. Pradeep remembered, "I was not skilled in any trade—that ruled out getting employed in a factory. So, I thought to myself that I better try fishing in the waters of taxi business in Delhi and see if I could 'net' a job somewhere. At least I hoped that I could earn more than I did from my land (*zamin*)." Rajdeep ended up employed by a gynecologist in Gurugram who needed a chauffeur to drive her from one private clinic to another where she saw her patients, while the extroverted Pradeep found work, through word of mouth, among his Jat brethren in Delhi, as a driver with a tourist cab company.

Feminized Brunt of Neoliberal Reforms

Seasonal or long-term migration of male members of the household such as that of Pradeep, his brother, and his sister's husband in Rajasthan, and that of Ahmeduddin in West Bengal, has been causal in the increase in female-headed households in rural India. In India, as of 2011, 10.9 percent of all households were female headed, due to male migration, desertion, widowhood, or divorce (Census of India 2011c). Commercialization of daily needs, rising costs of food staples, inability of wages to keep pace with inflation, the move from subsistence farming to cash crop production, and loss of employment in the agricultural sector due to diversion of land for other uses has placed the additional burden on women for adopting coping strategies to make ends meet.

Pluriactivity of rural households has emerged as a livelihood risk diversification strategy, one in which women's labor is pivotal. Poverty has led to increased female participation in agricultural and nonagricultural wage work. One study estimates that women's participation rate increases by 24 percent with every 1 percent increase in the poverty ratio, a term used to define the number of people falling below a defined poverty threshold (Pattnaik et al. 2018). Resultantly, poor rural women like Kamlesh are now faced with time poverty, as they have had to shoulder extra responsibilities due to increased pressures on their productive and reproductive labor. For example, Kamlesh undertook casual agricultural wage work, tended her own field, and provided care for her aging parents-in-law who lived in the joint family setup with her. Pradeep's wife, Rajjo, could ill afford to take a day off from farming even though she was heavily pregnant with her third child. In West Bengal, Ahmeduddin's wife, Aliya Begum, had fared worse, as the family had no agricultural land to cultivate and thus lacked reserves of grain to fall back on during lean periods. With irregular remittances from her husband, she and her eldest daughter had taken to working as casual wage workers primarily in the construction sector in a nearby town. Though the work was low paying and extremely physically arduous, they had no other choice but to take whatever job came their way.

Ahmeduddin and Aliya had a BPL (below poverty line) card, a government of India initiative used to identify families living below the government-determined poverty line. Once issued, a BPL card entitles identified families to anti-poverty initiatives such as subsidized food staples, cooking fuel like kerosene, and housing and health care. In 2013, India passed the National Food Security Act. This technically allowed Aliya to access up to five kilograms of rice per person per month, sold at a subsidized rate by an increasingly pared-down state-run public distribution system (PDS), through a chain of PDS distribution fair-price shops, colloquially known as ration shops. However, this allocated amount was never enough to last the whole month. Worse, with rampant corruption in the PDS, oftentimes, subsidized items were siphoned off by merchants and sold in the open market at highly marked-up rates.[13] This is where Aliya would have to procure most of the family's staples with the meagre wages they earned as construction workers.

The global process of capital accumulation has exacerbated gender inequalities in India, particularly as not all members of a family are affected in the same way by the state's retreat from social services and welfare policies. Instead, poor Indian women, like women in other countries undergoing neoliberal reforms, have become the "shock absorbers" for neoliberal capitalist policies (Garikipati and Pfaffenzeller 2012). Female-headed households (FHH) have borne the biggest brunt of the privatization of services and utilities: according to the Census of India (2011c) report, the poverty levels in such households are 20 percent higher than the national average.

In rural areas, the reduction in PDS coverage as part of a government streamlining strategy, in conjunction with the decrease in smallholder food production, shift to commercial monocrop agriculture, and rise in food prices due to a lifting of controls, has resulted in chronic food insecurity and chronic energy deficiency for impoverished women who head households (Krishnaraj 2006). They also have lesser household assets and lesser educational attainments, are more impoverished than the women in male-headed households, and live more precarious existences. In Odisha, one of the main bride-sending states, female-headed households such as that of Janaki make up 22.1 percent of all households. This high number of FHH can be attributed to Odisha emerging as the leading state for the supply of migrant labor, with a 2010 study done by the comptroller and auditor general of India showing an increase of 116 percent in rural migration.[14]

Although male out-migration has emerged as a major cause for female-headed households, early death or sickness of men in the family are other contributory factors. Janaki's husband had died early in their marriage, making her the head of the household. In contrast, Sukanti, also from the Baleshwar district of Odisha, had become the de facto head of the household when her husband had become lame because of an injury and could not work as an agricultural laborer anymore. Two of Sukanti's daughters were married in Rajasthan and one in Haryana. Her youngest daughter, Bullu, married to a Yadav man from Rajasthan, was visiting with her young son and daughter when I met them at Sukanti's mud hut in

Kusumpada village. Tall cacti marked one boundary of her homestead, while the other was defined by the neighbor's betel-leaf plantation. Sukanti sat outside her hut on a slightly raised platform on which a fresh coat of cow dung and clay had recently been applied. Bullu sat next to her, combing her four-year-old daughter's oiled hair into two tightly woven plaits. Thin and bent over, Sukanti, who was only fifty-five years old, looked much older than her age. Speaking about her life of hardships, she stated, "We are wage earners—we have no land of our own nor do we do farming (*chaasi*). My three daughters and myself have borne many hardships to get food. With my husband bedridden, I worked at various houses in the villages. If you don't believe me, I can tell you the names of the houses where I worked as domestic help. I also picked up work in the fields whenever I could. As my son was too young, I ran the household with the help of my daughters."

Sukanti's family and other rural families that I met in the four years of my research, also with daughters who were in cross-region matrimonies, led a very precarious existence—one in which a slight change in their lives, such as the death or illness of a family member, migration of a family member, or desertion by the earning male head of the household, could completely change the everyday reality and oeuvre of life choices for the remaining family members. Significantly, by 2009, 75 percent of women in rural areas were working in agriculture, compared with 59 percent of men (NSSO 2014).[15] A study done in Cooch Behar revealed a higher participation rate there of women from poor households as casual agricultural wage laborers (Pattnaik and Lahiri-Dutt 2020, 30). The high involvement of women in agriculture has been ascribed to the increased feminization of agricultural jobs that were previously performed by men, fewer lease-in land opportunities where family labor is put to work, and a shift from joint male and female tasks to female-only tasks. Wage disparities between the genders, with women being paid less than men for the same jobs, have also led to this wage-cutting strategy being implemented by rural agricultural households. Feminization of agriculture, including a high incidence of girl-child labor within the age group of seven to fourteen years, has also become prevalent in large-scale commercial and luxury crop farming (Venkateshwarlu and Da Corta 2001).

Feminized migration to urban centers, especially that of single and unmarried female family members to work in the informal economy, mainly as domestic workers, has also emerged as a household survival strategy for socioeconomically vulnerable rural families. These "chain-based" migrations occur through referrals by other local women who have found wage work in cities. Notably, this distress-driven rural–urban migration is overwhelmingly present among women of Dalit and tribal communities from states like Odisha, Jharkhand, and Chhattisgarh, where large-scale resource appropriation and land acquisitions by global capital have occurred with the connivance of the state (Deshingkar and Akter 2009). In Odisha, more than half of rural Dalit households such as Sukanti's have the highest rate of rural out-migration for both men and women. A vast majority of female economic migrants find employment as live-in domestic workers in urban middle- and upper-class households.

Emblematizing this trend, Sukanti's oldest daughter, Bindu, migrated to Kolkatta to find work as a domestic worker as soon as she turned sixteen. This work paid her much better than the wages she could obtain as a casual wage laborer in agriculture locally. The second eldest daughter also migrated to Hyderabad to find employment as a domestic worker in a middle-class household. Sukanti's household, like many others, was largely sustained by the remittances of the two daughters. And, once her daughters were married off in North India, Sukanti said, "my son had to leave the village and go to Surat for work." It is worth noting that, since the advent of neoliberalism, Odisha has witnessed a sharp growth in domestic-remittance dependency, so much so that by 2007–2008, rural Odisha ranked sixth in the remittance economy in India (NSSO 2014).

Land Acquisitions and Feminized Dispossessions

In the Cooch Behar district of West Bengal, land acquisitions appear to have crept up gradually and silently over time—and piece by piece—in the villages dotting the countryside. Usha Rani Das's house was situated next to the main arterial road connecting her village, Purbi Jodaipur, to Tufanganj, the block headquarters and a subdivision town in the Cooch Behar district of West Bengal. The government, by invoking eminent domain, or the right to expropriate private property for public good, had acquired part of her homestead land to build the arterial road. Usha Rani, a Dalit, lived in a tin-roof-covered, brick-walled, two-room house with her husband, who was partially paralyzed by a stroke; her twenty-one-year-old daughter, Mamata; and two grandchildren from her elder daughter Monika's first marriage. Incidentally, Monika was now married to a Haryanvi man from the Rohtak district.

Usha Rani worked as a plucker in a small tea plantation located just across the road from her house. Until a decade ago, the farmer who had owned that small piece of land had given it, on a sharecropping basis, to landless and marginal farm-holding families (*halua*). The fertile land gave two good crops of paddy each year. However, with the global consumption of tea on the increase and with the state providing tea growers with incentives, West Bengal has seen a rise in the small tea grower sector in the recent past.[16] The farm owner, recognizing the potential for greater profits, decided to take back his land, took on a couple of adjoining plots of farmland on a long-term lease, and grew tea plants instead. Such owner-supervised small tea plantations are quite different than the sprawling *cha bagaans* or tea estates set up during the British colonial period, in the sense that these are usually less than two acres and take their plucked leaves to small tea-processing factories dotting the North Bengal countryside. The scale of such land acquisitions by small growers can be assessed by the fact that the small tea sector accounts for 40 percent of the tea produced in North Bengal, of which Cooch Behar is a part.[17]

Haripada Das, Usha Rani's husband, was an itinerant seller of *chana* (dried and salted chickpeas) and *papad* (a thinly rolled fried lentil snack), who had previously earned Rs 50–60 on average per day. But the stroke four years ago and the accompanying partial paralysis had put an end to his earning abilities. Usha Rani's caregiving responsibilities increased as a consequence, and so she was pleased to find work in the small tea plantation, where the job of plucking was labor intensive and totally feminized. She earned a daily wage of Rs 50, a rate that often fluctuated based on the quantity of tea leaves that she could pluck in a day's worth of labor.

One study reveals that land acquisitions and land grabs, in general, worsen existing inequalities that poor rural women have customarily suffered from, including differential access to land or customary rights over its use and the lack of land titles and rights (Behrman et al. 2012). Despite around 65 percent of rural women relying on agriculture as their main source of income, a mere 13.5 percent have landholdings in their name (Agarwal 2012). In the case of India, the customary prevalence of patrilineal land inheritance deprives women of whatever monetary benefits or job offers come from such land deals. According to Levein, whose work looked at land acquisitions for SEZs in the state of Rajasthan, "women are almost universally excluded from negotiations over land sales, even in cases where the title is in their name. . . . The replacement of an agricultural economy over which women exercised some control with a real estate economy controlled exclusively by men—and involving much greater sums— has, by many accounts, weakened their position and exacerbated domestic abuse" (2012, 959).

Enclosures and land grabs have also deprived women of their customary rights over common lands and forests, resulting in the loss of income from livestock rearing and the sale of forest products, and increased their household chore burden, as more time and energy must be expended to obtain fuelwood, fodder, water, and food (Levein 2017, 1128). The regions where land acquisitions have occurred are marked by greater incidences of female school dropouts, female family members entering the wage market as casual laborers, and lowered ages at marriage for daughters (Majumdar 2014). With the spread of neoliberal culture, capitalist relations have transformed the rural marriage-scape through the spread of dowry culture among communities that earlier did not subscribe to it. Emergent and increased dowry demands from local grooms also renders pauperized and dispossessed families vulnerable to cross-region matrimonial proposals.

Marginalization of Indian Muslims

"My father was a woodcutter. He isn't working anymore. The riots that occurred in our area—many people died.[18] Our homes were set on fire. Our land was seized by the Hindus. My own mother got killed in the fights between the Hindus and the Musalmaans [colloquial term for Muslims]. We ran away and hid in the forests for four days. It was a very difficult time until the government came and rescued us."

Mamtaaj, a Muslim woman from Assam who was married to a Meo man, said this simply as she sat cross-legged at the *dahleez*, or entrance, of her house in a village in the Mewat region of Haryana. Resting her back against the doorway, she spoke at length about her life in Assam as a young woman, her marriage to an older Meo man a couple of years after the riots of 1992–1993 there, and her struggle to obtain respect, as befitting any other bride, from her husband's family and the larger Meo community.

Hailing from the Goalpara region of Assam, she was more comfortable wearing a *dhoti* (saree), but had given it up for the *shalwar kameez*, the long tunic and baggy trouser outfit that Meo women wear. I had met Mamtaaj a day earlier as I was walking down the village lane to meet a cross-region bride hailing from West Bengal. She had accosted me then and asked, "*kyun ji*, are you the 'madam' doing interviews of *paros*?[19] I am from Assam—why aren't you speaking to me about my life? Is it not important for your research notebook (*kitaab*)?"

Mamtaaj was one of the few women who directly questioned me about my selection criteria for conducting qualitative interviews with cross-region brides. It was women like her that led me to question my feminist agenda and reflect on how I could make peace with the ethics of my feminist research practice, a process that led me to abandon my sociologically honed "determining factors" and offer all cross-region brides in a particular village the choice to speak to me about their lives. This not only extended the period of my research to four years but also meant interviewing 116 migrant brides, compared with the tame number of twenty that I had thought of when designing my research. The following day, having arrived at this resolution, I had shown up at Mamtaaj's place after her husband had left for his midday prayers at the village mosque.

She proudly showed me her house, consisting of two rooms—the outer one, painted a dark shade of ocean green, housed three plastic garden chairs with thin cushions on top and a plastic rectangular table. A small framed print of Kaaba adorned one wall. Through small gestures scattered around the room, I could see that Mamtaaj took pride in her housekeeping. Tinselly shiny biscuit packaging material that had been opened up and cut to form decorative scalloped edging lined three simple cement shelves. On these sat stainless steel plates, *katoris*, and glasses, along with one unopened box of tea mugs. A colorful cotton crocheted throw covered the table. The *dahleez*, or doorway, was also adorned with a decorative garland of pink and green plastic flowers. She spoke about the Hindu-Muslim conflict that had led her to make the journey from a village in Assam in East India to another one in Mewat in Haryana. "In my region in Assam—the Guwahati-Goalpara side—Muslims don't live in peace. There is continuous Hindu-Muslim tension."

In the early 1980s, a disturbing trend of using Hindu majoritarian ideology to the detriment of Indian Muslims accelerated, a trend that irrevocably tore apart the lives of poor Muslims like Mamtaaj. During this period, political realignments occurred to deal with a profound crisis in Indian capitalism. Indian ruling classes turned to Hindutva,[20] an anti-Muslim and anti-Dalit ideology that had taken shape in early-twentieth-century colonial India. Earlier, this ideology had been confined to a small stratum of the upper-caste lower-middle class in Northern India, but after the mid-1980s, it started spreading within rural India as well. Dominant-caste peasants, faced with increasing Dalit assertiveness and polarization within their own caste groupings, saw it as a workable ideology that could deflect anger away from their privileges.

It is also significant that the spread of Hindu fundamentalist ideology in society paralleled the imposition of neoliberal reforms in the Indian economy in roughly the same time frame. Both share upper- and middle-class interests and have sought to transform the relationships among the state, society, and the individual by attributing society's ills to the internal other. Hindutva scapegoats the Indian Muslims, and neoliberalism blames the state for its welfare and interventionist policies in social and economic spheres. Not only do these two reactionary ideologies share similar agendas around transforming the Indian state and society, they also draw from each other in gaining ground locally through the use of arguments about "leveling the playing field." Both seek to depoliticize society by suppressing democratic dissent and social movements or to minimize the role of the state by doing away with protectionism (for more, read Gopalakrishnan 2006; Vanaik 2001). Over the years, the Indian state has also played a key role in the willful neglect of its Muslim citizens. The Sachar Committee Report on the socioeconomic status of the Muslim community in

India exhaustively detailed the deprivations of the Muslim community, including its poor representation in bureaucracy, lower rates of participation in the economic workforce, and second-highest level of poverty (the first being that of the Dalits) (Chisti 2007).

By evoking the ideology of Hindutva, the Hindu Right has been able to extend its base among the dominant-peasant castes, or the Other Backward Classes (OBCs), across large swathes of rural North India.[21] By cleverly projecting Indian Muslims as the internal and the eternal "other" responsible for all ills besieging India,[22] and as a "pampered" minority continually appeased by the "pseudo-secular" Indian state and the ruling political party, Congress (Basu 1996), the Hindu Right has sought to engineer the social cohesion of Hindus, by "transform[ing] economic and social contradictions among castes, between castes and among classes into communal ones" (Shani 2011, 147). The hardening of religious and caste identity is a double-edged sword that has also allowed the provincial propertied classes from the OBC groups to "mobilis[e] poorer peasants [of same castes] behind them in agitation to break the monopoly of lucrative posts and influence held by the upper castes—and to join with the landlords to keep down the Dalits whose labour they also exploited" (Harman 2004, 58).

In December 1992, under the auspices of the Bhartiya Janata Party (BJP),[23] a virulent anti-Muslim campaign culminated in the destruction of the Babri Mosque[24] by Hindu mobs. Large-scale rioting against the Muslims in India followed and furthered their marginalization. The district of Goalpara in the east Indian state of Assam from where Mamtaaj hailed was also caught up in the aftermath of the fury. The ensuing ghettoization of the Muslims, and their de facto reduction to the status of second-class citizens whose loyalty to the Indian state was continually questioned, resulted in a siege mentality among the Muslims, irrespective of class or spatial location.[25] This led Mamtaaj's father to actively seek to marry her off in the Muslim-majority area of Meo in Haryana, where he hoped that she could find security in numbers.

Dalit Assertion and Dominant-Caste Backlash

The resurgence of Hindutva and the presence of the Hindu Right political party, the BJP, at the federal and state levels has also emboldened Hindu upper castes and the dominant-peasant landowning castes, or the OBCs, to openly use violence against the Dalits in many parts of India as a measured strategy to show the aspirational Dalits their proper place in the caste hierarchy. Across India, the incorporation of the poor, including the historically economically marginalized

Dalits such as Sukanti, Usha Rani, and Janaki, into the market system has resulted in their "exclusion from control over assets; exclusion from the benefits of economic growth; exclusion from the impact of physical and social infrastructure expansion; and exclusion from education and from income-generating opportunities" (Ghosh 2015, 44). In particular, the economic precariousness of the Dalits, who number 164 million, or 16 percent of the country's population, has increased in recent years. An overwhelming majority of Dalits in rural areas still continue to work as daily agricultural wage laborers, oftentimes in the fields of dominant-caste landlords.

The OBC castes, such as the Jats in Haryana, have emerged as the biggest oppressors and exploiters of Dalit caste groups, as they see the politicization and education of the latter as a direct threat to their privilege. In postcolonial India, constitutional provisions in the form of a 22.5 percent reservation of the total admissions to government or government-funded educational institutions, as well as to jobs in the state services and public sectors, have been extended to the Dalits. From the 1960s onward, this affirmative reservation policy intensified caste-identity politics, in which the dominant-peasant castes, belonging to the OBC category, sought to obtain similar benefits. As the children of dominant agricultural castes secured education and sought such reservations for themselves so they could obtain the increasingly scarce but highly coveted government jobs, they saw affirmative action for Dalits as a denial of their share of the pie (Kamat 1979, 354).

In Rajasthan and Haryana, for example, pitting dominant-peasant caste group members of the Jats, Ahirs, and Yadavs against Dalits for the small number of reserved government jobs particularly intensified the former's resentment in having to compete for positions they considered their prerogative. The dominant-peasant castes thus strategically used their numbers and economic clout to politically leverage the state to have themselves declared "socially and educationally backward" and managed to gain a 27 percent reservation of government jobs and admissions to educational institutions extended to lower castes belonging to the OBC category. What has been missed in this discourse of "quota politics" is the harsh reality that Dalits face continual discrimination and exclusion from employment despite the Indian state's affirmative reservation policies (Thorat and Attewell 2007).

The cleavage in Indian society and politics along caste lines, or its "mandalization," has also increased the political subjectivity of the historically dispossessed Dalits (Pushpendra 2002, 356–383), who tactically use their vote-bloc politics to obtain political power and address caste-based economic inequalities and social discrimination (Pushpendra 2002).[26] The Dalits' political and social assertion, partly a consequence of the state's affirmative policies toward them, also makes them resist exploitative and hereditary caste and labor practices, which, until a couple of decades ago, had been taken for granted by the upper castes as part of their implicit customary caste rights and privileges.

The OBCs, overwhelmingly consisting of peasant proprietors who relied on Dalit agricultural labor, have been hit the hardest by this newfound Dalit assertiveness (Teltumbde 2012, 70–71). In rural North India, including in Haryana, the period from the early 1990s onward has witnessed increased caste contestations between dominant-peasant caste groups and the Dalits, with the latter bearing the brunt of caste violence and atrocities (Teltumbde 2012, 45–47, 68–74). Even though the Indian state legally abolished the practice of untouchability in 1955,[27] Dalits are still subjected to daily humiliation, degradation, and exploitation through caste-enforced codes governing dress, behavior, housing, employment, and access to services and resources (Navsarjan Trust 2011). Other studies have also revealed the scale of social disadvantage that Dalit caste groups suffer in everyday life (Thorat 2010). In urban centers, although caste hierarchies might appear blurred, both economic and social discrimination against Dalits is widespread, ranging from exclusionary employment hiring practices to rental practices that render them unable to find housing (Deshpande 2011, 182–210). Dalits are also often clustered in low-paying jobs that echo their hereditary "low-caste" occupations (Prashad 2000).

Additionally, the dispossessions, on a pan-India level, have further accentuated the fault lines of caste. Private developers and agents have paid lower castes a lesser compensation than the general castes for the same amount of land (Levein 2012). The NSSO data for 2009–2010 showed that, in that period, 92.1 percent of the rural Dalits were either landless or owned less than one hectare or roughly 2.5 acres of land (NSSO 66th Round 2012, cited in Rawal 2013–2014). Their precarious economic plight, due to their ownership of marginal or nil landholdings and their heavy dependence on casual wage employment in agriculture, has increased with the land grabs, forcible land dispossessions, and mechanization of farming.

Dalit women, being thrice discriminated against on the bases of class, caste, and gender, bear the biggest brunt of structural violence. *Dalit Women Speak Out*, a study spanning interviews with five hundred rural Dalit women in four Indian states, reveals the extent of atrocities that they endure on an everyday basis (Irudayam, Mangubhai, and Lee 2014). The systemic discrimination that the Dalits have historically suffered ensures that Dalit women have higher levels of illiteracy, caused by their social exclusion, ill health, lack of productive assets including land, and lack of access to social services that are increasingly privatized or come with user fees (Navsarjan Trust 2013). Dalit women face more intensified levels of poverty and deprivation than other women (see Navsarjan

Trust 2014). Three-quarters of India's one hundred million Dalit women live in rural areas; as landless laborers, over 52 percent of these women work as low-paid, casual wage workers in the fields of dominant-caste landlords or in commercial agriculture (Sabharwal and Sonalkar 2015, 52). They also face higher levels of seasonal unemployment than the non-Dalit female workforce (Sabharwal and Sonalkar 2015).

Further, Dalit women are routinely subject to gendered forms of caste violence that include forced prostitution, rapes, assaults, and humiliating public naked parades. According to Surinder Jodhka, who has theorized on caste in North India, caste is "a system that institutionalizes humiliation as a social and cultural practice" (2015, 12). Dalit women become tools that upper castes use to assert upper-caste dominance, emasculate Dalit men, and strike fear in Dalit communities for resisting upper-caste hegemony (Rao 2009; Teltumbde 2008; Teltumbde 2010). Rashida Manjoo, UN special rapporteur on violence against women, summed up the female Dalit condition in her statement: "The reality of Dalit women and girls is one of exclusion and marginalization, which perpetuates their subordinate position in society and increases their vulnerability, throughout generations" (Human Rights Watch 2013).

The socioeconomic discrimination and gendered caste violence are intergenerationally experienced at multiple levels by Dalit girls, too. My own evidence from the field had previously shown that Dalit young women and girl children in the two North Indian states were faced with increased gender-based violence, oftentimes by dominant-peasant caste men. A meeting with a focus group of mixed-caste women, with Dalits in the majority, brought this into sharp focus. The women had gathered to sit on a *chabutra* (raised platform) under the shade of a majestic *peepul* tree in Ghani Palthana village in the Rohtak district of Haryana. The courtyard of the *anganwadi* (government-run mother and childcare center) offered these women the privacy to speak about the gendered woes of local Dalits in Haryana. Since it was a holiday, there were no children or staff to disturb their narrative. Only the sounds of a tractor being repaired in a nearby lane and the soft cooing of pigeons in the *peepul* tree formed the backdrop to the women's voices. Many of them knew firsthand the gendered nature of caste violence, and so they worried about the safety of their daughters:

> It has become difficult for women from our community [Dalit] to step out of their homes. Young girls going to school are accosted by Jat youth in the fields or on the roads. They target low-caste women as they know they can get away with it. They don't commit dishonor (*beyijjadi*) against upper-caste women as they fear reprisals. If our girls travel in a bus, the men trouble them there too. They force themselves on the girls

(*jabardasti karte hain*). If the girls protest, they are killed. And if they live, they are so shamed by the community pointing fingers at them that they hang themselves (*beyijjadi ke karan majboor hokar phanda laga leti hain*). That's the main reason why our girls are unable to continue their education. For their own safety, parents from Dalit communities such as us have started taking our daughters out of school and keeping them at home.

Unsurprisingly, Dalit girls have the highest school dropout rate in rural areas (UNICEF 2014). Early school dropout, for Dalit girls, is due in large part to the inability of impoverished parents to pay for their education and the necessity of having all available hands in the family earn an income; however, these dropouts are caused just as much by the caste-based humiliation and abuse the schoolgirls suffer daily from upper-caste teachers (UNICEF 2014). These girls make up a large percentage of the unmarried female economic migrants to urban centers; they are absorbed within the informal economy, where they encounter caste disparity in employment and wages and certain jobs are off-limits to them because of their "untouchable" status (Sabharwal and Sonalkar 2015, 53). Early school dropouts are also caused by the corporatization of education and the fear of the girls being sexually abused while their parents spend long hours away from home earning a wage; these factors have emerged as important drivers for the lowered marriage age of Dalit girls in recent years (Human Rights Watch 2014). This might also be a significant causal factor in the increased incidence of dowry-free cross-region marriages of Dalit women to North Indian men.

On one hand, poor Dalit parents are opting to marry off their daughters early, whereas, on the other hand, the combination of the agrarian crisis, emergence of a neoliberal monetized culture to govern social relations, and spread of the consumer economy has normalized the commercialization of dowry demands (Kapadia 2002). Brides' parents are now forced to give cash and consumer goods like a TV, a fridge, or a washing machine as part of the dowry. The practice of dowry, which was earlier confined to the upper castes, is now being increasingly adopted by Dalits. Previously, they would marry off their daughters by giving five utensils. Rural distress, experienced alike by young Dalit men's families, has made them regard dowry as a capital accumulation strategy, the gendered impact of which I discuss in detail in chapter 3. Additionally, increased Sanskritisation, a term coined by the sociologist M. N. Srinivas (1952) to describe the emulation of the practices and rituals of upper castes by impoverished Dalit families as a strategy to obtain class mobility, has also led them to giving lavish feasts and huge dowries. The combination of the commercialization of dowry and Sanskritisation has thus led poor Dalit families into taking loans from informal moneylenders at high rates of interest and entering into debt bondage to marry off their daughters. This neoliberal-reform-induced economic marginalization, coupled with the historical socioeconomic one that the Dalits have had to endure on an ongoing basis, sets the backdrop for the gendered dispossessions Dalit women have to bear, including the foreclosing of matrimonial choices in their home communities and regions.

Intercaste Marriages: Churning a Caste Turmoil

Along with a sharpening of caste and class identities, there are also countertendencies toward the dilution of caste identities, which paradoxically has led to hardening of the caste divide in the two states of Haryana and Rajasthan. This is especially evident in urban areas, where there is a weakening of caste norms, as increased urbanization coupled with wider educational and employment opportunities facilitates interactions between young men and women from different castes at schools, colleges, and universities. The partial blurring of caste distinctions in these spaces also leads to contentious "love marriages" between Dalits and upper castes. As mentioned in the introduction, most marriages in India are "arranged" by parents, who take factors like caste and social status into consideration. Individual autonomy and the choice or consent of their wards is usually bypassed by the elders to cement an alliance with a "favorable" family in their own caste group. The increase in "love marriages" in India today is attributed by right-wing ideologues to the percolation of "problematic" Western ideas among India's youth.

In the instance of Haryana, such love-based alliances are vehemently opposed, especially those between dominant-caste women and Dalit men, as these social upheavals threaten to destabilize the dominant-caste hegemony. Within the research regions in North India, the antipathy to such locally transgressive intercaste unions was expressed in a guarded manner by many villagers belonging to the dominant-peasant caste group of Jats, who stated that, "societal rules established centuries ago were created for a reason" and "boundaries between groups have to be respected." While articulating such sentiments, they sought to stress that *they* were not against intercaste marriages, but instead were ostensibly voicing common opinions. However, Pushpa—a middle-aged Jat village woman from Palagarh village in the Rohtak district of Haryana who worked in her village as a community health worker, commonly known as an ASHA (accredited social health activist)—was forthright in stating hostility to the idea itself: "We will not allow for intercaste marriages here. If it happens, then the caste council will have a meeting and the family will be excommunicated from the community. We have many villages in Haryana: such transgressions will create a big social upheaval here."

The fear of intercaste marriages creating a "big social upheaval" is unsurprising as, historically, caste has been a "system . . . in which differences in the distribution of economic and political power are expressed through . . . restrictions" (Jaiswal 2000, 34). With patrilineal inheritance of land and the dependence on land and landownership acting as major determinants for caste status and hierarchy, maintaining caste endogamy in marriage relations became necessary to "regulate and reproduce . . . the hierarchy of social groups" (Jaiswal 2000, 9). Within Haryana, it was not uncommon to encounter nonelected and regressive Jat caste council (*khap panchayat*) members like Meher Singh Dhaiya making statements such as, "If our daughter dares to marry a local Dalit, we will use our belt buckle to teach her a lesson of a lifetime. Such alliances cause schisms (*darar*) in our society (*samaj*)."

Furthermore, the very act of some Dalit youth entering into "love marriages" with dominant-peasant caste women is taken as a direct threat to the masculinity, privilege, and power of the dominant-peasant caste men. In the conjugal research regions of North India, adult hegemonic masculinity is defined by qualities such as a stable job, marriage, and fatherhood, with the failure to meet these norms placing men in a subordinate masculine status. Entry into the brotherhood of hegemonic masculinity has become harder for young men from the dominant-peasant caste because of the multiple constrictions within the local marriage market and in terms of employment opportunities. Prem Chowdhry, in her work on masculinity in Haryana, has postulated that such subordinate masculinities are opportunistically harnessed by unelected and highly conservative bodies like the caste councils, or *khap panchayats*, to "offer the means through which contradictions between men are dissolved and masculine hierarchies (including those based on age) are legitimised and sustained through a public show of masculine collectivity, aggression and solidarity. This all-male public spectacle enables the marginalised categories [of masculinities] among the dominant caste male populace to come into their own" (2005, 5189).

Land Inheritance: Tracing the Roots of Gender Dispreference

Jat resistance is highest for alliances undertaken by their women with Dalit men. These marriages are interpreted as a Dalit conspiracy to gain control over Jat land, as Dalit husbands make their Jat wives claim inheritance rights over paternal property.[28] Satbir Singh Petwar, the then Sarpanch (elected village council chief) of Petwar village, whom I met in Narnaund town in Haryana, saw such marriages as a Dalit conspiracy: "The woman [from the Jat caste] in an intercaste marriage is the first to come and demand a share of parental property. For example, there's a boy from a low caste, he is very shrewd and cunning. He sees an innocent girl from a rich upper-caste family. He is from a low caste and so he lures her into marriage deliberately with 'sweet nothings.' Deep inside, he harbors greed for her father's money and land."

The Jats, in particular, strategically use constitutionally illegal caste councils (*khap panchayats*) to interpret marriages or "associations" of their women with Dalit males as serious violations of caste and customary rules. They issue caste diktats, ranging from social ostracism to sanctions against entire "erring" low-caste groups or even to the deaths of defiant couples, with unmarried dominant-caste males actively participating in acts of violence.[29] This insecurity of dominant-peasant castes can be traced to the Hindu Succession Act of 1956 that granted equality to women in inheritance rights. Shamsher Yadav, who belonged to the dominant-peasant caste of Yadavs in the Rewari district of Haryana and who wielded considerable clout in his village, Garhi Hakimpur, and in the neighboring villages thanks to the vast tracts of land he owned in the region and his status as a retired Indian Army man (*subedar*), stated the reason for the disquiet:

> The inheritance rights that the government has bestowed on women shouldn't exist. They should not have the right to inherit *both* from natal and conjugal families. The main problem is that if there are three brothers, the land will get divided three ways. But if there are two sisters, then it gets divided five ways. The brothers have already paid for her wedding and accompanying expenses and so she should be happy with it. But that is not the case as there is so much emphasis placed on land. With land becoming so expensive these days, let us assume that two killa of land is sold for 20 million Rupees. Earlier, it would have been all divided between the three brothers, but nowadays, the sisters take the land and get a share of the money.

Since ownership over the majority of landholdings accords these castes socio-economic dominance, the fear of the fragmentation of their lands, especially by non-dominant-peasant caste sons-in-law, has always been present, but became more pronounced with the passage of the Hindu Succession Act of 1956. As Virendra Vidrohi, the secretary of the NGO Matsya Mewat Shikhsha Evan Vikas Sansthan, active in the Alwar region of Rajasthan, said, "In this region, son preference is strong. The main source of income is agriculture. The question of who will own land after me—who'll inherit it and cultivate it—it raises the specter of son preference. There's distaste of giving property to the son-in-law. He should not get it at all as the property rights really belong to the son."

As mentioned earlier in this chapter, a thin minority of the rural dominant-peasant caste elites own a large proportion of the land, while the majority of the peasantry consists of small and marginal farmers with small landholdings. This section of small and marginal farmers from the dominant-peasant castes has more to lose from the real or imagined fragmentation of their meager landholdings through inheritance claims. Their anxiety about holding on to their small patch of land is further fueled by their rural elite brethren, who transform their disquiet into an emotive issue with a "caste" twist: Dalit men seeking to wrest control of their land through proxy and hence displace dominant-peasant caste's socioeconomic dominance in rural society.

Despite literally making women sign off their claims asking for a share of the paternal property,[30] these caste groups have lobbied unsuccessfully to have the Hindu Succession Act rescinded several times (Chowdhry 2011, 261). Balwant Devi, who was married to Shamsher Yadav, had served one term as the elected head of the local village-level governance institution, the Gram Panchayat, in her village, Garhi Hakimpur, in the Rewari district of Haryana. Similar to her husband, she was quite vocal about her opposition to the law that provided gender parity in inheritance rights: "Nowadays, girls demand a share of their property and force divisions within families. The sisterly love towards the brothers is not like it was in earlier times. The women ask for everything and then get the property divided up for their share."

Balwant Devi exhibited a Gramscian contradictory consciousness, one that had been deployed to increase the gender subordination of the women from the dominant-peasant castes. To elaborate, the women, while displaying an awareness of their oppression and subordination at an individual level, enact their resistances without a clear consciousness of the hegemonic ideological constraints that provide the legitimacy for their oppression and subordination. In this sense, they exhibit a Gramscian "contradictory consciousness" (Gramsci 1971, 76); their rebellions, or challenges, as they occur at an individual level, are not waged to overturn or dismantle the dominant ideologies of caste, religion, or patriarchy through collective action; they are instead waged in the name of only their own individual rights.

A variety of selective cultural and ideological controls are deployed through which the women are made to "voluntarily" relinquish their inheritance claims. The valorization of sister-brother love, the transient status of a daughter in her natal family, the substitution of dowry for inheritance, and the assurances of the natal family and her brothers' continual "protection" of the bride even in her new conjugal home are employed as patriarchal constraints to thwart any possible future claims from her.

Furthermore, inheritance claims by daughters appear as a causal factor for an increased girl dispreference. A focus group of Jat men from the village of Nagla Kasauda stated openly to me, "After marriage, her husband can lay claims to property." Additionally, the circulation of the idea of a Dalit "strategic plot" to deprive the dominant-peasant caste groups of their land through instrumentalist unions with their women might be another precipitator for the increased female feticide prevalent among the small and marginal landowning families in these caste groups.

The prevailing sentiment among dominant-peasant caste groups in this area is that they would much rather face a female shortage in their communities than worry about future fragmentation via a daughter's husband. Given such entrenched views about inheritance rights for women, it was unsurprising to have Balwant Devi narrate that that she had herself gone in for a sex determination test twenty years ago when, having given birth to five daughters, she was pregnant for the sixth time: "I paid Rs 100 to get an ultrasound done then. The doctor confirmed that I was pregnant with a male child. . . . So I did not get the abortion (*safaai*) done."

Dowry Demands Fuel Bride Shortage

Commonsense understandings of rural North Indian society link girl dispreference to the increased prevalence of the dowry economy (John et al. 2009). The tradition of seeking hypergamous alliances—that is, alliances with grooms who are socioeconomically better placed than the bride's family—places a small pool of "eligible" men and their families in a better bargaining position to make astronomical dowry demands, such as for a car or a motorcycle or other consumer durables like a washing machine. Once acquired, these items are then flaunted as visible symbols of the groom's marketability and the family's status within the caste subgroup, thus fueling a vicious cycle for those within their caste and kin networks to upstage such grooms by asking for even more blatant displays of dowry spending. According to Palriwala, the rise in dowry demands after economic liberalization allowed "the middle and lower class . . . to acquire desired consumer goods, capital for investment, bribes to 'buy' secure jobs, or an investment which may draw in further wealth" (2009, 161).

The hyper-commercialization of marriages, coupled with the agrarian crisis affecting rural farmer households, has worsened the plight of dowry providers

who have nil or marginal landholdings, as they have reduced income from agriculture and hence less disposable money to spend on dowries.[31] The pressure
to secure hypergamous alliances through bigger dowries is the second biggest
cause for rural indebtedness in Haryana (Chhikara and Kodan 2013, 356). The
Muslim community also is not exempt from this, as women increasingly face
harassment for not bringing adequate *jahez*,[32] consisting of money and goods,
to their marriage (Waheed 2009). Among Muslims, dowry is regarded as a "can-
cer or running sore (*jahez ka nasur*) that has been adopted quite recently in
imitation of Hindu practices" (Vatuk 2007, quoted in Jeffery 2014, 175).

In this context, the use of slogans like "spend Rupees 500 now and save yourself the headache of spending Rupees 500,000,"[33] by clinics offering ultrasound
services to check the sex of the fetus, tap in to the insecurity of families who
would otherwise have no choice but to seek to arrange hypergamous matrimonies by spending heavily on dowries. Despite India passing the Pre-Conception
and Pre-Natal Diagnostic Techniques Act in 1994, which banned prenatal sex
determination and sex-selective abortions, those who have mobile ultrasound
units ply their trade, and doctors offer clandestine "affordable" abortion services
to rural families burdened with an unwanted female fetus. Bimla Devi, the president of Shakti Parishad, a rural women's organization managed and run entirely by rural women from the Rewari district of Haryana, who had for years
unsuccessfully attempted to file complaint cases against doctors and clinics that
offered such services on the sly, had this to say: "The ultrasound technicians and
the gynecologists use 'code' words. If it is a female fetus, they will tell the parents-
to-be, 'bring a package of *jalebis* to celebrate the birth' and if it is a male, the
package of sweets is changed to *laddus*. Similarly, the cost of aborting the fetus
is coded: five jalebis means the cost of the abortion is Rupees 5,000, or ten jalebis
is Rupees 10,000." Pradeep also admitted in a moment of candor that, having
two daughters already, he had wanted to ensure that the third child was a male:
"Here, everyone gets it [sex determination] done on the sly (*chori chuppe karte
hain*). We find out about the clinic by asking around. Even though the government does crackdowns (*chappa*), these continue to operate. The testing and the
cleaning (*safaai*) [abortion] is fairly common among us Jats."

Pradeep never disclosed whether he had made his wife undergo an abortion.
Nor did Rajjo ever divulge which pregnancy resulted in the birth of the newest
addition to their family: a male child. But this fairly widespread practice of sex
selection through the introduction of new reproductive technologies has ad-
versely changed the societal composition in rural Haryana and Rajasthan. Satbeer, a landless truck driver from the Rohtak district of Haryana with a meagre
income of Rs 8000 per month, who had experienced the fallout of the female
deficit firsthand, was quite bitter about it. In his mid-thirties and lacking what

he termed a "muscular" male figure, Satbeer puffed furiously on his *beedi* as he recounted how he had unsuccessfully tried for seven years to get a Jat wife. He placed the blame of his bachelorhood entirely on the pervasive attitude of girl dispreference and sex-selective abortions: "There is a shortage of women among our caste. We [men like himself] are paying the cost of the sex-selective abortions (*safaai*). Earlier, I would have been able to marry here. . . . I am now going to Assam to get a bride for myself from there. Just like the others."

SOME MEN ARE MORE INELIGIBLE THAN OTHERS

Historically, among certain Hindu caste groups in North India such as the Jats, the practice of *atta-batta* or *adla-badla,* a bride swap between two families in which a family would swap a daughter for a daughter-in-law, was used by some families to ameliorate a natural bride shortage. Perforce, families desirous of cementing a marriage alliance with another were "encouraged" to follow this practice. Today, girl dispreference, the rules of *got* (clan) and village exogamy, caste endogamy, and hypergamy have brought a rupture to this female-deficit smoothing strategy and further contributed to the tightening of the marriage market for the economically disadvantaged stratum of these caste groups. Relu Ram, a Jat father-in-law from Jatianawas, a village in the Jhunjhunu district of Rajasthan, stated, "We were compelled to seek a bride from outside as we are not well off. Our son was not educated, nor did we have a daughter. Amongst the Jats, the custom of '*adla-badla*' also prevails: get your daughter married in exchange for a bride for your son from the same family. Since I did not have a daughter, I had no option but to marry [my son to someone] from another region."

The common refrain in the villages is that the practice of sex-selective abortion is a major contributory factor in creating the contemporary marriage squeeze there for local men, and thus also the need to seek wives from other states. Cultural preference for male offspring is ascribed to the customs of patrilineal inheritance of land and other productive assets; old-age insurance, relating to having a son to take care of elderly parents; and performance of funerary rites by the eldest son. Discrimination against daughters is also attributed to the unequal status of women in society and the pervasiveness of the institution of dowry. Desire to limit family size is also linked to birth order: families do not show a preference for a son for their firstborn, but if the first child is a girl, often they access medical intervention to ensure the second birth results in a son (Jha et al. 2011). The resultant consequence was summed up pithily by Rehana, a Muslim mother-in-law from a village thirty kilometers away from Jatianawas in the Jhunjhunu district of Rajasthan: "The men are unable to get married simply because pregnant women get ultrasound checks done of the fetus. If it's a boy, they continue with the pregnancy, and if it's a girl, then it's aborted. If only boys will be born, how then will we find brides for them? Will the girls fall from the sky then for them?"

However, most scholarly discussions on the ensuing bride shortage, or the "male marriage squeeze," present the deficit as cutting across the entire spectrum of North Indian society (Das Gupta et al. 2003; Mukherjee 2015). The skewed sex ratio is presented as the biggest contributor to the rise in the numbers of men from North India seeking brides from outside their local and customary marriage pools. Although it cannot be denied that sex-selective abortion of female fetuses has highly distorted the male–female sex ratio and reduced the pool of potential brides of marriageable age, evidence from the field reveals other underlying causes of rejection precipitated by girl dispreference and attendant sex-selective abortions that have resulted in the squeezing of men in their local marriage markets. In my countless conversations in Rajasthan and Haryana, villagers acknowledged the role of girl dispreference and sex-selective abortions in creating the bride deficit, yet they were equally quick to underline that the bride shortage was not experienced by all castes, nor were all men confronted with a marriage squeeze.[1]

Replacement of Family Female Labor

Here, whilst arranging a match, the girl's family looks at the employment of the man, the amount of land he owns, and other assets to ensure that their daughter and her kids will be well looked after. That's what each parent aspires to. I had very little land. Worse, I was illiterate. My mother had fallen ill. There was no one to cook for us (*roti bunune ku hisuub nuhin thu*). We would rely on the largesse of others to feed us. My parents also advised that once they were dead, I would have difficulty fending for myself on my own. I was forty years of age when I finally decided to go to Maharashtra to get a wife.

Pavan, who said these words, hailed from a village in the Rohtak district of Haryana. He owned a mere half a killa (half acre) of land, insufficient for supporting his family, which also included his ailing parents. He worked as hired help in a "tenthouse" (an establishment that provides catering and tents for marriages and other events) to supplement his ever-diminishing income from agriculture. Having just returned from an all-night shift working at a *jagran* (all-night religious song vigil) for the tenthouse, despite his tiredness, he had met me to provide an answer to my vexing query as to what constituted the final tipping point that made men like him withdraw from the local marriage market and reach out to a mediator to broker a noncustomary cross-region marriage.

Interviews with men like Pavan and their family members (n = 38) revealed that the men choose to wait until it becomes almost impossible to fend for themselves, that is, until their mother becomes too aged or infirm to look after their basic needs, or when the wives of other brothers refuse to look after the unmarried brother-in-law's daily needs. The men stated that while their sexual needs can be met locally with cash transactions, their desperate quest for a "wife" emerges when the female labor in the family has to be replaced.

As discussed in chapter 1, the spread of agrarian distress in India has fundamentally transformed the way female family labor within the household is both viewed and used. With the increasing push toward industrial agriculture in post-reform India, where both the inputs and outputs of agricultural production are increasingly controlled by big corporations, small and marginal farmers undertaking contract farming find it increasingly difficult to make money from farming. The Indian state has aggressively promoted agribusiness-led contract farming as a solution to the problems besetting Indian agriculture. Agribusinesses and farmers enter into advance contracts for a particular agricultural product with a pre-agreed-upon price, quantity, and quality, with all risks borne by the growers. The "self-exploitation" of farmers under this type of inequitable contractual arrangement also increases gender inequalities. Female family labor is increasingly prized as marginal, and landless farmers utilize this labor as a commodity in the casual agricultural wage market to supplement their ever-diminishing subsistence income. This trend of feminization of agrarian distress (Pattnaik et al. 2018) is evident in the increased entry of lower-class women from dominant-peasant caste groups into the wage market.

The shift in farming practices from the farmers' own resource-based activities to industrial agriculture relying on inputs has also increased rural household indebtedness, due to an increased reliance on informal moneylenders who charge a usurious rate of interest (Chhikara and Kodan 2013). To compensate for the decline in income and the higher agricultural input costs, these farmers are resorting to growing high-value crops that in turn demand higher inputs of labor, thereby increasing their own and their family's labor. During focus groups and interviews, marginal and small farmers, such as those from Meerpur village in the Nuh district, recognized that "hired labor is hard to find. If we hire labor, then what returns will be left for us? We do not have big pieces of land nor are we landlords. All our earning from the land will go to pay wages. It better to get a wife than a hired laborer. If there is no female in the house, then the man has no other alternative but to also sell his milch cattle (*maveshi*)."

Chet Ram, from Dhani Raghowas in the Rewari district, knew this dilemma only too well. Both his hands were atrophied and stunted from the poliovirus he had acquired as a child. Though he owned three killa of land (three acres), he could not have hoped to manage to make a decent livelihood from it if he were to hire casual agricultural wage labor. His marriage to Chandana, a poor Dalit woman from Odisha, was thus a win-win for him, as she was able to be put to work tending the family fields and looking after a couple of high-milk-yielding water buffalos, which Chet Ram had purchased almost immediately after his marriage. As he explained, "The money earned from both the farm and the sale of the milk will stay in the family. Not that there is much to earn from farming."

Rejection in the Local Marriage Market

The rejection of some men in the local marriage market is shaped by the fact that a prospective groom's steady employment ranks first among items on the desired checklist for families with daughters of marriageable age, a fact that Prem Chowdhry has underlined in her work on rural Haryana (2019). Villagers, including men in cross-region matrimonies, unequivocally state that, in the contemporary moment, only men who have government jobs (*sarkari naukri*) face no shortage of marriage proposals, while others like Dhoop Singh's son Rajesh get passed over. Dhoop Singh had tried to get his son married locally within his Jat caste pool for six long years, failing which he contacted his second cousin (*mamera bhai*) who lived in an adjoining village to help find a wife from the same place that he had brought his own *bahu* (daughter-in-law) from. Pulling deeply on his hookah, Dhoop Singh bitterly recounted,

> If a man has a government job, then the entire world seeks him. If not, then the fact of his owning one hundred acres of land cannot fetch him a single marriage proposal. My son was less educated. Nor did he have a regular job. He did have twenty killa [twenty acres] of land in his name, which is, by no measure, a small sum of land. The value of the land, immense in today's scenario, has no value. Even if a man works as a peon in government service, he will be the first to get married here. . . . Only men with government jobs are valued (*sarkari naukri danke par hain*).

Dhoop Singh's story reveals a pecking order for eligible males that exists within the local marriage market. This informal hierarchy places landed men with a government job at the top, followed by men with larger landholdings at a distant second level. At the lowest rung are those that are landless or marginal landowners, in precarious and informal employment, or considered "social rejects" because of old age, widower status, or undesirable traits of alcoholism or substance abuse.

The custom of hypergamy, in which a female marries up the social scale, has also transformed a small pool of educated men with government jobs from a thin stratum of rural communities in Haryana and Rajasthan into highly prized "eligible grooms." This is another way in which the strengthening of the neoliberal culture of capitalist relations, where social relations are monetized and determined by market forces, has reshaped marriage in India (see the 2005 edited volume *Dowry & Inheritance* by Basu for an excellent collection of essays on this). As discussed in chapter 1, this trend has transformed the practice of dowry, traditionally viewed as *stridhan* or gifts given to the bride by her family at time of her marriage, to one that now consists of cash and noncash gifts, including household goods, jewelry, and even the latest models of cars. Dowry has emerged as "leverage" to secure advantageous marriage deals for women. The reasoning stated by villagers such as Neetu from Rundh Murkedi is simple: "If we have to pay dowry anyway for securing hypergamous alliances, it is best to leverage this payment for a secure future of our daughters. These days, income from farms is uncertain. Men with a government job have security of employment (*pukki naukri*)." While large numbers of women's families vie for such men's hands in marriage, the downside is experienced by men belonging to the lower classes. This pyramidical marriage eligibility structure, both class- and asset-based, effectively serves to define which men can get married locally and which are pushed out of the marriage market and forced to seek caste-transgressive unions from other parts of India.

Dhoop Singh's bitterness can be understood within the context. With increased urbanization and real estate speculation, even farmlands in the interiors of Haryana have witnessed a meteoric rise in prices, thus making men like his son, Rajesh, quite rich by local standards. However, as a focus group of women from Dhoop Singh's village stated, "A government employed man is the girl's family's demand." Government jobs offer a stable and continuous source of employment and other perks, such as subsidized health care and a guaranteed pension. The declining rate of return from farming caused by the intensification of market-led agrarian reforms, as well as the diminishing of overall employment opportunities in the agricultural sector, have made a wide swathe of low-class men such as Pavan, who possessed marginal or small landholdings, unviable as husband material. Additionally, there has been a marked rise in unemployment and underemployment due to a decline in the creation of jobs within the manufacturing sector. For instance, one study reveals that "overall labour intensity in organised manufacturing fell from an average of 1.45 in the 1980s to 0.33 in the 2000s" (Sen and Das 2014, 3). It has also been estimated that, on average, 4.7 million young Indians enter the job market each year.[2] All of these factors operating simultaneously and in combination with each other have led to a high unemployment rate in India. According to a survey by the Labour Bureau of India, in 2015–2016, the unemployment rate stood at a five-year high of 5 percent.[3] Given these sobering statistics, it appears unsurprising that government-employed men are more sought after.

Linking Bride Shortage to Economic Precarity

"It is predominantly among the Jats that the brides from outside are being brought in. They face a shortage of girls." I found these words echoed by caste Hindu villagers across the two states. With the discontinuation of the caste census after India's independence, it is hard to obtain hard data demonstrating a low child sex ratio (CSR) among certain Hindu caste groups more than others. However, assumptions on caste-specific girl dispreference can be made based on Census of India 2011 data, which ranked the three Ahir- and Yadav-dominated districts in the state of Haryana—Jhajjhar, Mahendargarh, and Rewari—as first, second, and third, respectively, out of ten top districts with the worst CSR in the entire country; Sonipat and Rohtak, part of the Jat heartland, were ranked sixth and ninth (Census of India 2011b). Similarly, L. S. Vishwanath, who has linked the trend of female infanticide among certain castes in colonial India to present-day census results, states that, "given the low female to male sex ratio in the Jat dominated districts in U.P. and also in Punjab and Haryana, it is not difficult to surmise that this caste which resorted to female infanticide in colonial times is now practising female foeticide" (2007, 277).

Here, the data from the primary survey that I conducted among cross-region brides in Rohtak and Rewari provides a more accurate socioeconomic picture of the men in such alliances in the research areas. One of the questions in the conjugal region survey sought out details of the caste/religion of the men in cross-region marriages (see Table 1). A quick glance reveals that, among the Hindus, Jats and Ahirs together constitute 31.71 percent of the total men who have married outside of their caste and state. If the data is viewed by district, an overwhelming 490 men, or a total of 78.08 percent of such grooms from the Rohtak

TABLE 1 Caste / Religion of men in cross-region marriages

CASTE	ROHTAK	REWARI	MEWAT	ALWAR	TOTAL (NO.)	TOTAL (%)
Ahir♦	1	31			32	2.07
Bharbhunja•	1				1	.06
Bisht*	1		6		7	.45
Brahman*		4		16	20	1.30
Chamar•	27	1	6		34	2.20
Dhanak•	3				3	.19
Dhobi•	1		3		4	.26
Dom•	2				2	.13
Fakir (Muslim)			10		10	.65
Gujjar♦				1	1	.06
Harijan•		2	1		3	.19
Jat♦	456		2		458	29.64
Jogi♦	2	8	1		11	.71
Khati•	9				9	.58
Kumhar♦	1		2		3	.19
Luhar♦	7		11		18	1.16
Meghwal				1	1	.06
Meo (Muslim)			682	62	743	48.09
Muslim (General)			26		26	1.69
Nai•	2	2	15		19	1.23
Pandit*	24				24	1.55
Prajapat♦	4			1	5	.32
Quraishi (Muslim)			3		3	.19
Rajput*	8	11			19	1.23
Saini*	6				6	.39
Sakka (Muslim)			13		13	.84
Sharma*				1	1	.06
Teli♦	1		2		3	.19
Thakur*	1				1	.06
Valmiki•	9				9	.58
Undisclosed	8	4	34		46	2.98
TOTAL	584	63	817	82	1546	100

Source: Author's research study in Alwar, Mewat, and Rewari (2011), and Rohtak (2014).

* GC or General Caste, a category of higher-ranking caste groups that do not qualify for any affirmative action of the state.

♦ OBC or Other Backward Classes, an administrative category created by the Indian state. It refers to caste groups, overwhelmingly drawn from the Shudra caste group, considered to be economically, educationally, and socially depressed.

• SC or Scheduled Caste, a term used for caste groups that lie below the fourfold varna or caste hierarchy among the Hindus. The politically self-aware term is Dalits.

district, are Jats, and 49.20 percent from the Rewari district are Yadavs or Ahirs. Such numbers demonstrate the presence of a female shortage in these two dominant-peasant castes more than any other caste group among Hindus.

Paradoxically, these caste groups face a bride shortage precisely because of their sociopolitical ascendance to a dominant-peasant caste status in North India. This is directly attributable to their ownership of the majority of land, which is pivotal to their economic and political dominance, both regionally and nationally. To provide a perspective, even though the Jats in Haryana constitute 25 percent of its population, they own more than half of its cultivable land.

Patrilineal succession to land is a major contributory factor in girl dispreference, as these groups are threatened with the inheritance claims of their daughters regarding this asset. Further, there are internal stratifications within each of these dominant-peasant caste groups, as only a wafer-thin minority among them can be termed rural elites because of their ownership of large tracts of agricultural land and their attendant social clout. The vast majority of their populace comprises marginal or small peasants and landless agricultural laborers, with the latter depending on their elite-caste brethren for their livelihood as tenant farmers or agricultural wage laborers. It is only this stratum of economically marginalized dominant-peasant caste men, and not all men from these groups, that is confronted with the specter of a bride shortage.

Here, the results from the conjugal region survey on the reasons these men could not get married locally and hence had to enter into cross-region marriages acquire significance (see Table 2). In the Rohtak and Rewari districts, totals of 297 and 50 of such men, or 50.86 and 79.36 percent, respectively, cite not having a regular job or owning nil or less land as the sole reason for being rejected in the local marriage market. This is corroborated by findings listed in Table 3 about the occupation of the men in cross-region alliances. These findings reveal that a substantial number of these men work as laborers either in the farm sector or in agriculture-allied sectors or are employed in insecure or ill-paying jobs. Table 4 lists the size of the landholdings of men in cross-region marriages in selected areas of Haryana and Rajasthan; further, it shows that a large proportion of such men in these two districts are either landless or have marginal landholdings of less than one hectare that translates to a measure of two and a half acres. These two categories alone make up 66.06 and 90.09 percent, respectively, of the men in cross-region alliances in Rohtak and Rewari. If the category of small landholding (up to five acres) is added to these numbers, the percentage climbs to an overwhelming 82.18 and 95.25 percent, respectively, for Rohtak and Rewari. Significantly, none of the men in cross-region marriages own large landholdings of more than twenty-five acres. Ironically, their economic precarity, which causes their rejection as grooms locally, is also the biggest driver for marriage migration.

TABLE 2   Reasons for men to seek cross-region marriages

REASON FOR MARRIAGE	ROHTAK	REWARI	ALWAR	MEWAT	TOTAL (NO.)	TOTAL (%)
Less land or no land	186	43	42	401	672	43.46
No regular job	111	7	17	245	380	24.60
Old age / Over age	158	4		17	179	11.60
Love marriage	19		2	1	22	1.42
Death of first wife	9	3	9	72	93	6.01
Physical handicap	11	4	5	19	39	2.52
Alcoholism	8	1			9	.58
Divorce	15			5	20	1.30
Arranged marriage*	27	1			28	1.81
Second marriage♦			4	19	23	1.48
Mentally challenged	8			3	11	.71
Illiteracy	6				6	.38
Family feud•	7		2		9	.58
Social ostracism	2				2	.12
Undisclosed	17			35	52	3.36
TOTAL	584	63	81	817	1546	100

Source: Author's research study in Alwar and Rewari (2011), and Rohtak (2014).
* Same-caste marriage following rules of caste endogamy and village and got exogamy. These alliances were with same-caste families from villages in neighboring provinces.
♦ This is applicable only to the Meo. As Muslims, they can have up to four wives. The second marriage occurs with first wife still residing with the husband.
• Family members creating hurdles in the man's marriage locally.

Social Rejects and Marriage Rejection

Men are considered "social rejects" for a variety of reasons. They may have undesirable social traits such as alcoholism, substance abuse, or a history of anger or intimate partner violence, suffer from some physical deformity, be a widower, or have been deserted by a wife, causing them to also face the increased specter of singledom in rural North India. Mahmood, a twenty-four-year-old Meo man, was one such person who got rejected locally because of his so-called "dim-wittedness."

I met Mahmood's elder brother Amjad one humid August afternoon while returning to Meerpur village from Punhana, the *tehsil* (administrative block) headquarters of the Punhana block in the Nuh district of Haryana. I had hitched a motorcycle ride with Saddif, a Meerpur resident I had met while on my way back from research in a nearby village, and we were hailed by another motorcyclist. Saddif introduced Amjad by saying, "His brother has gone to get married in Jharkhand."

Amjad wore a big smile as he greeted us, *"As salaam aleykum."* He proceeded to take out his cellphone and show a low-resolution picture, from his WhatsApp,

TABLE 3   Occupation of men in cross-region marriages

OCCUPATION	ROHTAK	REWARI	MEWAT	ALWAR	TOTAL (NO.)	TOTAL (%)
Laborer	141	46	471	62	721	46.63
Farmer*	227	3	213	10	453	29.30
Driver♦	84	4	33		119	7.70
Shopkeeper•	19	3	23	2	47	3.04
Cattle rearing	2	5	3		10	.65
X-ray technician				1	1	.06
Maulvi				3	3	.19
Goatherd			1		1	.06
Itinerant salesman			5		5	.32
Rickshaw puller				1		.06
Barber	2				2	.12
Tailor	1		4		5	.32
Mason	7		17	1	25	1.61
Carpenter	5			1	6	.38
Gardener	1				1	.06
Photographer	1				1	.06
Cable operator	1				1	.06
Engineer	1				1	.06
Milk seller	3		3		6	.39
Factory worker	21	1			22	1.42
Government job	1				1	.06
Shop employee	9				9	.58
Electrician	10				10	.65
Private sector employee	23				23	1.49
Street vendor	3		2		5	.32
Sweetshop helper	5		2		7	.45
Horse cart owner			7		7	.45
Unemployed	9		15		21	1.36
Undisclosed	8	1	18		27	1.75
TOTAL	584	63	817	82	1546	100

Source: Author's research study in Alwar, Mewat, and Rewari (2011), and Rohtak (2014).
* This category includes those owning less than 2 acres of land.
♦ The category of drivers includes those driving trucks, minivans, auto-rickshaws, or tempos.
• This category includes grocery stores, mobile repair shops, tire puncture repair shops, sweetshops, and ͏̈́͏̈́͏̈́ ͏̈́͏̈́ ͏̈́͏̈́͏̈́ ͏̈́͏̈́

of a teenage girl standing in front of a mud hut, wearing an embroidered green-and-red colored saree, with a red *chunni* covering her hair. "This is the photo of my younger brother Mahmood's wife-to-be. The *nikaah* will happen tomorrow morning. See the clothes she is wearing. My mother bought them and sent them for her." From what I could make out from the photograph, the bride-to-be ap-

TABLE 4 Size of landholdings of men in cross-region marriages in select areas of Haryana and Rajasthan

SIZE OF LANDHOLDING AREA (ACRES)	ROHTAK (NO.)	ROHTAK (%)	REWARI (NO.)	REWARI (%)	ALWAR (NO.)	ALWAR (%)	TOTAL (NO.)	TOTAL (%)
Landless	162	27.74	33	52.39	49	59.76	244	33.5
Marginal < 2.5	218	37.32	23	36.50	13	15.85	254	34.9
Small 2.5–5	100	17.12	4	6.35	8	9.75	112	15.3
Semi-medium 5–10	65	11.14	2	3.18	6	7.32	73	10
Medium 10–25	39	6.68	1	1.58	6	7.32	46	6.3
Large > 25	Nil	–	Nil	–	Nil	–	Nil	–
TOTAL	584	100	63	100	82	100	728	100

Source: Author's research study in Alwar, Mewat, and Rewari (2011), and Rohtak (2014).

peared tense, unsmiling, and quite young. I wondered about the reasons that had made her and her family agree to this marriage, and what dreams she had nurtured about her life as a married woman. Instead of voicing my thoughts, I looked again at the photograph and commented, "She looks wonderful in those clothes—so well chosen by your mother (*ami*)." This appeared to please Amjad, who then proceeded to tell me that "he [Mahmood] has 60 percent intelligence—he is only 'loose' in his head (*sirf dimag se thorha loose hai*). His memory is not so good. You cannot really call him mad as he is able to work. He is uneducated and rears pigeons. He lacks social skills."

Amjad's comments about his own brother need to be understood in the context of the considerable stigma attached to intellectual disability in rural India, attributable in large part to the lack of diagnosis and specialized services (Rohwerder 2018). Consequently, men like Mahmood, labeled *seedha-saadha* (simple-natured), are misunderstood and marginalized by the local community. Very much like Pradeep's eldest brother, Bijai, who was considered a *bhola* (simpleton or dimwit) and similarly stigmatized by the villagers, Mahmood also found it hard to marry locally.

Mahmood and Amjad's family owned two acres of productive farmland that also boasted a borewell—in a region where a majority of Meo households were marginal landowners or landless (see Table 5 for the average size of landholdings for Nuh), their family stood out. However, the family was well aware that, as a social reject, Mahmood could never get married locally even with the poorest of the poor Meo families. This made them seek a cross-region bride, as they had heard that desperately poor Muslim families with daughters in regions like Bihar, Assam, Jharkhand, and West Bengal who were unable to pay dowry to local men, were open to proposals from Meo men and were also willing to overlook some

TABLE 5 Operational land-holding pattern for Mewat district, Haryana

SIZE GROUP (IN ACRES)*	NUMBER OF FARMERS	NUMBER OF FARMERS (%)	AREA	AREA (%)
Below 1.25	34959	45.89	10407	9.23
1.25–5.0	24168	31.73	24943	22.09
5.0–12.5	13122	17.23	40280	35.68
12.5–25.0	2974	3.9	19895	17.62
25.0–50.0	723	.95	9802	8.69
50.0 and above	221	.3	7535	6.68
TOTAL	76167	100	112862	100

Source: Adapted from 2014 Director of Land Records, Haryana, cited in Sehgal Foundation, 2015, *Identifying Backwardness of Mewat Region in Haryana.*
* Measurements of hectares in official records have been converted to acres.

"blemishes" (*daag*) in their desire to "settle" their daughters. Mahmood's three brothers, in particular, were keen to find a wife for him: "We have agreed to bear the expense of his household. Our wives are unable to take care of their own households—can you imagine them taking on his extra load on top of everything? That is why we have decided to get a bride from outside (*bahar se*). Each brother will get half an acre of agricultural land in inheritance. Mahmood can lease that land to a tenant farmer and earn some money from that. His wife can help him manage that land."

Land, Inheritance, and Marriage

Mahmood's brothers, who were willing to chip in for his wedding expenses and future household costs, and equally divide up the two acres of land four ways, stood out as a rare example. Yet, in common with many other men's decisions to opt for cross-region matrimony was the inability or outright refusal of the women in the household to attend to Mahmood's, or all of the men's, daily needs, including providing food and washing clothes.

A significant finding of my research shows that, with the prevalence of patrilineal inheritance, the marriage of other male members in the family, particularly in instances where small measures of land are at stake, has emerged as a direct threat to the proportion of inheritance that other married brothers and their children stand to gain from the men's bachelor status. This is noteworthy, given that 34.91 percent of men in cross-region marriages in this study owned less than one hectare or two and half acres of land (see Table 4).

As mentioned in chapter 1, almost all the research regions have witnessed a sharp rise in land prices due to real estate speculation and state-led land acquisition for industrial complexes and the rezoning of agricultural land for industrial or urban planning use. The regions surrounding the National Capital Region of Delhi such as Rohtak, Rewari, and Alwar have had the sharpest hike. Even in the industrially backward region of Nuh, a focus group of men from Meerpur village stated that, "Earlier one killa [one acre] of land in these parts would cost Rupees 200,000–250,000. Today, the same land fetches a price of Rupees 1.4 million. If the plot is near a main road, the price has shot up to 4 to 5 million Rupees for one killa [one acre]."

In Haryana, from the 1990s onward, the state government has put into place new policies for land acquisitions and compensation, commonly known as the "Haryana model" (Kennedy 2019). The compensation structure has benefited dominant-peasant caste groups such as the Jats, who own a significant proportion of Haryana's land. The changed political economy has made even rural families with small landholdings, whose earnings from agriculture have eroded because of the agrarian crisis, view their land in a different light. A focus group of men from Dahiya Khap Panchayat elaborated on the new neoliberal mindset of the landed Jat youth: "Earlier our forefathers would think of amassing land for the future generations, but the boys today think the reverse. They think of how quickly can they sell the land and then, with the money, buy cars, guns, and eat lavishly in big hotels."

According to Phool Kumar Petwar, who headed the Petwar Tapa,[4] the pernicious hold of neoliberal culture has resulted in land no longer being "perceived as a legacy for future generations. It is now valued only for its market value. This has changed the way people relate to each other in a family. Brotherly love (bhaichara) doesn't exist anymore because of this."

Petwar's conclusions were echoed by the villagers as well as by the men in cross-region marriages, who stated that it was in the realm of arranging matrimony for male siblings that the most perceptible shift in brotherly love, or bhaichara, would be witnessed. Customarily, marriages are arranged by elders in the family, including older brothers, who are usually married off first. The reshaping of families by capitalist relations, where money is paramount in determining family relationships, is a phenomenon that Satbir Singh, at the time the Sarpanch of Petwar village, traced back to occurring with increasing intensity "from the late 1990s and particularly from 2000 onwards when government made changes in laws around land use." He elaborated that changes in laws related to land use and the conversion of agricultural land into commercial and industrial use had led to a sharp escalation in land prices caused by land speculation. This led close family members of many aspirant bachelors to try to actively put a wrench in their chances of getting married locally. Such efforts were directly attributable to a desire to prevent increased fragmentation of marginal landholding through the marriage of an unmarried brother and the consequent birth of his children, who would stand to inherit the land.

Satbir, the unmarried truck driver in his mid-thirties who was now contemplating traveling to Assam for a bride, affirmed, "When I was younger, if a *rishta* or a marriage proposal did come, my other brothers would not show interest in pursuing it. They were greedy for my land. They would nix (*tangri lagaa detey*) my matrimonial chances." Pradeep, the cab driver from Jhunjhunu who was trying to get his elder brother Bijai married off, had similarly encountered resistance about Bijai's marriage from his own wife, Rajjo, and his second eldest brother, Rajdeep. Rajjo had expressed her discontent to Pradeep in private about the anticipated three-way division of the homestead and agricultural land that would occur with Bijai's marriage. On the other hand, Rajdeep had openly argued with both his brother and their mother. Pradeep ruefully divulged, "the property angle (*zamin ka chakkar*) [has] distorted relations and created schisms within the family."

The escalation in property prices and the changed value of land has also brought an attitudinal shift in locally rejected bachelors who, prior to this, might have been content to remain unmarried. They appear keener to seek cross-region marriages, either on their own initiative or with the help of elderly parents. A focus group of Jat men from the village Nagla Kasauda in the Rohtak district of Haryana revealed the true linkages among the monetization of family relations, land, and marriage: "These days, a man who is unable to get married thinks that his brother's wife does not treat him nicely or feed him well. So why the heck should he give his property share to her children? He feels he is better off selling a piece of his land to get a wife to look after his needs. Earlier, the men lacked money and therefore could not contemplate such an action."

Karam Beer from the Rohtak district, who had tried hard to get married locally, did exactly this. He sold a small portion of his three *bigha*[5] of agricultural land (three quarter of an acre) to raise the necessary capital to pay the broker's fee and the cost of travel and wedding expenses. He was illiterate and worked as a *raj mistry*, or mason, a job that was both irregular and seasonal. Early every morning, he would travel to a small town near his village and wait hopefully at a road crossing, along with several other hopefuls, for a contractor to pick him out for *dehadi* (daily wage work). If he was lucky, he would get work for ten to twelve days in a month. He stated, "My hair had turned grey as I aged. All my friends and relatives were married and had grown-up children. Only I was a bachelor. I was tired of begging scraps from my own family members to feed me. How long could this go on? So, I sold a small piece (*tukda*) of my inheritance (*hissa*) and used it to get married."

In Table 2, which lists the reasons for seeking cross-region marriages, a total of 162 men, or 22.24 percent of all the men surveyed in Rohtak and Rewari, cited being "over age" as their reason for being forced to seek a wife elsewhere. The men try finding a match locally within their caste marriage pool, but at around thirty to thirty-five years of age, it appears that an eligibility cutoff occurs and they are declared "too old" in the local marriage market.

Here, I broaden the conceptualization of dispossession elaborated on in the introduction and extend it to the masculinity of rural North Indian men. As mentioned, neoliberal privatization of social services, health, and education has led to the increased aspirations of women's families to secure husbands who offer financial stability through coveted government jobs. The rejection of economically precarious men in their local marriage market and the attendant shame of this dismissal results in the loss of their masculine honor within their tightly knit, caste-specific male groups and in the larger village community. The stigma of being a *daagi*, or one with blemishes, is emasculating, as such men become the butt of snide, dismissive remarks in homosocial environments of leisure and at *khap* meetings. This notion of masculine dishonor is multiplied by the fact that the local rejects, instead of getting a handsome dowry in marriage as they would have if they married locally, have to pay huge sums to facilitate their own cross-region weddings. This irony is not lost on rural men, who waste no opportunity to rub the loss in through comments like, "he [referring to a man in a cross-region matrimony] had to pay a fortune to a marriage agent to 'buy' a bride from Bihar," and "rejected material (*maal*) here ends up getting a wife whose antecedents are unverified (*jaat paat ka kuch pata nahin hai*). Who knows from where they get *these* women [referring to the cross-region brides]."

The dual stigma of being unmarried and unemployed also confers a societally "immature" masculine status to the men. This sidelines them from participating equally with other men in their community, thus creating a "crisis of masculinity" among them (Chowdhry 2005, 5192). The ensuing masculine identity crisis emerges as another causal factor precipitating the rise in noncustomary cross-region matrimonies. According to Pradeep, who was actively searching for a cross-region bride for his elder brother Bijai, it also makes bachelors more suspect in the eyes of local families: "People are not so welcoming as they think that these bachelors might try to ensnare the women into sexual relations. They do not get respect. Marriage gives them respectability."

Reinscribing Caste Hierarchies through Long-Distance Matrimonies

In the caste Hindu-dominated research areas of Rohtak and Rewari in Haryana and Jhunjhunu in Rajasthan, the elites from the three dominant-peasant subcastes—the Jats, Yadavs, and Ahirs—control most of the land. Ritually, these three castes are located in the bottommost Shudra *varna*, that is, just above the Dalits in the Brahmanical caste hierarchy. Following India's independence, redistributive land reforms were undertaken in the 1950s to end landlordism, impose a ceiling on landholding size, and confer landownership rights to existing tenants. However, these reforms ended up largely benefiting sections of caste groups, like the Jats and the Yadavs in North India, employed largely as agricultural managers or tenant farmers for upper-caste Brahmin and Rajput landlords. The displacement of the upper castes' land by these groups marked the latter's complete ascendance as dominant-caste groups in rural North India. In the subsequent decades, these dominant-peasant caste groups, by forming formidable caste blocs in Indian politics, have succeeded in blocking further land reforms meant to benefit the landless and marginalized Dalits.

The heightening of caste-based atrocities against the Dalits in Haryana and Rajasthan reveals a latent insecurity among their aggressors, the dominant-peasant Hindu castes, in their bid to hold on to their newly acquired sociopolitical dominant-caste status. This comes in light of the affirmative reservation policies of the Indian state toward the Dalits. Despite and in contradiction to their dominant-peasant caste tag, the economically depressed and landless men from these castes face rejection in a local marriage market already tightened with a bride deficit caused by hypergamy, caste endogamy, and sex-selective abortions.

As discussed earlier, the men and their families, despite knowing that the chances of securing a bride locally are slim, usually continue persisting in their search within the local caste (*jati*). However, with continued failure and increasing "old age," they usually take stock of the situation and realize that their only recourse is to remain single or transgress customary marriage norms to obtain a wife from another part of India. As Satbeer, the truck driver from Rundh Murkhedi village in Haryana, said, "A man first tries to get a match from within his caste and community. His honor (*izzat*) is not lost then. However, when it is not possible, his helplessness forces him to seek a bride from elsewhere."

Ostensibly, the female shortage caused by sex selection within their caste is the primary motive for obtaining "low-caste" wives from distant parts of India. However, what emerges is that the compulsion to do this, and risk losing highly valued caste honor, is necessitated only when men find it difficult to meet their day-to-day household needs, an important consideration given that women also perform 80 percent of the agricultural and animal husbandry chores. Krishna Devi, a mother-in-law of a cross-region bride from Bengal, affirmed, "I am too old now to be doing things. We are no longer worried about matching caste." The tipping point that makes families transgress caste rules on marriage appears to be the need for a female body to perform unpaid labor—both productive and reproductive—even though they invite social sanctions against them by doing so. A focus group of Jat men from Nagla Kasauda in Haryana affirmed, "It is like this: you have to continue your lineage and also need someone to cook for you and take care of the fields (*khet*). It is because of helplessness (*majboori*) that such marriages [cross-region] take place. We deliberately turn our face away from the caste transgression in such alliances (*muh morh dete hain*)."

However, the adjustment process is not smooth for either the incoming brides or the families into which they marry. Relu Ram's daughter-in-law, Barfo, belonged to an Indigenous group (the Adivasi) from Chhattisgarh, whose mode of subsistence was the sale of forest produce and not settled agriculture. She was also alien to the practice of taking care of milch cattle. Her mother-in-law, Khajani Devi, stated that when Barfo had first come to them, she had had to expend a lot of time and energy to teach Barfo about the household and field-related chores: "We had to teach her practically everything. . . . It took her a long while to learn the routine here. Her inability to understand our language was also a big hindrance in her adjustment process. If I asked her to collect cow dung, she would bring me a shovel."

The common refrain among the dominant-peasant caste men and their family members (n=62 out of a total of 75 interviewed) was that the culturally alien work ethic and food habits make it difficult for the incoming cross-region brides, who experience adjustment problems as they cannot easily perform the chores that local women have grown up learning. Given this, it bears asking why locally rejected Jat males are not undertaking marriages locally with women from the supposedly "female-rich" Dalit castes. The families would not have to incur travel expenses or pay mediator fees, nor would the local low-caste brides require training to meet expectations around the local work ethic.

The survey results reveal that an overwhelming number of cross-region marriages undertaken by dominant-peasant caste Hindu men from the two states are transgressive of caste. To illustrate, survey results from the Rohtak district (see Table 1) reveal that 77.69 percent of the men in cross-region marriages were Jats, while brides in Rohtak, self-identified as Scheduled Caste (SC) or Scheduled Tribe (ST), totaled 214 (see Table 6). Similarly, the Rewari district survey shows that, of thirty-one cross-region marriages undertaken by Ahir caste men (see Table 1), twenty-four brides self-identified as Scheduled Caste or Dalit (see Table 6). In the natal states of Odisha and West Bengal, 53.9 percent, or 104, of the surveyed families with daughters in cross-region alliances were of a Scheduled Caste (see Table 7). The evident intercaste nature of these alliances poses

TABLE 6 Caste/Religion data of cross-region brides from select conjugal regions

CASTE	ALWAR	MEWAT	REWARI	ROHTAK	TOTAL (NO.)	TOTAL (%)
Hindu GC♦	16	–	23	142	181	11.32
Hindu OBC•	–	4	12	158	174	11.26
Hindu BC⚥	–		–	9	9	.58
Hindu SC*	3	8	24	193	228	14.76
Hindu ST*	–	–	–	21	21	1.37
Muslim	63	646	4	15	728	47.11
Sikh	–	–	–	3	3	.20
Christian	–		–	3	3	.20
Buddhist	–		–	1	1	.06
Undisclosed	–	159	–	45	204	13.20
TOTAL	82	817	63	584	1546	100

Source: Author's study in Alwar, Mewat, and Rewari (2011), and Rohtak (2014).
* Hindu SC and Hindu ST stands for Scheduled Caste and Scheduled Tribes, respectively, and are counted as Dalit.
♦ GC, or General Caste, refers to the three caste groups of Brahmins, Kshatriyas, and Vaishyas, which do not benefit from affirmative action by the state.
• OBC or Other Backward Classes refers to caste groups considered educationally and socially depressed, most often from the fourth varna of the Shudra.
⚥ Hindu BC—Backward Classes

TABLE 7 Caste/Religion of cross-region brides from select natal regions

CASTE	BALESHWAR (NO.)	BALESHWAR (%)	COOCH BEHAR (NO.)	COOCH BEHAR (%)	TOTAL (NO.)	TOTAL (%)
Hindu SC*	26	38.80	78	61.90	104	53.9
Hindu ST*	1	1.5			1	.5
Hindu GC♦	8	11.94	16	12.70	24	12.43
Hindu OBC•	31	46.26	9	7.14	40	20.72
Muslim OBC•			14	11.12	14	7.25
Muslim	1	1.5	9	7.14	10	5.2
TOTAL	67	100	126	100	193*	100

Source: Author's research study in Odisha (2011), and West Bengal (2014).
Note: A total of 154 families were surveyed in the two states, but some families had more than one daughter married across regions. This number denotes a total of women in cross-region marriages from the survey of such families.
* Hindu SC and Hindu ST stands for Scheduled Caste and Scheduled Tribes, respectively, and are counted as Dalit.
♦ GC, or General Caste, refers to the three caste groups of Brahmins, Kshatriyas, and Vaishyas, which do not benefit from affirmative action by the state.
• OBC or Other Backward Classes refers to caste groups considered educationally and socially depressed.

a dilemma, as trenchant opposition to local intercaste alliances and related perpetrations of caste atrocities against local Dalits overwhelmingly comes from Jats (Teltumbde 2012; WSS 2014).

Here, a brief digression into caste and marriage rules becomes necessary. Although *anuloma*—that is, marriage between high-caste men and women lower in the caste hierarchy—is conceptually allowed, in practice, such marriages do not have large-scale acceptance as they have the potential to disrupt the "status quo in social and economic relationships between two caste categories" (Chowdhry 2011, 234). With women considered as "gateways ... to [the] caste system" (Chakravarti 2003, 67), a woman's body is regarded as a vessel that can be "internally defiled" with the semen of a lower-caste man (Dube 1996, 13–14). In that sense, marriages of upper-caste women with lower-caste men threaten to dilute hierarchies by challenging the concept of "caste purity." The highly exploitative caste system that grants to the upper castes land, resources, political and economic power, and customary access to the labor of the castes below them can be maintained and reproduced only if stratifications between various caste groups are strictly maintained.

Historically, in Haryana, a small number of wealthy landowners were able to overcome a female shortage through marriages with local low-caste women (Chowdhry 2011; Darling [1925] 1977). During the colonial period, these marriages were contested by the groom's community, and subsequent to the marriage, the low-caste bride was made to break off all contact with her family, so that the "myth of [the bride] belonging to a higher caste" (Chowdhry 2011, 120, also 121–153) would not get demolished. Moreover, the circulation of a local proverb, *beeran ki kai jaat nahin* (what caste can a woman have), emphasizing the fluidity of a woman's caste and its dependence on the caste or religion of the man she married (Pandey 2001, 165), also helped keep the veneer of caste approval intact. Yet, despite the popularity of the adage "whoever marries a Jat becomes a Jatni," meaning that the woman acquires the caste identity of her husband, such women and their offspring were not accorded equal status with same-caste brides (Chowdhry 2011, 120–153).

The context for such marriages in contemporary India is totally different. As mentioned in chapter 1, affirmative reservation policies around jobs and education for historically marginalized castes, Dalit political awareness, and "taboo" love marriages between Dalits and upper castes pose a threat to the hegemony of dominant-caste groups in Haryana, thus making them more anxious to assert their dominance, especially in rural areas. The group of Jat men from Nagla Kasauda village in the Rohtak district of Haryana who had argued for cross-region matrimonies as an unavoidable necessity for the future well-being of some families were also quite emphatic in stating that the Jat community (*biradari*) would not allow local caste-transgressive unions to occur:

> Over here, love marriages are taking place between Harijans (Dalits) and the Brahmins or the Jats even though the caste difference is huge. However, such marriages are not occurring through community consensus.
> Q: Why not through community consensus?
> A: Our societal structures does not allow this to occur. If someone marries a woman from another region, no one is wiser about the caste of the bride. It is an unknown. Here, if such a marriage takes place, it will lead to caste conflict. That is the main reason why intercaste marriages cannot take place here.

Marrying a low-caste woman from a far-off region thus becomes a preferred option for the Jats and other dominant-caste groups—with several spin-offs, one of which is the creation of fabricated caste genealogies for the migrant brides. Such alliances do not pose a challenge to the existing unequal caste hierarchy, as the vast geographical distance between the two regions has restricted social policing about the women's caste identity. One fictive justification for these non-customary marriages is made on grounds that two *jatis* are similar, on the same caste scale, and merely known by a different name, even though they are geographically distant. However, it needs to be understood that each *jati* and *got* has spatial limits—Jats are confined to the North Indian states of Haryana, Punjab, Rajasthan, and parts of Madhya Pradesh and Uttar Pradesh, and are not found elsewhere. In addition, potential grooms also do not insist on finding caste equals to marry, as they often have a fuzzy understanding of the natal-region caste groups or their ranking in the caste hierarchy, because of the alien sounding *jati* and *got* names and the absence of exact caste equivalents to facilitate comparisons. Finally, sourcing local low-caste women for wives could be interpreted as a tacit approval of alliances between their own women and Dalit men. As discussed, with women having legal equal inheritance rights over paternal property, they act as "potential introducers of fresh blood and new descent lines through their husbands" (Chowdhry 2007, 264). Given this, long-distance alliances allow the Jat community to maintain a status quo in opposing the marriage of Jat women with local Dalit men in Haryana. The men's families are able to maintain a stoic public facade and vociferously claim that the cross-region brides are not of "low-caste" stock by hiding or fabricating their identities. An interview with Mukesh Devi, a Jat woman from Uncha Tendroli village in the Rohtak district with a daughter-in-law from West Bengal, brought this out sharply: "If we bring a woman from elsewhere, we tell our kin and villagers that she belongs to caste groups such as the Jats, Thakurs,[6] or Gujars over there. We reassure everyone that she is the same caste as ours. However, if [our men] marry a low-caste woman from this region, the truth will come out in a moment that the bride belongs to a Scheduled Caste—that she is a Chamar or a Churhi."[7]

Families therefore recognize that the "truth" about similar alliances, when undertaken locally, cannot be hidden and that "objections" can be raised, with serious repercussions ranging from ostracism to excommunication by the caste group. This was reiterated by a focus group of Jat men from Nagla Kasauda: "If someone marries a woman from another region, no one is wiser about the caste of the bride. It is an unknown."

Conjugal family members often assert that the brides belong to the Jat or the Yadav caste in West Bengal or Odisha, with the only difference being that these castes have a different name there. However, historically, when one group of a caste subgroup, or *jati*, adopted a different economic activity with a changed social status and power, it eventually would lead to a rupture in "social interaction with its other caste constituents" (Jaiswal 2000, 5). The contention that entering into non-endogamous alliances through cross-region matrimony does not breach caste rules is also negated, as the two *gots*, in a majority of cases, have come from different socioeconomic strata and occupations. According to Kosambi, the migration of a *got* to another region altered its ranking in the caste hierarchy; and, if the differentiation persisted, that *got* regarded itself as different and no longer intermarried within the subcaste (1997, 15). Crucially, as Mukesh Devi, a mother-in-law, revealed, the incoming brides of Dalit background are advised to hide their caste identity, a fact confirmed by brides in Hindu households (n=29). The brides mentioned that they are asked to hide their true Dalit status and instead state that their families belong to the Jat or Yadav caste. This is hardly surprising, as the Dalits face systemic and structural discrimination because of their low-caste status and are subjected to daily humiliation, degradation, and exploitation through caste-enforced codes governing dress, behavior, housing, employment, and access to services and resources (Shah et al. 2006).

Moreover, when families were questioned about the response of the community toward caste transgression in cross-region marriage, they typically responded with "we will cross that bridge when it comes" (*tab ki tab dekha javega*). This false bravado about caste ostracism is also fueled by a hope that their family will be an exception to the rule and spared the ignominy of bringing home a low-caste cross-region bride. Caste councils, or *khap panchayats*, also offer tacit approval of these marriages, as they do not directly challenge existing local unequal caste hierarchies. On this, Nafe Singh Nain, president of Sarv Jat Khap Maha Panchayat (Supreme Council of Jat Caste Groups), whom I met in his home in Vinodha Kalan village in the Jind district of Haryana, stated, "There are many bachelors in every village who go and bring wives. They bring a woman from some other caste from another region because they are helpless (*majboor hain*) and cannot marry locally. But within the village, we won't have marriage with different *jatis*. . . . Different caste groups have been historically created for a reason and should be kept intact."

In this light, cross-region marriages have to be viewed as shrewd and carefully crafted tactics that allow the conjugal families from the dominant-peasant castes to circumvent rules on intercaste marriages and avoid caste sanctions. They permit the caste Panchayats to sidestep the quagmire of the intercaste nature of these alliances, by simply stating that the caste identity of these women is "ambiguous" or that the women come from similarly placed Jat communities that are just labeled differently in another region and language. The practice thus lets both villagers and kin networks use the fabricated caste identities of the cross-region brides as flimsy excuses for turning a blind eye to the blatant caste infractions of these alliances. Most importantly, it provides continued legitimacy to the upper castes, allowing them to maintain intact the local unequal hierarchies of caste relations and power by opposing intercaste alliances on the home turf.

The Puzzle of Marriage Rejection among the Meo

The Meo are a study in contrast to the dominant-peasant Hindu caste groups in Haryana and Rajasthan. The socioeconomic and political dominance of the Jats, Ahirs, and Yadavs, and the socioeconomic marginalization of the Meo, can be traced back to the colonial period, the repercussions of which are felt in contemporary India. At that time, significant changes occurred in landownership and caste-specific occupations, in conjunction with the colonial state's use of the ethnic and religious "divide and rule" policy. The Meo, quite unlike the Jats or the Ahirs, historically owned the majority of lands in the region known as Mewat and also ruled Mewat autonomously. However, after the Rebellion of 1857 against the British, in which the Meo actively participated, Mewat was deliberately divided up, by the colonial rulers, between the Hindu princely states of Alwar and Bharatpur under British Paramountcy, with another part directly administered by the British. It also led the colonialists to classify the Meo as "the boldest of criminal classes" (Aggarwal 1971, 40)—and thus began the process of "othering" them. As Mayaram wrote, "The nineteenth-century story for the Meos became one of growing impoverishment and indebtedness . . . in contrast to the Jats to whom benefits accrued from the canal-irrigated areas and who were consequently constructed as loyal peasants" (2003, 33) to the Imperial Crown.

From the mid-1920s, state-sponsored policies further assisted the ideological transformation of the Meo into the "internal other."

These politically motivated attempts to create "Hindu indigenization" and "Muslim otherness" wreaked havoc on the Meo during the Partition of India in 1947, when they were violently targeted by Hindu caste groups like the Jats, Gujjars, and Ahirs with the tacit support of the Hindu princely states of Alwar and Bharatpur. During this time, close to half of the Meo population migrated to Pakistan, while their lands were appropriated by the Hindu caste groups of Jats and Ahirs, who had previously lived alongside them. The failure of the post-independence Indian state and the Congress Party, the ruling political party at that time, to intervene and help return forcibly occupied land to the Meo, taking it back out of the hands of the dominant-peasant caste groups of the Jats and the Ahirs, affected the collective psyche of the Meo and increased their economic vulnerability. Until 1947, the Meo had been made up of small and medium landowners who possessed most of the fertile land. Present-day Meo are predominantly small and marginal peasants, owning between one and two acres of land. Subsistence rain-fed farming is complemented with income from farm and non-farm rural labor, such as cattle-rearing and agricultural wage labor.

In post-independence India, the social identification of the Meo religious identity as "Muslim" in a Hindu majoritarian society, along with increased religious intolerance on one hand, and their rejection by the mainstream Muslim community for not being "Islamic" enough on the other, has set the tone for Meos experiencing other forms of discrimination. Their socioeconomic marginalization, evident through Meo-majority areas ranking low in all development indices, stems from the indifference of political classes, willful neglect by bureaucracy, and prevailing anti-Muslim prejudice. Despite the vast gap on all counts between the dominant-peasant Hindu caste groups and the Meo, they have, it appears, one thing in common: cross-region marriages.

Contentions about female feticide as a major contributory factor are contradicted by my fieldwork among the Meo community in the Nuh and Alwar districts of Haryana and Rajasthan and affirmed by Census of India data. Meo-dominated areas boast the best child sex ratios in the country, with Nuh showing 906 females for 1,000 males in the census of 2011.[8] According to the Census of India (2011a), Punhana *tehsil*, one of the two primary research areas covered for information about the Meo (Alwar being the second), boasts the highest CSR, 917 girls to 1,000 boys, in Haryana. This figure is in line with previous censuses, in which the two regions have consistently recorded high CSRs. This can be partly attributed to the Meo not having the financial means to pay ultrasound clinics and doctors for sex determination and sex-selective abortions. Low literacy rates among them is also ascribed to the favorable CSR.[9]

Prima facie, then, the Meo do not appear to suffer from the bride deficit that plagues the dominant-peasant castes in Haryana and Rajasthan. Nor also do they appear to face the crisis of "patrilineal inheritance" that apparently besieges the landed Jats and Yadavs, wherein daughters demand a share of parental land, a factor laying the foundation for girl dispreference and sex-selective abortions among some groups. In fact, focus groups of Meo men and women and informal conversations with Meo villagers sought to emphasize this difference from the caste Hindus. This is significant because, very much like the caste Hindus, the Meo consider land to be subject to patrilineal inheritance. Despite Muslim laws granting women inheritance rights, succession to their father's property is usually denied to daughters under customary Meo laws (Shamsh 1983, 166; Sikand 1995). Inheritance of property by widows is also frowned on, and, in many instances, women themselves forgo their inheritance rights under social pressure. Additionally, the caste-class conflict between dominant-peasant castes and the Dalits, with the added scenario of intercaste marriage among them adding more fuel to the fire, is also absent here. This then creates a puzzling research question: If the Meo community is not confronted with a female shortage, why then has the practice of cross-region marriages with mainstream Muslims—shunned a mere generation ago—taken root? What other reasons precipitate the willingness of the Meo to breach their customary marriage practices and risk social ostracism?

Here a brief detour is in order, to explain the marriage traditions of the Meo, as a distinct ethnocultural entity among Indian Muslims. Notwithstanding the "Islamization" of their community that has gathered force since the 1930s, the Meo still perceive themselves as a *jati*, replicate the Hindu caste system in their elaborate kinship system governing social rules, and adhere to traditional Hindu caste rules on marriage, including endogamy and exogamy. Although Islam, as a religious ideology, advocates an egalitarian society, Indian Muslims have historically reproduced the stratified caste edifice of the Hindus among them, in which social stratifications are echoed in caste hierarchy (Bhatty 1996). Certain groups, because of their foreign ancestry, are labeled "high caste" (*oonch zat*). Meanwhile, others, either converts from the local population, such as the Meo, or those whose occupations are labeled impure or polluting, are bracketed under the "low caste" (*neech zat*) category (Bhatty 1996, 249).

The Meo shun the Islamic practice of marriage between cross or parallel cousins, even though it is widespread among the larger Indian Muslim community. Only those families with a non-Meo bride—that is, a woman from the larger Indian Muslim community—have incidences of marriage between first cousins. This is frowned on by the Meo, evident from the comments of a focus group of village men from Meerpur village in the Nuh district that "we do not consider such alliances valid. In fact, we condemn them."

Lastly, although polygamy is permissible under Islam, a majority of the Meo men remain in monogamous relationships (Chauhan 2004; Shamsh 1983). This is significant, as the majoritarian Hindu discourse about Muslims in general, and the Meo in particular, attributes the cross-region marriages of the Meo men to the ability of Muslim men, under the Muslim Personal Law, to have four wives in India (Rahman 2009). A look at Table 2, which covers reasons why men seek cross-region marriages, belies this misconception. Of the 817 cross-region marriages surveyed in the Punhana block of Nuh in Haryana, only nineteen of the men had entered into second marriages. Of these, thirteen did not get along with their first wives, whereas six others got married a second time as their first union was childless.

There is also extreme antipathy around giving daughters to men who are colloquially labeled "*dooj baar*"—that is, getting married for the second time because of the death of a first wife, desertion, divorce, or because the first marriage had not yielded any offspring. Subhan Khan, a landless Meo man from Nindoli village in the Alwar district of Rajasthan, eked out his living as a casual wage laborer in agriculture. He shared, "Here, people do not entertain a marriage alliance with men who are getting married '*dooj baar*' [for the second time]. I would be rejected with families saying, "we will not marry our daughter to a '*dooj baar*.' . . . So then I went to Bangal [West Bengal] to find a wife."

The clue to why a significant number of Meo men seek cross-region alliances can be found in Table 2. Very much like the low-class, poorly educated men from the dominant-peasant Hindu castes, here too, an overwhelming 646 out of a total of 817 Meo men from the Nuh district cited poverty and economic destitution as the sole motive for them being rejected locally. This includes owning less or no land as part of their economic destitution. This rejection factor is corroborated by examining the occupations of these men (see Table 3). Wage work, either in agriculture or the agriculture-allied rural sector, is listed as the main occupation by an overwhelming number of men from the Meo-majority regions of Alwar and Nuh. Tellingly, none reported holding a government or private sector job or being employed in a factory. A focus group of Meo men from Meerpur village described the situation: "Who goes out to marry? It is a man who has no land or the man who has a small patch. Employment is very hard to find here. If he has no land, he is rejected by most parents here. What will he feed his family with? There is almost no way that he can find a bride locally. Of course, there are Meo parents who marry their daughters to poor Meo men, but they are more desperate than the men's families."

In the Nuh district alone, the average size of landholdings is quite small, with the number of marginal and small landholders pegged at a quite high 77.62 percent in 2014 (see Table 5). This number is significant, as over 95 percent of Nuh's population lives in villages and is dependent on income from either agriculture or an agriculture-allied sector. Dependence on rain-fed irrigation due to the near absence of irrigation facilities makes tilling the small handkerchiefs of land financially risky and tenuous. The percentage of people who are below poverty level is 27.69 percent, or more than one-fourth of the total population (Rural Development Department, Haryana nd). With such a high number of Meo living in rural areas and leading a hand-to-mouth existence, parents of daughters old enough to marry prefer to find grooms who can financially support a wife, through either agriculture or other secure sources of income.

The male marriage squeeze among the Meo—who, again, do not suffer from a female shortage, unlike the Hindu caste groups—thus emerges as a direct outcome of their socioeconomic impoverishment and marginalization, hastened by the advent of the fundamentalist ideologies of neoliberalism and Hindutva since the 1990s. Meo-inhabited regions have borne the brunt of willful neglect by the majoritarian Hindu-leaning Indian state. Postneoliberal economic and industrial growth has totally bypassed the region of Nuh, where there is none of the investment in real estate, urban development, or setting up of industries. Inequity is visible even in the compensation given by the state government for land acquisition: in 2010, agricultural land in Nuh brought Rs 1.6 million per two and half acres or one hectare, while the neighboring Hindu-predominant area garnered Rs 5.5 million.[10] The situation is no better in Rajasthan, even though the district of Alwar has seen considerable postneoliberal industrial expansion, especially after 1998 (Planning Commission 2006, 95–96). Meo-dominated areas there have been bypassed in favor of Yadav- and Jat-dominated ones, such as Bhiwadi, Behror, Neemrana, and Tijara, which emerged as investment hubs for industry and real estate (MSME-Development Institute 2016).

Despite being granted OBC (Other Backward Classes) status in Haryana and Rajasthan, and even with the attendant affirmative reservation that provides them access to state or state-funded educational institutions or employment in government or public-sector jobs, the Meo have not been able to avail themselves of the benefits of this status because of a lack of state investment in education in their regions. This is quite unlike the caste groups of the Jats, Ahirs, Yadavs, and Gujjars in Haryana or Rajasthan, who, since having acquired OBC status through their political clout, have used it to further their economic and political interests.

Virtually no institutions of higher learning like colleges, universities, or polytechnic institutions exist in Meo-dominated areas; there are only four colleges for the entire region and no technical university in the Nuh district. The absence of technical colleges means that the Meo youth cannot be trained in trades or absorbed by industries coming up in the nearby industrial hub of Bhiwadi in

Rajasthan. Moreover, with fewer numbers of secondary or senior schools in the larger Nuh region, illiteracy is rife. There, men's and women's literacy rates are 69.94 and 36.60 percent, respectively, the lowest in the state of Haryana (Census of India 2011a). This institutionalized discrimination against the Muslims, evidenced by the state's neglect of technical education, infrastructure development, and incentives for setting up factories, has also led this region to have a small industrial footprint; though fertile agricultural land has been acquired for SEZs, employment is limited to skilled labor, and even that is limited to only one industrial area (MSME-Development Institute nd).

As a consequence, apart from agricultural wage labor, the only other occupations Meo men are able to become employed in are low-paying and unstable: they work as dumpster truck drivers or crane operators, or as daily wage laborers in the illegal mining quarries and brick kilns dotting the region. However, with the government clampdown on illegal mining mafias, this source of employment has also dried up for the Meo. Only since the mid-2000s has their close proximity to the National Capital Region of Delhi allowed them to take some advantage of the booming service, construction, and mining sectors, and find employment at the lower rungs of these sectors. Notwithstanding this, the high rates of unemployment among Meo youth because of the high illiteracy rate, lack of skilled training, and lack of opportunities for higher educational attainments are causal factors for rejection in the local marriage market.

Even though the "land of the Meo" is advantageously located close to industrial and service sector hubs in the National Capital Region, the Meo have not been able to cash in on the spin-offs of urbanization and industrial growth, largely because of their Muslim identity. Institutionalized prejudice against Muslims and the deepening of the Hinduization of India has led to active discrimination against the hiring of Muslims in both public- and private-sector jobs.[11] The "disadvantage" of being Muslim—magnified by their lesser educational attainments and the saturation of the urban informal labor market by the displaced and dispossessed masses coming from other parts of India to join the reserve army of labor in cities—translates into fewer and lower-paying jobs for the Meo. All these factors, in combination, have tightened the marriage market for the unemployed, underemployed, landless, and marginal landowning Meo men who wish to secure a Meoni[12] bride.

These narratives serve to underscore that reductionist claims of female feticide as the major pull factor for cross-region marriages are riddled with flaws. Instead, situating these matrimonies within the intersections of political economy and agrarian distress in North India, the patriarchal harnessing of female family labor through marriage and for social reproduction, caste contestations between the OBC and the Dalits, land inheritance rights, and the internal othering of the Meo Muslims allows for a more complex interplay of reasons to emerge as precipitators for these transgressive alliances.

Although the routes to the bride deficit, or male marriage squeeze, as a societal crisis are different for the Meo and the dominant-peasant castes of the Jats and Ahirs, they share one striking similarity: not all males from these two groups are rejected in the local marriage market. Instead, it is the men suffering from higher rates of poverty and illiteracy and negotiating precarious livelihood strategies who experience this rejection. These men, predominantly from the lower classes of the two groups, such as the landless laborers and marginal landowning peasants, have been rendered "ineligible" as grooms locally and are thus forced to seek cross-region alliances.

THE LAMENT OF THE POOR
Distant Marriages of Loved Ones

Nooru, engrossed in making cow-dung cakes with her *nanad* (husband's sister), looked up and cast a curious glance at me as I was welcomed by her in-laws, Mohammed and Saripan. She had arrived in Meerpur the previous evening and was already at work, engaged in doing household chores. Her elder brother-in-law (*jeth*), Amjad, whom I had met during my last visit to Nuh a couple of months earlier, had called me, saying, "They [the bridegroom and his eldest brother] have finally brought home the bride. Her father is also here. Come over tomorrow to talk to them about your research. You will also be able to take part in the *muh dikhai*[1] for the bride."

The next morning, Saripan and I hugged each other as I congratulated her on the good fortune of having another *bahu* (daughter-in-law) in the household. With a tone of pride in her voice, Saripan said to me in a whisper, "She is a sweet girl. She is literate—has passed her eighth grade. Our son, Mahmood, will not have any difficulty with an educated wife by his side." Nooru kept casting shy darting glances at me while washing her hands clean of the cow dung at the handpump in the courtyard. Wiping her hands dry, she went to the *chulha* to make tea. Saripan asked me to sit down next to her on a charpoy nearby as I gave Nooru a 500 rupee note as her *muh dikhai*. It fetched me a quick dimpled smile from her as she took the note from me and then promptly handed it over to her mother-in-law, Saripan, who sighed audibly in contentment at this "correct" gesture of Nooru's. The slight lull allowed me to look at Nooru more carefully. Slim and slight, she did not look any older than sixteen years of age, a suspicion that was confirmed later when she told me that she had been studying in grade nine until just two days before her marriage. She had tied her curly hair into two girlish plaits, and a pink sequined *dupatta*, supposed to cover her head, kept slipping down as she made the tea.

Her father, Mammal, was out taking a tour of the village with Saripan's eldest son, Mobin, who had gone to her home village for the wedding. On their return later that morning, Mobin showed me videos that he had taken on his cellphone of the farewell (*bidaai*) that Nooru got from her mother, sisters, and other village women as she got into the van that would take her on the first leg of the two-day journey to reach Meerpur village in the distant state of Haryana. In these two days of travel, the first time that she had ever been away from her village, Nooru had seen the terrain, the fauna, the language spoken by people, and the attire worn by women change considerably. Only the presence of her father and her father's elder brother (*tau*), who were accompanying her to the village, provided her some reassurance.

Later that day, Nooru told me that she had enjoyed her studies and already missed her school and her friends.

> My two elder sisters are married in our village. We had four marriage proposals for me, but all fell through. One man demanded Rs 80,000. The other asked for Rs 100,000 and a motorcycle—that one wasn't educated at all. His family had a two-story house and some land. Then there was another who was going to get married for the second time. My father is a cowherd. He cannot sell his skin to raise money for my marriage, can he? This "boy" is good—at least he is better than the ones demanding so much money. His family did not ask for any dowry (*dahej*). Instead, they [the groom's family] paid for all the expenses of the wedding (*ulta, uuheen paisa deeheen*).

When asked about her husband Mahmood's *seedhapan*, an all-encompassing euphemism adopted locally for a wide range of intellectual disabilities, and how that shaped her existence with him, Nooru bit her lips, kept silent, and looked away at a distant point. The silence stretched as I could feel her anguish in being asked this very personal question. Then she turned to look at me directly and said quite simply these words: "We are poor people. And as a poor girl, I have no choice about the type of man I get to marry. Poverty does not allow me that opportunity (*mauka*). Compared to men who live in mud huts who demand huge dowries, *this* man [my husband] is a better option."

Her resignation to this fate of living her future life with Mahmood, a man who she could not relate to as an equal and one who was not fully capable of earning a living, was poignantly sharp. As was the heartbreaking fact that the neoliberal accumulative process that was unfolding in India with greater ferocity had taken yet another gendered victim and dispossessed them of more than their dreams.

Nooru informed me, in a matter-of-fact tone of voice, that her husband's family had changed her name from Nooru to Salma, a change brought on by the fact that another female in the family was also named Nooru. In one fell stroke, she had not only been uprooted from her family and the land that she had grown up in, she had also been divested of her name, one that her parents had given to her so lovingly and one that she identified herself with. Despite these multiple dispossessions and dislocations, occurring to her at many levels in her intimate life and with rapid-fire speed, Nooru appeared to be trying hard to reconcile to her changed life circumstances: "I don't know what is in store for me in the future or what destiny has written for me. I will somehow bear it (*hum dekh leyheen*)."

Coercive Accumulation and Rural Impoverishment

Nooru's father, Mammal, having returned from exploring the village and inspecting the two-acre piece of agricultural land that the family owned, worried about why a *shehri* (city person) was taking notes about his daughter's marriage. Once reassured about the purpose of my research, he sat on his haunches as he spoke to me about his efforts to get his youngest daughter married in his region (*desh*). A few years ago, Mammal had tried his luck migrating to Delhi to earn more money than he did as a cowherd. He found work as a cook-cum-helper in a small restaurant there and had skimped and saved to raise a very modest dowry for his two older daughters. However, for the marriage of his youngest daughter, he could not foresee migrating back to the city. He was older now, lacked the stamina to endure the long and physically arduous hours at work, and was acutely aware that he could not raise the kind of capital required to marry a daughter off in today's changed socioeconomic climate compared to what had been possible ten years ago.

> These days, even the "good for nothing" men demand a motorcycle and Rs 100,000 in cash as dowry. Earlier, they would settle for a good watch, a cycle, and Rs 5000–7000 in cash. I am a cowherd (*goru charaat rahin*), herding cattle for other people in the village. I earn Rs 300 per cattle per year. I am lucky if I get fifty animals. In a good year, the number is seventy to ninety. What I earn is appallingly low as far as earnings go. The cost of living is going up each year and is sucking the blood in our veins dry. The village commons (*jangalat*) in our area has been taken by the government and handed over to the private industrial

houses and investors (*kampany*). Barbed wires and security guards do not allow us to use our land anymore. Now, I have to go much further to graze cattle.

A closer examination of the socioeconomic conditions of the natal regions and the particular communities from which a majority of cross-region brides come clearly reveals the myriad processes that have dispossessed women of matrimonial choice locally and made them "voluntarily" opt for marriage migration with North Indian men, both Hindu and Meo. For instance, Mammal and Nooru's village is situated within the mineral-rich Bokaro-Dhanbad-Giridih pocket of the eastern state of Jharkhand. This pocket has witnessed a flurry of mining leases given to big industrial giants for resource extraction, while, at the same time, forests and village commons have been summarily taken away for state-led "development" projects without including the affected rural communities in consultations. What makes the example of Jharkhand, which was carved out of the larger eastern state of Bihar in 2000, unique is that it possesses 40 percent of India's mineral resources and is one of the largest producers of coal, iron ore, and mica in the country. These rich resources have made mining and resource extraction a major industry in the state. In the year 2017 alone, during a two-day Momentum Jharkhand Global Investors Summit, 210 memorandums of understanding (MoUs) were signed and 121 proposals received in the mining sector and industries.[2] Changes in the local land acts there now allow agricultural land to be used for nonagricultural purposes. The Jharkhand provincial government has also displayed its coercive force toward protesting communities by opening fire on, killing, and summarily arresting protestors.[3] The coercive accumulation of resources has resulted in the expropriation of land held by local communities and the loss of community members' traditional sources of livelihood. Mammal's elder brother, a cow herder like him, was forced into becoming an economic migrant and relocating to Ranchi, Jharkhand's capital, where he now plied a rickshaw for a living. The percentage of Jharkhand's population living below the poverty line stands at 39.1 percent, with the Dalits and the Indigenous tribal communities faring worse, at 40.4 and 49 percent, respectively (Government of Jharkland nd). Muslims make up 13.8 percent of Jharkhand's population and suffer from a low work-participation rate.

The conjugal region purposive sampling survey of married women, who self-identified as non-Haryanvi or Rajasthani, reveals that in the state of Jharkhand, ninety-nine women (out of a total 1,546) had migrated as brides into Haryana and Rajasthan (see Table 8). Of these, a majority (n=67) were married among the Meo in the Nuh district of Haryana, while another twenty were married among the Hindus in the Rohtak district of the same state. The survey also

TABLE 8 State breakdown of the natal regions of the cross-region brides in select research areas of Haryana and Rajasthan

PROVINCE	ALWAR	MEWAT	REWARI	ROHTAK	TOTAL	TOTAL (%)
Andaman & Nicobar				1	1	
Andhra Pradesh	5	131		2	138	
Assam	12	175	6	66	259	
Bangladesh		2			2	
Bihar	10	156	10	71	247	
Chhattisgarh				12	12	
Delhi		1		23	24	
Gujarat		4			4	
Himachal Pradesh			2	16	18	
Jammu & Kashmir				2	2	
Jharkhand	10	67	2	20	99	
Karnataka		2		2	4	
Madhya Pradesh	5	7	1	14	27	
Maharashtra	3	25	4	25	57	
Nepal				3	3	
Odisha	5	7	8	31	51	
Pakistan				1	1	
Punjab				8	8	
Rajasthan				10	10	
Tamil Nadu			2		2	
Tripura			3	19	22	
Uttar Pradesh	9	6	3	109	127	
Uttarakhand	1			32	33	
West Bengal	22	173	22	87	304	
Not disclosed		61		27	84	
TOTAL	82	817	63	584	1546	

Source: Author's research study in Alwar, Mewat, and Rewari (2011), and Rohtak (2014).

showed a significant number of the brides (n=355) originating from the states of Odisha (n=51) and West Bengal (n=304) (see Table 6 for a detailed state-based listing of the brides' natal regions).

Similar to Jharkhand, the state of Odisha, a big sender of cross-region brides to Haryana in particular, has aggressively wooed both foreign direct investment and domestic capital by offering tax incentives, deregulations, and special concessions. By 2014, it had signed ninety-three MoUs with foreign and domestic capital for steel, power, crude oil, ports, SEZs, and cement, among other sectors.[4] As well, the more than 150,000 acres of land granted to such development programs have begun causing displacement and dislocation in rural Odisha. This is significant, as over 87 percent of Odisha's population is rural and consists largely of agricultural laborers and marginal farmers; over 60 percent of its population depends on the agriculture and allied sectors for sustenance.

In the research areas of Baleshwar in Odisha and Cooch Behar in West Bengal, where I undertook a micro-study of ten villages each, landless households stand at a staggering 81.05 and 83.80 percent, respectively (Socio Economic Caste Census 2011b). Forty percent of Odisha's population is made up of Scheduled Tribes and Scheduled Castes, or SC (Dalits); 18.8 percent of Baleshwar's people are Scheduled Castes, while 11.28 percent are Scheduled Tribes; and Dalits constitute 50.17 percent of Cooch Behar's populace (National Informatics Centre Cooch Behar 2012), with the Koch Rajbanshis as the main SC or Dalit community and the Muslims, at 23 percent, as the biggest religious minority group.

The coastal district of Baleshwar has fared better in the poverty ranking than other parts of Odisha, yet its level of rural poverty is very high. The primary source of income for marginal and landless farmers in the Bhograi Block is betel-leaf farming[5] and paddy cultivation; for this, farmers take on land on a sharecropping or tenancy basis and utilize the labor of female family members to offset labor costs. The stakes are high in betel-leaf farming, as it is labor intensive and subject to the vagaries of nature. Bishnu Parda from Gagan Pada village had to give up working as a casual agricultural wage worker because of a leaking heart valve. With his now-dead father having sold their only patch of land to marry off Bishnu's three elder sisters, the family was left with nothing except the homestead land. While his wife still continued to work as a casual agricultural wage worker, Bishnu had taken to cultivating betel leaves on an open patch of two hundred meters (two decimals in local parlance) located on the side of his homestead. He described the economy of this cash crop: "Our economy is dependent on paddy and betel leaves (*dhano aar paano*). If the demand for our betel leaves is okay, we earn, people get employment, and we are able to meet our necessities. If the flood destroys our paddy, then we are in trouble. It leads to situations where we get food for one day and starve for the next three days."

The study of select villages in the Baleshwar district in Odisha shows that most of the cross-region brides belonged to either the OBC or SC caste and came primarily from families with no landholdings (see Table 7). As evidenced in Table 9, out of the fifty families surveyed in select villages from Baleshwar district of Odisha, thirty-six owned no land and only one was a marginal landholder. A total of forty-three undertook tenant farming or low-paying agricultural wage work, the rate for which is one of the lowest in India (see Table 10). This is a very high percentage of families that had no assets to call their own. Agricultural income being insufficient, they supplemented their income with livestock rearing, fishery, and horticulture. Almost all families fell into the category of BPL, or below poverty

TABLE 9 Landholding size of families with daughters in cross-region marriages from ten villages each from Cooch Behar, West Bengal, and Baleshwar, Odisha

LANDHOLDING	BALESHWAR (NO.)	BALESHWAR (%)	COOCH BEHAR (NO.)	COOCH BEHAR (%)	TOTAL (NO.)	TOTAL (%)
Landless	36	72	41	39.5	77	50
Homestead only	13	26	9	8.6	22	14.3
Marginal (<2 acres)	1	2	53	51	54	35.06
Medium (2–5 acres)	–	–	1	.9	1	.64
Large (>10 acres)	–	–	–	–	–	
TOTAL	50	100	104	100	154	100

Source: Author's research study in Odisha (2011) and West Bengal (2014).
Note: These families had more than one female in a cross-region marriage.

level, or were just above it. With either little or no land assets, a majority of the families either took land on for sharecropping for paddy cultivation or did seasonal low-paying agricultural wage work, which pays one of the lowest rates in India (Deaton and Dreze 2002). In the Baleshwar region, the largest percentage of cross-region marriages is localized to the Raju caste with OBC status. They have developed an "extensive marital relationship with Khandayats" (Jeyaseela 2006, 357), a cultivating peasant caste. Although an elite group has emerged from this caste cluster with substantial influence in state politics,[6] a bulk of them live in distressing economic conditions in the rural areas.

West Bengal, another natal or sending region, was ruled by the Left Front for thirty-four years, from 1977 to 2011.[7] In its early years of rule, the Front undertook pro-poor rural land reforms with Operation Barga, under which it gave agricultural land to tenant farmers and sharecroppers. But by the early 2000s, the Left Front had embraced the neoliberal agenda. It tabled the Bill on Land Acquisition for Special Economic Zones in the Indian Parliament in 2003, the passing of which in 2005 gave teeth to corporate land-grabs in the name of development. Big capital was attracted to West Bengal through offers of concessions and with forcible land acquisitions from the rural landowners who were undercompensated (Das 2015). Very much like Odisha, the state justified the use of excessive force against peasants protesting acquisitions.[8]

Cooch Behar, the easternmost district of West Bengal, suffers from its geographical remoteness. It has no industry except tea plantations to absorb the labor force. Ironically, the spread of unregistered tea plantations is one cause for increased landlessness and consequent unemployment of its rural peasantry. The main crops are rice, jute, and tobacco. Over one-quarter, or 34.74 percent, of its people are agricultural laborers, of which 47.5 percent are women (Census of India 2011d). The Rajbanshis, the state's Indigenous population, designated as the SC category, is the

TABLE 10 Livelihood of parents with daughters in cross-region marriages from ten villages each from Cooch Behar, West Bengal, and Baleshwar, Odisha

LIVELIHOOD	BALESHWAR (NO.)	BALESHWAR (%)	COOCH BEHAR (NO.)	COOCH BEHAR (%)	TOTAL (NO.)	TOTAL (%)
Agriculture (own farmland)	–	–	2	1.9	2	1.3
Barber	–	–	2	1.9	2	1.3
Betel-leaf farmer	2	4	–	–	2	1.3
Carpenter	–	–	1	.9	2	1.3
Construction worker	–	–	2	1.9	2	1.3
Cook	1	2	–	–	2	1.3
Daily wage laborer*			41	39.5	41	26.5
Domestic servant			4	3.9	4	2.5
Farm laborer	34	68	13	12.5	47	30.4
Fishing	2	4	1	.9	2	1.3
Mason	–	–	2	1.9	2	1.3
Migrant laborer♦	–	–	11	10.5	11	7.1
Rickshaw puller	2	4	3	2.9	5	3.1
Street vendor	–	–	2	1.9	2	1.3
Tenant farmer	9	18	15	14.5	24	15.5
Van driver	–	–	5	4.9	5	3.2
TOTAL	50	100	104	100	154	100

Source: Author's research study in Odisha (2011), and West Bengal (2014).
Note: These families had more than one female in a cross-region marriage.
* This category includes those who seek daily casual wage employment in agriculture-allied sector or nonfarm sector.
♦ This category includes migration for work on construction sites or at brick kilns.

majority here. More than half of its rural population lives below the poverty line and is landless. State-led privatization of social services and decentralization of public services has led to increased economic distress, with a strong correlation between chronic hunger, landlessness, and food insecurity intersecting with social and other forms of historical exclusion of certain groups (see Roy and Sen 2011). The study of ten villages in Cooch Behar revealed that a total of 80.16 percent of cross-region marriages were undertaken by two main marginalized communities: 61.90 percent by the Dalits and 18.26 percent by the Muslims. Nearly 39 percent of these families were landless and approximately 9 percent owned just the homestead land (see Table 8). A total of 69 of 104 families were dependent on agriculture wage labor, tenant farming, or the agriculture-allied sector for their livelihood. In the last ten-odd years, seasonal male migration to other parts of India had emerged as a significant household strategy to augment family income (see Table 9 for details).

Men from these parts are considered skilled masons, so they were able to find work easily in the construction sector in the National Capital Region of Delhi or Kerala. With secure work for five to six months and daily wages of approximately Rs 200, they preferred this over casual employment in the informal economy in the neighboring states of Assam, Tripura, or Mizoram. The household women who stayed behind often engaged in the home-based, informal industry of beedi-making that flourishes there because of the local cultivation of tobacco. Many families, it appeared, lived solely through a remittance economy.

During fieldwork, it was not uncommon to hear the rural poor share their worry about constricted and gainful employment opportunities, increased alienation from their lands as they mortgaged these for money to pay medical bills, and rising household expenses. Interestingly, in both Odisha and West Bengal, the same villagers would often add that the *aboshtha* or conditions, were slightly better than they had been before thanks to a number of government social welfare schemes for below poverty line families such as theirs that gave them some relief. Interestingly, after the large-scale censure of neoliberal reforms, schemes such as the National Rural Employment Guarantee Act, instituted from 2005 onward to provide livelihood security in rural areas as well as an old-age pension, widow pension, and subsidized food, have also faced widespread criticism for corruption and leakage of funds. Notwithstanding, the Indian state, adhering to a neoliberal model of minimizing public spending and encouraging privatization of services, has gradually withdrawn from subsidizing education, water, electricity, and agricultural inputs. Ahmeduddin, the landless Muslim from Cooch Behar who seasonally migrated to Bihar for work under the *dadan* system, said,

> Even today, I lead a hand-to-mouth existence. You will not believe that I do not have money to buy a pen or a notebook for my youngest daughter.... We have mortgaged our house to a moneylender and that is how our life is being run (*shuud chalachi*). Life was even worse before I migrated [for work]. Do you see that *kadamb* tree in the corner of our courtyard?[9] We used to eat the fruit of that tree to kill our hunger pangs. One chili and one garlic pod per person was the most we could afford. That was the misfortune of our family when my daughter got married in Haryana.

Dowry as a Capital Accumulation Strategy

Scholarly works reference the rise in dowry demands by eligible local men, particularly from East India, as the singular precipitating factor behind the increased acceptance of "dowry-free and all wedding expenses paid" cross-region matri-monial proposals from North Indian men in East India (Mukherjee 2015). What is of significance is that the transactional nature of dowry and the centrality of cash and other assets in firming up marriage alliances between families is of re-cent vintage among the socioeconomically marginalized Dalits and Muslims in India, two groups from which a significant majority of cross-region brides come. Among the Dalits, the custom of bride price used to prevail, and new brides would be given a small number of cooking utensils as part of their bridal trous-seau (All India Democratic Women's Association 2003). Indian Muslims have also increasingly adopted this upper-caste Hindu cultural practice, despite Is-lam not recognizing dowry as an approved custom (Vatuk 2007). It is necessary to examine why, in this contemporary moment in India, such shifts are emerg-ing in cultural practices related to marriage-making, and why rural men and their families are increasingly adopting the practice of dowry and then using marriage to facilitate an asset transfer from the bride's families in the form of cash and other resources.

Marxian feminist economist Himani Bannerji calls for conceptualizing pa-triarchy and capitalism as conjoined ideologies, wherein "capitalist growth and human dispossession are twins" that operationalize gendered violence (2016, 13). In India, the structural violence of neoliberalism gets initiated at an intimate gendered level through the commodity fetishism of eligible local grooms. This novel articulation of gendered violence is a clear manifestation of the deepen-ing inroads of a neoliberal cultural mindset that commoditizes social relations, one that is set into motion by the capitalist accumulative force within India. This gendered violence is then reinforced through patriarchal ideology governing un-married female sexuality and gender norms about marriage. In this context, dowry should be interpreted as a (mal)adaptive reaction to the economic dis-possessions and increased precarity of employment in rural India. The inten-sification of rural poverty, caused in large part by the agrarian crisis, the development-led dispossession of the rural populace, and the paucity of employ-ment opportunities, has resulted in rural males regarding dowry as a capital accumulating and, by extension, poverty alleviating strategy. It offers such dis-possessed males, and by extension, their families—who are landless, precariously employed, or underemployed, or who face the specter of dislocation to the city as economic migrants—a form of economic security that they otherwise lack. Taking advantage of the woman's family's internalization of a patriarchal ideol-ogy, which links female sexuality and family honor to the woman's chastity, and of the societal stigma associated with having an unmarried daughter at home, the men seize the moment of marriage negotiation to make excessive dowry de-mands. Simultaneously, the increased materiality of marriage and the linkage of a man's worth to the amount of dowry that he is able to garner provides these economically marginalized men with social status: the success in accruing a higher dowry is the "most public acknowledgement of a man's worth that he is likely to experience" (Kapadia 2002, 17–18). According to Patricia Jeffery, in contemporary India, dowry has to be recognized as a "polyvalent institution that also connects with conspicuous display in status competition in a hierarchical society and with people's rising aspirations to possess consumer goods" (2014, 172). The integration of social relations into the market economy as capitalist relations and the rise in the dowry economy forces eligible brides' families to spend more than their means allow to meet the inflated dowry demands of local men. This causes impoverished families to face the specter of debt bondage and land alienation to get their daughters married locally.

In West Bengal, in particular, the practice of dowry, or *pon*, among the Hindu lower castes and the Muslims is a relatively new phenomenon (Ghosh 2010a; Gupta 1997). The inability to provide an adequate dowry is related to a higher incidence of domestic violence against women by their husbands and in-laws (Babu and Babu 2011, 38). West Bengal witnessed a rise in dowry deaths by nearly 82 percent between 1998 and 2007 (Ghosh 2010b, 6). Cooch Behar has also seen a rise in crimes against women, including dowry-related harassment and deaths (Ghosh 2010a, 58). The period between 1995 and 2007 saw a 74 percent rise in all-India dowry deaths,[10] with Odisha ranking second in the country for dowry-related deaths and suicides (Ghosh 2010a). By 2014, the Baleshwar district had the highest number of dowry-related deaths, suicides, and torture in Odisha.[11] Achala, a cross-region bride who hailed from one of the chosen research villages in the Baleshwar district, was quick to emphasize that she had voluntarily opted to marry a man from Rewari. She had seen her elder sister's marriage "turn hellish due to her husband's constant demand for more dowry. He would not even allow her to return home for a visit. That is why I preferred to marry here as the man wasn't asking for any dowry. I just did not like dowry or what it does to people. I wanted a man who would not be violent because of his greed (*hadap*) for dowry and money."

The men's families capitalize on the societal disapproval of families with unmarried daughters to maximize asset transfers during marriage deals. Implicit in these marriage deals is the underlying threat that if the transfers do not take place as agreed, either the marriage proposal may be called off or the bride, post marriage, may face harassment and/or domestic violence in her husband's household. This fear of daughters being harassed, beaten, or even killed by their husbands or in-laws for their failure to bring adequate dowry was one that Sitabi, a Muslim woman from West Bengal married to a Meo rickshaw puller in the Alwar region of Rajasthan, mentioned as central in her cross-region marriage: "Girls would get burnt or thrown out of their homes for bringing less dowry. My mother and brother did not want that to happen to me. What would they do if I were burnt?"

Dispossession of Matrimonial Choice

"Poverty is a powerful force that shapes people's destinies. It torments the life out of you (*garibee zabri cheez hai. Sataa kar rakh deti hai*). If I was not poor, do you think that I would have been married here?" These three sentences, spoken by Mehrunissa, from Razzakpur village in the Nuh district, as she fed her toddler daughter spoonfuls of *khichri*, effectively sum up the dispossession of matrimonial choice that impoverished rural women face in certain parts of rural India. It is a dispossession that not only reduces their marriage options locally but that also forces women like her to marry men who are considered "rejects" in their own marriage markets. In doing so, it unfolds myriad other dispossessions and dislocations, including that of cultural alienation and uprootedness from the support of their natal families because of the vast geographical distance between the two regions.

Mehrunissa's husband, Jamshed, was much older than she, landless, and worked as a bus driver for a private company. He had been a *dooj baar*, or seeking to marry for the second time, before their marriage. Jamshed's first wife, a cross-region bride from Assam, had deserted him because of his wayward ways. In the Meo society, men who are labeled *dooj baar* are usually rejected as husband material by parents of young Meo women. Like Nooru, Mehrunissa was also from Jharkhand. Her father made a precarious living as a goatherd, rearing goats and selling them, and had no resources to fall back on to provide a dowry for his daughter's marriage. For him and many others like him that I met in Odisha and West Bengal, the helplessness and inability to pay the excessive dowry demanded by local men; the "duty" to marry off adult unmarried female family members; the societal shame, or *lajja*, of not marrying them off at the right time; and pressure to keep the family honor in the community intact had forced them into accepting marriage proposals of men from "distant lands who asked for no dowry, just the girl." Oftentimes, based on the reality of marriage options available locally, the parents and even the brides themselves strategically opt for such alliances. Rabiya, an Assamese woman, "voluntarily" married a Meo man unable to walk due to polio-afflicted legs:

> I agreed because my parents were very poor. Over there [natal regions], girls like me cannot get married because of poverty. I might have got married to a man who worked in brick kilns. This man has a shop and

earns reasonably well. He cannot walk well due to polio, but at least I have no shortage of food. There is no want. Is it in my fate to feel sad? I do not have that luxury to indulge in such emotions. Yes, I feel bad about leaving my parents behind, but do I, as a poor person, have any option?

Although these marriage alliances might be said to constitute strategic and spatial hypergamy, largely thanks to the image of North India, and the state of Haryana in particular, as a place of wealth and jobs for migrant labor from Eastern India, the women from impoverished families, more often than not, end up in marriages with low-class and landless men who eke out precarious livelihoods. In such strategic hypergamous matrimonies, women might marry up the geo-economic hierarchy, but they might be disadvantaged in other ways through their marriages to men who are social or "economic losers" locally. Constable labels this "marrying down" in an otherwise economically more prosperous region or country as "paradoxical hypergamy" (2005b, 167). In the case of these brides, they are also disadvantaged by their supposedly undesired caste and/or ethnicity and internal other status in conjugal homes and communities (a fact I explore in chapter 5).

Here, it is worth revisiting the conceptual model of "gendered geographies of power" advanced by Mahler and Pessar, which underscores how the social location of an individual within "power hierarchies created through historical, political, economic, geographic, kinship-based, and other socially stratifying factors" (2001, 6) both affects their access to resources and shapes their agency. Poor women of marriageable age who voluntary opt for cross-region matrimonies exhibit their gendered, yet quite compromised, social agency in doing so. Their agency is "compromised" as it does not occur freely, but instead occurs within the constraints of operative power hierarchies and scales to improve their lives.

This conceptual understanding about the neoliberal accumulation process and its interaction with other forms of historical and contemporary exploitative and unequal power relations and ideologies such as patriarchy, caste, and Hindutva, as in the case of India, is germane for understanding the increased commodification of marriage, heightened dowry demands of local men, and consequent rise in cross-region matrimonies from certain regions of India, and in some communities more than others. The Indian state, through its adoption of neoliberal reforms and its acting as an agent for global capitalism, I argue, has emerged as an active enabler and facilitator of this particularized form of matrimonial dispossession for socioeconomically marginalized women from certain "underdeveloped" parts of India more than others. In this, the hegemonic hold of patriarchal ideology governing the disciplining of female sexuality through marriage plays an active role, often articulated through statements such as, "After the girl matures, she has to be married off to prevent dishonor to the family," "Whether you are married near here or far, you'll have to lead a married life," and "How can she remain a burden (*bojh*) on the family, social rules demand that she be married off."

What emerges as a significant finding of this research is that the women and their families undertake a constant weighing of pros and cons of the various constricted choices available locally. The lack of access to resources or land entitlements that could potentially allow poor women to seek adequate and alternate livelihood opportunities and not be regarded as economic burdens on their families is a big player in this decision-making. Faced with zero-sum choices and hegemonized by the heteropatriarchal discourse that frames marriage as normative, the women then "voluntarily" or "strategically" agree to cross-region proposals. Using this framework of analysis thus allows for recognizing the economic source of women's oppression and exploitation and the erosion of gender rights in India.

Failure to secure a match locally because of high dowry demands that arise from a number of reasons, including dark-skin tone discrimination (discussed later in this chapter), patriarchal concerns about sexual "purity," and the diminishing "market appeal" linked to the women's increasing age, makes the women particularly pliable to the "dowry-free and all wedding expenses paid" marriage proposals of North Indian men. The intersection of poverty, heteropatriarchy, and the lack of alternate choices, either social or economic, for the women is thus taken advantage of by the North Indian bachelors seeking brides, as well as by the marriage brokers, in the business of arranging cross-region matrimonies by offering the inducement of "dowry-free weddings." Nooru's eldest brother-in-law, Mobin, who had accompanied his younger brother, Mahmood, to his wedding in Jharkhand got a glimmer of the reduced choices faced by the poor there. He observed,

> No industry (*factory ya karobar*) exists there. You either work in the fields or migrate to the city. There is poverty in those parts. Those who are capable have all migrated to Kalkatta [Kolkata], Bambai [Mumbai], or Surat. Show me a person who detests his daughter so much that he would want to marry her off so far away from her loved ones. They are rendered helpless (*majboor*) by their poverty [and so have] to agree to marry their daughters so far [away] to "blemished men" (*daagi aadmi*) such as Mahmood.

The common refrain of parents with daughters in cross-region alliances is, "if I had an alternative, I would never have married her off so far from us." It is imperative to acknowledge that poverty "merely exacerbate[s] the vulnerability of marginalized and disadvantaged groups" (Sanghera 2005, 7). Doing so allows us to appreciate how compromised and constricted the choices of families and the women themselves become around marriage options. It inexorably pushes them to override concerns about the vast distance separating the two regions; the disparateness in customs, language, and food habits; and the absence of social policing mechanisms, including running background checks on the grooms, and enter into marriage alliances with North Indian men. Adopting the analytical perspective of feminist political economy and meshing it with Dalit feminism prevents making the error of regarding the brides as mute victims of patriarchal ideology or trafficking. Instead, by placing people's subjectivities, however compromised, right in the center of knowledge production about these matrimonies, the blame can be placed squarely on the structural and systemic conditions in contemporary India as "enablers" in increasingly dispossessing poor people and preventing them from making advantageous life choices.

Disenfranchising Dalit and Muslim Women of Marriage Options

Neoliberal dispossession and neoliberal accumulative processes in India thus extend to intimate social relations, shrinking marital choices and affecting women belonging to certain socioeconomically marginalized communities such as the Dalits or the Muslims more than others. As detailed in chapter 1, these groups have historically suffered from higher percentages of landlessness, a lack of productive assets, and high poverty rates. These two groups also have the largest percentage of people living below the poverty line.[12]

As revealed in surveys conducted in natal and conjugal regions, the women from both the Muslim and Dalit communities bear the brunt of the multiple and overlying axes of oppression caused by patriarchy, caste ideology, religious fundamentalism, and predatory capitalism. For example, the socioeconomic precarity of the Dalits is exploited by marriage mediators who deliberately seek out "Mahadalit" or Dalit families. Ajay, a Jat landless man from the village Uncha Tendroli in the Rohtak district of Haryana, married to a Dalit woman from West Bengal, was now in the business of brokering marriages for men from his region. He exclusively sought out women's families that were very poor: "What does very poor mean? It implies a person who is either landless or has very little land, has no other resources at hand and no earning occupation. Usually, it is a Dalit family. They are not well-off (*pichde hue*). . . . So, we exploit their helplessness about getting their daughter married and get them to agree to our proposals."

In the case of Muslim cross-region brides such as Mehrunissa and Nooru, structural constraints such as underdevelopment coupled with limited avenues for gainful employment for women in their region, Jharkhand, put together with the willful state neglect of Muslim-majority areas, dispossess them of choices in marriage, both locally and across regions. The same institutionalized neglect that condemns the Meo to poverty because of their Muslim tag similarly haunts Indian Muslims from the natal regions. The rural Muslims face higher levels of dispossession, poverty, and constriction of employment choices. The increased prevalence of dowry among them, hitherto a practice usually exhibited by the caste Hindus, has also increased the vulnerability of poor rural Muslims with daughters of marriageable age.

A recent study using the Indian Human Development Survey of 2004–2005 and 2011–2012 revealed that the Muslims lag behind even the socioeconomically marginalized Dalits in all indices, such as education, employment, and earnings. For example, in West Bengal, Muslims earn 79 percent of what the Hindu Dalits do in the same region, while this number drops to 68 percent for Haryana. In West Bengal, Muslims are among the poorest, and in Haryana and Bihar, less than 10 percent of Muslims hold a salaried job.[13] In Nooru and Mehrunissa's natal state, Jharkhand, 14.53 percent of its population are Muslims.

The disruptive forces of dispossession, dislocation, and/or landlessness are intensified for the Muslims in India. They suffer from greater difficulties because of the systemic discrimination against them, with the rural Muslims experiencing greater levels of poverty, food insecurity, and unemployment than other religious groups. A recent study of Muslims in West Bengal—27 percent of its population—found that over 80 percent of rural Muslims are economically more disadvantaged than rural Hindus.[14] Further, it found that 38.3 percent of rural Muslim households are subsisting at income levels half of that of the poverty line, and these constitute the largest percentage of marginal landowners and landless laborers.[15] Muslim women also face higher levels of dowry harassment and dowry-related deaths.

The Muslim population in Cooch Behar—23.34 percent of its total populace—similarly suffers from a higher rate of indebtedness and higher numbers of BPL families (Centre for Studies in Social Sciences nd). My own research revealed that, of a total of 126 surveyed families in cross region marriages, 18.26 percent were Muslim (n=23) (see Table 7). All these families were either landless or owned just their homestead land. Their main source of livelihood was either as daily wage laborers in agriculture locally, or as migrant laborers in brick kilns in the neighboring state of Bihar. The Muslims are socioeconomically more deprived than their Hindu neighbors and have a higher rate of illiteracy, a greater lack of civic amenities, and less access to government schemes (Centre for Studies in Social Sciences nd).

Imtiaz's homestead in the village of Dakhin Nuapur in Cooch Behar consisted of a collection of mud-brick houses with thatched roofs that opened onto a central courtyard. He worked as a housepainter in the nearby small town of Tufanganj, while all the adult women from his family worked as construction workers, carrying heavy headloads of bricks or cement and mortar eight hours a day for which they earned Rupees 100–120 per day. He had started looking for a match for his daughter as, he firmly believed, "a daughter has to be married in some way or another." However, excessive "demands" (local term used for dowry) from local men made him accept a marriage proposal from a Meo man:

> This man from Haryana was much older than her—thirty-five as compared to my daughter, who was barely twenty then. He asked for no money. The man paid for all the expenses—saree, Qazi's fee, the nosering (*nakphul*)—everything. We agreed as our hands were tied. There was no way we could have married her to someone here. It was not my desire to marry her off there, but what other option did I have? You have seen the state of my house. My dire economic situation (*arthik aabhab*) and fear of social stigma (*samajik bhay*) made me agree to this alliance.

Similar to the Hindu families in natal regions that receive dowry-free and all-expenses-paid marriage offers, the economic vulnerability of pauperized Muslims such as Imtiaz or Nooru's father, Mammal, in regions like Jharkhand, Assam, Bihar, and West Bengal, where sizable population of Muslims reside, have caused them to emerge as soft targets for marriage proposals from Meo Muslim men rejected in their local marriage market. Unlike the Muslims in North India, who regard the Meo as tainted because of their Hindu ancestry and continued belief in Hindu customs, the Muslims in West Bengal, in particular, do not see them as that different from themselves and are thus more accommodative to their proposed alliances. As Imtiaz put it, "They also believe in Allah and so do we. They do *namaaz* and read the Koran just like us. We are all Muslims (*mushalmaan janno*)."

The increased spread of Hindu supremacist fundamentalism and the selective violence against Muslims in Northeast and East India has also caused a spike of marriages involving Muslim women from these areas, who have left for the Muslim-majority areas of Nuh and Alwar.[16] The desire to "settle" daughters in Muslim-majority areas stems from justified fears of the targeted rapes of Muslim women by Hindu rioters.[17] As Mamtaaj, an Assamese woman now married in Meerpur village in the Nuh district, said to me, "I got married here after the Babri Masjid [mosque] riots. Muslim women were raped and, as a result, lost their honor. It was difficult to get married there." The deliberate destruction of Muslim houses and livelihoods and the people's displacement from their regions exacerbate their poverty, as happened in the case of Nagma, a Muslim woman originally from Bihar, but now married to a Meo man from Razzakpur village in the Nuh district. As she slapped cow-dung patty cakes on an open patch by her house, she related, "[My] family lost everything in the Hindu-Muslim riots of 1989.[18] The Hindus seized all our land. My parents died in the riots. The proposal for marriage from my husband here came with no dowry demand. This was the best option."

Fair Skin as Marriage Capital

Other predisposing factors work in conjunction to equally dispossess poor women from marginalized communities of a chance of local matrimony. In particular, the association of fair skin with beauty and high status results in dark-complexioned women from poor families finding it harder to marry locally (Kukreja 2021).

Colorism is discrimination based on the lightness or darkness of skin tone that is experienced at an intimate level by a dark-hued person (Hunter 2007). Parameswaran and Cardoza argue that "dark skin has been a source of stigma for Indian women [since] long before the arrival of globalization" (2009, 218). Idealized feminine beauty in India has been weighted heavily in favor of light or "fair" skin, despite the majority of the population being of darker hue. In contemporary India, the interconnections between colorism and gender discrimination play out most prominently in the marriage market and the mate-selection process. As mentioned earlier, the integration of social relations into the market economy is exhibited by the increased dowry demands of local grooms. Preexisting asymmetrical patriarchal gender relations are further intensified during matrimonial negotiations with men demanding higher dowries for women who are darker colored. Ironically, despite India being a country where a majority of its population is of dark complexion, lighter skin tone is highly valued, as it signifies a higher social and caste status (Ayyar and Khandare 2013). Assumptions are made that people's dark skin is a consequence of doing manual labor in the harsh tropical sun, and that such physical-labor-induced skin tone is the preserve of the Dalits. Consequently, darker hue acts as an impediment for women in securing a suitable marriage partner, as evidenced from a cursory glance at the matrimonial advertisements placed in leading newspapers, wherein descriptions of an ideal bride include "fair-skinned" as a desirable attribute.

This "politics of skin tone" and the concept of beauty as "capital" has been aggressively pushed by global capital in India, with huge amounts invested in advertising the social benefits of acquiring a lighter skin tone.[19] The country has emerged as one of the biggest markets for skin-whitening products, with an annual expansion rate of 18 percent as of 2012.[20] By 2016, the sales of skin whiteners made up 46 percent of total facial cream sales in India.[21] It has been estimated that 60 to 65 percent of India's female population in the age range of sixteen to thirty-five have used such products in their quest to enhance their "beauty."

During my own research, I observed that most rural homes had tubes of "fairness" cream lying casually along with hair oils (and *kumkum* or vermillion in Hindu homes) on ledges below small plastic-framed mirrors hung on walls in the sleeping areas. Discussions with local research assistants revealed the insidious correlation of feminine dark skin color with exorbitant dowry demands made by local men. Women research assistants admitted, on the side, that they too used skin-whitening creams to avoid the daily humiliation of being "dark-skinned" and the future threat of rejection in their local marriage pool. Unsurprisingly then, despite the expensive price tag of these creams, a factor to bear in mind given that the majority of the rural families who I met were leading a hand-to-mouth existence, these tubes are regarded as paltry investments that promise bigger returns at the time of "arranging" women's matrimonial alliances. With the huge inroads made into rural markets by the cosmetic industry, evidenced by big posters of these products plastered on the sides of small tin-shack shops, many dark-skinned poor women in eastern India are buying into the seductive "therapeutic narrative" that the advertisements for skin-lightening creams appear to offer. The seemingly transformative powers of the skin-whitening creams, as presented in television and print advertisements, offer visions of a better marital future, one that Sukanti's daughter Bullu, who was visiting her, confessed to being taken in by as she came closer to the age when her mother would start looking for marriage partners for her.[22] By regularly spending the seemingly small amount of Rs 20 for a 25-gram tube, Bullu hoped to acquire better marketability and a lesser dowry "demand" in the local marriage market that prized light skin and possibly thwart a marriage to an unemployed or alcoholic local man rejected by others. She tried using it as a magic charm, without success, to ward off the worst-case scenario—a "cross-region" marriage that would take her away from her mother and her ailing father.

The toxic linkage between colorism and the patriarchal compulsion to "marry off" an adult daughter was one that another bride, Chandana, the younger sister of Janaki, the cook-cum-mother of a cross-region bride herself, had experienced firsthand. As Dalits, and with the household managed solely by the mother, the family struggled to make ends meet as agricultural wage workers. With skin-tone discrimination in local marriage markets rendering dark-skinned women as "second-class" bride material, ironically, local men try to show their largesse in "accepting" dark-hued women as their wives *only* if the women's families give bigger dowries.

Female-headed households such as Chandana's face an even greater foreclosing of local matrimonial options. Oftentimes, with the death of their husband, young women's mothers, left solely in charge of taking care of the household and the surviving family members, are not able to single-handedly cough up the exorbitant dowry requirements of local men. For female heads of households from socioeconomically marginalized communities, their gendered identity and limited or nil access to productive resources and land, along with the gender discriminatory wage gap, further make raising this dowry an unachievable goal. The addition of another variable such as skin tone to the equation of dowry payment further constrains local matrimonial choices and compromises the brides and their families into accepting proposals they would otherwise not court.

Chandana had chosen to marry a man from Dhani Raghovas in the Rewari district of Haryana. He was fourteen years older than she and had a physical disability that made him an immediate reject in his marriage market, despite owning four acres of land. When Chandana first met him, she immediately saw his right arm hanging loosely by his side, a reminder of the polio virus that had taken its toll on his unvaccinated body when he was young. However, Chandana, a Dalit, opted to marry him despite the evident *daag*, or "blemish," even though she had, in her heart of hearts, dreamed of a strong and physically able man as her groom. Chandana and Janaki had lost their father when they were fairly young, and as they were growing up, their mother had struggled to find work as an agricultural worker in the village to help the family survive. Chandana recollected, "I had no father. My mother said, 'I cannot cater to the dowry demands of men here. It is better to accept this proposal. How [else] can I marry you off?' She and I then consulted amongst ourselves. When a girl becomes 'mature,' people make barbed comments about her unmarried status. It was better to accept this proposal. Looking at the poverty of my mother and thinking of my circumstances, I made the pragmatic decision to accept this marriage."

The rejection of darker-hued women in the Indian marriage market is an anomaly, as India is a tropical country with harsh sunlight. However, it is also unsurprising as the idealization of whiteness as the norm is widespread in rural India, where a dark-skinned daughter, right from her birth, is constantly reminded of her misfortune in possessing a dark skin tone. In West Bengal in East India, where many of the cross-region brides came to North India from, darker skin tone is referred to as *moila rang*, literally translated as dirty color. Here, dark skin is associated with ugliness, savagery, dim-wittedness, and an uncouth nature. Hunter, in her study of colorism among African Americans in the United States, contends that the family itself has been a site for reproducing and articulating dominant discriminatory practices and beliefs (2005). In India, comparisons between female relatives on the basis of skin tone tend to "scar" the darker-skinned women with lowered self-esteem (Badruddoja 2005). These women have no respite, not even within the four walls of their own home, where they are continually exposed to "painful barbs" (Hunter 2005, 85) about their darkness.

Within families, this color discrimination, or colorism, also creates bitterness between siblings, as the darker-skinned daughters are forced into cultural exile far away from their loved ones, their community, and region, while their lighter-skinned sisters are able to get married locally with a lesser dowry. Ajay Das from Kusumpada village in Odisha knew this quite intimately. His family had gradually sold all their land to marry off his other two sisters, and he was left with only the homestead land. Unable to sustain his family on the seasonal and low-paying agricultural work of betel-leaf farming, he had chosen to migrate to Surat, an industrial town in western India where he found work in a cotton mill. He was home for a few weeks for the festival of Durgo Pujo and Diwali when I met him. Our conversation on colorism ensued:

> We have three sisters. One was married in our village and another in a nearby village. For the other one, the dark one, people came to see her, but nobody selected her. So, we got her married in Haryana.
>
> Q. Why in Haryana?
>
> A. Because she was dark and none selected her here.
>
> Q. Just because she was dark?
>
> A. Well, people demanded more dowry [for her], which we could not muster. For that reason alone, we did this.
>
> Q. What amount would be spent if she were married here?
>
> A: We would be spending about 2 to 3 lakhs of rupees.
>
> Q. If your sister were fair in complexion, then would she have been able to marry here?
>
> A. Oh yes. She would have married here. Good looks and fair complexion—then definitely it would have happened here in the village.

The colorism discrimination dividing up families like Ajay described was one that Kaushalya, a bride from Maharasthra married to Pavan from the Rohtak district of Haryana, felt deeply. Her other sister, slightly lighter-skinned than she, was married in a village not far from their family. Kaushalya viewed her cross-region marriage from the perspective of being an exile from her community, her culture, and everything that she had grown up with. She said,

What crime had I committed by being dark skinned that I was pun- ished by being married so far away from the family? My sister who is lighter in color got married in my parents' neighboring village. It is only because we had to give a bigger dowry for me that I was married so far away, otherwise I would be living in my region (*desh*), close to my family who could offer me support in a time of need. Why would I come here? Dark-skinned people have a right to live, don't they? The dowry is less for fair skin, but for darker skin, it is more. Why is it like this? If you take dowry, take it without discrimination—why take more for darker skin?

The rejection of pauperized dark-complexioned women in the local marriage market also creates a situation ripe for marriage brokers and traffickers to step in and take advantage of their socioeconomic vulnerability. Subhash Bhanja, a Dalit landless agricultural wage laborer from Kusumpada village in Odisha, was more than happy when a woman from the same village brought a marriage pro- posal: "About four to five local families had come to see her [the sister]. They did not select her as she was darker in color. We did not make any inquiries about the Rajasthani man when he agreed to the proposal. We were just happy that she got married." The ineligibility of such men, whether because of their eco- nomic instability, physical disability, history of domestic violence, or substance abuse, is often overlooked in the patriarchal desire, or haste, to "settle" the "girl" with whoever is willing to marry a dark-skinned woman.

Birth Order of Daughters

In addition to all the other constraints operating simultaneously, birth order also determines, to a large extent, the marriage options for daughters. The regions from East India such as Bihar, Odisha, Assam, or West Bengal from which an overwhelming majority of cross-region brides hail do not suffer an adverse CSR, largely because of cultural norms different to those of the North Indian states of Haryana and Rajasthan regarding daughter aversion.[23] Because of this, these regions are often termed as female rich. As a consequence, families with greater number of daughters, if they do possess some assets, usually exhaust them, either by selling or mortgaging, to meet the wedding expenses of the eldest daughter(s). Consequently, those daughters lower in the birth order are disadvantaged, as their parents are left with nothing to use to raise money for their dowry. Chaitali, a cross-region bride who hailed from Mednipur in West Bengal and was mar- ried to a man from Uncha Tendroli village in the Rohtak district, said, "All my other sisters who were elder to me were married locally. My father had sold off his entire two killa [two acres] of land to pay for their marriage expenses. He had no money left to even undertake tenant farming. He was landless and working as an agricultural wage laborer when it came my time to be married off."

Sometimes, parents pragmatically—and legitimately—opt for cross-region alliances instead of mortgaging their land to raise dowry money. As one father from Cooch Behar, Imtiaz, shared, "[I] worry that if I sell everything for the marriage of my daughter, what will happen to the rest of my children? How will I feed them? I have to take care of their future too." Conversely, some daughters who are the eldest in the family, such as Manjuli, a Bengali woman married to Raju, a Jat marginal landowning farmer from the Rohtak district, "voluntarily" agree to a cross-region marriage to preserve the meagre family assets "for the future of the siblings." In doing so, they demonstrate their compromised agency within the restrictive intersecting dispossessions brought on by patriarchal ideology and neoliberal accumulative processes. Although Manjuli was not happy with the type of man she had married, she did not have a moment's regret about her "sacrifice," made for the well-being of her entire family: "My parents were poor. If I had to be married there, then our small piece of land would have to be sold. My family would have gone into debt peonage. I have five brothers and sisters and [there are] just three acres of land. I was the eldest in the family. My father said he would sell the land. I told him, 'No, don't do that.' When this proposal came, I accepted it for the future of my siblings (*bhobhishya khatir*)."

Marriage options are also constricted by the fact that natal regions such as West Bengal, Odisha, and Assam are also prone to natural disasters. Every extreme climate event such as a flood or a cyclone further pauperizes the historically marginalized communities, as they miss out on state compensation and alternate livelihood opportunities because of their lack of ownership of land or productive assets. Equally affected in such cases, men's families seize on marriage as a moment to recoup similar losses by making outrageous dowry demands, thus effectively foreclosing local marriage options for poor women. For instance, the super cyclone of 1999 in Odisha devastated large tracts of land, killed and displaced large numbers of people, and destroyed livelihoods, as floodwaters salinated agricultural land.

Damini, a cross-region bride from the Balasore district who had become a marriage broker, admitted that she sought out impoverished families in villages devastated by the cyclone, such as that of Biju and Sondhya. I met the twosome at Damini's house in Dhanauti village in Rewari district. They had accompanied their daughter, seventeen-year-old Megha, to her husband's home in the same village. The fare for their travel had been borne by the man. Biju was from a Dalit caste that hereditarily picked coconuts for a living. It was a risky livelihood, as he would climb trees, sans protection gear, with just a coir rope tied around his ankles to help him shimmy up. Before the cyclone, he had made a measly Rs 10 per coconut tree, not enough to support a family. But with the destruction of 80 percent of Odisha's coconut tree cover in the super cyclone of 1999, his livelihood had taken a major hit, and the family was reduced to total penury and destitution. The offer of a marriage proposal by Damini was a "godsend" to the couple, who were clueless about how to marry off Megha.

In a different scenario, the death of a mother and subsequent remarriage of the father can shift the man's loyalties toward his new family members with the birth of stepchildren, as well as create extra financial stress. It also creates hierarchies of favored and disfavored daughters within the household, as the stepmother's vested interest lies in ensuring that her children's future is not shortchanged by the marriage of her stepdaughters. The absence of any dowry demand whatsoever from North Indian rural males thus becomes a big incentive for such families, as it preserves the meager family assets for children from the second marriage.

Cross-Region Matrimonies as Resistance

A small percentage of cross-region marriages occur not as a consequence of dispossession of matrimonial choices, but in defiant opposition to the patriarchal ideology that places a singular emphasis on virginity as a prerequisite for marriage. Women are written off in the local marriage market after their supposed transgression of patriarchal rules governing female chastity, such as by having an "affair," being divorced, widowed, or deserted, or leaving their abusive husband and returning to their family. This is another group of women that often exercises agency by voluntarily opting for cross-region matrimonies with North Indian men. These women defy the dominant knowledge production of them as mute victims. Circumscribed by societal norms and taboos around unmarried women, lower educational attainments, and the lack of economic opportunities and inheritance rights that could make them economically independent, women like Deepika, a widow with a small son, recognize that they are "viewed suspiciously by married women who fear that we will entice their husbands (*shami*). The village men, too, do not leave us alone. It is better that we get married in Haryana. At least, we get some respect (*ijjat*) and security because of our marriage."

TRAFFICKED? OR MARRIED? WHEREIN LIES THE TRUTH?

"I was quite young when my father passed away. I had little money, no land, and two younger sisters to marry off. An acquaintance from this village brought the marriage proposal. He was related to a woman married there [Uttar Pradesh in North India]. In fact, I had first asked him, 'We have two sisters to be married. Get us some proposals.' When he did, at first, I refused. I was worried about their well-being—it is so far away and we know no one there." Bijoy, who spoke these words, sat leaning against a thick bamboo beam that held up the thatch roof of his house. Bijoy was landless and worked as a *mistri* (mason), a seasonal job, as the monsoon months meant no work available locally. I was in Nimaipur, a village in the Bhograi block of the Baleshwar district in the eastern state of Odisha, to meet with the natal families of women in cross-region marriages. The survey with the migrant brides in the research areas in Rajasthan and Haryana had revealed patterns of chain bride migration from some areas more than others (see Table 8 listing natal states of the brides). I had collaborated with a local Baleshwar-based NGO (PRAVA, or Professional Assistance for Voluntary Action), to conduct a survey of ten randomly selected villages.

Both the Baleshwar district and the Bhograi block had a significant number of women in matrimonies with men from Rajasthan and Haryana, as well as from another neighboring North Indian state, Uttar Pradesh. Nimaipur, a village with approximately 580 inhabitants spread among around 120 families, had seven women from six families in cross-region alliances. Two were Bijoy's younger sisters, Anita and Sunita, married to two brothers from the Mathura district of Uttar Pradesh.

"My eldest sister is married here. You see, my father was alive then and he was able to raise some money for the dowry by taking loans. I was quite young then. Since his death, it has been very difficult to make both ends meet," Bijoy continued, as his sixty-five-year-old widowed mother, Puspalata, walked over to listen in. "The 'charge' [local term for dowry] is very high here." Similar to Bijoy's initial reaction to the proposal, Puspalata had also rejected it, worrying that, "if I was dying, I would not be able to see the face of my daughter before my death. It would take her two days to make the journey. By that time, I would have been dead for a long time."

However, a family conversation about their "harsh material conditions" and the no-dowry carrot being offered made them change their mind. Anita, the prospective bride, who had resisted the match by arguing that she would not be able to visit them as easily as other women married locally, was persuaded by her mother: "I told her [Anita], 'Dear, you do not have your father, only your one brother. How will he manage your wedding? You *have* to get married, it is the societal custom (*niyam*). It is a good match. We will take care of you.'"

Anita's eventual consent is unsurprising, given that arranged marriage, a process in which mate selection is undertaken by the family and kin elders, is still the norm in India. In India—unlike the West, where the paramountcy of romantic love and individual free choice usually determine the selection of one's life partner—marriage is commonly considered a coming together of two families from the same caste and socioeconomic strata and involves a rigorous screening process that examines the background of the two families to ensure compatibility. The concept of companionate marriage based on romantic love and individual choice is of fairly recent vintage and largely localized to urban centers of India, but even here parental approval is sought before the nuptials. In this context, cross-region matrimonies breach another pillar of customary marriage-making in India with an almost negligible background check or "vetting" of the prospective grooms and their families. According to Bijoy, "we went ahead trusting the mediator. He was known to us. Our poverty would have not allowed us to marry them here."

On being asked about the transactional nature of Anita's marriage—whether the family had received any cash from either the mediator or the groom—Bijoy replied, "The groom's party bore all the expenses related to the marriage and travel. I did not take any money from them. I spent *our* money only on the wedding reception and the few days of hosting them here. The mediator (*madhyasta*)—he got paid Rs 1000 by the groom."

Bijoy and Puspalata knew, from hearsay, that other mediators charged a lot or did *dhandha* (trade) in women, but they said it had not happened in Anita's case.

But the twosome acknowledged that the mediator and the groom had "exaggerated the amount of land the family owned and the income the man earned—as small lies that almost all families tell to get a match."

Bijoy had accompanied his sister after her marriage to her new home in a village in the Mathura region: "I stayed there for fifteen days to assess the place and to see the truth and the lies of the people." After a year and a half, Anita called up Bijoy to ask whether the family was willing to marry the youngest sister, Sunita, to her younger brother-in-law. Bijoy recollected, "The family was good and Anita was happy. The two sisters would be together and be a support to each other. It was arranged directly—no mediator involved." Puspalata had also visited her two daughters three times and had stayed for six months the last time she was there, enjoying her time with her grandchildren. Puspalata reminisced about the dire conditions that had led to the marriages: "The marriages happened twelve years ago. It was after the cyclone. There was no work anywhere to be found. People said to me, 'Why did you give them away to such a far place? Will they visit you again? Suppose they are killed? It is a completely unknown place.' I did not answer and thought, why should I bother about their opinion. Will they help me or appreciate my problem? No, they will not."

Puspalata referred to the 1999 cyclone, recorded as the most intense one to have occurred to date. According to government records, around nine thousand people lost their lives, while the unofficial records estimated the fatalities to be around thirty thousand. The super cyclone decimated Odisha's countryside, with storm surges salinating fertile lands, destroying standing crops, uprooting coconut trees—a major source of livelihood and food—and killing livestock. Twelve years later, stumps of decimated coconut trees, one long-lasting impact of the cyclone, were still visible, and villagers pointed out to me farmlands that had become inarable. "That was the time when many of the women in the region started getting married outside [of the region]," said Bijoy. It was evident not only that any adversity or sudden-onset natural disaster could tip poor families such as Bijoy's further into economic precarity, but also that hardships like this accentuated already existing gender inequalities, such as the inability to marry locally because of increased dowry demands from similarly economically vulnerable local men.

Hari and his mother, Prabha Devi, lived a small distance away from Bijoy. Hari's youngest sister, Sarmila, was married to a man from Mathura. When I arrived to speak with them, Hari and his entire extended family were busy piling freshly harvested paddy into a mountainous pile in the open courtyard, which would then be covered with a protective cover of tarpaulin until it was threshed. Sarmila and her husband, Vinod, were also there. Hari was a sharecropper and saving the harvested crop from the elements was critical for the family's financial well-being. I waited until he took a break, and then we spoke. Hari recounted,

> I told the mediator that I would agree to marry my sister to the man he had proposed, but before that, I needed to check, for myself, how he and his family lived, and what their [material] conditions (*abastha*) were like. I went with three other people in my family to his village. All four of us inquired from the villagers and neighbors whether the man was any good, if he were an alcoholic, or if he had any bad habits. The villagers told us, "Have no fear, give your sister here [in marriage]. The man and his family are good people." So, I decided to go ahead with the proposal and marry her off there.

One of his sisters had married locally, as she was fairer in skin tone than Sarmila. As discussed in chapter 3, men demand a higher dowry for darker-hued women like Sarmila. Prabha Devi was bitter about people's greed in trying to milk poor families of more dowry, "just for dark skin. Everyone wants fair skin. We are so poor that we could not even buy her a pair of silver earrings. I had to settle for gilt [silver plated] ones."

Failing to secure a marriage for Sarmila locally, the family was open to a proposal that a local mediator, Sanupal, brought to them. Sanupal had similarly arranged for ten such cross-region weddings and was known to "place" the women in good families. Hari put an unusual demand before Sanupal—that he visit Vinod's village to verify his background before saying yes. He explained why he took the trouble: "She is *my* sister. *I* am responsible for her. People had warned of trade (*dhandha*) in women—that women are sold and killed there—I wanted to see things with my own eyes and confirm where she was going. I did not speak Hindi, but one cousin, who had migrated to Delhi for work, did. He accompanied me."

Vinod was landless, uneducated, and worked in a *halwai* (sweetshop) in a small town near his village, and so was poorly paid. These three factors in combination struck him off as "suitable" marriage material. "Women's families aspire for grooms with a government job (*sarkari naukri*) and not one who fries *jalebis* and *samosas* all day long," said Vinod, with a wry grimace, later that evening. Failing to marry locally, he took a loan to pay a villager and his Odiya wife (as people from Odisha are called), who mediated cross-region matrimonies: "I asked him to get me a good wife, just like his. I paid a total of Rs 20,000—it included his commission and other costs such as buying sarees, gifts, travel, and food." When I met them, Vinod was in Nimaipur only because Sarmila was pregnant with her first child, and her family had asked that she come home for the delivery. Vinod stressed repeatedly that Sarmila and he were married "according to customs (*reeti-rivaj*)" and that "she had not been sold (*beyki nahi gayi hai*) as happened in the case of Hari's neighbor, Binata Devi's daughter."

Binata Devi lived in the same neighborhood as Bijoy and Hari. When I got there, Binata Devi was cooking a frugal meal of boiled rice and a fistful of red lentils in an aluminum pot over a smoking wood stove in her courtyard. Widowed, she lived alone. She said, "This homestead is all that I have. I have simply nothing else. Not even a tap for water. I am too old to work now."[1] Binata Devi's eyes immediately clouded with tears at the memory of what had transpired with the youngest of her five daughters, Jharana.

Mousami, a woman Binata Devi knew from the village, was married to a man in Rajasthan. Mousami had approached Binata Devi to send Jharana along with her to look after her newborn infant and to take care of the livestock. The mother had agreed because of their desperate food insecurity. Jharana's paternal uncle, Bhagaban, who knew Mousami, went along with the twosome to Rajasthan. On his return, he informed Binata Devi that all was well with Jharana and that she had settled in quite nicely with Mousami.

"But when my daughter did not come back after a few months, Bhagaban told me that she had been married off to a man there. Who gave him and Mousami the right to marry off my daughter?" Binata Devi remarked angrily as she showed Jharana's only photograph—a tiny image on an official Indian Election Commission card. Furious with what had transpired, Binata Devi and her brother, Jagadish, had approached the elected village council, *gram panchayat*, seeking justice. Mousami and Binata's brother-in-law, Bhagaban, were called to a village council meeting in Nimaipur, where they admitted to both forcing Jharana into marriage and being paid Rs 26,000 by the man who had married her. The two agreed to take Binata Devi and her brother, Jagadish, to see Jharana.

Jagadish, who lived adjacent to Binata Devi's homestead, sat quietly as she cried, remembering the visit. Jharana was not living a happy life. Married to a man who often came home drunk with two or three men in tow, Jharana would lock herself up in a room to prevent the drunk men from sexually assaulting her. She would be beaten up by her husband for the slightest of reasons. Seeing Jharana's hellish life, Binata Devi pleaded with her daughter to return home, but she had refused. "I said to her, 'Even if we have to beg to survive, don't stay there and get beaten up by him.' My daughter said it was her fate (*naseeb*)." Wiping her tears with the edge of her saree, Binata Devi continued: "You are asking about the marriage of daughters. I gave birth to my child, brought her up by working as a wage laborer until she grew up. Can you ever feel what I am going through, thinking of her? You must have your own children—what is the worth of the children for a mother? Tell me. I would rather poison and kill my daughter than give her in marriage there [North India]."

Within a span of a day in Nimaipur, just like with my first day of fieldwork in Haryana, I had come face-to-face with three different and disparate trajectories of matchmaking and cross-region matrimony. I realized that these challenge assumptions about the homogeneity of the modes through which cross-region marriages are arranged, the players involved in marriage mediations and their motives, and the roles of the women and their parents in either accepting or being deceived into such proposals.

These disparate narratives also challenge the dominant discourse in mainstream Indian and international media—one picked up by scholars and activists—that has presented *all* cross-region alliances as instances of bridal trafficking. Out of a total of seven cross-region marriages in that village, only one, that of Binata Devi's daughter, Jharana, neatly fit the category of a woman coerced into a bad marriage, with money changing hands for the so-called sale of the bride. These narratives also reveal that the processes of mediation, motives, and strategies are replete with contradictions and ambiguities. In that context, I considered, is there any space to recognize the presence of partial truths or negotiated existences?

Framing the Bride-Trafficking Discourse

Contemporary cross-region marriages can be considered to have begun occurring in North India in roughly two phases. In the first phase, lasting roughly until the early 1990s, they occurred sporadically and were not specifically aimed at filling a female deficit in these communities. Livelihood strategies such as employment in the Indian Army or the long-haul transport industry would take Haryanvi or Rajasthani men to distant regions of India, where, eventually, their contact with local communities would result in marriages with local women. Organized criminal gangs and commercial marriage brokers were also absent in this phase.

But by the mid- to late 1990s, as the female deficit increased, such men and their wives began getting tapped for obtaining brides by the women's extended natal family or community. Additionally, men, locally called "agents" and employed in the army or in the long-distance transport business, would also field informal requests to find wives for their village men. Both forms of matchmaking allowed the nascent but gradual emergence of female migration chains. As the demand increased, a new breed of altruistic and commission-based marriage brokers emerged to facilitate cross-region marriages, including cross-region brides and their husbands, as well as criminal gangs that traffic women. Other unlikely actors include fathers or brothers of the women, as their migration for work to North India brings them into contact with prospective grooms there.

The dominant discourse within India, framed by a handful of anti-trafficking activists and organizations, appears to leave no room for a heterogeneity of experiences, motives, and circumstances that spur such alliances, especially from the natal communities.[2] This creates a reductive construction of such marriages by framing them in simple binaries of traffickers cheating unsuspecting brides and their parents, with assertions being made that the women are forced into sexual slavery by North Indian male buyers. Contentions are made that poor parents are pushed into selling their daughters to agents who prey on their poverty; that women are forced into sexual slavery by North Indian male buyers; and that organized bride-trafficking rings operate in the bride-deficit regions of Haryana and Rajasthan (Blanchett 2003; Pandey and Kant 2003; Rahman 2009). Shafiqur Rahman, a prominent India anti-trafficking activist and founder of the anti-trafficking NGO Empower People, asserted in an interview with me in New Delhi that "in 100 percent of cases, these aren't marriages. These are trafficking. . . . The men buy women, sell women, and do trafficking of women. Each girl has been sold 4–10 times."

Local and international media have played a significant role in disseminating "trauma narratives" by employing emotive stories of wife sharing, sexual slavery, and bride trafficking, using words like "slave brides" or "India's Bride Buying Country" in their headlines.[3] Without offering analytical insights, Orientalist representational tropes involving archetypal imageries of "native" brides as "victims" of "patriarchal violence" and the grooms as "sex-starved beasts" are deployed. Victim accounts and unsubstantiated estimates are reproduced uncritically from NGO reports, and, quite often, the same people figure constantly in media reports, either as anti-trafficking experts or as victim-survivors.[4] Deliberate agenda-setting is also evident in an interview that Shakti Vahini's Ravi Kant gave to me in his Delhi office: "The media served as an important tool to influence public opinion." The consequent public outrage about "violence against women" has helped create a high profile for anti-trafficking organizations' activities and their paternalistic "rescue-based" interventions. As Constable wrote, "it seems ironic that some of the activist groups that most strongly oppose the demeaning treatment and condescending images of women, ultimately traffic in those very images themselves" (2006, 19).

Aiding this assumption about widespread bride trafficking and of brides as transactable commodities who are sold to the highest bidders is the language used by potential suitors and conjugal families in describing these noncustomary matrimonies. Terms such as "we have *bought* the bride" (*kharid kar layen hai*) are commonly used when describing the process of cross-region marriage-making. The paying of a commission or brokerage fee to a marriage broker, a fee that includes the marriage package of all costs related to travel, food, lodging, and the marriage ceremony, is misinterpreted as a transaction cost for the purchase of a wife. In large part, ethnocentric notions about Biharis and Bengalis (as discussed in chapter 3 and further elaborated in chapter 5) provide justification for such conclusions. The burden then falls on the "bought" wife to prove the genuineness of her marriage and to dispel entrenched beliefs about her "sale."

Interestingly, scholars working on the subject of cross-country marriages in Southeast and East Asia have urged caution in bracketing such marriages into neat categories, as the "ambiguities . . . make it difficult for an intimate insider— let alone an outside observer—to pronounce with any degree of certainty where the distinction lies between real and fraudulent marriage" (Freeman 2011, 108). They have argued that marriage migration needs to be understood as part of the coping strategies used within the larger contexts of globalization and structural adjustment programs in sending countries (Hsia 2004; Hsia 2008). Marriage migration with calculated risk-taking by women in deliberately transforming themselves into market commodities not only muddies the boundaries between victimhood and agency, it also runs counter to discourses of passive victimhood. A study of Vietnamese women's marriages to Taiwanese men terms this "active submission as agency" (Tseng 2015, 118).

Problems of Quantification

Notwithstanding such cautionary notes stressing a heterogeneity of experiences, anti-trafficking activists continue to underline, without substantiation, the magnitude of bride trafficking with statements like "there are about five to ten thousands [*sic*] women forced into marriage by coercion or trade in Haryana" and "every year, thousands of young women and girls in northern India are lured or sold into involuntary marriage" (Pandey and Kant 2003, 7). The NGO Empower People has similarly claimed that "100,000 girls [are] trafficked every year [i]n the name of bride trafficking."[5] Similarly, the UNODC *Country Assessment* for India has made uncorroborated broad generalizations that "every year, thousands of young women and girls are lured into the idea of a happy married life with a rich man in Punjab or Haryana," and that "most 'purchased brides' are exploited, denied basic rights, duplicated as maids, and eventually abandoned" (UNODC South Asia 2013, 10).

When questioned about the methodology used to arrive at such numbers, the anti-trafficking activists behind these reports have no answers, such as Ravi Kant, president of Shakti Vahini, another leading Indian anti-trafficking NGO, who stated in his interview, "[We] cannot give you a figure or a percentage.... There is no data on this, but the numbers may run into thousands." Other NGO reports have stated that "the information gathered is mainly based on interceptions [and] media reporting, as provided by the local people, the buyers and their families, the victims and their families and a few of the agents who have been bringing the girls to sell them" (Pandey and Kant 2003, 3).

Scholars working in this area of global sex trafficking and moral panic have urged caution, as "most reports go on to quote large numbers without any indication of what they are actually referring to" (Doezema 2010, 5), with extrapolations made from unstandardized data-collection methods that lack empirical rigor (Weitzer 2014, 12). They contend that the data is often anecdotal and full of unverified assertions, and that the numbers are deliberately manipulated to create a moral panic (Chuang 2010; Weitzer 2011). Problems of quantification also occur because trafficking is an illegal activity, further making accurate figures hard to obtain (Van Liempt 2006). Globally, other interlocutors pick up such unsubstantiated figures for reference, thus contributing "to the construction of both the dominant paradigm or discourse of trafficking, as well as the mythologies of trafficking" (Sanghera 2005, 5).

It was this vagueness over numbers and generalizations that led me to design two close-ended baseline surveys to assess the extent of bridal trafficking and to ascertain the modes through which these marriages occur. One purposive sampling consisted of all cross-region brides in 226 villages from select research regions in Haryana and Rajasthan, and another of natal families that was conducted in clusters of ten natal villages each from the two sending regions of West Bengal and Odisha. The survey model has often been derided for its tendency to bring out generalizations, without enabling the researcher to look at more complex underlying reasons; in this case, however, the paucity of data, either about the exact numbers of cross-region marriages or the socioeconomic backgrounds of the grooms and brides, made it a vital research instrument for uncovering trends and patterns in marriage-making (see Tables 11 and 12 for details on modes of marriage mediation). Significantly, the design of the two purposive samplings, with details on caste, religion, landownership, and livelihood strategies of natal families, also allowed for contextualizing the "matrimonial vulnerabilities" of some groups of women more than others (see Tables 7, 9, and 10).

TABLE 11 Mode of mediation for select conjugal regions

MEDIATOR	ROHTAK	REWARI	ALWAR	TOTAL (NO.)	TOTAL (%)
Agent	49	9	3	61	8.36
Cross-region bride	173	10	20	203	27.84
Husband	181	21	16	218	29.90
Husband-bride duo	58	12	17	87	11.93
Sister	12	3	5	20	2.74
Self*	24	3	9	36	4.93
Love marriage	8	4	2	14	1.92
Husband-trafficker	–	–	4	4	.55
Bride-trafficker	6	–	3	9	1.23
Migratory father/ brother	11	1	–	12	1.65
Maulana	–	–	3	3	.41
Undisclosed/not remembered	62	–	–	63	8.64
TOTAL	584	63	82	729	100

Source: Author's research study in Alwar and Rewari (2011), and Rohtak (2014).
* This includes marriages through Jamaats.

TABLE 12 Mode of mediation for select natal regions

MEDIATOR	BALESHWAR (NO.)	COOCH BEHAR (NO.)	TOTAL (NO.)	TOTAL (%)
Bride	19	26	45	23.31
Bride trafficker	1	2	3	1.55
Husbands of cross-region brides	10	16	26	13.47
Local locators	23	41	64	33.16
Love marriage	1	5	6	3.10
Migration for work (bride)	–	3	3	1.55
Migration for work (male family member)	2	11	13	6.73
Sister	9	14	23	11.91
Trafficker	2	3	5	2.61
Not remembered		5	5	2.61
TOTAL	67*	126*	193	100

Source: Author's research study in Odisha (2011), and West Bengal (2014).
* Includes siblings in cross-region marriages, with 50 and 104 families surveyed in Baleshwar and Cooch Behar, respectively.

Bridal-Slave Discourse

The quantitative data revealed vast variances in the way cross-region marriages were mediated. Certainly, some women were trafficked for marriage, but they did not make up the majority. Instead, belying the dominant "all brides as trafficked" narrative, an overwhelming number of marriages were mediated by the migrant brides and their husbands or by marriage agents who charged a fee (see Tables 11 and 12). Importantly, the natal region survey (Table 12) revealed a new and a significant insight: the role of local locators in arranging nearly one-third of such matrimonies (their mode of mediating is discussed later in this chapter). It can be argued that, during the surveys, people might not have made a "full disclosure" in stating the mode of marriage-making. Yet, correlating data from the conjugal and natal regions reveals almost similar marriage-mediating trends.

Additionally, instead of exclusively relying on the survey to arrive at conclusions about patterns of cross-region marriage-making, interviews with the brides and their natal families formed an intrinsic element of the study to reveal details. From a total of 116 interviewed brides, a significant number (n=80) emphasized that they were married according to the religious customs of their community (*reeti rivaj ke saath*) (n=43), or that documentary proof about their marriage existed either as a registered marriage certificate or a *nikahnama* (Islamic marriage contract) (n=37). Brides also openly disclosed whether they were trafficked or sold (n=5). This sample can be taken as representative of the total of cross-region marriages surveyed. During interviews, women stressed that though they might have been deceived about the men's socioeconomic status or their physical ability, they were not "bonded" (*bandhua*) slaves.

Brides actively sought to dismantle the victim discourse and to underscore their non-trafficked status by citing their ability to speak freely with me for the interviews without being monitored, their freedom to use cellphones to speak to their natal families, and their ability to travel back and forth between their natal and conjugal homes. However, Ravi Kant, an anti-trafficking activist, in an interview that I conducted with him in his Delhi office in 2012, rejected such testimonies by asserting that "*all* women are trafficked and victims of bride-trafficking. They suffer from 'Stockholm syndrome'[6] and cannot understand their victim-status."

The New Marriage Brokers

Traditionally, Jati priests, or the Brahmins, and a specific caste group, the Nai, or the barbers, whose nature of work brought them in intimate contact with the community, would be asked to find suitable matches. Kin members with an extensive social network in their caste group also acted as informal go-betweens. The role of the matchmaker was crucial for checking the antecedents of each family, including the *got*, socioeconomic status, and character of the groom or bride. Usually, the *bichola* or *bicholia* (common terms for matchmaker) was given some token remuneration, either money or gifts, as a gesture of goodwill by both parties, to acknowledge their efforts in locating the right match. In West Bengal, the social legitimacy of this customary sum is evident in the term *Ghatok Bidai* (literally translated as "farewell to the mediator"), which is used for the payment given to them, whether in cash or kind. The context of cross-region matrimonies has made these traditional matchmaking practices redundant and given rise to a new set of mediators. Their matchmaking, with motives varying from altruism to pure profit-making, is integral to the continued spread of cross-region matrimonies in rural North India, yet they occupy an ambiguous position of (dis)respectability in rural society. Similarly, Maunaguru, in *Marrying for a Future*, underlines that "brokers are 'pathways' in the matchmaking process" (2019, 23) for marriage-making between the diasporic Sri Lankan Tamil community and Tamils located in Sri Lanka. In their case, the dispersal of Sri Lankan Tamils overseas caused by the protracted civil war in Sri Lanka, broken networks of kin members, and need to prove the "genuineness" of diasporic matrimonies to immigration authorities has reconfigured marriage-making. This disruption has led to the emergence of a new breed of commercialized marriage brokers who are widely perceived as unpopular figures because of their "ambiguous behavior, untrustworthiness, [and] profit-making motivation" (2019, 27).

The Bride Matchmakers

Cross-region brides themselves arrange the largest numbers of marriages, oftentimes matching men in their conjugal families or extended kin network with female relatives from back home (see Tables 11 and 12 for details on the mode of marriage mediation). Their matchmaking ranges from informal one-off alliances to brokering marriages for commission, the latter of which treads very close to what can be termed bride trafficking.

Brides as Informal Mediators

The biggest group of bride mediators in this study arranged cross-region matrimonies organically, without any incentive for profit and for a variety of reasons. Kusum, a woman from the East Indian state of Jharkhand, had mediated just two marriages, for female relatives, to men who were known to her husband's family and who lived in adjacent villages in the Rewari district. She described the creation of such female migration chains: "This is how it happens: suppose I get married here first. I will then go and arrange marriages of a couple of other women from my family or of neighbors in the village. Those women then mediate a couple of other such marriages. A majority of the weddings here are conducted through this method." This chain migration from within kin member groups or within one's natal or neighboring village(s) has also created clusters of brides from one region, which emerged in some parts of the conjugal research areas. For example, Chandana's village, Dhani Raghowas, included one such cluster of brides from the Baleshwar district of Odisha.

Interestingly, Kusum's own marriage had taken place because of her impoverished village barber father's request that another man, whose daughter was in a cross-region alliance, secure a similar marriage for Kusum. In a majority of instances, brides like Kusum face requests from both natal and conjugal communities. Their natal relatives and neighbors from back home request that the women arrange similar dowry-free matrimonies for their female wards. On the conjugal side, they are also asked by conjugal kin members or villagers to "arrange a bride just like you (*tumhare jaisi*)" for unmarried male relatives or neighbors. The pressure to accede to requests, particularly from the conjugal side, is tremendous, because of the threat of domestic violence or abuse by their husbands or in-laws if they refuse, their low bargaining power as daughters-in-law within the patriarchal familial setup, and their lack of fallback options. The desire to gain respect and recognition within their new families and communities are other motivators. Most of the women stressed that they would arrange a couple of marriages only if *they* themselves were happily married there.

Such chain migrations also enable the women to expand their social networks and overcome their cultural loneliness, a fact noted by earlier scholars (Kaur 2004, 2597). Sitabi, a woman from West Bengal married to a rickshaw puller from Khusropur village near Alwar city, could not relate to local women because of differences in culture and customs, nor was she welcomed into the close-knit community of Meo women in the village. Soon, she was back in her village to "persuade" a neighborhood woman Miskina's family to agree to her marriage with a landless agricultural wage laborer from the same village. Sitabi recounted, "I won't speak to my Meo neighbor [because of the repercussions], but with Miskina, I can speak out about what is troubling my heart. I trust her. That's why I got her [married here]. The main benefit is that we can meet and chat with each other. We can share our sorrows. We speak the same language. We do not feel alone."

Additionally, among the Meo community, Muslim cross-region brides arrange for the matrimonies of their sons or other conjugal male relatives with their immediate natal female family members, like nieces (n=5), this despite the Meo shunning the Islamic practice of marriage between first cousins. Akhtari Bano was one such woman, who had obtained her brother's daughter as a bride for her own son, Salman, named after Salman Khan, the Hindi movie actor, whom Akhtari Bano idolized. She was from Hyderabad, and "there, Muslims (*Musalman logan*) marry cousins. Meo do not like it but it [the custom] is changing. I got my niece for Salman. My brother was spared the cost of dowry. The family lives in love and affection (*pyaar-mohabbat*)."

Moreover, both surveys and interviews revealed that some marriages are arranged by female siblings, like Anita, the bride from Nimaipur in Odisha, who got her younger sister, Sunita, married to her younger brother-in-law. This disproves the anti-trafficking activist Shafiqur Rahman's contention that "the women traffickers pose as sisters just to dupe everyone. In actuality, they are pimps trading in women and pretending to be sisters." Contrarily, natal region surveys in Odisha and West Bengal revealed that a significant proportion of women are actually blood sisters: in Cooch Behar, of a total of 126 women in cross-region alliances, forty-four were sisters; and in Baleshwar, Odisha, twenty women of a total of sixty-seven were sisters (see Tables 11 and 12). Also significant is that the sibling marriages mimic the female migration chain pattern evident in intra-Asia marriages (Freeman 2011), with a lapse of time happening between the two marriages. Interviews with groups of married sisters in conjugal regions (n=5 pairs) contradicted the "madam in a brothel posing as a sister" scenario that Shafiqur Rahman has insisted is the truth.

I met with Vahida Bano, a Maharashtrian Muslim woman married to Usman, who lived in Chak Peepalraha village in the Jhunjhunu district. She helped her husband with his traditional shellac bangle-making, and she packed up colorful *lac* bangles decorated with glass and beads in long thin cardboard boxes as she recounted, "Three sisters got married here and only one of us was left behind in Akola. If she were married there, we would not have been able to meet her. That's the main reason why we decided to get her married in Rajasthan. At least this way, even after the death of our parents, we sisters would be able to keep in touch and our families interact with each other."

Contrary to the popular perception that cross-region brides are only too willing to mediate marriages for the material benefits these bring, a dissenting note was struck by many women, including those who had arranged one-off marriages in the past. Brides mentioned having the hardest time convincing people that women are not available for sale in natal communities. Purnima, a bride from Bihar married in Rohtak to a landless blacksmith, had this to say: "Over here, close to twenty people have come to me and requested that I help their sons get married. 'Get us a girl from there [Bihar].' I tell them flatly that girls are not available for sale there. Nor is there a glut of unmarried women as you all assume it to be."

Nurnesa, a Muslim woman from West Bengal who had mediated just one marriage—that of her younger brother-in-law Yasin to Khadija, a woman from her own natal village—refused to mediate for other Meo families. She just did not want to take the risk of a marriage going sour: "At the time of the wedding, the family might promise everything but later on, they might reject her. Who can we trust? Obviously then, all the problems will descend on me. It'll strain my relations with people back home. I will not be able to travel there. That's why I categorically refuse to mediate."

Very much like Nurnesa, Manjuli, a bride from Odisha now married into the Rohtak district, who had opted for cross-region matrimony to prevent the loss of her family's meagre landholding through catering to local men's dowry demands, categorically turned down matchmaking requests from natal families and women. She said, "I flatly refuse. I myself have put my neck in the noose and hung myself—why make the others suffer as well? The caste ostracism hurts me a lot. I tell my friends back home flatly that over here, life is really hard. I say, 'if you still want to get married, it is better you go and drown yourself.' That's what I tell them."

The refusal to mediate any or any more cross-region marriages is a decision that brides make based on a clear-eyed evaluation of their compromised existence in conjugal communities. These also constitute refusals to accede to the popular perception about the disposability and salability of women by parents in East India, as much as a rejection of conditions in rural North Indian communities, where they would not want other women to live their lives as married women.

Bride Brokers

For the brides, the transition from informal matchmaking to profit-oriented brokerage is based on several interrelated factors. As more families start seeking the women's assistance, the unequal power dynamics within the family and community are shifted in the women's favor. They start being treated with deference by the very same people who had despised them not so long ago. Chee, Yeoh, and Vu, in their study of Vietnamese brides in Malaysia, note that the lack of familial support or resources and the unequal power dynamics make matchmaking attractive to these brides (2012, 95). However, this favorable power dynamic is transient and lasts only until the marriage has happened. For some brides, a taste of this changed dynamic and the willingness of the men to pay a commission make them transition to mediating marriages purely on a commission basis. Others become brokers reluctantly—they are urged to do so by their husbands and in-laws because of the high monetary returns.

Other studies interpret such mediating as a strategy to improve the women's social isolation (Chaudhry and Mohan 2011), but I contend that mediation should also be interpreted as an act of subversive resistance, deliberately undertaken by the two sets of mediator brides, informal and profit-based. It is a tool that they tactically employ to negotiate, resist, and cope with the patriarchal controls and violence they encounter in their conjugal homes. The earnings silence their detractors within the family and allow them to negotiate more freedoms for themselves. For instance, they are able to subvert social disciplines that impose restrictions on their movement. Citing the necessity to run background checks on the prospective families and discuss details with them allows the women freedom to travel between villages.

Manasi was one such Odiya woman married to a Dalit man, Bhuru Lal, in the Rewari district. She had begun by mediating a marriage for her widowed elder brother-in-law (*jeth*), "to overcome loneliness here. But then people started coming and requesting us to arrange marriages. I am very happy as there might come a day when we will have a large group of women from my region here. We will be able to travel back on the train as a large group. We will not be alone." Manasi now charges a fixed commission that includes the cost of travel and lodging and the marriage, for the groom as well as two of the groom's accompanying male family members. She mentioned that "marriage-making has made my life a bit easier here. I can pretend I am busy arranging a match while actually I am gossiping with my mother in my language. My husband leaves me alone too." Brides such as Manasi are also able to buy time off from chores in the household and in the fields by strategically making extended phone calls during periods when they are expected to work. Matchmaking also allows them the privilege of maintaining contact with their natal families, as they now have legitimate reasons to make phone calls back home and converse in their own language, thus giving them privacy from prying conjugal relatives.

They are also able to negotiate flexibility regarding the continuous demands made on their productive labor thanks to the family-sanctioned trips back home, which allow them to take longer periods of time off from the drudgery of their household and agricultural chores. The sojourns back home to arrange marriages are also important in their multiplicity: the women have an opportunity to generate a small income, but, equally importantly, they can also enjoy themselves by traveling alone and spending time with friends and relatives back home, while being unencumbered by the conservative social mores of rural North India. The women expressed this through comments like, "I do not have to wear a veil [back home]. I can move freely. But here [in Haryana], I cannot even walk across un-accompanied to the shop next door without people commenting about my supposed lax morals."

Tapping into their social networks for potential brides, using their parents as marriage scouts, and enjoying the convenient base of their natal homes all make this process occur smoothly, as evident from a comment by Damini, another Odiya bride broker: "I call up my brother in Odisha and ask him to search out a girl who can be married here. After locating a family with a girl of marriageable age, he then talks to them about the proposal. Once we get the green light, then I take the groom and his relatives with me back home for the marriage."

Such bride brokers often work in tandem with their husbands to draw in potential male clients, partially by projecting a "good wife" persona as an advertisement for their ability to fetch wives "just like her."[7] Manasi elaborated on this strategy: "The parents usually have a lot of questions for me: 'Suppose I marry my daughter [to someone] in Haryana? Will she remain happy there or not?' I tell them, 'Look at me, I have visited my family several times after my marriage. You have seen me before. Have you found that I was unhappy? Did I complain or cry that I wasn't being fed or looked after properly? Or that I have nothing decent to wear or that my husband beats me up? I have never complained about any of this.'"

Brides as Traffickers

Unlike the categories discussed above, the tactics of the final category of match-maker mimic those of traffickers and agents. This category of bride brokers appears to have no compunction about invoking notions of societal shame around keeping an unmarried daughter at home to pressurize natal families into giving in to their proposals. They gloss over or falsify details about the men's physical ability, age, marital status, and earning ability to make them appear to be attractive "husband" material. They resort to deception and coercion in bringing the women, including near relatives, to the conjugal regions on the pretext of providing a helping hand with housework or caring for the bride-trafficker's children. The women are then married off to anyone who offers their asking price. This happened in the case of Binata Devi's daughter, Jharana, who was sold by Mousami, and with Imrana, sold by her maternal aunt in Alwar.

I met Imrana, a woman in her early thirties from Assam, in Rasoolpur village in the Alwar district. She sat on a charpoy in a small room holding my hands tightly clasped in hers as she recounted, "I was brought here when I was barely twelve and then sold by my maternal aunt to an old man. She had told my mother that I would help her with household work. In actuality, she had reached a deal with an old man." With the help of sympathetic neighbors, Imrana had managed to escape the abusive marriage after a couple of years. Instead of returning back to Assam, she decided to work for a local family as domestic help. A year later, she remarried locally, to another Meo man, Ballan, a carpenter she met while working there: "He is a good man with a clean and simple heart. He loves me and takes good care of me."

In other instances, it appears that the situation is not such an open-and-shut case. Oftentimes, the women bring their siblings or female relatives without the intention to "sell" them, but local families' demands for women and the lure of a hefty commission, ranging anywhere from Rs 40,000 to Rs 70,000, make them change their attitudes and behaviors. For women married to poor, destitute, and underemployed men, these cash inducements appear attractive, in that they will help to ease their own poverty, and so the female wards in their care are transformed into tradeable commodities. Although I am certainly not offering an excuse for such heinous practices, I recognize that the harsh material reality of the brides in their new homes and the glitter of easy money are precipitating factors in eroding their moral scruples and humanity as they transform into "traders" or traffickers of their own loved ones.

Farjana's story is illustrative. As an eleven-year-old, she had come to the Alwar district with her elder sister Mallika to take care of Mallika's household after the birth of her children. "But with the money that my husband offered her, she 'sold' me. She was poor and I guess the money was more important to her than her own sister," said Farjana, as she sat on the ground quilting a beautiful multicolored throw made of a patchwork of old fabrics in her home in Khadrauli village in the Alwar district. When asked whether she had ever confronted her sister about it or thought of escaping, Farjana replied, "I had to be married sooner or later. A girl cannot remain unmarried. The twist of fate (*kismet*)[8] played tricks on me. I stopped associating with my family from then on."

The Husbands: Informal Matchmakers and Marriage Brokers

The husbands of cross-region brides also emerged as another significant category of cross-region marriage brokers (see Tables 11 and 12). Here again, very much like with the bride mediators, the men's mediation ranges from informal and altruistic one-off matchmaking to profit-oriented marriage brokering with a fixed commission. What is common is that they all tap in to their wives' social and kin networks to locate potential brides.

Husbands as Informal Matchmakers

Altruistic husband mediators consist of men considered to be in successful cross-region marriages, with "a wife who treats her in-laws and her husband well and looks after the house and children properly." The social pressure of familial and kin ties is brought to bear on these men to encourage them to mediate alliances similar to their own. Chet Ram, a man from the village Dhani Raghovas in the Rewari district, whose hands were laid waste by the polio he had contracted when he was quite young, stated, "My maternal cousin's wife is from Odisha. Since he had developed a 'link' to that place, I requested him to find me a wife just like his from there." Of the thirty-six husbands interviewed, eleven mentioned requesting a male relative to mediate a cross-region marriage for them. Such cross-region marriages do not involve a commission; instead, the prospective grooms pay for just the travel expenses of the husband mediators and their cross-region wives to the natal regions. As Nooru's elder brother-in-law, Amjad, described, "Neither the man nor the bride's family made any money. It was a selfless deed (*bina swarth ke*). We just paid for his family's tickets to the village—that is all." These one-off mediator husbands rely primarily on their wives and, by extension, their in-laws for both locating and persuading families to marry their daughters off to aspiring bachelors.

Husband Brokers

The lure of easy profits and the ability to use their wives or in-laws to locate potential brides and act as translators cause many husbands to transition from altruistic to commission-based marriage brokering. This was elaborated during one focus group of Meo village men: "Some of the men who can't get married locally go to Assam or West Bengal, get married, establish connections, and then start doing the business (*dhandha*) of arranging brides for other Meo men. Earlier, this wasn't possible. Now, every second person says, 'Let me arrange your marriage (*laa main teri shaadi karwa deta hoon*). It will cost only 5,000 to 10,000 Rupees.'"

These men are usually economically destitute, landless, and have precarious livelihood sources to begin with. The offer of prospective grooms that they "will pick up the tab on all expenses" is lucrative, given that the daily wages for male unskilled workers in agriculture are Rs 310 in Haryana[9] and Rs 201 in Rajasthan.[10] Even getting to mediate one marriage "with commission" provides a big financial relief. To illustrate, in 2014, some brokers such as Ajay, from Uncha Tendroli village from the Rohtak district of Haryana, were charging "a flat rate of Rs 60,000 per marriage of which 20,000 was the net profit." His wife,

Chaitali, had come from the West Mednipur region of West Bengal. With the uncertain income he made as an agricultural wage laborer, it was not hard for Ajay to coax her into helping arrange marriages of women from her region to men there. Meeting them in their home, I could see that they were comparatively well-off in light of the circumstances of other landless wage laborers in the same village. Their single-storied house boasted an anteroom, with a big television and a washing machine standing as testimony to their success in mediating cross-region matrimonies.

When questioned about the high fee that the duo charged local families, Ajay sought to justify it, contending, "I need some money for my own survival. Tell me, why should I take all the effort and run about to arrange weddings? It is entirely up to you to label my work either as pimping or brokering (*dalali ya naukri*)." Sukh Chain, a poor-sighted and uneducated man who lived in the same village as Ajay and Chaitali, had approached them to arrange a match for him. Landless, he ran a small *kirana* (grocery store) from a room of his small house that opened out onto a village lane. He had taken a loan from a Jat farmer to pay the sum of Rs 50,000 to Ajay for securing his marriage to Babki, whose village was adjacent to that of Chaitali. It had been an easy match to arrive at, as Babki had been rejected locally because she suffered from a speech impediment. Although Sukh Chain justified paying the high fees by acknowledging that "no one will work without any personal benefit," he, like other villagers, considered husband brokers like Ajay to be greedy and unscrupulous, and contemptuously referred to them as *dalals*, or agents. This stigmatization of profit-oriented brokers on account of their dubious brokering practice is one that Maunaguru also encountered in his study of Tamil marriage brokers in Sri Lanka (2019, 53–55). To counter this stigma, one such broker in his study had chosen the term "marriage facilitator," to "eliminate the stigma of profit making . . . [and] mak[e] it seem more service oriented" (2019, 53). In the instance of Indian cross-region matchmaking, profit-oriented brokers, both women and men, seem to prefer the traditional terms *bicholia* or *bichola* over agent or *dalal*, which are words imbued with malpractice and dishonesty.

Army Men and Truck Drivers as Brokers

Another category of marriage brokers, referred to locally as agents, or *dalals*, comprises men with some contacts in the natal regions, because of the nature of their employment in the army, construction industry, or long-distance transport business (see Table 11 on conjugal region mediators). In the nascent phase of cross-region marriages—that is, until the mid- to late 1990s—"armywallas," a colloquial term used for servicemen who had married women from other regions of India and returned home to their villages after retirement, were sometimes asked by their relatives to arrange cross-region marriages. With the creation of "links" for chain migrations, and the willingness of locally rejected males to pay considerable sums of money for marriage, this informal matchmaking is now commoditized with a predetermined fee.

Religious Preachers (*Maulvi*) and Religious Congregations (*Jamaat*)

Additionally, the Meo have two other distinct and unlikely cross-region marriage brokers: the *maulvi*s, or Muslim religious preachers, and the *jamaat*s, or religious congregations (see Table 11 on mode of mediation in conjugal regions). The *jamaats* allow Meo men to travel to other Muslim-majority parts of India on religious tours. Some others who become *maulvis* earn a living teaching in the madrassas, or Islamic religious schools in other parts of India. Such contacts allow them to become acquainted with local poverty-stricken Muslim families with daughters of marriageable age. Mubina Bano, a woman from Hyderabad who got married through a *maulvi* and now lived in Razzakpur village in the Nuh district, explained the process: "The Meo *maulvi* learned about our poverty and broached my parents with a marriage proposal for his brother-in-law who couldn't get married locally." Ashrafi, a Meoni widow with no land or resources, said, "My son studied in a madrassa and went on a *jamaat*. The *maulvi* in a madrassa in Bihar arranged a match for him—in fact, my son got married to his niece." She added that, if it were not for the *jamaat*, it would have been impossible for him to get married locally.

Significantly, these *maulvi*- or *jamaat*-mediated marriages, though few, do not incur any commission or cost related to travel or other extraneous expenses. Also, the method through which these matrimonies occur appears to eliminate deceptions about the grooms. In addition, the husband and the wife tend to be closer in age to each other, unlike the wide age gap found in other cross-region alliances.

Locators in Natal Regions: Critical Cogs in Mediating Cross-Region Marriages

Here I examine the role of an overlooked yet very critical component of cross-region marriage brokering: local locators. All marriage brokers, including bride brokers, are totally reliant on the local people in the natal regions for "locating" potential brides. These locators—called *ghotoks* in West Bengal and *madhyas-tas* in Odisha, terms used locally for traditional marriage mediators—are advantageously placed. They are naturally embedded in the source communities; they speak the language of the area; and they have extensive kin and social networks in a number of villages that they can tap in to.

The largest group of such locators comprises the immediate family members of cross-region brides, who oftentimes become informal locators by default. Their underlying fear of the ill treatment of their daughters and their customary low status as "wife givers" make it difficult for them to refuse requests for matchmaking coming from the conjugal homes. In other instances, mothers are urged by their bride daughters to become locators for them. The incentive of a shared commission also makes many natal families graduate to active scouting. Their impoverished status—which led to them finding cross-region alliances for their daughters in the first place—coupled with the promise of easy financial returns coming to them as go-betweens, whittles away their reservations about mediating. This was precisely the case with Biplab Das, the father of two daughters, Aparna and Mamata, who were in cross-region marriages with two men from the same village, Dhaiapur, in the Sonipat district of Haryana.

Biplab Das lived in Purbi Jodiapur village, in a sprawling compound that housed three families—all had one of their daughters in a cross-region matrimony in Haryana, thanks to his mediating. Biplab, having migrated to the industrial hub of Dharuhera, near Delhi, had met Ram Bhajan, now Aparna's husband, where they both worked in an automotive factory. Knowing Ram Bhajan well, and the fact that he had asked for no dowry, made Biplab, a migrant worker with two daughters of marriageable age, propose the hand of his eldest daughter, Aparna, to him. Biplab's transition into becoming a locator occurred by happenstance when he was approached by his neighbor living in the same compound for a similar "no-dowry" match. A phone call to Aparna and Ram Bhajan by Biplab had the twosome become marriage mediators, first on an altruistic basis and then commission-based.

Oftentimes, and contrary to popular perception, poor parents, of their own accord, also seek out such locators to help marry off their daughters. Biplab's neighbor, Usha Rani, a Dalit woman who worked as a plucker in the newly emerging tea gardens in their village, was one of them. She explained, "I chose to go to him [Biplab Das]. His daughter is married in Haryana. She is a mediator (*ghotok*) and has arranged marriages of village women. I asked his daughter to find a suitable man for my daughter too."

Other independent commission-based locators include teashop and Dhabba owners, drivers of passenger minivans that ply on rural routes, and traditional local matchmakers who are willing to broker cross-region matches. The active search begins once the conjugal-region broker contacts the locator with details about the prospective groom. This usually happens after the finalization of the brokerage fee, based on, as Ram Bhajan explained, the "number of blemishes (*tota*) the man has. We show brides based on all these factors (*usi hisaab ki ladki dikhate hain*). If he has more blemishes, then he will not get a young and a beautiful wife."

The modus operandi for all locators, Ram Bhajan explained, is to "travel from village to village and scour for poor parents with four to five daughters. Poor means someone who is landless or has very little land, has no other resources, and does not have a regular source of livelihood." Damini, a bride broker, offered more insight on this: "My mother is on the lookout for families that are 'soft.' Those with widowed mothers or where the father has remarried. The step-mother has an interest in saving for her own children." In the latter instance, the pressure to save meagre material assets for other children from the second union and the desire to "marry daughters off 'cheaply'" is unrestrainedly exploited by locators, who offer a "dowry-free, all-expenses-paid" marriage proposal to parents. The locators also search for "families with daughters who have left their abusive husbands, those who are deserted, or widowed" as "these are more receptive to cross-region proposals and don't make much of a fuss." It is worth noting here that cross-region matrimonies offer such women a second chance at marriage, one that might not be possible locally.

Locators also allay parents' concerns about marrying their daughters into distant regions without familial support networks or any cross-checks. Parent locators do this by showcasing the "successful marriage" of their own daughter(s) as much as by putting continual pressure on parents about the "societal shame" (*samajik lajja*) of having an unmarried daughter sitting at home. Manjuli, a bride from Odisha married into the Rohtak district, recounted, "Each day, the village man who was the agent there would come to meet my father and try to wear down his resistance. Morning and evening! He finally convinced my father that the proposal was good and that the man belonged to a respectable family."

The potential bride's parents take the risk that their daughter will not be trafficked or sold based on the locator's "trust" factor and social legitimacy, and on the fact that, as natives of the region, if anything goes wrong, they can be "caught by their throats and held accountable," as Bullu's mother in Odisha explained. Manasi's mother in Baleshwar, Odisha, had become a bride locator for her daughter. Manasi said, "It is only once the phone call comes from my mother that a family has been located and appears open to accepting cross-region proposals that I take the man and a couple of his relatives with me to my natal region."

Significantly, all mediators, including Ajay, stressed that, "the women's families do not sell their daughters. The commission is divided up between the local locators and the agents like me." The rate varies based on the groom's marriageability factor and the effort required to convince reluctant parents to agree to these unequal matches. In the Cooch Behar district of West Bengal, in 2014, a locator's commission ranged from Rs 5,000 to 7,000. Biplab Das justified his fees by saying, "the '*ghotok bidai*' or the mediator fee here is normally Rs 5000–7000. We make the effort and spend time and energy. It is not possible to do it on a charity basis. Tell me, is it? It is a win-win situation for both: the woman gets married and we are able to feed ourselves" (*ekta meye uddhar holo, ekta aamar pet ta kaam chaale*).

Treading a Dangerous Line between Deception and Trafficking

Although those in the business of brokering matrimonies might stress that such brokered marriages are a "win-win" for the pauperized natal families bound by social pressure and a patriarchal burden to "settle" their daughters in marriage, what also emerges from the one-on-one interviews with the brides and their natal families is the widespread nature of deception that mediators and the locators resort to. Of 157 interviewed brides and natal families, seventy-three, or over 50 percent, affirmed some measure of deception had occurred about the men's economic status, physical ability, or marital status (see Tables 11 and 12 for details).[11]

Bundo, one such woman who had experience with this deception, hailed from the central Indian state of Maharashtra and belonged to an Adivasi (Indigenous) community. She recounted, "In fact, we were not told that he [her husband] limped and used a cane. We had met him always sitting down. But after the wedding, when he got up, we realized the truth. My mother wailed seeing this and cursed the mediator for this deception. They asked me to break off the marriage. . . . But my marriage with him was in my fate (*kismet*)."

Similarly, Chabirani, a mother I met in a village in Odisha, cursed the locator as she remembered the deception carried out during her daughter's marriage: "The man's [groom's] hand was covered by a shawl. It was only after the marriage was conducted and my daughter was sent off to her new home that she told us his hand was 'useless' and that this was deliberately hidden from us. If we had known about it, we would not have married her off to him." The common Indian adage that "a thousand lies have to be told for a marriage to take place" acknowledges the role of exaggerated claims, lies, and deceptions that each side resorts to in order to clinch the matrimony. Families engaged in matrimonial discussions also employ the tactics of reading between the lines, as each side knows that a fair bit of deception and exaggeration takes place; they consequently deconstruct claims through cross-checking. For cross-region alliances, the long distance between the two places of residence and the absence of the old mechanisms of cross-checking, such as through relatives married there, prevent the women's families from getting an authentic picture. This inability to verify claims does result in deceptions such as those detailed by Bundo and Chabirani. Of the 116 women and fifty natal families interviewed for this study, a total of ninety-four mentioned that a full disclosure had not been made about the men's economic status, physical ability, or marital status. Such deceptions, conducted to earn easy profits off arranging brides for men, transform women into transactable commodities—with no consideration of the long-term impact on their lived experience as married women.

In this context, it is not unsurprising to find natal communities attempting to distinguish between those who traffic brides and those who do not, by using the terms "sale" (*bikri*), "trade" (*byopaar*), and "marriage" (*bibaha*), as well as statements like, "he sold my daughter to a worthless man," "he traded my daughter" (*aamaar meye re byopaar*), and "I married my daughter off in a temple following all customs" (*jhiyo re bibaha kori diyo*). They also employ distinct terms of address for different groups of marriage brokers, based on the monetization of the mediation or lack thereof. The terms agent and *dalal*, with their negative connotations of deviousness and greed, are used interchangeably for any profit-oriented mediators, who charge a fixed commission to broker cross-region marriages on a regular basis. The traditional mediator terms *bicholia* or *bichola* are often used for informal matchmakers who are brides, or their husbands, who mediate one-off marriages altruistically or for token payment. Additionally, their exact familial relationship to those for whom they mediate is used, such as "my *mausi* [maternal aunt] acted as the *bicholia* for my marriage." What also appears common is that informal matchmakers, usually the brides themselves or their husbands, are given small gifts, or *negs*, such as clothes, food rations, or a gold nose pin, as an expression of gratitude by the men's families. Their travel costs to natal regions are also borne by the families.

In contrast, profit-oriented marriage brokers not only locate families with marriageable daughters in far-off regions within India, they also charge a variable all-inclusive "commission" or "fee," ranging from Rs 40,000 to 170,000. As discussed, this includes costs for the travel and stay of the mediator, the prospective groom, and a few accompanying relatives, as well as some wedding expenses. The rate is also dependent on the men's rejection factors in the local marriage market. Of note is that the entire amount has to be paid up front to the broker. This appears to be an unwritten rule followed by all categories of brokers, altruistic or commission-based, as, "once the marriage is done, the groom knows he has got what he wants. Why will he bother paying us what is owed?"

Is It Marriage or Trafficking?

So, when does a marriage become an instance of trafficking? What constitutes a lie that both sides can live with versus one that results in the marriage being termed as bride trafficking?[12] In May 2011, India ratified the United Nations Treaty against Transnational Organized Crime, which contains the Protocol to Prevent, Suppress and Punish Trafficking in Persons, especially Women and Children—commonly referred as the Palermo Protocol. Though the Protocol includes no separate provision for forced marriage, Article 3a recognizes any action as trafficking if there is force, coercion, deception, or fraud involved for the purpose of exploitation, or if profits are derived from the exploitation of the trafficked person through sexual exploitation, forced labor or services, slavery or practices similar to slavery, or servitude.

In July 2018, a draft Trafficking of Persons (Prevention, Protection and Rehabilitation) Bill, tabled by the government of India's Ministry of Women and Child Development, was passed to unify the multiple existing laws on trafficking, to set up anti human trafficking units, and to offer victim status and rehabilitation services to victims of human trafficking. Incidentally, the Indian approach has been critiqued by activists for its adherence to a "failed 'raid-rescue-rehabilitation-criminalisation' model."[13] Further, the various laws and their unclear stance on trafficking makes for ambiguous interpretation by police officers and the consequent harassment of anyone assumed to be involved in the trafficking of women or girls.

What emerges as a fact is that the lure of high profits and the ripple effect of generating new clients with each successful marriage they broker causes marriage brokers—such as the brides, their husbands, and other agents, as well as locators—to tread a narrow but dangerous line between trafficking and mediation. The greed for profit makes the marriage brokers fear that if they refuse to mediate for men with serious drawbacks, their clientele can potentially turn to other brokers willing to undertake higher degrees of risk in natal regions. As Sree Chand, a husband broker from Uncha Tendroli village in the Rohtak district, explained, "We lie to them [the woman's family] that the man has a huge house, he holds a good job, earns well and his family is well established. It is only through a web of lies that we are able to get the man married there."

Incidentally, marriage brokers such as Sree Chand emphasize that balancing deception and transparency in their communications with natal communities is fraught with complications. Any exaggeration of claims or withholding of facts about prospective grooms means they run the danger of becoming persona non grata in natal communities, a death-knell for their future marriage brokering services. They also have to place a significant number of women in "successful" marriages for their business to thrive. The feedback from the married women to their parents or the natal community and the fear of social reprisals adds pressure regarding their transparency.

Although such deception-laden marriage mediating surely cannot be condoned, the practice must be situated within the larger context of neoliberal restructuring of social relations, wherein people are reduced to transactional commodities with an exchange value. In the instance of cross-region matrimonies, this structural violence, under neoliberalism, through morally lacking social relations, is gendered in nature.

Trafficking Gangs and the Trade in Brides

Obtaining accurate and exact numbers about bride trafficking can be difficult, as some women choose to not define themselves as trafficked or as deceived into marriage, but it is also inaccurate to homogenize all marriages as constitutive of trafficking and involving victimhood for the brides. Other scholars working on trafficking have also noted difficulties inherent in collecting data about trafficking (Van Liempt 2006). Moreover, no standard profile can be made of the traffickers, as they are as varied as the circumstances of their victims (Feingold 2005, 28). For example, a majority of the trafficked women, such as Jharana and Farjana, are tricked by people either related or known to them, such as distant female relatives who have married into the region or women from their natal village (discussed earlier in the section on brides who become traffickers). Cross-region brides and their husbands whose mediating has become commercialized also walk a thin line falling somewhere between the relatively innocent mediating, brokering with its inherent deception and trafficking.

Further, contrary to the claims of Shafiqur Rahman, who contends that "the men buy them and sell them [women]. It has become a lucrative trade for them," the trend is not large scale. Instead, both the quantitative and qualitative research conducted in this study revealed only fifteen cases in which the purchase and sale of a woman had occurred either involving a bride broker, husband broker, or trafficking gangs. Mubarik, a mason from Sheikh Ismailpura village in the Nuh district, showed no hesitation in speaking about the transactional basis of his relationship: "I am not lying that I paid some money to get this wife from a relative of mine." *Dooj baar*, and with children from his first marriage, he saw nothing morally wrong in buying his "already married" wife, Tahira, from her first husband "to ensure that the household continued to function smoothly" (*ghar basane ke liye kharida hai*). As a landless rural man who was able to find occasional employ as a mason in nearby towns, for him, paying Rs 20,000 seemed to be cheaper than the other option—approaching a mediator to arrange a cross-region wedding, who would have charged him more than that amount.

Speaking with Tahira later on in her native Bengali, I asked her why she did not run away or seek help from NGOs active in the region. Nursing her three-month-old infant girl, she replied in a resigned tone: "Return where? My family was desperately poor—that is how I got married here in the first place. Who is there to support me—a woman with children? My first husband sold me to this man. This one troubles me, but at least he is not going to sell me."

Tahira "chose" to continue in her "marriage," illegal in both the eyes of Indian law and Islamic marriage customs, because of her almost total lack of life choices. Her father used to work as a deckhand for a fisherman in West Bengal and had married Tahira off to her first husband hoping that she would have an easier life in Nuh. With no capital or resources, he felt bound by his patriarchal "duty to settle" her. For Tahira and countless other women, patriarchal ideological constraints truly conjoin with the capitalist dispossessions that besiege India's poor with compromising life options.

Mubarik, however, is a clear-cut case of an abettor to trafficking, as he deliberately sought out Tahira's former husband to "strike" a deal over her. In that sense, he clearly fits the stereotype of "husband trafficker" that anti-trafficking activists argue about (Rahman 2009). Demands by men like Mubarik to secure "wives," by hook or by crook, are primarily necessitated by their urgency to find a female replacement to ensure the smooth functioning of their households. Such a violent articulation of the gendered cost of social reproduction, while revelatory of the erosion of the moral compass under the gradual expansion of the free market economy, is also indicative of the low worth accorded to women in general.

The commoditization of marriage and intimate relations has also fueled the rise of trafficking gangs who "arrange" brides for a price, a clear glimpse of which was offered by the efforts of Pradeep, the cabdriver, and his family in Ramsar village, to find a woman to marry Bijai. "We are going to 'buy' a bride. We will pay money and get her. We have spoken to two to three 'agents' here and whosoever finds the right match, we will buy her from him," said Pradeep, after having spoken to men he himself called "dubious." His mother, Phoola Devi, also saw nothing amiss in this "deal-making" as she elaborated on the negotiations with the agents/traffickers:

> The agent said, "You need to have Rs 70,000. I will show you at least ten to twenty to choose from. Keep the one that catches your fancy and suits your family." Everything revolves around money—if you have money, the agent talks to you. He might spend Rs 20,000–30,000 to get a woman and, from us, he will charge Rs 50,000. They size up the family's capacity to pay. Sometimes, they demand 100,000 from one and 50,000 from another. They buy a woman from somewhere to bring her here and sell her off. Once she is sold to us, we bring her home.

The complicity of the families who source brides from mediators known for their clandestine operations and "cash only with no questions asked" policy cannot be denied. People like Pradeep and his mother Phoola Devi abet trafficking by creating a "demand," and by willfully choosing to turn a blind eye to the overtly shady operations of such traffickers. They also choose not to ask probing questions, such as how these women have ended up in the trafficker's "care," or for details about the women's families. The bottom line for such grooms and families is to obtain a guaranteed "workhorse" for the best price with no questions asked. This attitude is evident from demands, such as those placed by Phoola Devi and other families, that the agent "bring a woman from a poor family, one who will be able to work well, that is she can cook and also do agricultural chores (*khet mein kaam kar sakey*)."

The fact that a family can pick and choose a bride that "catches their fancy" and that "suits" their needs and their paying ability establishes a woman's objectified status. Families seeking brides through traffickers not only internalize and reproduce market economy ideology and language when describing a "transaction," they also act as consumers in a purely capitalist sense in the way they describe the process of obtaining a woman. The traffickers' assurances of a "product guarantee" to assuage the fears of the "buyers"—that is, assuring the prospective groom and his family of the soundness of their investment—also ingrain the "woman-as-a-product" attitude among such families. For instance, Satinder, an agent from Kesariya Garhi villager from near Pilani town in Rajasthan, who was negotiating with Pradeep, stated, "I guarantee that the woman is of 'good quality.' She is a hard worker and will not run away." The use of words like "guarantee" and "good quality" speak to the degree to which these brides are commodified to rope in prospective buyers. Through the trafficker's employment of the phrase "hard worker," the woman is likened to a piece of merchandise—with the ability to perform adequately assured to the family. In the end, a combination of dissension among family members about the dubious process of marriage-making that was being proposed and their worry about being taken advantage of in a marriage scam caused Pradeep's family's deal with Satinder to fall through.[14]

My discussions with state authorities and local activists in Jhunjhunu city revealed that trafficking gangs are more active in the Jhunjhunu district of Rajasthan than anywhere else.[15] This activity was also ascribed to the dispersed layout of the villages and the restrictive mobility of women there, which prevents easy detection. The absence of informal mediation networks, because of the relative newness of such marriages, appeared as another factor encouraging the traffickers to flourish there.[16] O. P. Kataria, the additional superintendent of police (S.P), Jhunjhunu district, Rajasthan, stated, "The ones who are trying to get a bride for their son—why don't they think that if someone is arranging a wedding for money, there is something fishy there. Why don't they verify facts or ask hard questions from the agents about the women's background? Why don't they find out more—such as the address or details of the parents? They just give money to the agents and bring the women back home with them. They are equally guilty."

Mythology of Parents Selling Daughters

Bride seekers like Phoola Devi try to justify their unethical stance by arguing, "Over there [natal states], people who are poor are unable to marry off their daughters there. There are also some parents who take money from agents and sell their daughters off to them. Folks like us then pay money to the agent and buy the woman from him." What makes them arrive at such conclusions? Jo Doezema (2010) uses the terms "myths" and "mythologies" to refer to powerful political discourses that create an exaggerated moral panic about trafficked women victims to legitimize rescue crusades. She argues that such narratives are deliberately disseminated by "discourse masters," that is, people who are ideologically invested in keeping such mythologies alive (Doezema 2010). In this regard, the role of mainstream anti-trafficking activists cannot be condoned. Although they rightfully critique the traffickers for treating women as commodities, their attempts to generalize this discourse to *all* cross-region marriages creates problems for a vast majority of brides who are not trafficked and who then have to bear the burden of proving the "genuineness" of their matrimonies.

More importantly, traffickers are overwhelmingly invested in keeping this mythology alive for the easy profit it generates for them. When quoting their commission or fees to prospective grooms and their families—as in the case of Pradeep's negotiation for his eldest brother, Bijai—the traffickers state that a sizable part of it has to be paid to the girl's parents to "buy" their acquiescence. However, marriage brokers such as Ajay, a husband from the Rohtak district, admit that "the girl's family isn't given any money at all. They are just told that the expenses for the wedding, the feast, and for the clothes will be paid for by the groom." Apparently, this strategy is adopted deliberately in order to thwart questions about the high commission and the percentage of profit the mediators make with each successful marriage alliance. The traffickers or marriage brokers make a risky gamble with their pitch of daughter selling, as they can land directly into the hands of law enforcement agencies and be charged with abetting trafficking.

The myth of sale also conveniently feeds into prevailing racist and denigrating stereotypes about natal communities, particularly Bihar, Jharkhand, Orissa, and West Bengal, naming families as savage, emotionless, and poverty-stricken folks willing to sell their daughters for whatever money they can lay their hands on, as evident from Phoola Devi's comment that "over there [East India] people sell their daughters." With the marriage brokers maintaining a tight upper hand due to their familiarity with the local language, quite often prospective grooms and an accompanying handful of relatives are unable to establish a direct line of communication with the women or their families to ascertain the details by which an agreement is arrived at. The payment of money for marriage ceremonies, clothes, and the feast is deliberately *presented* as a transaction of the bride/ commodity. The grooms accept, prima facie, what the mediators tell them about the "sale," as it aligns with their negative assumptions about natal communities.

A focus group of mixed-caste men in a village in the Rohtak district acknowledged that this erroneous belief was because "all the expense there, whether it is for food or for travel, all is borne by the man's family. That is the main reason why people here assume that she has been bought." Karam Beer, a house painter from Rundh Murkhedi village in Rohtak district, who had sold a small part of his land to finance his marriage to Dharani, an Odiya woman, affirmed: "We marry the women and do not buy them. . . . I have been to my father-in-law's place and am welcomed like a son-in-law (*damaad*) and not a thief (*chor*)."

Nevertheless, the "bought" status of the new bride gets conveniently entrenched in everyday discourse in conjugal communities, with repercussions for the brides (a theme explored in subsequent chapters). Women's husbands and conjugal families themselves are also invested in keeping this mythology alive. Conjugal families and communities often employ the terms *beyki hui* or *kharidi huie*—roughly translated as "bought" and "sold"—when referring to cross-region brides. They conveniently pick up this myth of "bought" brides for their own agenda and evoke it at moments when the brides try to question or resist unreasonable demands made over their labor. This was the case with Bundo, an Adivasi bride from Maharashtra, who recounted what happened when she protested the excessive load of farm work she was asked to perform: "My mother in law claimed that money had been paid to my parents. I retorted: 'Not a single rupee has been taken by my parents. How dare you lie?' The truth came out when I confronted the mediator. He and his wife had taken the money from them saying that my father had to be bribed to agree to the marriage. He had to tell the truth to my in-laws."

"It Feels Like I Am in a Prison": Regulating Freedom of Movement

The myth of bride buying is also strategically evoked when the women start desiring to step out of the confines of the house and move away from the constant supervision exercised over their movements by other female members. In rural North India, the prevalence of classical patriarchy with a patrifocal and patrilineal form of family structure creates subordination of and control over women, especially the new incoming brides, who begin at the bottom of the power hierarchy as "effectively dispossessed individuals" (Kandiyoti 1988, 279). Cross-region brides' intra-household and intra-gender bargaining ability, particularly in the regulation of movement, is compromised by weak "fallback positions" in terms of support networks thanks to the vast physical distance between the natal and conjugal regions.

During one-on-one interviews with the men's family members, although the families overtly insisted that the women were treated like other daughters-in-law in the household, in private, they admitted to regulating the women's activities, particularly in the early years of the marriage, either because of the fear of losing the huge sum invested in the marriage if the brides ran back home or their worry about having been tricked by marriage scamsters. Brides such as Kaushalya attested to the constant surveillance and harsh treatment that they faced more than the local brides: "My family didn't allow me to venture out. They asked me to remain inside the house all the time, whereas in Maharashtra, I had the freedom of movement. When I first came here, it felt as I was in a prison."

From a total of 116 interviewed cross-region brides, a staggering ninety-three, or 80 percent, reported facing some form of control that the local brides were usually exempt from. The reported degree of surveillance and/or restraint varies, from total confinement within the four walls of the house to restricted movement within the village to chaperoning by female family members as the new bride goes around doing household chores such as collecting water or firewood. The constant chaperoning prevents the new brides from speaking to other cross-region brides and women neighbors; it also dissuades local women from reaching out to them and striking up friendships. Other strategies involve locking up, at night, the room where the new couple sleep to prevent the bride from running away in the night. In another method, witnessed only in the Jhunjhunu district, where villages are located far from agricultural fields and where almost every family has a small house on its farm, families strategically relocate the newly married couple to a remote dwelling commonly known as the *kua*. The difficult access to any mode of transport from the *kua*, the new bride's unfamiliarity with the local terrain and the language, and the total absence of interaction with anyone other than immediate family members leads to this extreme choice in sequestering newly married cross-region brides. Pradeep's family also adopted this surveilling for Manju, Bijai's wife from Uttar Pradesh, by having the couple stay at Kamlesh's home, or *kua*, for four months. During my visit to Kamlesh's *kua*, I witnessed how Kamlesh's youngest daughter would accompany Manju to the fields whenever she went to answer the call of nature. On asking Kamlesh about this, she tried to justify this policing by saying, "She is new to these parts. She might get lost. That's why we don't let her go anywhere alone." Realizing that this sounded disingenuous, she sighed and acknowledged, "We have spent so much money on the marriage and then she might run away. That's what we worry about the most."

The claustrophobia brought on by the constant surveillance and regulation results in the women experiencing their lives as "being confined to a prison" (*pinjare mein kaid*). Further, the denial by the men's families to let them visit their natal families accentuates this prisoner-like perception. Out of the 116 brides interviewed, seventy-three divulged being refused permission to go to their natal region in the early years of their marriage. This stands in stark contrast to the relative ease with which the local brides can routinely visit their natal families during festivals, life-cycle ceremonies, and childbirth. Narangi Devi, a mother-in-law from the Rewari district, who had prevented her daughter-in-law Achala from visiting her family, said she did this because she "feared that she might not return here. We would lose all the money that we had paid to the marriage agent. That's the main reason why I did not let her visit home." Like Narangi Devi, others candidly admitted that the payment of a huge commission to mediators led them to take such measures to prevent the loss of their monetary investment in a "wife." A gradual easing back of such constraints around the bride's freedom, including the ability to visit her natal region, starts occurring as more time passes and after she bears children. The families hope that maternal love will act as a deterrent against desertion.

Significantly, villagers also play a role in the surveillance of the brides by acting as informal "eyes and ears" for the families, as explained by Manjuli, a bride from Odisha, who had sought to run away because of the culture shock she experienced in Haryana: "I had told my husband's family that I wanted to explore the village. In actuality, I was finding my way out of the maze of lanes to escape. I was accosted by two village women who questioned me about my movements. The twosome said they would take me back home. After 'escorting' me back, they scolded my mother-in-law and said, 'You better control your daughter-in-law's movements or else she'll run away.'"

Such behavior of local women is not surprising, as they often share caste and kin alliances with the families bringing in cross-region brides. This informal and often invisible community policing not only deters the brides from running away from abusive or difficult family situations but also makes it doubly hard for them to open up to the local woman and share their distress with them. Such fissures in empathetic solidarity for the gendered nature of the brides' oppression and exploitation allow more extreme forms of patriarchal subordination to occur, thus normalizing gender-based violence in all forms. These are the experiences that anti-trafficking activists and organizations singularly choose to present as evidence that the women have been trafficked. These normalized hostage-like situations, exclusively limited to the cross-region brides, cannot and should not be condoned under any circumstance. Such human rights violations constitute attacks on the women's freedom of movement and make them experience prisoner-like status on a daily basis within the households and in the villages. Although it might be convenient to lay the blame of such egregious violations on conjugal families, traffickers, and marriage brokers, the discourse has to shift to examine how the state enables these abuses. As Lucy Williams, in her discussion of cross-border marriage migration, has noted, "violence and subjugation of individuals by others never take place in a vacuum and social and state ideologies and policy regimes contribute to the creation of environments in which human rights abuses can take place and, indeed allow or condone abuses when they occur" (2010, 75).

The Brides and Their Parents: Enacting Agency, Initiating Checks

The practice of curtailing new brides' movements provides much fuel to the discursive framing of all grooms and their families as buyers who treat the brides like chattel, as much as it upholds Eurocentric beliefs about the victimhood of "Third World" women caused by violence from native males (Mohanty 2003). On the flip side, such neatly sutured knowledge formation also enacts another level of gendered violence, albeit intellectual, by denying the women any subjectivity.

Homogenized representations of these brides as passive victims who silently suffer violence and abuse from conjugal family members are shattered by some women's demands for intervention and accountability by marriage mediators, whether in the form of village men turned marriage agents or bride mediators, particularly in cases of domestic abuse or the husband's alcoholism. Nila was one such bride, married to Dhanpal, an alcoholic hunchback with a violent temper, from the Rohtak district. Dhanpal had ten acres of inherited farmland, and his relatives viewed Nila as an interloper who had denied them their share of Dhanpal's land. Her eyes took on an angry glint as she spoke about seeking accountability from Sree Chand, the *ghotok* (mediator): "I go to his house and demand that he intervenes to stop the beatings. I fight with him about making my life hell—as he knew from before about my husband's abusive nature and alcoholism. Everyone has learned about his duplicitous way of arranging weddings." Sree Chand, in a separate interview, acknowledged that the "slump" in his business of mediating was caused by Nila's vocal outspokenness and exposure of his devious matchmaking ways. Such demands for interventions or accountability were expressed by as many as thirty-nine of the 116 interviewed brides.

Other women, whose movements are highly regulated either because they are trafficked or because the family fears that they might run away, are also able to find spaces in which they exhibit their resistance. Their methods range from using verbal taunts about the policing methods to actual escape. To illustrate, Mohua, an Odiya woman married through a dubious marriage agent, was always locked up at night with her husband in a room to prevent her from running away. I met her in Odisha, where she now lived with her brother and his family and worked as a daily wage laborer in agriculture. She recollected how she had used every opportunity to taunt the family, saying, "Why do you lock up the room each night? You fear I will run away? I will do so eventually and you will be able to do nothing." She did end up giving the family the slip "by saying that she had to go to the latrine." In another instance, Ismatara, a Bengali bride who faced intimate partner violence in her marriage to a Haryanvi man, called her brother and told him that she could not continue in the marriage. He traveled from his village, Dinpur, located right next to India-Bangladesh border in Cooch Behar to take her back home. I met Ismatara and her brother, Shabban, in their village, where she now lived with his family and worked as a casual wage laborer in agriculture. Shabban stated, "Thanks to Allah that she is safe now. I could not have lived in peace if I had done nothing after hearing her cries for my assistance." These narratives of subjectivity, resistance, and autonomy, though small in number, run counter to the dominant perception of all cross-region brides silently suffering from abuse and ill-treatment at the hands of their husbands or in-laws—until rescued by anti-trafficking groups.

The one positive effect of the trafficking trope and its circulation by the media is the natal communities' heightened vigilance. Agreeing to marriage migration is risky, and the women and their families often appear to have no control over the outcome of this migration strategy. Therefore, to mitigate some of the risks and wrest some control over the way the future brides may be treated by their husbands, women's parents and communities have started taking proactive measures, with a resultant nascent emphasis on accountability and transparency for all marriage mediators. Ram Bhajan, who was married to Aparna from Cooch Behar and now worked as a marriage broker, reported, "I had to give a photocopy of my Aadhar[17] card to the women's parents. The families want evidence that I am not a trafficker." Marriage broker Sree Chand similarly stated, "One time, a woman called up her parents and complained that the man was landless and that I had deceived her. This created a major furor there. When I visited the place to arrange another wedding, I was hauled up in front of the village council (*panchayat*)."

Such consciousness on the part of natal communities is also organic, as feedback from cross-region brides—given either when returning home for visits or through phone calls—about the deceptions and lies of mediators has led to wariness on the part of other parents about readily acquiescing to cross-region proposals. As Ram Bhajan ruefully admitted, "the people there have become wiser."

The same social and kin networks that are tapped by the brokers and bride locators are also utilized to shame, denounce, and punish those who deceive the women and their families. This happened in Dinpur, a village four hours away by bumpy road from the town of Cooch Behar in West Bengal. The picture-postcard idyllic village, with cows grazing in the distance and groves of bamboo dotting the rural landscape, is marked by the presence of a razor-wire fence dividing India from Bangladesh. Parts of people's fields lie in no-man's-land—farmers are allowed only regulated entry to their farmlands. Living is hard there, with migration to the neighboring states of Assam or Tripura being the only option for livelihood. Lakshmi Rani, a widowed woman in her seventies, had succeeded in getting her neighbor, Anjan, "ostracized by the community. No one in the village speaks to him or his family. Nor can the daughter visit home." Anjan had acted as a locator for his son-in-law, who brokered several marriages involving a high degree of deception, one of which involved Lakshmi Rani's then sixteen-year-old daughter, Shompa.

One method of conducting verification checks (*janch pardtaal*) against fraud and deception involves, according to Imtiaz, a father from Cooch Behar, "going personally to the prospective grooms' villages to run background checks instead of taking the mediator's (*ghotok*'s) word at face value." Similarly, Purnima from Khaprauli village shared what transpired when the mediator came to her village in Bihar with a marriage proposal: "My maternal uncle came here [to Rohtak]. He came alone and stayed for eight days to verify the family and my husband. He asked around in the village about the man: whether he had a 'good' character, what type of a job he did and what he earned. He also asked people to frankly tell whether his niece would be happy or unhappy if she was married to this man. It is only after he was satisfied with his scrutiny that we agreed to this marriage."

Marriage mediators, sensing the reluctance of parents, have also begun suggesting that families make a trip, as Ajay stated, to "check out things independently and then proceed with the marriage only when satisfied." Such premarriage verification visits, sponsored by the mediators with expenses paid by the prospective grooms, are usually undertaken by the women's immediate male kin, like Hari, the landless sharecropper from Odisha who took a trip to Mathura for this purpose. Although the number of premarriage verification trips is fewer (n=7), postmarriage verification trips, in which the father and/or brother accompany the bride to her new home, are numerous (n=25).

These visits are important on several counts. First, anticipating such a trip places pressure on both the mediators and the prospective grooms to not make false claims. Here, the husband-wife mediator duo or the husband mediator has more at stake, as any deceptiveness can ruin their future matchmaking prospects in the village or community. Second, by making a visit to the conjugal village, the woman's family sends a clear message that in the case of ill treatment, her family will support her, notwithstanding the vast distance separating the two regions and families. Despite the best of intentions, misrepresentations and deceptions still occur. Apart from their unfamiliarity with agricultural traditions in conjugal regions, poor landless parents are often impressed with the sight of prospective grooms living in brick dwellings (*pucca ghar*), owning a buffalo or two, or possessing a small piece of land. This lulling of the parents into a false sense of the men's economic prosperity happens based on their comparison with the natal regions, where a majority of poor families live in one-room houses with thatch or tin-sheet roofs, and where brick houses and buffalos usually symbolize wealth.

Court Marriages and *Nikahnamas*

Formalizing a marriage in the courts,[18] instead of holding the traditional wedding ceremony officiated by priests, is another measure through which a small number of Hindu families (n=7) have begun to show a heightened consciousness of the difficulties their daughters face in married life. The registration of marriages in the courts offers legal protection to the women. Jasoda Das and her husband, Bhagirath Das, from the village of Tentuliapal in Odisha, had, on the advice of the elected village council chief (*gram pradhan*), insisted that their daughter be married in the courts. Jasoda elaborated on the rationale: "The certificate acts like a threat. The man cannot sell her off to another nor can he deceive us." This trend indicates a growing astuteness about the gender-friendly laws and the courts as a refuge for exploited and abused women. As Parbati, the Odiya cross-region bride mediator, explained, "They can testify in front of the judge and obtain justice. Not so if the marriage occurs in a temple." Examining documents that both parties stated were marriage certificates, I found that, in some instances, the documents were merely affidavits, "Declaration of Intention of Marriage," intended to be issued prior to the actual court marriage. More research is needed to ascertain whether this aberration is due to naivety about the intricacies of legal processes on the part of the parents or a new level of deviousness by the brokers for Hindu families.

In the case of Indian Muslims, including the Meo, formal proof of the marriage already exists in the form of a *nikahnama*, copies of which are given to the two parties. As one Bengali bride, Majeda Bibi, married to a Meo man, said, "If need be, in time of trouble (*mushkil*), [the *nikahnama*] can be used as proof of our marriage." The implicit threat of legal action presumably preempts the conjugal family's commodification of the brides. Husbands and their families also have begun to prefer formal registration of marriages, as Sumer Singh, a father-in-law, stressed while showing me the marriage certificate of his son, Amar, who had married Sarbati, a bride from Chhattisgarh: "The court paper shows the marriage is legal. It is a safeguard against anyone accusing us of trafficking."

Wedding Albums and Safety Deposits

Natal families have also begun taking wedding photographs as "an item of crucial documentary evidence" (Maunaguru 2019, 87). Instead of the usual nostalgia or keepsake value attached to photographs, these visual artifacts are transformed into "witnesses" (Maunaguru 2019, 90) to prove the authenticity of the marriage and to safeguard against fraudulent marriages. Ganga Chand Das, an Odiya man whose sister was married in the Mathura region of Uttar Pradesh, said, "We can show the police the photos of the men who married our daughters to identify them." A focus group of men from Rajasthan that also included male relatives of a man with a trafficked bride shared with me the fact that traffickers do not allow the sham marriages they have arranged to be captured on film for fear that the police can use these as evidence in case a "sale" goes wrong. In Cooch Behar, a new trend of parents (n=2) insisting on the groom depositing a sum of money in the name of the woman using a bank instrument called Fixed Deposit has emerged.[19] The rationale, as given by Shunjit Das, a father from Cooch Behar, is that "the money can provide financial security to the woman and her children if the marriage sours." These proactive measures by the natal families and natal communities run counter to the manner in which they are represented by the anti-trafficking lobby and the media, as well as by conjugal communities—as unconcerned about their daughters' welfare. Discursive representations of the brides as passive victims are similarly dismantled by their demands for accountability on the part of the marriage mediators.

The "victim" status is also belied by cross-region brides who have been widowed, deserted, or given a divorce by their husband, or who have chosen to leave their abusive husband of their own accord, of which there were a handful in this study (n=7). Contrary to expectations that they may want to seize such opportunities to return home, they often actively seek matrimony in the same region. Parbeen Bano was one such woman. Originally from Bihar, she left her first husband because of his abusive nature and soon after entered into a second marriage with another Meo man who, she said, "this time was a good man." Instead of returning home and facing hostility from her community, she said, "Here, *dooj baar* men are willing to marry a *dooj baar paro*, so I chose to remarry here."

The "repatriation and rehabilitation" rescue package stridently pushed by the anti-trafficking groups misses these nuances that shape the migrant brides' decision-making. That perspective also fails to recognize the social stigma that returnees face in their natal communities on account of their "lost" honor.[20] The women's reintegration is made doubly difficult with the gendered barriers to ownership of resources, which thwart them from obtaining economic independence. Sahin Bibi, married into a Meo family from Khadrauli village in the Alwar region, expressed this consciousness in very articulate terms: "I really have no options. If I return home, I will become a burden (*bojh*) on my parents. It will mean an extra mouth to feed. My brothers and their families will resent my presence. It is hard to earn a day's earning there in agriculture. There are very few jobs available. I do not even own a piece of land that I can till and feed myself. Other women in the village will look at me suspiciously and fear that I will steal their husbands."

Challenges to the Patriarchal Idealization of a Virgin Wife

Cross-region marriages also give women a space from which to challenge the patriarchal idealization of virginity as a cornerstone for marriage. Furthermore, inversions of and disruptions to hegemonic narratives of natal families being duped by dishonest brokers emerged from my fieldwork in Odisha and West Bengal, in that natal families, locators, and marriage mediators also enact deliberate acts of deception about the women, either independently or in collusion with each other. "Being a single woman carries huge stigma in our society (*samaj*)," said Nijammudddin, whose daughter had been in a failed marriage locally and then remarried a Haryanvi male. Families with daughters or sisters who are widows, were deserted by their husbands, have been sexually abused, or have children born out of wedlock[21] actively seek out locators or bride brokers to arrange cross-region matrimonies. For example, Parimal, a Dalit landless agricultural wage laborer from the Baleshwar district, discussed how his "youngest sister had got involved with a man. No local family would want her as a bride." Parimal sought the help of his other sister, already in a cross-region marriage with a Haryanvi villager. In another instance, this time of a woman who had been sexually assaulted by a Central Reserve Police Force member stationed in Assam, village council (*panchayat*) members advised her brother, Bhajendra Das, to "'find a Haryanvi man for her. The stigma will prevent her from marrying here.'"

The North Indian men become an obvious choice of marriage partners, as they "do not know about the women's past." In such instances, natal families take part in deliberately deceiving, either separately or in collusion with locators and marriage brokers, prospective grooms. Of the sixty-five interviews conducted in the two natal regions, thirteen families, or 20 percent, openly admitted to resorting to lies or hiding facts to facilitate the cross-region marriages of their female wards. In all such alliances, the parents acknowledged that the "truth" was either never revealed or only partially revealed to the groom—usually after the bride had borne his children.

It can be contended that, by deliberately facilitating such alliances, the brokers and the locators unknowingly question and loosen the patriarchal concept of the "virgin bride" and provide women a space from which to challenge this patriarchal idealization. Though the numbers are not substantial enough to indicate trends, these examples contradict totalizing narratives about the gullibility and naivety of natal families. Such instances also reveal their utilizing, to their advantage, the men's inability to verify facts about the women and/or their total dependence on the mediators. The deceptions, however, are also tinged with worries about the women's future well-being if the grooms or their families do indeed learn about the women's past.

In sum, what appears as a common leitmotif from my interviews and travels is that the reasons for marriage migration are complex and varied, with no one migrant-bride trajectory being the same as the other. But what is common in all trajectories is the increased economic precarity that fuels people to make such moves. Deepika, in her early thirties, who had "voluntarily" traveled to Haryana with the husband-and-wife broker team, Ram Bhajan and Aparna, explained her decision-making based on an honest appraisal of the life options available before her:

> My husband died when my son was five months old. My parents had died earlier. I moved in with one of my sisters in the city and started working as a domestic helper. But I found it hard to manage my life. My son fell sick and had to be hospitalized. I had no money for the fees. At that time, a man approached me and said, "Sister (*Didi*), are you willing to go to Haryana to be married?" I agreed, as I had no money and no other option. He knew a woman from this region and her Haryanvi husband who would arrange marriages of women. Did I feel scared that I might be sold off in marriage? I have faced economic difficulty. I had no other option but to take a chance on this.

THE STAIN OF THE INTERNAL OTHER

Dhani Raghowas, a village that lies on the southern edge of the Rewari district of Haryana, has the appearance of a frontier village. On its outskirts, an asphalt road that links it to National Highway 11 merges seamlessly with the encroaching sands of the Thar Desert. Scantily populated, the village seems suspended in a time warp, with no flashy signs of consumerism evident anywhere. Unlike in other villages, no billboards exhort soft drinks to quench the thirst brought on by the intense heat of the desert, which easily reach 120–122 degrees Fahrenheit during the midsummer months. Nor is there any signage from real estate agents encouraging villagers to sell farmland. The monochromatic monotony of brownness shrouding the village is broken only by the green leaves of the thorny babul acacia trees and clumps of the perennial long grasses that thrive in the sandy semiarid land.

This remote village was home to a group of migrant brides, all of whom hailed from one small geographic region of Odisha. Chandana was the first cross-region bride to come to Dhani Raghowas in 1998, and after her, five others followed in quick succession. Chandana's husband, Chet Ram, fifteen years older than she, had had both his arms wasted by a bout of childhood polio. With this disability making him ineligible in the local marriage market, he had sought the help of his nephew, who had a cross-region wife from Odisha, to arrange for a match from there for him. According to him, it was a good deal for both parties: "I had considerable land, but no luck in getting a wife here. Her [Chandana's] family was poor and had no chance of getting a match there." With her husband unable to do any agricultural work, Chandana alone tended the three acres of agricultural land that he owned.

As the first cross-region bride in Dhani Raghowas, Chandana had experienced a difficult life. In the initial years, she had appeared as both oddity and spectacle to the villagers. Her different mode of dress, language, and physical features, coupled with rumors of her being "bought," caused villagers to flock to Chet Ram's simple two-room house for a look. There was also intense speculation about her caste ranking, as Chandana was not able to correlate her Teli caste from Odisha with known *jatis* present in the caste hierarchy in Haryana. Unable to forge friendships with local women, and fielding requests from local men to arrange dowry-free matches with women from her region, Chandana was tempted to mediate, as she saw it as a way to end her cultural loneliness. On a visit back home to the Bhograi block in Odisha, Chandana arranged for her niece, Jhimpi, daughter of her widowed elder sister Janaki, who worked as a cook in a roadside eatery, to marry a young landless agricultural worker in the same village. Having Jhimpi live less than two hundred meters away from her house had assuaged some of the alienation that Chandana felt in Haryana. She went on to mediate two other marriages for local men with women from her region, and thus built an Odiya community in Dhani Raghowas that became a cultural oasis and a refuge for these women: "We can drop in on each other when feeling low or missing home. It helps overcome the loneliness that we all feel here."

Kanaklata, who lived three hundred meters down the path from Chandana's place, was another such bride. In Odisha, her natal village was adjacent to that of Chandana. After the failure of her first marriage, caused by the violent temper of her husband, she had returned home to live with her brother and his family. On one of her trips back home Chandana, who had known Kanaklata from before, approached her with a match, a widower with four daughters. Kanaklata recollected, "Over there, I could never have gotten remarried—it is just not the custom there. The feeling of constant obligation to my brother did not sit well with me. When Chandana mentioned this match, I said to myself, 'What do I have to lose?'"

Tall and gaunt in appearance, with her face lined with worry, Kanaklata disclosed that life was hard for her, as her husband, Mangal Singh, was quite controlling and constantly monitored her movements. Proud, she did not want to admit she had made a mistake and return back home yet again to her brother in Odisha: "With what face will I return? I have nothing to fall back on. No way to earn a living or survive." For the majority of rural Indian women, unequal access to land rights and other assets results in the lack of security to become independent and have a secure livelihood. Despite the Indian state granting equal

inheritance rights for women in matters of property, the reality is that customary laws and ingrained beliefs about patrilineal inheritance of land prevent many
women from claiming this right.[1] In fact, a recent study done by the National
Council of Applied Economic Research reveals that rural women own less than
2 percent of India's agricultural land, thus increasing their dependency on male
kin members for economic sustenance.[2]

Together, the two women nostalgically reminisced about Durga Pujo, a ten-
day festival dedicated to the goddess Durga, celebrated with pomp and enthusi-
asm by Hindus in the East Indian states of West Bengal and Odisha. It was at
that point that Nirmal Devi and Rajlata, two village women to whom I had been
introduced earlier in the day by one of my research assistants, a local member
of Shakti Parishad, came by to take me to another meeting.[3]

As we walked toward the slightly more densely populated part of Dhani Raghowas, Rajlata casually inserted a question asked of me, ad nauseum, during
the entire course of my research: "What caste are you?" This four-word query,
seeking to locate my exact ranking in the caste hierarchy, is symptomatic of the
deep embeddedness of the oppressive and discriminatory caste ideology in
people's lives. It also reveals the pernicious hold of caste ideology that even my
supposed privileges of class, education, and urbanity could not erase—for these
women and others in the rural communities, my identity was defined first by
my caste and then by other factors. Notwithstanding India projecting itself as
modernizing, caste identity continues to govern and shape people's social encounters and access to resources, education, jobs, and other services (Deshpande
2011; Deshpande 2013).

The Burden of Low Caste (*Neech Jaat*)

Shakuntala's two-story house, where four other women had gathered, was undergoing renovations of its tiled walls and floors. In its central open courtyard,
the group of six women were quick to state, "They [the brides] are all low caste
(*neech jat*). Despite *these* women and their families pretending that the women
are same caste as us, we see through it all. We wanted to make sure that you are
aware of this." All the women present belonged to the Yadav caste, one of the
three dominant-peasant caste groups prominent in Haryana (the other two the
Jats and Ahirs). Dhani Raghowas is a Yadav-majority village, where the Dalits
make up a quarter of its population.

Shakuntala, as their undeclared leader and spokesperson, said that, "the migrant brides were lying about their 'real' (*asal*) caste. The entire village knows
the truth." They stated that other Yadav women in Dhani Raghowas kept up a

facade of caste geniality with the migrant brides because of the sharing of kin ties with others in the village. I noted that this often led villagers such as those from Dhani Raghowas to declare, overtly, that they did not display caste discrimination and that they treated the brides as caste equals.

The women were part of a self-help group (SHG) run by a local NGO, the Social Centre for Rural Initiative and Advancement, and, when questioned about the principles of female empowerment and equality that the SHG members were asked to inculcate, they unequivocally stated, "Female empowerment is important, but not at the cost of our caste identity (*jaati apni jagaah aur mahila utthan apni jagah*). . . . In villages, caste is *the* primary identity." They then voiced a concern, echoed countless times by members of dominant-peasant castes across Haryana, about the presumed loss of their traditional power and prestige caused by constitutionally enshrined "reservations" that have enabled the historically marginalized Dalits to have access to education and government jobs.

Because of the affirmative reservation policy, the Dalits are sarcastically referred to as *ghar jamais*, or freeloading sons-in-law of the state, by the dominant-peasant castes in North India. What is conveniently sidestepped in this caricaturing is the harsh reality of the Dalits leading a socioeconomically precarious existence thanks to a continued lack of access to resources. In Haryana, Dalits own a paltry 2 percent share of the land despite making up 20 percent of its population. With over 80 percent of the populace living in rural areas, most depend on farm and nonfarm rural labor as their primary sources of livelihood. In Rajasthan, Dalits constitute nearly 17 percent of the population, yet they hold very marginal ownership of land and are heavily concentrated in caste-relegated, low-paying occupations or agricultural wage work. In both states, although the extractive patron-client caste relationship (Jajmani system) may have declined, unequal relations linger because of the dominance of dominant-peasant castes, also described by the commonly used term OBCs (Other Backward Classes), over landholdings and other assets that provide employment opportunities in rural India.

In this context, it was unsurprising that this group of Yadav women worried that the authority of dominant-peasant caste groups—and by extension, of *their* men—was gradually eroding. In addition to blaming the affirmative policies of the Indian state, the group added, "If more low-caste women from other parts of India get married to Yadav men, local low castes will get emboldened too. They too will start asserting authority and dominance (*woh bhi rob dikhaenge*). Their men and women will use cunningness (*chalaki*) to get married to the dominant castes."

It is revelatory that, as much as the public face of caste violence has been that of men from dominant castes in Haryana and Rajasthan, women are culpable, too, in the continuation of caste-based gender oppression and are ideologically invested in maintaining caste boundaries. Here, the concept of "border guards," a concept that Nira Yuval-Davis uses in her discussion about the ideological reproduction and maintenance of an imagined community's unity, allows us to understand how caste allegiance trumps gender solidarity (1997, 23). Yuval-Davis argues that women oftentimes act as symbolic border guards to police and enforce such borders and regulate who lies outside the pale of their community (1997, 37). They do so by creating themselves as the model (Yuval-Davis 1997, 58), with the promise of social power granted to them through their acquiescent participation in this oppressive policing.

Noted Indian historian Uma Chakravarti similarly argues that this fracture in gender solidarity along caste lines is unsurprising, as "stratification within women," based on caste hierarchies and in which certain categories of women have benefited from the subjugation of other women, has existed since Rig Vedic times (2004, 277). With patriarchal ideology investing in women as repositories of "tradition" and "honor," women internalize patriarchal norms and police themselves and other women in name of "culture" and tradition. Economic dependency on male heads of households, through lack of ownership of land or other assets, also ensures their conformity to approved social behavior. In both Rajasthan and Haryana, the dominant-peasant castes own an overwhelming proportion of land and resources and, with it, the ability to wield extensive social and political clout. Consequently, women such as those from the Yadav caste in Dhani Raghowas, though subordinated by patriarchal and caste ideology, are made complicit in the "perpetuation of the caste system . . . through their investment in a structure that reward[s] them and subordinate[s] them at the same time" (Chakravarti 2004, 293–294).

Caste-Exclusionary Practices

As I traveled across villages in Haryana and Rajasthan, I found that rural folks were keen to embrace surface symbols of globalization and modernity such as Westernized attire or hairstyles. Yet at a deeper level, there appeared to be no evident thinning or rupturing of caste boundaries. Dalit scholars such as Sukhadeo Thorat (2002) have similarly noted almost no change in the rule of caste endogamy in rural areas. The increased hardening of caste beliefs has been affirmed by statistics released by India's National Crime Records Bureau on caste-related violence and crime against Dalits, which reveal a 25 percent increase in the period between 2006 and 2016, with a sharp rise of 5.5 percent in 2016 alone.[4] Incidentally, this data also shows that urban regions are not without caste violence. In light of the ever-increasing caste-based violence and discrimination in North India, witnessed in almost daily reports in newspapers and official reports, it would appear presumptuous and naive to assume that dominant-peasant castes would choose to single out local Dalits for a range of caste-based discriminations and violence and yet not display any of this poisonous rhetoric against suspected low-caste or Dalit cross-region brides.[5]

In the rural hinterlands of Haryana and Rajasthan, an unapologetic and spirited defense of caste ideology and caste-based exclusionary practices reigns supreme. Take, for example, a group of Jat women in the densely populated mixed-caste village of Mandaherhi, located in the Rohtak district. They had witnessed many Jats from within their village and kin groups get married to women from distant parts of India. About the migrant brides, they said, "Who knows from where they [the men] have sourced them? The compulsion to have someone run the house forces them to seek a wife from another caste. They are not from the same caste or economic class as us. We do not associate with them easily."

Interestingly, unlike the Yadav women from Raghowas, who did not appear to display any gender solidarity with the cross-region brides, my discussion with women in the group revealed complex and contradictory reactions. For instance, they did not interact easily with cross-region brides in their village because of their caste ambiguity. Yet, they showed sympathy for the brides, who they said were exploited for their labor by conjugal families: "With homes adjoining each other, there is no privacy. We know exactly what goes on in their homes. The helpless (*bechaari*) women are made to work long hours. Sometimes, we tick off their in-laws with a sarcastic comment about it." Such encounters, rare as they are, offer a slight glimmer of a comradeship that transcends caste boundaries.

Kin relatives and villagers also did not appear to buy in to the argument put forward by many families and husbands, that "it does not matter what caste the woman originally hails from, she assumes the caste of her husband after marriage. A woman married to an Ahir will be called Ahiri." Men such as Sube Singh, a middle-aged Jat male who plied a shuttle minivan between his village and the nearby town of Rohtak, detailed the fallout of these caste-transgressive alliances: "Such marriages breed ill-feelings within the family. We do not know which caste the woman belongs to—is she a Harijan or some other low caste? That is the reason why relatives generally stop associating with that family."

Consequently, kin- and caste-based concerns about caste purity and pollution often result in the targeted seclusion of families with cross-region brides whose caste credentials are suspect. This happened in the case of Hukum Chand, who hailed from Bardhakhui village in the Alwar district and had married a woman from eastern Uttar Pradesh. Playing with his seven-month-old son, Vivek, in his lap while his wife, Saroj Bala, busied herself making *pakoras* on the *chulha* at the side of the open courtyard, Hukum Chand stated, "In the case of social events or weddings, those who are ostracized are not invited nor does anyone go to their house. They are singled out while the rest sit together and celebrate events as a community. Worse, if a death occurs in that ostracized household, no one from the caste or kin group (*biradari*) attends any of the ceremonies."

Such community-wide caste ostracism, enforced to ensure the exclusionary nature of the caste collectivity—also known as *hukka-pani band*, or the nonsharing of the communal smoking pipe—offers clues to the desperation of families to create a fabricated, locally acceptable caste status for such brides. In this context, it is unsurprising that cross-region brides married into caste Hindu families are often quick to assert, in public, that they are not Dalits. A study undertaken in one village from Uttar Pradesh, a North Indian state adjoining Haryana, similarly reveals the unease of low-caste cross-region brides in openly sharing their caste status (Chaudhry 2018, 08). This unease has to be contextualized within the caste milieu of the region.

Despite the number of cross-region brides from my study shown to be from Dalit families (see Tables 6 and 7), their desire to be perceived differently is due to the widespread nature of caste exclusionary practices vis-à-vis these brides and the conjugal families among the Hindus in Haryana and Rajasthan. It was to avoid this ostracism that Hukum Chand had insisted on a court marriage in Varanasi, "so that I could show this certificate, that listed our castes, as proof that Saroj is not from a *neech jaat*." However, he ruefully admitted that even this strategy did not cut any ice with his *biradari*, or kin group. Saroj stated that, though she had not had a "day's sadness since her marriage" to Hukum Chand, she could not say the same for her interactions with women from his village: "The women would question me, 'Where are you from and which caste do you belong to?' When I would mention my caste, they would say I resembled some other low-caste group.... They'd bring it up at all places. Suppose you were sitting outside the house, they might be passing and raise this. Or if we went to the fields for work, they'd bring it up while working there."

Here, the role of dominant-peasant caste-based caste councils, or *khap panchayats*, which are nondemocratically constituted, male-dominated, and highly patriarchally conservative bodies, yet wield considerable clout in determining social relations within rural North Indian communities, bears a closer look. Phool Kumar Petwar, who, until recently, had been the presiding head of Petwar Tapa, stated unequivocally, "Even though we know that inter-caste marriages are taking place, *khap panchayats* cannot openly affirm these alliances. If we do so, then social restrictions (*maryada ki had*) will cease to exist. Boundaries between different castes that have been historically created for a reason will get erased. Nor can we condemn these openly as the courts will act against us and lock us up. But the reality is that we do not accept such marriages or the women. We look down on them with distaste and aversion."

His perspective resonated in Dhani Raghowas, where Yadav women such as Shakuntala and Nirmal Devi maintained a façade of caste amiability, while simultaneously looking down on the cross-region brides because of their presumed low-caste status. In this context, it needs to be understood that, on an everyday basis, the denial and withdrawal of friendship by the dominant-peasant caste women are covert mechanisms through which caste hierarchies are maintained, while overtly allowing the caste and kin women to maintain a mask of caste geniality with the brides and their families.

Dalit feminism argues that the intersectionality of the multiple oppressions along the axes of gender, caste, patriarchy, and class have to be placed at the center in any discussion about gendered caste violence. Instead of normalizing and equating caste violence with gender oppression—as a form of oppression that all incoming brides have to deal with in any marriage—the dynamics of the unequal and oppressive caste-centered power relations have to be openly called out. The failure to situate these caste-transgressive marriages within the "ax[e]s of patriarchy . . . [and] caste oppression" (Rege 2006, 74), and persistence around seeing the brides as "somehow unmarked or disembodied from their caste or religious identity" (Rao 2003, 2), might result in scholarship that, perhaps not intentionally but consequently, offers a modern justification of caste oppression.

Taboos of Food and Association

An early wintry chill hung on in the morning air despite the sunrise. I was in a village in the Rewari district, spending time with Manasi, a Dalit bride from the Baleshwar district of Odisha. Manasi was just beginning to light the hearth fire to make tea and *rotis* for the family, myself included, when Suman, a high-caste woman who was my local research assistant, walked through the door. Calling me aside, Suman expressed her open displeasure about my breaking caste rules by sharing food with Manasi and her husband's family, both Dalits. She cautioned me about maintaining the *maryada*, or honor, of societally established caste boundaries.

Apart from endogamy, intercaste relations and caste hierarchies are defined through food, as rules governing its preparation and commensality are crucial to maintaining hierarchies of exclusion and inclusion—or purity and pollution. Dalit scholars point to the use of clothes, food, and language in the politics of identity creation and differentiation of caste collectivities.[6] In this context, within rural communities, internalized notions of caste hierarchy and ritual taboos on association are tested when communal space has to be shared with these brides as "caste equals." With the preparation of food falling into women's domain, village women come to play a central role in keeping the "purity" of their caste group intact. A few brides (n=9) mentioned their exclusion from weddings and other life-cycle ceremonies of kin members because of being regarded as *neech jaat*, and hence not being allowed to participate in food preparation during such events. This was affirmed by Meena Devi, a Jat woman from Rajasthan. Her village, Banherapur, comprising several dispersed *dhanis* or hamlets spread across low-rising mounds that crossed the arid land, had cross-region brides from West Bengal, Bihar, and Maharashtra. On the subject of food taboos, she stated, "If a bride is from our caste, we have no taboos for her. How can we allow a woman with unknown or dubious caste identity to handle utensils or food? She is barred from participating in the preparation of communal meals."

Brides (n=12) from across Haryana and Rajasthan mentioned that the ritual notions of caste pollution through food and drink are invoked in everyday encounters to remind them of their ritually taboo status, thus making them continually experience having a "stigmatized body" (Rao 2009, 270), the low-caste identity of which cannot be erased through marriage to a perceived upper-caste man. Unsurprisingly, Nafe Singh Nain, president of Sarv Jat Khap Maha Panchayat (Supreme Council of Jat Caste Groups), has asserted that caste taboos about purity and pollution enforced through eschewing intercaste dining are maintained, as "no one drinks water from such households." In this context, Chandana from Dhani Raghowas discussed the everyday impact of caste regulated boundaries: "You know I am from Odisha. Here, they are Jats and Yadavs. If I visited anyone, they would remark, 'Oh, don't drink water from *this* glass, instead cup your hands to get water.' I found this upsetting and so gradually stopped going to people's places. Why hurt myself?"

Additionally, the food habit of most Hindu dominant-peasant castes in conjugal regions is largely vegetarian, with wheat, lentils, and milk and milk products such as yogurt and ghee constituting the daily diet. Caste-based communal ostracism is also closely linked to the mainstream upper-caste association of a non-vegetarian diet with low-caste status.[7] Despite the abundant evidence of diverse eating habits among various caste groups in different parts of India, this flawed food-centric discrimination that operates through the denigration and ridiculing of nonhegemonic cuisine is evoked to intensify the othering of the low castes. Food rules are used as an informal codification system within the caste system, with certain foods and cuisines emblematic of pure and impure caste status.[8] For instance, Rajbala, a neighbor of a cross-region bride, Manjuli, from Odisha, stated, "When she first came here, her body emitted the stink of fish. We simply couldn't sit next to her. Gradually, as she started eating our food, that smell less-ened." Manjuli, though Bengali, had grown up in Odisha. She resisted such prob-lematic and simplistic dualisms that seemed to define women like her in Haryana by saying, "I have eaten fish since childhood. I tell the women here, 'I was born in a fish-eating family. How could I have known that I would be married here.' I do not cook or eat it here." Like Manjuli, a majority of the brides from regions or communities where meat is a normal part of the cuisine adapt to local diet by giv-ing up their cuisine. Others feign prior vegetarianism, display abhorrence to eat-ing meat and eggs, and even ask visiting family members to pretend the same. Sukanto Das, the brother of a cross-region bride who lived in Purbi Jodaipur vil-lage in the Cooch Behar district, elaborated: "Over there [in Haryana], we are considered low caste (*choto jaat*) because we eat fish . . . and meat. . . . When I vis-ited my sister, she cautioned me against telling anyone that we eat eggs, meat, or fish. The husband's society (*samaj*) is not nice. If they learn that we are meat eat-ers, they will stop speaking to her and her in-laws (*tader aadmi bolbe na*). Her husband also warned me that his community looks down on Bengalis as low caste simply because we are nonvegetarian."

Caste Epithets as Disciplining Tools

Dominant-peasant caste women also resort to the intentional use of caste epi-thets to mark caste boundaries and to assert caste superiority over cross-region brides. At the very base level, caste slurs are deployed as verbal weapons, to as-sert caste supremacy and show brides their proper "designation" within the family hierarchy (n=27). As one woman in a focus group consisting overwhelm-ingly of Jat women from Ghani Palthana village stated, "We do it deliberately. For we know it will hurt them. Calling them Churhi or Chamaran rankles them."[9] Chandana, the Dalit bride from Dhani Raghowas, stated that the vil-lage women, "do not insult you openly to your face. Instead, they taunt us about our caste behind our back. It hurts us—we are aware that they do it. We are help-less and cannot respond back." Veiled taunts about "low-caste" status take a vicious turn when, for example, a child gets hurt while playing or during an al-tercation over the resource sharing of water or firewood. These barbs about pre-sumed low-caste status are deployed as weapons to shame Dalit brides publicly and intimidate them into submission.

A study on systemic caste violence, based on five hundred Dalit women's tes-timonies, revealed that name-calling "communicates a world view in which Dalit women have no entitlements" (Irudayam et al. 2014, 103). The use of lan-guage as a discursive tool to subjugate and subdue certain categories of people is neither new nor innocent; caste epithets, as coded texts carrying the full force of historical discrimination and caste violence from upper castes, are harnessed to teach Dalit women not to overstep boundaries and to continually keep them suspended in a subservient state. Unlike the physical scars of caste-inflicted violence or evidence of spatial segregation, the invisibility of language makes it harder to prove the damage caused to the psyche of marginalized Dalits. In India, caste slurs are punishable under the Scheduled Castes and Scheduled Tribes (Prevention of Atrocities) Act and Rules (1989). The Supreme Court of India, in a 2008 judgement, also noted that caste slurs are "often used by people belonging to the so-called upper castes or even by OBC as . . . words[s] of insult, abuse or derision."[10] In the case of cross-region brides, the use of caste-specific verbal abuse is done with a deliberate intention to destroy and deprive Dalit brides of a sense of self and identity. Disturbingly, the caste stigma of a low-caste bride and the association of caste epithets with either such women or their children do not fade away with time. Meher Singh Dahiya, secretary of Dahiya Khap, recounted an incident from his village while also providing a warning about the future: "Earlier, such marriages were quite rare and the family would be recognized by the caste of the woman they'd bring. During my childhood, a Jat married a Valmiki (Dalit) woman here. For the last fifty years, I've been hearing "child of a Churhan" (*churhi ke*) as referents for their family members. If you ask anyone, 'Where did you go?' he replies, 'To the Churhi's house.' A similar stain (*dhabba*) will taint this group of women and their children."

It appears that not much has changed in the last fifty years. The most common articulation of prejudicial behavior against this current group of children is name-calling, commonly understood as a form of peer victimization used to reinforce exclusion from peer social groups (Verkuyten and Thijs 2002). In Nuh and Alwar, focus groups of Meo men and women revealed that, "the common abuse is 'child of a Paro' (*aie paro ke*). This expression is also used to taunt [about the mother's undesired caste/ethnic status]. People do not use the right language in speaking to such children." In contrast, in the Rohtak district, it is boys that appear to be at the receiving end of ethnic epithets such as "Bihari" or *biharan ke*—that is, a child of a Bihari woman—from both their peer groups and adults.

Such incidents were recounted only in the Rohtak and Nuh districts of Haryana and Alwar in Rajasthan. It can be speculated that the extension of such slurs to children in other research areas might not have occurred because cross-region marriages are a relatively new phenomenon there, the children are younger in age, or the numbers of children are fewer. These children might then pose a lesser threat to established hierarchies than, say, in Nuh, Alwar, and Rohtak, where the numbers are higher and the children have reached a marriageable age.

Caste Dynamics within the Intimacy of the Home

"Even my own wife, Rajjo, addresses her [Bijai's wife Manju] as *'aie churhan.'* There is constant bickering in the household as the two sisters are dead set against her. They are extremely upset about the family bringing in a low-caste (*neech jaat*) woman as his wife," stated Pradeep, the taxi driver, in a rueful tone, as he recounted his eldest brother Bijai's marriage to Manju, a low-caste woman from Uttar Pradesh. Rajjo and her sister, Sadhana, were extremely upset about having to welcome an "unknown caste woman" as their *jethani* or eldest sister-in-law. What galled them further was that they had to keep up a pretense within the larger Jat community in the village and among their kin network that Manju was a Jat, just like them. They did this not because Phoola Devi or their husbands had asked them to do so. They were well aware of the consequences of not keeping up the pretense, as they had participated themselves in the informal yet widespread community-based exclusionary practices against families that had cross-region brides in their village. They worried about the stigma of having a woman from an uncertain caste in their family, casting a long shadow over their own young children's future life prospects.

Consequently, Rajjo and Sadhana tried to make Manju's life difficult in her new home. As Pradeep put it, "There's constant disharmony and bickering in the house. Ever since we got *her* [Manju], our family life has become hellish." The two sisters hoped to drive away Manju "voluntarily" by using every opportunity, within the intimacy of the house, to humiliate her. Phoola Devi, who sought to reason with the two or advocate on Manju's behalf, also attracted their anger. They stopped cooking communal meals and finally asked their own mother-in-law to leave the homestead. However, on being reminded by their husbands, Pradeep and Rajdeep, that the ownership of the family farmland was in Phoola Devi's name, Kamlesh, Pradeep's sister, told me bitterly, a temporary truce was brokered with them, motivated solely by greed (*lalach*) about inheritance.

With such a deep-rooted prejudice against low-caste groups displayed even by families entering in to long-distance intercaste marriages, it is foreseeable that brides like Manju will not be left untouched in facing caste othering from their new relatives within the intimacy of households. Anupama Rao has noted that the body acts as the "experiential site" for caste violence and stigma, which are enacted against it with "intimate practices of prejudice" (2009, 268), rendering systemic caste violence invisible. The most striking aspect of caste-based oppression here is that such "intimate practices of prejudice" take place mostly within the four walls of the house—shared by both those perpetrating the violence and the one at the receiving end of it. Living in a joint family setup under a common roof makes it harder for dominant-caste female relatives to avoid intimate contact with the cross-region bride. It also makes it easier for them, 24/7, to treat the bride differentially. Sometimes, families exhibit overt caste prejudice by not allowing the brides to perform prayers at the family altar. Bullu, the Odiya woman I had met in her mother Sukanti's home in a village in Odisha, was a case in point. Married into a Yadav family in Rajasthan, she recounted, "My mother-in-law didn't allow me to offer water to the Holy Basil (Tulsi) for over a year after my marriage just because they weren't sure which caste I belonged to." Resentment around treating the bride as "caste equal" outside the home is displayed by a refusal to share intimate space with her or take her to social events.

Public caste shaming, denigration, and caste-exclusionary practices are not unfamiliar to the Dalit brides. Growing up in rural communities, they learn to recognize, from an early age, the operationalizing of caste-linked unequal power relations in the lives of their family members as much as reconciling themselves to the circumscribed life opportunities caused by caste-enforced barriers. They carry this ingrained knowledge with them to their new communities in North India, but find particularly hard to accept the continual onslaught of caste discrimination within the intimacy of their marriage and household. The perniciousness of caste ideology that legitimizes the exercise of quotidian caste prejudice and caste exclusionary behaviors has many brides contradict the majoritarian view that they live in *mauj* (luxury). The brides do, however, admit that, despite being married to men who are poor, landless, or underemployed, these marriages offer them food security. But the fact of their acquiring caste upward mobility is vehemently contested by many brides. In this regard, comments such as those of Sampa, from Midnapore in West Bengal, married to a landless Jat man from Rohtak, were echoed by other women: "We were better off in our own regions. At least then I would not have to continually hear insulting remarks about my caste or my ethnicity. The folks here call us low caste all the time. If I had got married back home, I would not face such taunts then."

Undertaking Patriarchal Bargains with Caste

For cross-region brides, the stress of adjusting to new families and their lowered position in the family power hierarchy as a daughter-in-law is magnified. Compared with local brides, cross-region brides fare poorly in household bargaining outcomes because of their poor fallback position (Agarwal 1997) (a theme elaborated in chapter 6). In the case of Dalit brides, caste prejudice and caste exclusionary practices worsen their intra-household and intra-gender bargaining outcomes. This creates another subcategory of marginalization that cross-region brides experience within the conjugal households and communities: putting down caste-suspect and Dalit brides through continual caste-linked denigrations is a strategic tool, developed over centuries, that not only shames the women about their Dalit identity but also serves to erode resistance against demands placed on their reproductive or productive labor.

In a patrivirilocal family setup, oftentimes the mother-in-law weighs her strategies and makes an opportunistic "patriarchal bargain" (Kandiyoti 1988) with caste ideology, wherein she pragmatically ensures that the new bride's life is not made difficult by other women in the household, as happened in the case of Phoola Devi trying to reason with Rajjo and Sadhana. This in no measure implies the mother-in-law is free of caste prejudice; the necessity of a pliable and docile "worker" who acquiesces to her commands and does her bidding warrants that a veneer of caste "assimilation" be maintained to prevent the bride from outright rebellion. Yet within the intimacy of relations, the bride is still subject to varied caste-disciplinary mechanisms that continually remind her not to overstep boundaries of caste collectivities.

For example, Kaushalya, a bride from Maharashtra, was still forced to maintain a separate cooking area despite having been married for six years. She found the caste-based contradictions in her existence as a daughter-in-law, and as a farmworker who was providing much-needed labor for the family, hard to swallow: "From day one, my mother-in-law set up a separate cooking region for me—because of casteism (*chua chuut ke maare*). My in-laws do not accept even a glass of water from my hands. But they have no hesitation in eating the *rotis* made from the wheat that I harvest."

It becomes apparent that the conjugal families, notwithstanding their need for female family labor for social reproduction, are not shorn of their caste-prejudiced beliefs and behaviors during interactions with caste-suspect or Dalit brides. Caste ideology legitimizing caste violence, discrimination, and exclusionary behaviors is both internalized and normalized by upper castes; it does not operate on the simplistic principle of an on/off caste discrimination switch that can be deployed unconnectedly vis-à-vis local Dalits and not the Dalit cross-region brides. Conjugal family members, including the husbands, employed in their interviews politically correct statements such as "all humans are equal"; "we do not believe in caste discrimination like untouchability"; and "caste discrimination is something of the past." However, upon being questioned about whether this rhetoric is similarly applicable to local Dalits, their supposedly "broad-minded" façades crumbled, with them making the unequivocal statement that "it is a different matter with them."

Caste Fabrications Keep Local Hierarchies Intact

Importantly, the continual emphasis made by families with Dalit cross-region brides that such brides are not low caste also allows these very families to continue exercising caste prejudice against local Dalits as a way to reinforce unequal relations of power locally. They have much to lose socially from their caste groups if they are perceived as being lax in practicing caste discriminatory practices vis-à-vis local Dalits. Dhoop Singh, an elderly Jat farmer, seventy years of age, had a high stature in the Jat *biradari* because he owned a significant tract of land. Despite this, he was unable to get his youngest son, Rajesh, married locally thanks to his failure to study beyond primary school. The family managed to get him married to Nutan, a dark-hued woman from the Deoria region of Uttar Pradesh. With Dhoop Singh's stature in the Jat community getting a severe beating because of this alliance, he worked harder to prove his anti-Dalit stance. On being asked about this contradiction, and whether having a Dalit daughter-in-law made any difference to his attitude toward local Dalits, he quoted a local proverb, "what caste can a woman have" (*beeran ki kai jaat nahin*), to emphasize the fluidity of a woman's caste and its dependence on the caste or religion of the man she marries (Pandey 2001, 165). Having a Dalit daughter-in-law did not change his views on the continuation of local unequal caste hierarchies, his stance on maintaining the social domination and authority of Jats locally through authority or violence, or his practice of caste discrimination against local Dalits. The facade of the higher-caste status of these brides, vociferously asserted by families in cross-region alliances and tactically acknowledged by dominant-peasant caste groups, also prevents local Dalits from acknowledging contradictions in the dominant-peasant caste stance on opposing local intercaste marriages and caste-exclusionary practices.

Here, it is worth acknowledging the complex contradictions of the lived reality of Dalit brides. Dhoop Singh's daughter-in-law, Nutan, a tall dark-complexioned young woman, twenty years of age and a high school graduate, expressed that, despite her father-in-law's public posturing, neither he nor other family members practiced "*chua chuut*" (casteism) toward her. Conversations with other cross-region brides (n = 9) also revealed that not *all* such brides experience caste violence in the form of exclusion, discrimination, and caste slurs within their conjugal homes. The gamut varies and is determined by various factors, including the necessity of having a female to perform domestic chores within the household, the region from which the bride is sourced, and the economic clout of the conjugal family within the community. For instance, caste taboos are rarely invoked for fair-skinned women from Himachal Pradesh, on the grounds that "they share the same cultural values and beliefs." This reinforces the need to acknowledge the many variations in both the experiences of cross-region brides and their access to power within conjugal homes—instead of "universally grouping" them into an "already constituted, coherent group with identical interests and desires, regardless of . . . contradictions" (Mohanty 2003, 21).

A significant number of interviewed brides (n=35) brought up "caste concerns," a code word for caste-based discrimination, during one-on-one interviews, indicating its pervasiveness. Concern around possible human rights violations, given the contemporary Indian reality of caste hardening, make it imperative to take such testimonials seriously and not dismiss them on the grounds that, because experiences of caste discrimination are not shared by all, they are not worthy of consideration. A 2014 survey found that over 27 percent of Indians practice untouchability and over 30 percent do not allow a Scheduled Caste person to enter their kitchen or handle utensils, with these numbers being higher in rural areas than in urban ones.[11]

Othering in the Meo Heartland

In contrast to the caste Hindu-dominated areas such as Rohtak, Rewari, and Jhunjhunu—where the virulence of caste prejudice is unleashed through a combination of subtle and overt exclusionary and discriminatory practices against cross-region brides because of their presumed low-caste status—the Meo do not appear to practice this form of caste-based discrimination against the cross-region brides brought into their community. Nonetheless, the Meo, while not subscribing to the Brahmanical caste rules of purity and pollution that are maintained through regulations on inter-dining and association, do believe that they are a distinct ethnic group whose distinctiveness is maintained through strict marriage rules. As with the caste Hindus, the entry of non-Meo women as brides creates rancor among families because of the brides' suspect religious identity and the perceived future dilution of the distinctive Meo ethnic stock through their children. The larger community also views these women as oddities whose ordinary everyday lives, to some extent, are transformed into a spectacle for village women and children.

Mubina Bano, who originally hailed from the central Indian city of Hyderabad, knew the pain of rejection from her husband's Meo community only too well. Mubina's single mother worked as part-time domestic help in middle-class households in Hyderabad. Unable to feed her family adequately, she had married off Mubina to Abdul Rashid, a marginal landholder, with the hope that she would have a better life. Slim and tall, with sharply etched features, Mubina Bano sat on a small bench under a thatch-covered verandah of her one-room house. Her fourteen-year-old daughter, Naseema, who sat beside her, had become her widowed mother's constant companion after the death of her father three years ago.

Adjustment was hard for Mubina Bano. She had lived her entire life in the city and suddenly had to do very rural-specific chores, both in the household and in the family plot, that were totally alien to her. Uprooted from her community, she found it hard to build another one in Nuh, as village women would laugh at her inability to carry a pot of water on her head or make cow-dung patties in the right shape. However, she stated that this was not the most painful thing she had to contend with: "I am called a *paro* by the villagers. It feels strange and sad. What hurts is that there is a lot of respect for the local brides. These women are called by their first names: so and so is Rehana, Parveena, or Ruksana. And us? We are all simply called *paro*. No first names for us. It just doesn't feel right. It shows the lack of respect people here have for us."

Mubina Bano eloquently summed up the anguish experienced about this all-encompassing label of *paro*, used exclusively for cross-region brides in Meo-dominated regions of Alwar and Nuh in Rajasthan and Haryana, respectively. According to Virendra Vidrohi, an activist associated with the NGO Matsya Mewat Shiksha Evam Vikas Sansthan, in the Alwar district, "Historically, the River Yamuna formed a natural boundary to the region populated by Meos. Any person who hailed from '*us paar*' or 'the other side' of the river was called '*par ka*' or 'from the other side.'" In the contemporary period, this historically created geographical descriptor used for all "non-Mewatis" is now singularly employed as an epithet for women who come into Meo families as brides from other parts of India. The term *paro* does not just imply spatial alienation; it is now saturated with the negative values of poverty and deprivation. Similar in hate value to the epithet low caste (*neech jat*), it provides the Meo an opportunity to "other" and culturally denigrate cross-region brides. Villagers, including a focus group of Meo men from Meerpur village in the larger Mewat region, affirmed that, "nowadays, the term is understood as an abusive expression. Employing it against someone is akin to swearing. It is considered both abusive and hurtful to either call a woman *paro* or label her as such."

The Stigma of Non-Muslim or *Kaffir*

The increased influence of an orthodox Muslim religious movement, the Tablighi Jama'at or TJ for short, among the Meo in the last three decades has led to an "Islamicization" of its society. This is evident from the shedding of the earlier

syncretic and pluralistic culture that included many Hindu life-cycle ceremonies such as *kua-pujan*, or the worship of the well by new mothers, as well as
reducing visits to Sufi shrines for wish-fulfilment, among others. An increasing
number of Meo men also opt to wear the so-called "Islamic" attire of white kurta
pyjama instead of the traditional *tehmat* or *lungi*.

In contrast, the assertion of an aggressive Hindutva, supported by the Indian
state and governed at the central and provincial levels by a Hindu Right political party, the Bharatiya Janata Party, has led to public lynchings of Meo men by
so-called cow-vigilante groups of rural Hindu men in the recent past.[12] Such vigi-
lantism, threatening the livelihood of the Meo, based on animal husbandry and
agriculture and their ability to feed their families, has created a siege mentality
among the Meo and paved the way for the TJ and its conservative agenda to gain
further inroads among the Meo.

Interestingly, despite becoming more Islamicized and besieged by the forces
of Hindutva, the one thing that the Meo, who pride themselves on being a distinct ethnic group, have not shed is their adherence to the *gotra* system, that is,
clan-based groupings very similar to that of caste Hindus. The continuation of
the *gotra* system is dependent on a series of rules that govern marriage, among
other things, which limits marriage within the *jati* of Meos and the fifty-two *gotras* that constitute it, with a taboo placed on marriage within the *gotras* of the
father, the mother, and the paternal grandmother (Chauhan 2005). The Meo,
very much like the Hindu caste groups, are governed by customary nonelected
all-male caste councils that arbitrate over infractions of caste endogamy or other
taboos related to marriage, including evoking a range of social sanctions against
the erring person or the family.

Until recently, the Meo married only within their clans, a custom that has
become lax with the spread of TJ ideology. My own research data, corroborated
by interviews with local activists, has shown that cross-region marriages among
the Meo do not date back more than thirty years, with a majority being of recent vintage. This is also in line with the findings of Shamsh (1983) and Jamous
(2003), who did their fieldwork in the 1980s and 1990s, that the Meo did not enter into marriage with other Muslims then.

With such a backdrop, suspicions about Meo men entering totally taboo in-
terreligious marriages cause further anxiety in this close-knit community. Until
the early 2000s, a majority of the cross-region brides here were suspected of being Hindu (*gair jaat samajhte the*). "Even after fifteen years of marriage here, I
am called a *paro*. The women say that I am an outsider—*gair jaat*—someone who
is not really a 'pure' Muslim (*pak musalmaan*)," said Nurnesa from Nindoli village in the Alwar district of Rajasthan. Nurnesa and her younger sister-in-law,

Khadija, both from West Bengal, were married to two brothers, Subhan Khan and Yasin Khan. Nindoli village had just four cross-region brides when I met them, of which three were from West Bengal and one from Assam.

Cross-region brides, such as Nurnesa and Khadija, married into Meo families are often asked by extended family members and village women to recite passages from the Koran in an attempt to separate those with an "authentic" Muslim identity from Hindu women posing as Muslims. There is also a failure among the Meo to recognize that the Muslims in West Bengal, Assam, and Bihar have culturally more in common with the Hindus there than with the Muslims in Rajasthan, due to the "sharing of space, regional ethos and cultural traits [which cuts] across religions and sectarian differences" (Das 2006, np). As a consequence, cross-region brides who have pierced noses, wear sarees, or share some cultural traits perceived as Hindu are erroneously branded as the religious other.

This religion-based suspicion about suspect Muslim identity was one that Nurnesa's husband, Subhan Khan, was very familiar with. Having returned from a day's wage work at a farm owned by a Yadav farmer, he took a moment to wash off the day's dirt before speaking about the stigma of suspect Muslim identity: "The doubt always remains: Is she a Muslim or a Hindu? Both Nurnesa and myself have been saying that she is a Muslim. But the women here associate the nose-pin and saree that Nurnesa wore when she first came here as a Hindu-only fashion (*taur tareeka*). Nowadays, everyone is rigidly judged with a complete lack of understanding that she can be a Muslim despite wearing a saree."

The hardening of attitudes and the linkage of attire with religion appeared to change somewhat as the Tablighi Jama'at gained more ground locally after the Babri Masjid demolition in 1992. With Meo men joining the TJ and getting trained as *maulvis*, they are fast emerging as matchmakers for poor unmarried Meo men, as they travel to Muslim-majority regions of Bihar or Andhra Pradesh to preach or take over religious duties. As mentioned in chapter 4, they are thus able to identify poor Muslim families with daughters of marriageable age. While only these brides are spared the ordeal of having to prove their "Muslimness," ironically, the stigma of not being Muslim (*kaffir* or *bejaat*) does not appear to rub off. Ashrafi's daughter-in-law, Vahida, was a Muslim bride from Bihar, who Ashrafi's son, Altaf, a *maulvi*, had married when he had gone on a *jama'at*. Despite Ashrafi's protestations that Vahida was a Muslim, the village women, she said, "think that she is not one of us—that she is a *bejaat*—*kaffir*—belonging to the Hindu faith. If a Muslim marries a Hindu, family honor is lost."

The contentious nature of the "assimilation" and "integration" of the brides within the kin networks is further evidenced by the experience of some families who are unable to obtain local brides for brothers of men with cross-region wives (n=7). The stigma of having a "*neech jaat jethani*" (low-caste sister-in-law),

a *kaffir*, or a *paro* with a suspect religious identity deters local families from negotiating matrimonies with these local men. In a majority of cases, such stigmatized families have had to bring in another cross-region bride, as happened
in the case of Yasin, Subhan's younger brother. When the time came to marry
off his younger brother, Yasin, local families rejected him by claiming that the
stain, or *dhabba*, of a *paro* and a *gair jaat* (person with unknown religious antecedents) would tarnish their Meo daughters. In the end, the family had no choice
but to ask Nurnesa to find a bride for Yasin from her natal region in West Bengal. In this context, the addition of religious identity and religious fundamentalism to the already existing matrices of patriarchal and gender oppression
placed on the cross-region brides further alters the relations of dominance and
subordination for this set of brides.

The Violence of Erasing Cultural Identity

Nurnesa and Khadija had to additionally contend with village women ridiculing
their work habits as they cooked on the *chulha* on one corner of their courtyard or
when they spoke in their mother tongue, Bengali. This ridiculing about women's
native language was also present among Hindu households. The process of "making the women more like us" involves both an idealization of the self as innately
superior and a filtering out of the locally undesirable cultural characteristics (*taur
tareeke*) of the brides. These include visible cultural markers like language, dress,
and food habits. Here, the concept of creating "authentic clones,"[13] in which sameness and difference are simultaneously enacted for performing authenticity work,
becomes useful in understanding the status of cross-region brides. It recognizes
the centrality of asymmetrical power relations—emerging from the historical process of colonialism and the contemporary neoliberal project—in shaping the trajectory of extraction of labor from workers and in creating idealized workers who
are simultaneously denigrated for their race, ethnicity, or spatial location. According to Mirchandani, whose work examines the experience of Indian call-center
workers, the process of authentic cloning involves "the establishment and recognition of the social location of actors" (2012, 135). Such workers, though they are
desired for their affective labor in the global neoliberal economy, are continually
reminded of their low ranking in "an imagined and experienced hierarchy"
(Mirchandani 2012, 138) of race and ethnicity. Similarly, the cross-region brides
are lauded for their docility and servility in the face of the extraction of their productive and reproductive labor by the conjugal families, yet are constantly ap-
prised of their hierarchical low placement in the conjugal caste and ethnic order.
Their "(in)authenticity" is always emphasized by defining their difference from the

normative local brides through comments such as those made by the group of Yadav women in Dhani Raghowas: "They can never become truly like us. Difference will always remain" (*farak hamesha rah jayegaa*).

The legacy is devastating for the brides.[14] Unlike the call-center workers, who enact their authentic cloning in the public arena of their work sphere and only while they are at work, the brides have to do it continually—while also being subject, again, continually, to caste hatred within the private sanctity of their homes. Further, unlike the call-center workers, who remain anonymous and invisible to callers even as they undertake their expected authenticity work, the cross-region brides, because of the nature of the relationships they are in, are denied that invisibility and anonymity. Their distinct physical difference forces them to remain hyper-visible, both within the private space of the household and in the public sphere of the village and their kin group. They also lack the easy opt-out option of not reporting to work the next day.

Cultural assimilation such as that experienced by migrant brides is not a benign process. The price of entry into a collectivity is set by a dominant group. It involves the use of force, in which the violence of making people shed their cultural identity and instead adopt that of a dominant group is experienced by those whose "belonging" is suspect (Yuval-Davis 1997). The process of cultural assimilation takes different forms in rural Haryana and Rajasthan. For some brides, the cleansing of their cultural heritage and imposing of the (believed) cultural superiority of their conjugal communities gets articulated through the unilateral decision of their husbands and in-laws to change their names to those considered more locally appropriate.

Marunima's name was changed to Mumtaaj. Marunima was a young Muslim woman barely nineteen years of age. Hailing from Akola in the central Indian state of Maharashtra, she was married to a Muslim man from Chak Peepalraha village in the Jhunjhunu district. Her father worked in a dairy in the town but, after contracting tuberculosis, had become bedridden. Marunima, who enjoyed going to school, dropped out to provide care for him, as her mother worked as domestic help in the newly emerging middle-class households in Akola. The result of the increased push toward privatization of health care under the neoliberal restructuring of social services in India, and the reduction of India's public spending in health care to a mere 1.3 percent of its GDP,[15] has included a gender dimension that Marunima knew intimately. The inability to secure an adequate dowry for her marriage, brought on by the family's deepening poverty because of out-of-pocket health-care costs, essentially dispossessed her of a marriage choice locally: "Poverty snatched away any choice for me to marry there."

Marunima was anguished about the name change unilaterally imposed by her in-laws: "My name is given no value at all. My parents had given a lot of love and thought into choosing this name for me. It is as if with my name change, my own original self was being erased" (*naam ke saath jaise mujhe hi mita diya*). A few other brides (n=6) also brought up this name-based discrimination during interviews, thus proving its significance for the women. The only justification offered by conjugal families, including that of Marunima's, was that the women's original given names were unpronounceable and alien-sounding. However, the grief this caused for the women was evident in their rightly interpreting this move as a deliberate erasure of their cultural identity. Although perhaps not deliberate, such name stripping and supplanting with locally approved names is another way to alienate the women from their culture and to demonstrate the low value accorded to it.

Similarly, linguistic bigotry is manifested in the rural hinterlands of Haryana and Rajasthan for a vast majority of cross-region brides. Although the brides linguistically adapt themselves by learning the local language—simply as a survival strategy, to be understood—they find that the locals are not so accommodating toward them speaking their own mother tongue. Linguistic bigotry here takes the form of villagers ridiculing their language, along with a clear subtext of intention to reinforce inferiority (*majak udate hain*), as in the case of Nurnesa and Khadija. Women from the neighborhood would rudely caricature the alien-sounding Bengali language, hurting the two women to no end. Neighborhood children would also jeer at them as they conversed in Bengali. Given their cramped living quarters, the twosome lacked privacy even to converse with their family members in West Bengal.

During focus groups such as the one of Jat women from Mandaherhi village in the Rohtak district of Haryana, Madhu Bala and other village women revealed, "Whenever we are tired of working in the fields and need a break, we pester the brides to speak anything in their language. When they do, we find it sounds funny and weird (*ajeeb*). We just crack up in laughter hearing them speak." Conjugal family members also participate in linguistic bigotry, enforcing strict rules about speaking exclusively in the local language, even with other women from the brides' natal regions. In part, this disciplining is derived from the family's anxieties around possible rebellion on the part of the brides.

Consequently, the women end up censuring themselves by not speaking their mother tongue—to their children, other brides, or their families via cell phones—in the presence of family members or villagers. This conformity, while sparing them the agony of having their language made fun of, also results in a gradual loss of ability to converse in it, a fact ruefully acknowledged by brides who had been married for longer periods.

Sitabi, a Muslim bride from West Bengal married to an impoverished and landless Meo rickshaw driver from Khusropur village in the Alwar district, could no longer converse in her mother tongue because of the enforced linguistic disciplining she faced. In the harsh midday heat of July, she sat fanning herself with a cloth-covered hand fan as she told how she was unable to speak in Bengali with her close friend, Miskina, a cross-region bride from her village whose marriage she had mediated, as they would be made fun of by anyone within hearing range. Speaking in one's own tongue exacted a heavy price, as female relatives would report back to the women's husbands that the brides were, as Miskina recounted, "cooking up a conspiracy and so they would get beaten up."

Language is a key to cultural identity, so this forced suppression, as in the case of Sitabi and Miskina, results in the denial of transmission of their native language and culture to their children and the consequent erasure of children's cultural identity derived from their mother's side. Sitabi admitted that neither of the two women's children could speak a word of Bengali, a fact that hurt, as it was a part of their *pehchaan* (identity). Conjugal family members and villagers, blissfully unaware of this toll, proudly tout the success of the women's linguistic assimilation through comments such as those made by Dhanwanti Devi from Banswa village: "You cannot make out they are not Haryanvi by speech. They have mastered it. It is only when you look at them that you realize that they are Biharan." Many a time, much to the discomfiture of the cross-region brides and despite my protestations, their North Indian mothers-in-law would order the brides, very much like circus performing animals, to speak Haryanvi in front of me to demonstrate the success of the women's assimilation into the local culture. Conjugal families and villagers, complacent in their belief about their own cultural superiority, fail to recognize the violent impact of such a forcible assimilation, which causes the brides' "entire self and body also [to] come into question, making every single physical, mental, and emotional manifestation seem inadequate" (Aranda and Rebollo-Gil 2004, 920).

Such experiences raise a few crucial questions: On whose terms are these adjustments or incorporations made to occur? Whose idea of nation and national identity is being reified, and who is being asked to shed their identity? Scholars have critiqued the concept of national integration, which draws heavily from modernization theory's notion of a homogenized nation-state, because its imposition of dominant cultural ethos occurs along with the forcible suppression of difference and the assimilation of minorities and marginalized groups (Jetumbde 2010, 31–32). Though modernization theory projects the notion of peaceful assimilation of disparate groups as part of a nation-building exercise, in reality, this exercise seeks to create a disciplined body of citizens out of peasants, ethnic and religious minorities, and other marginalized groups. Its aim is to homogenize, not to accommodate difference, resulting in marginalized groups being unable to articulate their separate and distinct identities.

With reference to India, the "problematic of integration"—termed as internal colonialist and paternalist (Saha 1986, 287–288)—has been critiqued because the supposedly voluntary cultural assimilation of visible minorities and Dalits occurs *only* on terms set by dominant-caste groups and Hindu supremacists. Hindutva, or chauvinistic Hindu cultural nationalism, articulates its assimilationist ideology by projecting a notion of India as a country of one people, one religion, wherein hierarchies of caste and differences of ethnicities are subsumed under a monolithic Hindu identity with the attendant forcible assimilation of minorities. This Hindu supremacist ideology argues that "all differences of ritual, belief, and caste are irrelevant" (Basu et al. 1993, 8–9) in the face of an overarching "Hindu solidarity" (Basu et al. 1993, 8–9). Similarly, the unquestioning celebration of national integration, and of the adjustment or gradual incorporation of the cross-region brides, without discussing the violence—literal and metaphorical—contained in this supposedly peaceful ethnic cleansing, runs the danger of reinforcing Hindutva's belief in a homogenized Hindu nation state.

The Stigmatizing Label of Biharan

Undergirding such distinct discriminatory and exclusionary behaviors toward cross-region brides is the prevalence of the deeply rooted chauvinistic ethnocentric beliefs in North India toward people from East and Northeast India, in which the regions are seen as "a periphery not only in terms of geography. It is also a periphery to the dominant image of caste, race and religion in India."[16] In the research areas of Rajasthan and Haryana, all cross-region brides hailing from the eastern states of India (such as Jharkhand, Odisha, West Bengal, and Assam) are usually lumped together under a homogenized category Biharan by the conjugal communities. A few largely negative characteristics, which one race scholar terms "ethnoracial mythmaking" (Treitler 2013, 7), are used to explain such othered brides' behaviors, values, attitudes, cultural practices, and material circumstances with the term Biharan—a term invested with connotations of poverty, crime, filth, and savagery. This branding also extends to entire swathes of brides who are dark-complexioned but hail from other states like Maharashtra or Chhattisgarh. Ethnic identifiers such as these are not only imbued with ethnocentric notions of superiority that denigrate their cultural identity as inferior but are also closely tied to caste prejudice that associates dark-colored skin with low-caste status.

Ethnoracism, often interchangeably called ethnocentrism, involves a peculiar mix of cultural chauvinism, wherein one ethnic group reifies its culture, derived from shared cultural and other characteristics, in addition to claiming intellectual and physical prowess (Treitler 2013). Very much like caste ideology, in the "ethnic project," ethnic groups are placed on a hierarchical ranking with the dominant ethnic group placed at the top and others placed relationally to it. Ethnocentrism is both socially constructed and intrinsically tied to the socio-economic and political necessity of certain dominant groups to reinforce un-equal power structures as a way to "hoard privileges for themselves" (Treitler 2013, 34). The dichotomous representation of one's cultural supremacy and the primal subordinate position of certain undesired ethnicities or regions occurs through language, food, customs, behavior, or physical features (Aranda and Rebollo-Gil 2004). This allows the dominant group to maintain its privilege and power over the dominated group(s) through exclusionary practices. Discrimi-nation based on race or ethnicity is experienced by all people belonging to mar-ginalized groups. Many times, race and ethnicity also overlap. In such instances, ethnoracism then operates between different racialized ethnic communities that get positioned differently on the race hierarchy (Treitler 2013).

In India, people from the eastern and northeastern states, and in particular from the state of Bihar, face ethnochauvinism in the rest of the country.[17] The roots of ethnic prejudice and racist attitudes against Biharis in North India can be traced to the onset of the Green Revolution, which created the pull for the seasonal migration of almost two-thirds of the rural landless and marginal land-owning Bihari men from the low-caste groups of Hindus and Muslims there (Ansari 2001; Deshingkar et al. 2006). In the contemporary period, Bihar, with the tag of being the poorest Indian state and having the lowest per capita income in the country (Deshingkar and Akter 2009), has witnessed a steady seasonal and cyclical outmigration of its populace to other parts of India; Haryana alone accounts for 11 percent of the migrant population from Bihar.[18] The majority of rural male migrants, unskilled and illiterate, end up working in the urban in-formal economy or in the agricultural sector. While the migration of the coun-try's poor is attributed to the failure of postcolonial India to develop Bihar, the role of British colonialists in making East India, or the Bengal Presidency,[19] chronically poverty-riven should not be ignored.[20] Hindi cinema has also con-veniently assisted in creating and disseminating, on a pan-Indian level, prob-lematic stereotypes of Bihar as a poverty-stricken, lawless, and corrupt state ruled by goons, landlords, and mafias that feed off the oppression and exploitation of its vast populace.[21] The hatred toward such "ethnic villains" (Treitler 2013, 4) is summed up through the common use of the expression, *Ek Bihari, Sau Bimari* or "One Bihari brings on a hundred maladies." Targeted ethnoracist violence against Bihari migrants in other parts of India ranges from vilification cam-paigns to social ostracism to denial of jobs to other discriminatory practices, as well as to physical attacks.[22]

In Haryana, although Bihari male migrants are crucial for making up for the shortage of agricultural laborers, especially during the transplanting and harvest seasons, they are excluded through a deliberate process of housing them separately in quarters built in the agricultural fields of their dominant-peasant caste employers. This distancing through segregation allows the perpetuation of stereotypes about Biharis as uncouth savages. The process of internal "othering" and the creating of "us" versus "them" dehumanizes the Bihari migrant through prejudice and misconceptions. For example, food stereotypes are used to allow North Indians to distance themselves from and exclude the Biharis.[23] Anju Devi, whose brother had married a woman from Bihar, summed up the widespread prejudice of the Haryanvis against migrant male laborers from Bihar: "We do not go near the Biharis. It is so because they eat *gutka-supari* and are constantly spitting. They also eat fish and meat. That's the main reason why we abhor them. Biharis eat everything and the laborers who come from Bihar—they live separately in the fields and cook there as well. A bad odor comes from them. Nobody wants to keep a Bihari in their house. We think it's better that they confine their way of living and eating to the fields. Nobody wants to venture near their quarters."

Anju Devi gave the interview as she played with her eight-month-old niece in Khaprauli village in the Rohtak district. Harsh and condemning in her stance, she did not appear to exclude her Bihari sister-in-law from this othering: "Truth cannot be denied (*sacch sacch hain*). We had to spend a lot of time teaching her *our* ways. Biharis have bad habits and are less clean." Significantly, ethnocentric prejudices are selectively exhibited toward certain categories of cross-region brides. Brides from Himachal Pradesh and from Uttar Pradesh are excluded from being labeled as Biharans, as it is argued that they are closer to the Haryanvis in cultural and social practices than the others. This was evident from many villagers' statements, such as the following made by a focus group of Jat women from Mandaheri village: "There is a difference in the way of living of Biharans from ours. Their dress and food habits differ. The ones from Himachal Pradesh maintain cleanliness like us and live the same way. But it cannot be said about the others."

At the very basic level, this "self-versus-other" rhetoric is used against the brides' style of dress, cooking, eating habits, and manner of speech. For instance, these othered brides, who are said to lack social graces, have to be taught the "right way" by the ostensibly more culturally refined local women to be accepted within families. Krishna Devi, from Tehrapur village in the Rewari district, whose daughter-in-law, Sharbana, was a Bengali, adopted a mantle of cultural refinement, relating, "She [the daughter-in-law] would eat the *roti* by breaking it very crudely, and eat using her hands. We advised her to always eat food with a spoon. Earlier, after eating, she would wipe her hands on her clothes. We had to teach her to use a towel instead."

A mixed focus group of Dalit and dominant-peasant Jat caste youth, incidentally all friends, from a mixed-caste populated village, Nagla Kasauda, in the Rohtak district, voiced another common misconception associated with the cross-region brides: "The term 'Biharan' implies low-caste status. It is because low-caste men from Bihar migrate here to work as agricultural workers. They come because they are poor and uneducated." Such ethnic mythmaking collectively pegs the women in two categories of internal otherness—low caste and undesired ethnicity.

Namita, a cross-region bride from the northeastern state of Tripura married to a landless Haryanvi man from Charwali Khas village in the Rohtak district, attributed this inaccurate branding to the fact that "folks here are ignorant that there are other states too in the east. . . . Well, even my *jethani* calls me Biharan. If my husband's closest family members call me that, how then can I expect that village women will desist from using that label?" Being called a Biharan angered her, as it not only erased her identity as a woman from Tripura, it also showed, according to her, an unwillingness to learn about other parts of India. This truism has also been pointed out by antiracist activists, who have referred to the widespread ignorance in the rest of India about the country's northeastern states.[24] Incidentally, cross-region brides from East Indian states such as Assam, Tripura, and Odisha who marry into Meo households, very much like the brides in the dominant-peasant Hindu caste communities, are also collectively branded as Biharans or Bengalans. As discussed above, while these terms carry the same prejudicial aspects of poverty and savagery, they are also, among the Meo, imbued with another layer of meaning: doubts about Muslim religious identity.

The ideological investment in undermining the cultures and ethnicities of the internally othered cross-region brides occurs through a number of strategies, including making natal communities the butt of ridicule. Villagers in conjugal communities make sweeping generalizations, such as those made by a focus group of elderly Jat men from Nagla Kasauda village: "Bihar is a backward and a disreputable area. Trucks are looted there commonly by people there." Another generalization extremely hurtful to the brides was verbalized by a focus group of Yadav women in Dhani Raghowas: "There is a lot of poverty there [in Bihar]. Parents are willing to sell their daughters for small amounts to obtain alcohol (*daru*). They have no feelings for their daughters or what might happen to them."

Ideologically, such totalizing narratives that center around denigrative ethnic mythologies reinforce the superiority of the North Indians. In this context and within the prevailing sentiment of ethnocentrism, the disturbing statements made by Om Prakash Dhankar, a senior party member of the BJP in Haryana—

that, if elected, he and his party would "get girls from Bihar for unmarried Hary-anvi boys"[25]—reinforces the low worth attached to women from Bihar in Haryana. Comments like these made by people who hold a political position[26] objectify the Bihari women as expendable commodities that can be "brought in" to over-come the bride shortage in Haryana.

Disturbingly, such ethnocentric statements and beliefs also create "savior" narratives of the Haryanvi and Rajasthani men, both Hindus and Meo. These local rejects are transformed into "knights" who rescue the women from their heartless families and inconsiderate local (natal region) men. To cite an exam-ple, Kaushalya, the cross-region bride from Maharashtra, was constantly told by her husband, Pavan, that, if it were not for him, she would have been sold by her alcoholic father to human traffickers. Kakoli, a Bengali woman living in Un-cha Tendroli village in the Rohtak district, recounted that both her husband and mother-in-law would make statements like, "Men in your region are bes-tial, drunkards and good for nothings. You would have suffered there. Here, your life is heavenlike (*mauj mein hai*)." Kakoli was hurt by such blanket branding of men. She knew that her father, who worked as a deckhand on fishing boats ply-ing the waters of the Bay of Bengal, cared deeply for his children. Contrary to the voices of the brides, which clearly display a complex range of factors that have dispossessed them of matrimonial choices in their natal regions, both men and whole communities in Haryana and Rajasthan project homegrown savior nar-ratives about themselves by having offered to "save" the brides through marriage from presumed eventual prostitution. The contradictions of such savior narra-tives were not lost on some of the migrant brides, who were quick to point out to me that their husbands were local "rejects" and so constituted "second-class" husbands who were elevating themselves as heroes (*hero baney chalet hain*). The brides were also quick to point out that such narratives would often be brought up at strategic moments, and played a big role in diminishing their bargaining power over the list of household and farm related chores (points discussed in the next chapter).

Ironically, labeling a significant majority of cross-region brides as Biharan, even when they are not from Bihar, has the unintended effect of creating divi-siveness among the group of brides as a whole. Women such as Manjuli who hail from other states, like Odisha, Assam, or West Bengal, make it a point to em-phasize their distinct and separate identity from Biharans, through statements like, "Bihar is located one place and Odisha is at another place. People migrate from Bihar for agricultural wage work. But in our region, no one migrates as agricultural laborers." Another bride, Bishakha, said, "We are not from Bihar. We are from a higher caste than them." In large part, their comments illustrate that their anxiety around distancing themselves from the Biharan tag stems from the dominant belief among Hindu conjugal communities, particularly in Haryana, that all Biharis are low caste. The emphasis placed by some of the cross-region brides, that "we are a higher caste than them [Biharis]," reveals their worries about being labeled, by default, as low caste, and having to face caste discriminatory and exclusionary practices as a result. Treitler, in her discussion on ethnoracism, calls this process "ethnic distantiation," wherein othered groups attempt to elevate themselves within the racial or ethnic hierarchy by distancing themselves from the ones lower than they are (2013). Problematically, the very act of these brides dissociating themselves from being identified as Biharan also reinforces the negative association of this tag.

Colorism Discrimination Is More Than Skin Deep

Colorism emerged as an additional prejudice that visually stigmatizes darker-hued cross-region brides as low caste or as being of an undesired ethnicity. Although conjugal families might themselves be dark-complexioned, they treat the brides on a relational scale of colorism. Postmarriage, dark-skin stigma alters the migrant brides' lived reality through the articulation of complex violence that Mathew (2013) terms colorism-related primary and secondary marginalization. Of 113 interviewed brides, fifty-seven migrant brides stated that they experienced some form of colorism-related violence. That this violence of colorism is deeply rooted in India and is not a Western import was brought out sharply in national debates in 2020 around dark-skin discrimination. Although the precipitator might have been the Black Lives Matter movement (the anti-racist movement that spread globally after the tragic death of George Floyd in May 2020 in the United States), calls for racial justice around the world resonated with dark-skinned Indian women who face dark-skin prejudice in their everyday lives. Until then, their concerns, and those of dark-skinned migrant brides, had been either silenced or ignored through discourses that speciously dismissed colorism as either something Indians have lived with for centuries—simply part of the local customary marriage-making practice—or as a Western construct (see Kukreja 2021 for details).

As discussed in chapter 3, colorism, or pigmentocracy, specifically denotes discrimination based on skin pigmentation (Hunter 2005; Rondilla and Spickard 2007). Colorism is distinct from racism or ethnoracism, even though it borrows heavily from racist ideology. Colorism further determines the racialized minority subject's dis/privilege at multiple levels (Rondilla 2009). According to Hunter, "colorism, like racism, consists of both covert and overt actions, outright acts of discrimination and subtle cues of disfavour" (2007, 241). It is experienced at two levels: first, a person with a darker skin is less privileged or looked down on within their own minority group, and second, that same person faces discriminatory treatment in the larger society because of the dominant discourse that favors whiteness.

Ayyar and Khandare contend that colorism in India pre-dates the colonial encounter and the subsequent circulation of Eurocentric norms of "whiteness" as the ideal beauty type, tracing it directly back to the caste system and the "mythical Aryan supremacist" (2013, 1) discourse around fair-skinned Aryans invading India and defeating the dark-skinned natives. Casteism equates dark skin with low caste or untouchable status and, by extension, with primitiveness, uncleanliness, and ritual impurity (Ayyar and Khandare 2013). The addition of dark-skin bias creates and reinforces further stratifications for already marginalized and discriminated caste groups in India (Mishra 2015).

In the instance of migrant brides, colorism-related primary marginalization forces them into cultural exile and to undergo a deeply resented violence of cultural assimilation. As discussed in chapter 3, "fairness" or the lack of it emerges as part of the variable marriage capital demanded by potential local grooms in the form of dowry. The penalization of cross-region brides like Bullu and Janaki from Odisha and Kaushalya from Maharashtra, because of their dark skin tone, haunts them even in their conjugal communities in North India. Postmarriage, their dark skin impedes their acceptance into conjugal communities as it embodies low-caste status and undesired ethnicity.

The secondary marginalization of dark-skinned migrant brides emerges from the association of their dark skin with low-caste status and undesired ethnicity. Take the case of Bishaka, a migrant bride from West Bengal, who had expressed her frustration earlier on being labeled a Biharan by the women in her conjugal village. Possessing a dark skin tone, she elaborated on the burden of "darkness." Sitting on her bed as she fed her year-old son, named Prince, she expressed unhappiness about the widespread and intersectional stigma that dogged cross-region brides like her: "The people here think that because I am dark in color, I belong to a low caste. They make fun of me and call me low caste." Her efforts to clarify that the majority of people in her state are dark-hued have fallen on deaf ears in the village.

Rajbala, from Rundh Murkhedi village, affirmed that fair-skinned women, such as those from Himachal Pradesh and Uttarakhand, appear to be exempt from being branded as low caste simply because "they are 'fair complexioned' (saaf-suthri)." Their nondiscrimination occurs largely because their skin tone is more in line with that approved by the dominant color discourse that privileges fairness with a higher-caste status. Race theorists working on colorism and internal discrimination have pointed out that deeply embedded prejudice about dark skin associates darker skin tones with "savagery, irrationality, ugliness and inferiority" (Hunter 2005, 2). Within both Haryana and Rajasthan, I found comparisons being made between the locals as fair, aesthetically beautiful, and civilizationally superior, and the dark-skinned cross-region brides as ugly, primitive in behavior, and less intelligent.

Additionally, with skin bias being "related to interwoven beliefs about light skin's signification of superior racial, regional, and upper caste/class identities,"[27] dark-skinned cross-region brides thus appeared damned to perpetual low caste and, by extension, low social status in conjugal communities. Paradoxically, the social capital of light skin, and its association with a higher-caste identity, appear to privilege lighter-hued Dalit cross-region brides solely because it allows for the easier fabrication of a higher-caste genealogy for them—quite unlike the experience of dark-complexioned women from a similar Dalit caste background, for whom the intersection of gender, caste, and ethnicity with colorism creates multiple oppressions. Pavan, the husband of Kaushalya, the dark-skinned cross-region bride from Maharashtra, elaborated: "If there are two women from outside and one is fair and the other dark, the common assumption in Haryana's society (*samaj*) is that fair-skinned people are from higher castes. Such women are assumed to come from well-to-do families and higher castes. The dark-skinned women are called Churhan or Chamaran—they are immediately understood as having low-caste origins."

Subscription to this belief results in bachelors demanding lighter-hued cross-region brides. Hindu husbands (n=9) stated explicitly that if they had had an option, they would have preferred a fair-skinned bride, preferably drawn from the neighboring region of Himachal Pradesh. Pradeep, the taxi driver from Jhunjhunu, and his family also had asked the marriage agent to find a bride from this region for his brother, Bijai, because "their color and physical features are similar to ours."

However, because of the inability to pay a higher premium to marriage mediators, who demand a bigger sum for sourcing a bride from Himachal Pradesh or securing a fair-complexioned wife from elsewhere, families such as Bijai's settle for the less desirable option of a dark-skinned woman, as the men are desperate to get married (*majboori mein lani pardti hain*). Nevertheless, the internalized skin-tone discrimination does not wither away. Men's families, it appears, do not fully accept such wives and thus create an internal hierarchy that privileges lighter-toned daughters-in-law over darker ones. Kaushalya, Pavan's wife, stated,

> The fact is that women here are fair skinned while I am darker. They do not like me. When they [my husband and his family] had come to Maharashtra [to find a woman] for marriage, they did not consider the

skin tone—whether a dark-skinned woman would fit the bill. Now, they worry about what their relatives might comment about my caste or skin color. If there is a festival, wedding, or any function within the family, I am not taken anywhere. Nowhere! . . . All the women will be fair skinned whereas I'll be dark. I'll stand out.

According to Hunter, the combination of dark skin tone and markedly ethnic facial features creates multiple layers of limited life opportunities (2007, 243) and lesser social and economic capital (2007, 246) for dark-skinned women, in general. The internalization of this color-based construction of ideal feminine beauty compromises the brides' ability to strike advantageous bargains, and it further tilts the already skewed gender dynamics of relation and power within the intimacy of marriage to the benefit of the men. Unsurprisingly, a number of dark-skinned brides (n = 11) stated that their husbands often reminded them of the "favor" they had done by marrying them.

Such rescue-oriented themes also reveal the strategic use of colorism by the husbands and their families to erode the women's bargaining ability around the use of their labor. "Color" becomes a convenient tactical tool that is brought into use by the family when more labor needs to be extracted from the bride, or when they want to quell the bride's resistance to discrimination on the multiple axes of ethnicity, caste, and color. The instrumentalist nature of the marriage was referred to bitterly by Bundo, a dark-skinned Adivasi bride from Maharashtra married to an autorickshaw driver from Dhaipur village in the Rohtak district: "Had they not seen me when they had begged my father to marry me? They needed someone to cook and clean for them. And now they talk about my color." She mentioned that her husband and his family members used the insulting term *kali-kalutan* to address her. Other dark-skinned brides (n = 7) also shared how insults such as "black crow" (*kala kaua*) or "black snake" (*kali nagin*) are often used both as descriptors and as forms of address for them by conjugal family members as well as by villagers. This skin-tone bias is also witnessed in the Meo community, where the dark complexion of the majority of cross-region brides becomes associated with the undesired ethnicity of Biharans. The normalization of colorism among the Meo is also evident in the extensive use of the terms Biharan and Bihari to pejoratively refer to any dark-hued Meo woman or child.

Intergenerational Racial Hierarchy

A worrying trend of intergenerational othering of some women's children started emerging during the four years of my fieldwork in Haryana and Rajasthan (see

Kukreja 2018 for more). Although the numbers are not huge, they suggest future discrimination in the making. The intersectional and overlapping discriminations of caste, class, ethnocentrism, and colorism result in the creation of a racial hierarchy, with those from the state of Himachal Pradesh ranked first because of their similarity in "racial" and cultural attributes to the locals, whereas others from the eastern states of Jharkhand, West Bengal, and Odisha are ranked the lowest. Villagers echo problematic racial fears of miscegenation, as evidenced by this response from a focus group of mixed-caste men from Nagla Kasauda village in the Rohtak district: "The women being brought in from there: they are short in height. Due to harsh summers there, they are also dark complexioned. People here are light skinned and of a taller build. Obviously, the 'breed' (*nasal*) will get impacted as their children will be darker in color and shorter in height."

Nira Yuval-Davis, in her book *Gender and Nation*, states that, "gendered bodies and sexuality play pivotal roles as territories, markers and reproducers of the narratives of nations and other collectivities" (1997, 39). With women constructed as "carriers of the collectivity's 'honor' and as its intergenerational reproducers of culture" (Yuval-Davis 1997, 67), cultural difference articulated through their bodies and their progeny is deliberately deployed in contestations and struggles over power relations (Yuval-Davis 1997, 37). Yuval-Davis's conclusions acquire significance within the caste-charged rural North Indian environment, where the maintenance of caste hierarchy is dependent, through caste endogamy, on a controlled biological reproduction of caste groups.

The linkage of physical attributes and ranking in caste hierarchy to intellectual ability and physical prowess has also been used historically by upper castes to justify the perpetuation of unequal caste hierarchies. The deployment of institutionalized racism by British colonial rulers through anthropometric data to classify India's native population and term certain caste groups like the Jats as "martial races" (Oommen 2002), on one hand, and the assertion by Indian nationalists during India's struggle for independence that Indians shed the "effeminate" tag by adopting the martial and masculine valor of some of its caste groups (Chacko 2012, 25–27), on the other, also play a big role in reinforcing this mythology in contemporary India.

Belonging to a group is not merely a product of social location but is dependent on how individual and collective identities are valued and judged and how meanings are imposed (Yuval-Davis 1997, 203). This results in boundaries being drawn in exclusionary ways for some brides and their children more than others. Yuval-Davis stresses that the inclusion of a child into a collectivity is not based on birth alone but on identification with a particular ethnic and national collectivity (1997, 27–28). The limited but suggestive evidence from the field reveals that the migrant brides' children are often projected as a threat to the supposed "pure" quality of the Meo and the dominant-peasant Hindu caste groups, a trend that bears ominous portents for their future integration into parental communities. For instance, the Meo use the analogy of crops and weeds to drum up community outcry against the women and their supposedly "mutated" offspring, as evidenced by a statement from a focus group of Meo men and women in the Nuh district of Haryana: "In a field sown with wheat, sometimes the undesired and lowly millet too starts growing (*gehun main jo jaon paida ho rahaa hai woh bhadda hain*). *Paro* children are like the millet—unwanted weeds born in a field full of pure Meo children. They are despised and given low status in society."

The corrosive combination of internal othering and ethnoracism with caste ideology or religious identity has allowed fears, in particular about Jat and Meo identity, to gain strength instead of being diluted or erased. Local communities in Rohtak firmly believe that cross-region marriages are "unnatural" and result in producing children that are "diseased," "flawed," or "inferior" to those born to unions with local women from the desired subcaste groups. The linkage of physical attributes and ranking in caste hierarchy to intellectual ability and physical prowess has been used historically by upper castes to justify the perpetuation of unequal caste hierarchies. Anxieties about erosion of Jat power and privilege are circulated through comments like "If the influx of the Bihari brides continues, our race will gradually get wiped out (*nasal khatam ho jayegee*). And then, the Bihari race will take over control and dominate us," and "Our households and our land will eventually be controlled by them. Haryana will be filled only with Bengalis and Biharis. The Jats will cease to exist." This ethnoracist mythology of Biharis overrunning Haryana and undermining the dominance of certain castes can be interpreted as an Indian take on the eugenicist discourse that valorizes the "biologization of cultural traits" (Yuval-Davis 1997, 20). This is best exhibited by a sentiment expressed by a focus group of Jat women from Mandaherhi in the Rohtak district: "My child bears my influence as he drinks my milk. Similarly, a child of a Bihari woman will grow in her womb and drink her milk—obviously, his character will be like the Biharis: full of deceit and cunning."

The Meo similarly revealed a problematic worry about the "dilution" of their ethnic identity through the entry of women from suspect castes or religions (*gair jaat* or *kaffir*) into their community. This undesired identity has resulted in a small number of families from the Meo community (n=7) encountering hiccups in securing suitable matrimonies for their sons. Misgivings are beginning to be voiced about the future matrimonial chances of the children of such transgressive unions, as evident from a statement by Phool Kumar Petwar, a caste council member from Haryana: "There will be fissures in our society. Civilized society will not arrange an alliance with a son of a Bihari woman. There will be obsta-cles for him to get married." Chaudhry's (2018) work on cross-region marriages in one village from Uttar Pradesh, a state adjoining Haryana, also seems to sug-gest similar roadblocks for matrimonies of children born of cross-region brides.

My own research, spanning forty-five villages across Haryana and Rajasthan, reveals the pernicious hold of the caste-ist belief in a graded hierarchy of people. Villagers do not hold back in expressing their worry that if, in the future, their daughters enter into matrimony with stigmatized cross-region male offspring, "their daughter's children too will be branded as low caste (*neech jaat*) or children of Biharis (*Bihari ke*)." Matters are further complicated by the marriage rules of caste, or *gotra* (*got*), endogamy, and village or territorial exogamy, as caste veri-fication of the antecedents from the man's mother's side will not occur—a com-plication that many villagers across both states were quick to comment on. According to some Jat men from Nagla Kasauda in the Rohtak district, "Our community will then ask the question, 'Whose children are these? Where's the mother from? What caste is she?' People will ask such questions and it will cre-ate a big problem later on." Just to illustrate, in one village in the Rewari dis-trict, villagers brought up an example of a local Ahir man, an army *hawaldar*, who had married a Bihari woman twenty-five years ago when his regiment was stationed in Bihar, bringing her back to Haryana. None of his children had been able to marry locally and instead had been forced to seek life partners from Bihar.

In this context, the role of *khap panchayats*, or caste councils, which still ex-ercise sway over the governing of social relations in rural North Indian com-munities, cannot be ignored. Caste councils such as the Dhaiya Khap Panchayat, highly regressive as they are in their views about women and caste, have come out openly to contend that as cross-region marriages increase in Haryana, "a new sub-caste group of 'mutated' children might emerge. Marriages will then occur only between them." Families in cross-union marriages with young children concede this harsh reality. Relu Ram, a Jat father-in-law from the Jhunjhunu dis-trict of Haryana commented, "In our region alone, there are nearly ninety who have done the same. We will marry within that group if we cannot get a match from our caste group."

Families with cross-region brides acknowledge the import of this stigmati-zation for securing matrimonies, not just for cross-region offspring, but also for other children in extended households. Pradeep, the cab driver whose eldest brother, Bijai, was married to the low-caste cross-region bride, Manju, acknowl-edged that, "societal lowering of family esteem is extended to other family members (*parivar neeche gir jaata hai*). Even my children will suffer in getting matches as our family is now branded as having an outsider bride." Brides in cross-region alliances such as Namita bravely assert, "If we are unable to find brides for our sons here, then we will fetch brides from elsewhere, just like we did" (*jaise hum laaye hain, waise hum bhi wahan se ley aayenge*). In doing so, however, it is feared that they will re-create the cycle of stigmatization for their children's wives and children.

DOCILE BRIDES, EFFICIENT WORKERS

Undertaking Everyday Negotiations
and Resistances

"I was afraid about what people here would be like. Would they accept me or like me? Each woman has this fear when she leaves her own family and its comfort and goes to a new family. What will the mother-in-law be like? Or the husband? One is naturally tense about it." Kaushalya, the dark-skinned Dalit bride from Maharashtra, having fed the water buffalo freshly cut fodder, decided to take a rest before she began the next round of household chores. Speaking to me, she recollected her anxiety as a new bride. Bidding farewell to her mother and sister, she had cast a long look at them, unsure when she would next see them again. As she left her village to take the train to Delhi, from where Pavan and she would travel on a bus to her new home, she "worried what life had in store for me as a married woman in this totally unknown place." This concern was not unfounded, as Kaushalya, unlike other women married locally in their own regions, was moving far away from her village and her familial support structure in Central India.

Marriage, in India, is a moment of traumatic rupture for any new bride—whether local or cross-region—as she steps out from under the security of her relations and away from her hierarchically elevated status as a daughter. In rural North India, with the prevalence of classical patriarchy with a patrifocal and patrilineal form of family structure, patriarchal constraints operate to create the subordination of and control over women, especially the new in-coming brides, who begin at the bottom of the power hierarchy. Restrictions on village and *gotra* exogamy in marriage among the Hindus and the Meo Muslims further heighten the vulnerability of these migrant brides, as they each leave their natal village behind and migrate to their new home, located a fair distance from their own family home. The result is that the new daughters-in-law enter their respective households as "effectively dispossessed individuals," with truncated rights and an inferior status within the family hierarchy (Kandiyoti 1988, 279). Apart from having to adjust to living in a new household and negotiating relationships with their new husband and his family, their changed status as daughters-in-law brings on new responsibilities and workloads, captured in thick detail in the book *Don't Marry Me to a Plowman* (Jeffery and Jeffery 1996), about rural women in Uttar Pradesh.

The stress of adapting to a new family, a changed status, and a lower position in the family power hierarchy is particularly magnified for the cross-region brides. Unlike most marriage migrations in rural India, which usually involve a distance of not more than three and a half hours of travel time from natal homes (Fulford 2013, 2), these women often come from distances involving two to three days of travel from their villages, which are located in distant states like Maharashtra, Assam, West Bengal, Tripura, and Odisha (see Table 7 in chapter 2 for details on the natal regions). For any migrant, the migration journey always involves multiple losses that are made more acute by nostalgia for home, and this is no different for the cross-region brides. At the most mundane level, many of the brides bring up the sharp difference in the physical environment—from the tropically lush green landscape of the east Indian states of West Bengal, Assam, Odisha, or Tripura to their new homes that are predominantly semiarid or desert-like—that is particularly jarring as they try to adjust to their new reality. Binta, a cross-region bride from Odisha, who now lived in Rundh Murkhedi village in the Rohtak district, articulated this yearning for her homeland: "There is a singular lack of greenery in Haryana. You cannot find fruit bearing trees either. That's the biggest sadness for me. In my region [Odisha], the landscape is lush green and abundant with mango trees everywhere. There, each house has guava and banana trees. Here, there is just nothing."

Binta's sensory yearning for her natal home is best understood through Raymond William's concept of "structures of feelings" (1961, 68). Structures of feelings is a concept employed for affective elements of consciousness that shape the feelings, moods, and emotions of individuals as the "felt sense of the quality of life at a particular place and time: a sense of the ways in which the particular activities combined into a particular way of thinking and living" (Williams 1961, 68). It also refers to the contradictions of the lived social yet personal and intimate experiences of marginalized "feeling" subjects whose subjectivities are silenced or devalued.

Marriage migration exacerbates these multilevel losses. The adjustments that brides such as Binta and Kaushalya have to make at a routine household level are harder than those for other brides, who, as locals, are at least on familiar cultural terrain in terms of language, social norms, caste behaviors, and familial expectations around their duties and responsibilities as daughters-in-law. Mubina Bano, the bride from Hyderabad who now lived in Razzakpur village in the Nuh district, elaborated: "Suppose I was married in my own place, it would still be *my* region. The language would be the same. When I came here, everything was different. The language was different. The way they cook *rotis* with hands, I was not used to that. They fetch water on the head while I carried pots on my side."

Apart from being torn from familiar cultural and social moorings, migrant brides have to additionally contend with unfamiliar languages; different ways of cooking, eating, and dressing; alien cultural norms and customs governing their behavior; and a lack of familiarity with the household and agricultural chores they are expected to perform from day one. Relations with close conjugal female family members, such as the mother-in-law, the wives of the husband's elder brothers, or *jethanis*, and the husband's sisters (*nanads*), thus acquire significance as they are the bride's only female contacts and guides in the initial period.

Kanaklata, the cross-region bride from Odisha who I met in Dhani Raghowas in the Rewari district, had her *nanad*, Suman, come to stay for a month with her. Suman, responding to a missive by her brother, Mangal Singh, left behind her children in the care of her mother-in-law to quickly bring Kanaklata up to par in handling chores related to the household, cattle husbandry, and the farm. Kanaklata recollected, "She is the one who taught me everything—right from speaking the language to making *rotis* and cow-dung cakes (*gosse*). That one month was spent learning chores that were totally alien to me."

Female relatives such as Suman are the ones most invested in making the brides "authentic clones" (Mirchandani 2012) of themselves. These women also teach the brides, married into Meo or Hindu households, the customs and traditions of their *jati* that incorporate the customs, among others, of veiling the face with a *ghoonghat*, wearing the *odhni*, and other self-regulatory practices. For almost all the cross-region brides, veiling, or the *ghoonghat*, is the hardest to learn and is resented the most, as the women come from regions where this custom is not practiced.

Negotiating Intra-Household Bargaining over Labor Demands

The initial period of marriage is also when intra-gender negotiation about the division of labor occurs. Patriarchal ideology co-opts older women into enforcing patriarchal norms and ideology, by offering them the rewards of a reduced workload, increased stature in decision-making, and control over the younger incoming female family member's labor (Kandiyoti 1988). Kandiyoti notes that, in the face of threats or slippages to the patriarchal order through the younger woman's resistance against the existing power hierarchy within the family, the older women resort to greater enforcement of patriarchal norms and ideology; this ensures that they are able to cash in on the incentives previously offered to them by their own in-laws to ensure their own compliance during their stint as daughters-in-law (1988, 282–283). In this context, the cross-region brides' total dependency on affinal kin women to inform them about gender roles and the family's expectations of incoming wives appears to set the stage for both the quicker and more efficient extraction of their labor and the transference of gendered demands on reproductive and productive labor.

Women such as Krishna Devi, a mother-in-law from Tehrapur village in the Rewari district, instrumentally help the brides learn the ropes as quickly as possible, in large part to reduce their own workload—which, in many instances, has increased as a consequence of household coping strategies against neoliberal reforms in agriculture. Krishna Devi, with her arthritic knees, found it increasingly hard to work as a casual wage worker in the fields of land-rich villagers who belonged to the same caste (Yadav) as she did. Her younger son Barjesh was, according to her, "a good-for-nothing fellow who does not stick with one job for long. With neither land nor a stable job, no parent was willing to discuss the marriage of their daughters [with him]. [So] I got a Bangalan so that *I could make her work*." This blatant rationale for the marriage—to get a workhorse—outlines that the strategy not only allowed Krishna Devi to reduce her own workload in the house but also enabled the efficient replacement of her labor with that of Sharbana's in agricultural wage work.

In this context, it is unsurprising that, in the contemporary period, the rise in cross-region marriages has occurred parallel to the entire region experiencing a severe agrarian crisis. The rural poor seek to cushion its impact by extracting more unpaid labor from female family members on family farms. The agrarian crisis has also caused women from landless, marginal, and small farm-holding families from both the Meo community and the dominant-peasant Hindu caste groups to enter the agricultural wage market as part of the household's coping strategy.

It can be argued that most brides in India have to contend with familial extraction of their labor for social reproduction, but it is worth noting that the ability of the brides to resist what they perceive as excessive demands on their productive and reproductive labor is "critically related to the proximity (or otherwise) of effective support networks, in particular, networks of natal kin" (Palriwala and Uberoi 2008, 30). These excessive demands can range from the older women in the household off-loading their own domestic and farm-related chores onto the bride's shoulders to buying more cattle to augment the family income through the sale of milk to forcing the bride to work as a wage laborer.

According to Kandiyoti, "women's strategies are always played out in the context of identifiable patriarchal bargains that act as implicit scripts that define, limit, and inflect their . . . options" (1988, 285). She stresses that patriarchal bargains are fluid and constantly negotiated between the brides and the female members of the affinal families (Kandiyoti 1988). This fluidity of bargaining ability allows the women to renegotiate, to their benefit, demands on their labor and the power they wield within intra-household relations. As well, any woman's successful intra-household bargaining outcomes are also based on a set of variables defined as the "fall-back position" that consists of social support systems "which determine how well-off [she] would be if cooperation failed" (Agarwal 1994, 54).

A focus group of Jat women, from the mixed-caste village Mandaherhi in the Rohtak district, detailed how the patriarchal bargains of new local brides get scripted out prior to their physical entry into their conjugal households as married women: "At the time of finalizing the marriage and the dowry payment, our parents tell our prospective in-laws that their daughters are not going to work in the fields. Consequently, we work in the fields if we wish to." While this type of refusal to work may not be true for all local women, comments like these, heard across several villages in the Rohtak and Rewari districts, are indicative of how dowry, a practice that marketizes marriage and commoditizes women, is used to deflect the commoditization of women's labor. Interestingly, local women's refusals to abide by patriarchal rules that legitimize the control in-laws have over the incoming brides' labor are immensely generative, as they put an end to the local women's labor exploitation. This generative aspect of refusal has been increasingly studied by anthropologists such as McGranahan, who stresses the "need to recognize and theorize refusal as an element of social and political relations" (2016, 320). The refusal of work, as a political act, challenges both the patriarchy and capitalist accumulative strategy.[1]

Studies have shown that the amount of dowry paid not only increases the overall stature of the natal families but also plays a crucial role in the women's ability to negotiate a better status in the conjugal household (Bloch and Rao 2002). Linkage is also found between an inability to bring adequate dowry and a higher incidence of domestic violence experienced by women at the hands of their husbands and in-laws (Kumari 1989). Unlike with local brides, whose families negotiate future demands on their daughters' labor based on the amount of dowry that they give, such bargaining appears to be absent or significantly reduced for the migrant brides. Mamtaaj, a Muslim bride from Assam married to a Meo man in Meerpur village in the Nuh district, summed their predicament: "The biggest difference is that we come from very poor regions and families. Our parents are not able to give a dowry. Whereas over here, families give money, jewelry, furniture, clothes, and even cars as dowry: the dowry often costs Rupees 1 or 1.2 million. The outsiders come empty-handed. Obviously, the locals who bring so much are valued and respected (*unki kadar hai*)."

The fact that the cross-region brides' parents, as wife-givers, are not able to give any dowry to the grooms because of their poverty compromises their negotiations for household labor allocation. Additionally, the vast geographical distance inhibits the natal families from giving gifts in cash and kind at significant life-cycle ceremonies like *Bhaat*[2] or *Chuchak*.[3] This creates rancor within families, especially after the birth of the women's children, when Chuchak has to be performed by the maternal uncles, who bring gifts for the newborn child and the husband's family members. A men's focus group from the Rohtak district elaborated: "They [the women's family] are usually so poor that they cannot even afford a train ticket. Gifts brought during *Chuchak* shows the prestige of the family. With the women's family not following this custom, it creates ill-will."

The increased financialization of social relations with the deepening of neoliberalism, evident from the coveting of life-cycle gifts, while increasing the value and respect of local dowry-bearing brides, also transforms negotiations over the use of their labor. Subhani, a Meo woman from the village of Sheikhpura in the Nuh district, articulated this difference by stating that, "these women [local brides] do not go to work in other people's fields. They just work in their own fields or fetch green fodder and firewood for their own household. The others are put to work as laborers in the farms of others." Bimla Devi, president of Shakti Parishad, a grassroots legal aid feminist group consisting entirely of village women from the Rewari district, elaborated: "Cross-region brides are praised as they agree to go for agricultural wage labor without demur, but the local brides will never do that." The generative element of local women's refusal to work as agricultural wage laborers paves the way for their ability to negotiate change within the unequal familial power relations. For the migrant brides, their inability to undertake similar refusals appears to be intrinsically linked to their poverty and lowered bargaining ability. These constraints make the latter exercise their refusal through other "very deliberate, willful, intentional actions" (Simpson 2016, 327) (discussed later in this chapter).

Myth of Bride Buying and Bargaining Outcomes

Migrant brides' bargaining ability is further compromised by the grooms unconventionally bearing all the wedding expenses. The family's payment of mediator fees and, in some cases, the additional small amount of money given to the natal families to help with wedding expenses, create an assumption that the brides are "bought" and are thus akin to bonded labor (*bandhua majdoor*). This marketized perception immediately changes familial power dynamics in favor of the in-laws. Kusum, hailing from an impoverished Dalit family from the eastern state of Jharkhand, had to contend with this "bought bride" syndrome with her mother-in-law. Kusum's future husband had paid for all the wedding expenses, including a token fee of Rs 11,000 for Sudha, the mediating bride, and her husband. However, her mother-in-law, Raj Rani, brought up the subject of "having bought" Kusum when the latter refused to go and work as a casual agricultural wage worker. Kusum was able to ensure that the commonly held misconception of "buying" a bride was corrected in her case, by asking her husband "to set matters right," but other migrant brides are often unable to resist the "slave-owner mindset" of their in-laws, thus increasing their vulnerability to being worked to the bone and abused.

The myth of bride buying combined with colloquial yet pejorative terms like *molki* or *kharidi huie* that roughly translate to "bought" are used strategically against the brides as convenient disciplining tools—to remind women of their subordinate position and to coerce them back into docility and labor compliancy if and when they resist what they deem unreasonable demands. These terms are also evoked when the women, feeling a bit more comfortable with their surroundings and able to converse in the local dialect, start asserting independence, step out of the confines of the house, and rupture the constant surveillance they experience from other female family members. By seeking to lower the women's self-esteem and underline their commodity status, families seek to immobilize, minimize, or thwart their resistive strategies and coerce them back into compliance. Within the village, too, the brides are reminded of their so-called bought status by other women, who use it to assert unequal power relations and to remind the brides of their low ranking within the social hierarchy. The internalization of the market economy ethos and the reinforcement of the women's value as expendable commodities—wherein inefficient or unproductive goods or wares are replaceable with more efficient ones—are evident in comments like the following made by Phool Kumar Petwar, a former *khap panchayat* member: "If they will not work as expected, then very much like a buffalo that does not yield enough milk, they can be dispensed with and replaced with another hardworking woman." The intermeshing of this market-driven ethos of expendability of women with patriarchal values about marriage, capitalist relations, and the stigma associated with desertion play a significant role in—as it was stated in a focus group of Jat women from Mandaherhi village—"extracting more work from outsider brides. They cannot do as they wish. They also have to work more than the locals."

The expendability of all cross-region brides is underscored by a common refrain used by the men and their families that the *baharwalis*, or outsider brides, are cheaper than buffalos. Such statements, used exclusively for brides from the eastern states of India while sparing those from Himachal Pradesh, Uttarakhand, and Uttar Pradesh, appear to be an extension of the overall "othering" and ethnic discrimination that people from East India, particularly from Bihar, suffer in other parts of the country. Mukesh, a man from Dhaipur village in the Rohtak district who married, as did his younger brother, a Maharashtrian woman—in fact, the brothers married two sisters—would frequently comment that "buffalos cost Rs 60,000 whereas a wife can be obtained for a mere Rs 30,000." These statements, often made in the presence of the brides, are deliberate strategies to lower their self-esteem, reinforce their subordinate ranking in the family hierarchy, and demonstrate their low market value and disposability and are, in actuality, labor disciplining tools. Mukesh acknowledged that he deliberately chose to say this to demoralize the two sisters: "We [the two brothers] are able to keep the two sisters under our thumb (*angoothe ke niche dabaa raakhe hain*). They are forced to keep mum."

Docile Cross-Region Brides versus Fiery Locals

Paradoxically, despite being denigrated as ethnically and caste inferior within the families, as discussed in chapter 5, cross-region brides are also projected as "model" daughters-in-law. Descriptions like "hard-working," "does not answer back," "quick worker," and "uncomplaining when asked to do more chores" are frequently used by the conjugal family members in describing them. The contradiction in simultaneously representing these brides as hardworking and as ethnically and/or civilizationally inferior is best explained through the concept of "stereotypical dualism" (Hulme 1986, 49–50), wherein stereotypes have two features: (1) several characteristics are collapsed into one simple image that represents the essence of the people; and (2) the stereotype is split into two halves— good and bad.

This is best exemplified by Krishna Devi, a mother-in-law from Tehrapur village in the Rewari district who elaborated on the lack of bargaining ability of her second daughter-in-law, Sharbana, the cross-region bride. Despite giving birth to a daughter ten days prior, Sharbana had been put to work both in the house and in agricultural wage work after a mere three days of rest, instead of the customary forty days that local custom dictates. Returning back after a full day's work on the *khet* (farm), Sharbana had barely enough time to breastfeed her infant daughter when Krishna Devi, lying on a cot in another room, called out to her. As Sharbana sat pressing Krishna Devi's aching legs, the mother-in-law compared her two daughters-in-law, the elder one, a local woman from Haryana who belonged to the same Yadav caste, and Sharbana, the younger one from West Bengal, by saying, "The Bangalan [Sharbana] is hard-working. If you tell her to do some work, she never refuses nor answers back when asked to do more. But if you ask the local bride to 'please do this,' she does it grudgingly, or worse, even refuses to do it. She will not even fetch a glass of water for me, whereas this one will do my bidding. *This one* is the better one. The other one is totally worthless (*khoti*)."

The elder daughter-in-law's parents had given a dowry and were based locally—in times of any trouble, she could reach out to them for help or mediation, quite unlike Sharbana, whose parents were landless seasonal migrant workers from West Bengal. Krishna Devi, while praising Sharbana's work ethic, also had no hesitation in labeling her as "a woman with less intelligence (*mand bhuddhi*)." Krishna Devi never referred to Sharbana by name. Instead, she chose to address her younger daughter-in-law as Bangalan, a term that carries the full weight of North Indian ethnocentric violence.

A large part of the ability of local women to derive strength (*majbooti*) from the nearness of their families is also made possible by the proliferation of mobile telephony, affordable cell phones, and a competitive market in cell phone operators across rural India. A focus group of Dalit women from Charakpur village in the Rewari district elaborated on how the intra-household and intra-gender dynamics have changed, for the better, for local brides thanks to the cell phone revolution: "We just give a phone call to our mothers, but the outsider brides (*baharwali*) cannot do that. We don't hesitate in fighting back as we have our family's support. Responding to our missive, our brother or our father come here in a moment to bail us out. The others can't threaten that they're going to their parents' as their homes are far away."

All the women in this focus group possessed a cheap handset that they tucked in the folds of their bodice for safekeeping and to keep their hands free for work. They cited the pervasiveness of cell phones as a significant causal factor in their success in obtaining better patriarchal deals for extra demands made on their labor. This was evident from the complaints of a number of mothers-in-laws that, "the phone is glued to the ears" (*chipka rahta hai*) of their local daughters-in-law, and that they "call their parents at a moment's notice" (*jhat phat phone ghuma deyti hai*). Amjad, the elder brother-in-law of Nooru (aka Salma), the

Muslim bride from Jharkhand in the Nuh district, knew this only too well from the differential treatment meted out to his wife, a local Meo, and Nooru, his younger brother Mahmood's cross-region bride: "They [the locals] have the solid backing of their families" (*unke paas peeche se thok hai*).

The long distance from the natal regions and the consequent weakened familial support networks are fully exploited by conjugal family members, as evident from statements such as those made by Sharifa Bano, a Meo mother-in-law from Rawalpur village in the Nuh district: "Unlike the locals, we are able to make the *baharwali* work for wage labor (*majdoori*) in other people's fields. They go without protest." Relu Ram, whose daughter-in-law, Barfo, was an Adivasi from the central Indian state of Chhattisgarh, accurately ascribed the brides' lack of protest to their vulnerability: "They have come from outside. They worry that if we throw them out, where will they go and who will take care of them?"

Contradictorily, while dowry provides munition for local brides to undertake varying degrees of refusal when it comes to patriarchal labor demands, this very refusal, subversive as it is in undermining patriarchal controls, is seized on by in-laws to denigrate them. To elaborate, local brides appear to draw flak from their in-laws for a range of infractions that include their supposed arrogant and rude attitude toward the elders. They are chastised for their generally more rebellious nature and sloppy work ethic; for their numerous visits to their natal families for protracted periods of time; for being constantly on their cell phones; and for calling their families or kin members at a moment's notice to intervene on their behalf against their in-laws, for any imagined or real slight. Such comparisons are based on the cross-region brides' compliance and submissiveness toward the labor demands—both reproductive and productive—made on them by the households. Further, these are deliberate strategies calculated to create discord and unhealthy competition between the two sets of brides, both within the household and in the community, to extract labor more efficiently and willingly from both sets of women. Ironically, both groups are similarly subordinated by the overarching patriarchal ideology because of their subordinate status as daughters-in-law. Part of the reason for this is that, for both sets of brides, their labor is being increasingly utilized for more family subsistence farming activities and/or paid wage work in agriculture—household coping strategies against the increased marketization of social services and provisioning that add to the women's overall workloads.

Here, I refer to James Scott's (1990) concept of hidden and public transcripts in shaping the everyday resistance strategies of subordinate groups. He explains public transcripts as the discourse enacted between the dominant and the subordinated, in which the latter appear to willingly comply with the demands of the former. Hidden transcripts refer to the "discourse that takes place 'offstage,' beyond direct observation by powerholders" (Scott 1990, 4), undertaken by both dominant elites and subordinated groups. In the case of the elites, hidden transcripts provide their true perceptions and outlooks regarding their subordinates, while, in the case of those dominated, these transcripts serve as sites of resistance and rebellion.

The valorization of the cross-region brides can be interpreted as "public transcripts." These are staged by members of the conjugal families, including the husbands, in the presence of both cross-region and local brides, to ensure the compliance of these two sets of women in the face of unequal and oppressive patriarchal power relations. Such public transcripts, if taken purely at face value and not examined critically, run the danger of being accepted as truisms. James Scott, in his work *Domination and the Arts of Resistance* (1990), warns against making naïve conclusions based on these public transcripts. He argues that public transcripts offer an illusion of consensus between the supraordinates and subordinates by serving as a "*self*-portrait of dominant elites as they would have themselves seen" (Scott 1990, 8; emphasis original).

Importantly, the hidden transcripts of these families, undertaken in the private sphere, run contrary to their public avowals of preferring these brides over the local ones. Such offstage discourse is made explicit through statements that they have to "somehow endure the fact of marrying these women because of their helplessness (*majboori*) to secure brides locally." In the case of the local brides, the public transcripts also serve as veiled threats, used to dissuade or prevent them from undertaking open resistance against existing unequal patriarchal relations of power. Such public transcripts also conceal the discrimination enacted daily within the private sphere vis-à-vis the cross-region brides, either through caste or ethnic othering by exclusionary practices or through unequal treatment in the division of household labor or allocation of resources.

The women's intra-household and intra-gender bargaining outcomes are also dependent on the earning ability of their spouses and their economic ranking within the household. Women whose husbands earn less than other male members in a joint-family household situation, are unemployed, or are physically handicapped appear to get short shrift, as they are dependent on the pooled income and resources of the family for their subsistence. Such reasons for compromised bargaining ability are not exclusive to cross-region brides, but also extend to the local women. However, it must be kept in mind that, very often, it is men who are considered social losers, as "blemished" (*daagi*) and thus rejected as grooms in the local marriage market that—because of their poverty, disability, or character flaws—seek out cross-region alliances. The men's own lowered status and worth in society and the family extends to their brides, with the consequence of diminishing their bargaining power. Other variable factors also influence the intrafamily bargaining dynamics and outcomes, such as the caste and ethnicity of the women; the way their marriages have been conducted, whether through a marriage agent or the bride herself; and the presence (or the absence) of "social support systems" (Agarwal 1997, 9) in the form of kin and caste networks.

For the migrant brides, such skewed bargaining creates discrimination in other arenas. Dual standards are often observed between the local and cross-region brides within households through the denial of jewelry, gifts, or the purchase of new clothes. Parbeen Bano, a cross-region Muslim bride from the eastern state of Bihar, married to Tahir, a Meo man from Ghasaulipur village in the Nuh district, said that, "whenever a customary gift of clothes comes to the family, the local brides get the first pick of the lot. I never get asked [by my mother-in-law] what set of *salwar kameez* I would like for myself. I always get their rejects. Just because I am a *paro*." Mubina Bano, a cross-region bride from Hyderabad who married a man from Razzakpur village, provided another example of such intrafamily discrimination: "For a local [bride], the families will buy a 2 *tola* gold necklace (*hansli*), but for the *paro*, a simple silver anklet is also out of question.[4] We remain bare-necked—just as we have come from our parents (*jaise aaiye the, vaise barattey hain*). Nor do we get any jewelry later on. The families say, 'Oh she is from outside (*paar*), why does she need anything?'"

Such everyday acts of discrimination and their treatment as inferior members of the family reaffirm the migrant brides' subordinate status and provide legitimacy for their abuse and neglect. Incidentally, their demand for parity through the equal intra-household dispensation of jewelry is based on the traditional custom of regarding jewelry as *stri-dhan*, or women's wealth, as a form of insurance they can use in times of personal or financial crisis. This is not surprising as, in both Haryana and Rajasthan, being given jewelry as part of one's dowry is still considered the sum of women's share in paternal property—in lieu of land, which remains the inheritance prerogative solely of men.

However, in instances where the families have more than one cross-region bride (n=23), either sisters or two cross-region brides brought in at different periods of time, the familial power dynamics appear tilted in the brides' favor. Here, it must be noted that the (cross-region) marriage of a female sibling into the same conjugal family as her sister is undertaken only if the first bride is relatively content with her married state. Together, the brides have more opportunities to maneuver advantageous patriarchal bargains, register stronger protests against caste or ethnic discrimination both within the family and in the community, and provide support to each other in the face of abuse or exploitation. In this context, Achala, a migrant bride from Odisha married into Banswa village in the Rewari district, who had arranged the marriage of her husband's younger brother with a woman from her natal village, stated, "Our mother-in-law (*sasu*) has to contend with the two of us and so cannot exert her dominance (*rob*) so easily over us. The family knows that if we stop working or return back home, their household will come to a screeching halt. Instead of us, *they* will become helpless (*laacharey*)."

"The 'Outsider' (*Baharwali*) Brides Treat Us Better": In-Laws Weigh Their Options

In the classic patriarchy operating in the conjugal areas of Haryana and Rajasthan, elderly parents customarily live in their own home with the eldest son and his wife, who are expected to take care of their well-being. Within this form of patriarchy, the desire to ensure old-age security and welfare causes mothers-in-law to try to maintain control over their sons. This is done through their close monitoring of, and continuous delegation of work to, their daughters-in-law, so that they do not have any spare moment to build intimacy and affection with their husbands (Kandiyoti 1988). On the other hand, they also do not want to antagonize the daughters-in-law, because their own well-being and the provision of their daily needs depend on the cooperation of these new entrants into the family.

However, negotiation over power relies on a number of variables, including economic or caregiving dependence on the younger generation. Upending the dominant societal and cultural norms that usually have the elderly parents live with the eldest son, a significant number of interviewed in-laws (twelve out of a total of twenty-one) had strategically chosen to live with their sons with cross-region wives. Dhoop Singh and his wife, whose younger son, Rajesh, was married to Nutan, a cross-region bride from eastern Uttar Pradesh, were one such couple. In relating why they had made this decision, Dhoop Singh stressed, "The ones from outside are imparted good values from their parents. They know how to keep a family intact. . . . The local brides are arrogant and do not serve our needs properly." Piroji and her husband, Mauji, had similarly opted to break the tradition of living with their eldest son and instead move in with their youngest son, Zakir, and his cross-region bride, Karima, who was from Bihar. The landless family lived in a two-room dwelling, a government social housing project for BPL families, located a short distance from the main village, Mian Ka Vas. Despite Piroji's advanced age and frail health, she went to work in the fields as hired help. With the rising cost of living, she said, "there is no other option" (*chara nahin hai*). When I met Piroji, Karima was washing Piroji's feet of the dust from the day's labor in a farmer's field. On being asked, "Don't other daughters-in-law (*bahus*) take the same care of you as Karima?" Piroji replied, "Others will kick you with their feet (*laat marangi*) instead of washing your feet."

Such statements asserting the "greater respect and care conferred to the elders by cross-region brides," which motivate the noncustomary relocation of the in-laws are essentially public transcripts—staged for both sets of brides, but with different end results in mind. For the local brides, these provide a cautionary note about the fallouts of transgressing their hierarchical and submissive role as daughters-in-law, including, importantly, a lesser or zero share in the family inheritance. This happened in the case of Phoola Devi, Pradeep's mother, who said, "Manju (the cross-region bride) is the better one. The other two do not cook meals for me or allow me to use the courtyard. They are worthless (*khotey sikkey hain*). I will divide up my property independent of how the twosome desire the division of land to occur."

Quite differently, for the cross-region brides, these transcripts are meant to affirm their continued docility and subservience to the established and unequal intrafamilial hierarchies of power and gender relations; the potential for better status and a share in the family's resources, including land and other productive assets, works as an inducement for the women to behave in the fashion expected of them. In actuality, the non-erosion of the older woman's authority; the compliance of the migrant bride in accepting her rank within the family hierarchy; the economic dependence of the son and his family on the father's income; the compromised bargaining ability of the migrant bride; and the dependency of older family members on the daughters-in-law, in general, to cater to their day-to-day needs and comforts, appear to guide such decisions. In other contexts, local daughters-in-law who possess better fallback options challenge the power and authority of the older generation, as happened in the case of Krishna Devi, mother-in-law of cross-region bride Sharbana, who said, "I don't live with my other daughters-in-law. They are with fiery temperaments (*tez tarrar*). They are not intimidated by us. They just reply that they will return back to their natal homes if we trouble them."

Problematically, the deliberate idealization of cross-region brides allows conjugal family members to control and regulate *all* groups of subordinate female relatives who are trying to wrest better patriarchal bargains. The artful deployment of this divisive dualism by rural families in Haryana and Rajasthan also neutralizes the brides' dissent, pits women within the same household against one another, and allows for the easier extraction of labor from both sets of brides. The decision to live with sons who have cross-region brides thus appears as a carefully thought out strategy, in which the older women (and men) weigh options about which daughter-in-law can best serve their interests, namely, through acceding to their subordinate status.

Self-Valorization as a Coping Strategy

Such instrumentalist representations of cross-region brides as good workers and caregivers are problematically appropriated by the migrant brides themselves to turn their exploitation and suffering into a virtue. Their reconceptualization of themselves as more virtuous and hardworking in relation to the local women is evident in comments like those made by Chandana, the bride from Dhani Raghowas: "We work both at home and in the fields. The ones from here are not able to manage that. It may be a rare local woman who is able to work long and hard in the fields and then take care of chores at home."

Paradoxically, the very patriarchal ideology whose oppressive hold makes the brides opt for cross-region matrimonies, evident through statements like, "a girl, once she reaches maturity, *has* to get married," is given a unique twist by the very same women in order to resist their multiple otherings on counts of religious prejudice, casteism, and ethnocentrism. Women such as Manjuli "frame" themselves as model wives: "There is a vast difference between the local women and us. They do not know how to respect family members or how to ensure that the family honor stays intact." Oftentimes, migrant brides also end up valorizing their commitment to marriage, despite experiencing intimate partner violence. As Purnima, another bride, explained: "We Bengali women know the meaning of marriage and honor, whereas local women do not. A husband is a husband for life. If our husbands are abusive or uncaring, we do not leave them and go running back to our parents the way they do." Such self-valorization, detrimental as it is to the self and done relationally to local women, is how they try and make meaning of their "place in an imagined and experienced hierarchy" (Mirchandani 2012, 138) of patriarchy, caste, and ethnicity. In some senses, this reification mollifies them as they try to make peace with the restricted oeuvre of life options available to them.

However, although this reverse othering of the local women as possessing less wifely traits enables the cross-region brides to feel a cut above the former, it also works to their detriment. First, it prevents them from questioning and resisting their own oppression and subordination. Second, it works to deepen the fissure between the two groups of women, both manipulated by the hegemonic patriarchal ideology through stereotypical constructs used in their subjugation and exploitation. Notwithstanding these drawbacks, the process of reverse othering allows the brides to subvert their marginalized position and turn their exploitation and oppression into an asset. The women's construction of this alternate valorized subjectivity occurs as a defense mechanism against the constant belittling they endure in the household and in the village, which is also brought on, in large part, by the marginal masculine stature of their husbands within their communities.

The Crisis of Masculinity and Its Impact on Marital Relations

The contemporary process of accumulation and dispossession by neoliberal capital and the agrarian crisis have left uneducated, poorly educated, and landless men in Haryana and Rajasthan more marginalized than others. The societal and cultural associations of maleness with the ability to earn a decent livelihood, marry, and procreate have created anxiety among this swathe of men, who, because of their social or economic unsuitability, are unable to attain these idealized masculine benchmarks (Chowdhry 2019). This crisis in masculinity[5] has led to increased violence in the private sphere (Nanda et al. 2014). One study reveals that economic stress—either because of the men's failure, as heads of households, to adequately provide for their families or because of their unemployed/underemployed status—has created anxiety about their ability to perform masculinity in the public sphere; they subsequently resort to intimate partner violence as a form of compensation (Nanda et al. 2014, 21).

In addition to the economic stressors, the feeling of being "less than others" or "not equal" is reinforced by the rejections from local families on the grounds that they are unfit husband material. They are also the subject of ridicule from other men, who often use innuendos like "they suffered from deficiencies (*usme kami thi*)" to describe their rejection locally as groom material. Pradeep, speaking from the experience of his eldest brother, Bijai, said that societally and within the kin network, "bachelors (*kunwarey*) are treated disparagingly and with suspicion. If an unmarried man visits any house, he is made to feel uncomfortable. 'Why isn't he married? Perhaps he has his eyes on women in the house.'" These men's internalization of social values and expectations about masculine norms and ranking in the masculine hierarchy associated with marriage and parenthood also compel them to seek wives from other regions.

Contradictorily, while the men opt for cross-region marriage to obtain a leg up in locally operative masculinities, they are emasculated by the facts regarding their initial rejection in the local marriage market, having to pay a commission to secure a cross-region bride, not obtaining a dowry, and flouting caste endogamy. These factors all peg them at a lower masculine scale than those married locally: "They are one number less (*ek number kam hai*) than those who marry locally respecting caste rules." This devalued masculinity has repercussions on their relationships with their wives. Their inadequacy around acting "male" occurs at multiple interlocking levels: they are poor, landless, unable to earn or to earn enough to provide for the household, and may have physical handicaps. For such men, "the home [is] sometimes seen as a zone of emasculation, given that the male head of the household is unable to provide for its material well-being" (Mehta 2014). Resultantly, the men appear to exaggerate their masculinity through a higher incidence of physical violence enacted visibly against their spouses.

These men, more than others, appear to display greater belligerence in their behavior toward their wives, either through strict control over their movements and freedom to meet other women within the village, or through acts of physical violence that even local men condemn as reprehensible. During the course of one focus group with Meo men from Meerpur village, the subject of masculinity came up for discussion. The nine or so men, whose ages ranged from the mid-thirties to mid-seventies, emphasized that, in relation to men with local wives, men with migrant brides exhibit higher degrees of control over their wives as a way to assert their masculinity. In another instance, Kanaklata, from Dhani Raghowas, similarly spoke about her husband's proneness to surveilling her movements and beating her for the slightest of causes. She acknowledged, "he does this to assert his manhood (*mooch ka rob*)." These acts of masculine compensation are undertaken to reinstate the men's position within the normative masculine club. Here, it must be clarified that spousal violence is not restricted to cross-region brides alone. The National Family Health Survey of 2005–2006 revealed that 27 percent and 50.2 percent of married women in Haryana and Rajasthan, respectively, had experienced spousal violence (physical, emotional, or sexual) (IIPS and Macro International 2007).

Women—and in particular, mothers-in-law—also play a role in reinforcing hegemonic masculinity. This implies the maintenance of patriarchal ideology, which the mothers are co-opted into through the inducement of their elevated status in the familial power hierarchy after the marriage of their sons. They do this by goading their sons to commit violence against their wives for small slights and imagined wrongs. For the cross-region brides, this combination of conjugal family women's attempts to buttress patriarchy and the men's anxieties about their marginal masculine status creates a particularly noxious intimate environment.

The degree and intensity of the controls and violence enacted on these women also depends on the mode through which they have been obtained, either through marriage with their parents' approval or through trafficking. In general, the men's payment of a mediator's or trafficker's fee to source cross-region brides, unlike the prevalent customary norm of grooms receiving money and other marriage gifts from brides' families in the form of a dowry, places them in a marginal masculine status compared to other men. Their masculine ego undergoes a severe bruising. Although such men did not themselves openly articulate such feelings of being emasculated, the topic often reared up during conversations with their wives and conjugal region villagers.

Accommodating Masculinity in Private

It would be erroneous to assume that all men in cross-region marriages subscribe to toxic masculinity and exhibit aggressive hypermasculine posturing vis-à-vis their wives. Scholars working on masculinity argue that, within the public sphere, "men may cultivate a façade of normativity while privately acting in unsanctioned ways" (Osella and Osella 2006, 19). In doing so, they contest the prevailing hegemonic masculinity. Similar to such findings, I found glimmers of contradiction in the tension between the public posturing and private personas of some of the men I met in Rajasthan and Haryana. At times, their violent abuse, manifested within the intimacy of the household, seemed to work to compensate for the inadequacies they experienced in the public sphere. At other moments, the men displayed empathy with their spouses and surreptitiously made small concessions to soften their lives, but in ways willfully hidden from the public gaze. Interestingly, the publicly hypermasculine persona and the private and more accommodating self often appeared to coexist in such relationships.

This "personal masculinity" (Bird 1996) varies from individual to individual. The men in this study (n=22) were found to do away with some elements of hegemonic masculinity within the intimate sphere of husband-wife relations. This behavior finds expression through a range of gestures and concessions, such as helping out with household chores or taking care of children, moving away from a joint family household to establish a separate household, or reducing demands on the women's labor in agriculture. Manjuli related how her husband, Raju, responded to her plea for a lesser workload: "He said, 'Just accompany me to the fields. I will do the work. You just chip in what you can.'" Often, such men express their subjectivity against the dominant masculine norm surreptitiously, in order to avoid being labeled as "henpecked" (*jooru ka ghulam*) and becoming subject to further ridicule from their male brotherhood.

The men's recognition that they are considered "inadequate" (*bechara*) prior to their marriage, and their realization of the change in their status—as married, with children, and without the need to depend on other family members for meeting their subsistence needs—causes them to take such measures. Tahir, a Meo man, who I met in his village in the Nuh district, was one such man. His first wife had died in childbirth, leaving behind a newborn son and a three-year-old toddler. He married Parbeen Bano, a woman from Bihar, who had left her abusive husband, another Meo, and decided to seek remarriage locally, rather than returning to social and economic uncertainty in her natal village in Bihar.

Seven years into his marriage with Parbeen Bano, Tahir said he was a content man: "Parbeen does not behave like an evil stepmother toward the two boys, and instead loves them as her own." Living in a joint family setup, he got to observe how Parbeen Bano was stigmatized and othered by women in his extended family because she was a "*paar ki*" (*paro*) and a Bihari. When Parbeen Bano asked him to set up a separate household, he agreed for pragmatic reasons: "If she takes care of me, then I should also do the same." Others such as Ashok, Nitu's husband, had decided to break away from the joint family setup because of the intense caste-othering that Nitu, being Dalit, had encountered within the intimacy of the joint household. Similarly, Satbir had built a room atop his family's single-story house in Rohtak to help Bishakha escape the excessive housework extracted by his mother and his sister. For men such as Tahir, Ashok, and Satbir, to formalize such a breaking away means running the danger of being disinherited from whatever meagre resources the family might own, as much as it results in being labeled as "living under the thumb of their wives" (*angoothey key nichey*). In that light, these measures are truly laudatory.

Other gestures include buying rice or stealthily bringing in eggs or cooked meat dishes for their wives. For instance, Bhuru Lal, a Dalit landless man from Murwara Khurd village in Rewari, married to Manasi, an Odiya woman, stated, "I buy rice for her and bring it home. Even I have adjusted to eating rice once in a day." Such gestures acquire significance given that the diet among the Hindus in Haryana and Rajasthan is predominantly vegetarian, with wheat as the staple grain, meat and eggs taboo, and rice looked down on as an inferior grain. Some men also take their wives out for a day to nearby small towns, where the women can relax and eat what they like without censure or ridicule—being away from the oppressive social norms. This was illustrated as a strategy in the interview with Raju, Manjuli's husband. He acknowledged that Manjuli, who was more educated than him, did not seem happy in her marriage, as she had desired a husband who was "modern and smart—with a personality." Raju, with his simple habits and shy nature, just did not fit the ideal she craved. Instead, he tried to bridge the gap between the two by "tak[ing] her to the city for an outing. We eat samosas and other snacks there and enjoy ourselves. It gives her a break from the nosiness of our neighborhood." Such actions by husbands, however small in number, not only demonstrate a softening of their stance toward their wives, but also indicate their subtle resistance against constrictive rules regarding intimacy, eating, and public behavior within their communities. These intimate and almost surreptitious acts of accommodation and respect are revelatory around how these couples try and work out a companionate relationship within the local constraints of societal norms and expectations about gender roles and gender behavior. Such examples also challenge the stereotypical characterization of these men as patriarchal monsters, forcing observers to see them, to some extent, as victims of societal and patriarchal norms and expectations.

Land, Inheritance, and Profits: Reshaping Intra-Household Relations

In instances where families own tracts of land that span more than two acres, it appears that cross-region brides face significantly higher levels of violence and abuse from their husband's relatives. As discussed in chapter 2, with the prevalence of patrilineal inheritance in North India, oftentimes, family members thwart the marriage prospects of younger siblings in the hope that the land share of the unmarried men will pass on to their own children instead. In the case of the Meo, the second marriage, or *dooj baar*, of childless men whose first marriages have either collapsed or whose wives have died are also not welcomed by their immediate family members for the very same reasons. This commodification of social relations, intensified especially after the neoliberalism-induced real estate speculation and rezoning of agricultural lands resulted in a sharp upward trend in prices, has created "schisms" (*daraar*) even within families owning less than an acre of land. Focus groups and interviews with villagers, including families with cross-region brides, affirmed, "Those who are married do not want bachelors to get married—they want to grab his piece of land."

With market-driven relations and property already driving a wedge between family members thanks to escalating land prices, the entry of these brides, as potential procreators of children who will have the first stake in their father's inheritance, further worsens intra-gender dynamics within the households. Pradeep's wife, Rajjo, had cautioned him against getting Bijai married, as it would imply that Pradeep's own children would be deprived of a greater share of land. In July 2012, seven months after the wedding, while discussing the charged familial relations, he candidly elaborated: "Now that Bijai's married, the land and the house will be divided three ways. Earlier, his share would have remained within the family and the division would have been fifty-fifty. This marriage has been a loss (*ghata*) for the family. The two sisters-in-law (*devranis*) fight and make life difficult for the new bride . . . They threaten to make her life so hellish that she will voluntarily choose to end the marriage by running away."

With land prices in all the research locations that fall within the National Capital Region (NCR) of Delhi witnessing a sharp rise—as much as Rs 10 million for an acre—including the Meo-dominated regions of Alwar and Nuh,[6] Phoola Devi's land was now worth a considerable sum. Additionally, with the intensification of the agrarian crisis in these rural regions, families such as Pradeep's are faced with constantly declining returns from agriculture, increased inroads to risky commercial contract farming, and rising debts to informal moneylenders. As a focus group of Meo men explained, this unviability of farming has made rural families now consider the meagre compensation paid by the state for land as cash in hand, which they can use for paying off debt and investing in nonagricultural livelihoods. As mentioned in chapter 2, the neoliberal culture has commoditized relations and toxically reshaped the way people relate to each other. A significant number of cross-region brides (n=21) mentioned being mistreated and made to feel unwelcome because of "the property angle" (*zamin ke chakkar se*).

Unlike the *nanads*, or the husbands' sisters, who have a lesser stake in patrilineal inheritance,[7] their husbands' elder brothers' wives, or *jethanis*, view the migrant brides as a direct threat to their own husbands' and children's future inherited share. As discussed earlier, the absence of familial networks to deter the brides' abuse emboldens the *jethanis* to deliberately mistreat the former. They offload more chores on them, make efforts to thwart their integration into the household through discriminatory behavior, and use abusive and derogatory language toward them.

Mohar Mohammad, a Meo *dooj baar* who had married Sitara from Bihar, spoke as he sat by the side of a *batewara*, a small hut-shaped storage space for dried cow-dung patties, in his village, Mian Ka Vas: "I wanted to have my own children—to whom I could pass on my name and my land." While Mohar Mohammad was happy that he now had a brood of children who would inherit his small share of family property, the same could not be said about his family members. His wife, Sitara, taking a break from household chores and sitting down to rest under the shade of a *kikar* (gum Arabic) tree in the mid-afternoon, elaborated: "My *jethani* is always bent on making my life miserable here. . . . I am made to work more in the house. She wants to accumulate (*hardapna chahti hai*) all the land. If I run away and desert my husband, then her children will get our share of the property. Don't you understand that? She wants my husband's share of land for her family."

Sitara's stressing of "don't you understand that" underscores the newly emerging centrality of capital and market ethos within the intimacy of familial relations in these parts. It also underscores the fact that, as discussed in chapter 1, a gap exists between women's legal rights and their actual ownership of land in South Asia, where women face significant barriers in securing their legal rights over land and in exercising control over the land they own. In Haryana, in particular, the rise in land prices has caused women's right to paternal property to become even more contested. It is not uncommon to find families using violence or intimidatory tactics, threatening to sever all ties with them, or resorting to social shaming to make women give up their rightful share.[8]

The barriers that prevent local women from realizing their property rights are heightened for cross-region brides, as evident in interviews with brides such as Bundo, an Adivasi woman from Maharashtra: "I am beaten up a lot by his [my husband's] family. In fact, they would like me to die childless so that I do not claim my husband's considerable property." Oftentimes, the presence of conjugal caste and kin personnel in the local elected government posts and police department also appear to restrain the women from seeking interventions against domestic abuse or denial of property rights, as the former's caste and kin loyalties appear to transcend their duties and responsibilities to their official posts. One bride, Sundari, who was repeatedly harassed by her conjugal family members while her husband had migrated to the state of Gujarat for work, recalled her futile efforts to seek help: "At the police station, the person in charge there, instead of writing down my complaint, would call up my conjugal family or the village chief and ask, 'What is the problem?' He would ask me to make peace with them. . . . He could not do that for a local woman, who would have been accompanied by her father, her brothers and cousins to ensure that the right procedure was followed."

Violence, an integral component in making local women, including daughters, sign away their rights to inheritance (Chowdhry 2012, 46), is similarly exhibited toward cross-region brides to deter them from staking claims to property. In Haryana and Rajasthan, customarily, a widow's claim to inheritance among the dominant-peasant caste groups, who own most of the land there, is frowned on because of the threat it poses to male lineal inheritance (Chowdhry 2012). A widow's ability to bargain for her inheritance rights becomes dependent on her access to mechanisms of policing and justice. However, for the cross-region widows, the absence of social legitimacy within the conjugal communities—caused by their perpetual outsider status, the relative nonexistence of marriage certificates, and the intimidating tactics of deceased husbands' relatives—leaves them without access to these mechanisms. Moreover, "the lack of familial support makes their position weak (*majbooti naa hain unki, peeche se koi na hai unka haq mangne ke liye*). The police also disregard their pleas for justice. In our region, cross-region widows and their children get only one third or half of the property that a local widow would normally get." Amjad, whose youngest brother Mahmood was married to Nooru (aka Salma), the young school-loving cross-region bride from Jharkhand, made this comment based on, as he said, the reality (*haqeeqat*) in his village.

The potential for such changed intra-gender dynamics within a family appears to be negligible in instances where there is no agricultural land at stake. Since over one-third, or 37.22 percent, of men (excluding figures from Nuh) who enter cross-region alliances do not own agricultural land (see Tables 4 and 5 in chapter 2), prima facie, their wives should not face the same degree of mistreatment as those whose husbands do own land. However, even the small plots of land on which houses are constructed in villages are becoming bones of contention with the skyrocketing land prices in rural Haryana and Rajasthan, due to the increased compensation rates for land acquisitions, ranging anywhere from Rs 3 million to the astronomical sum of Rs 15 million for an acre;[9] the proximity to the NCR of Delhi; and the gradual merging of the villages adjoining major cities like Rohtak, Rewari, Alwar, Jhunjhunu, and Nuh into urban territories. Further, if the husband dies before the division of the ancestral homestead has occurred, his widow's position becomes more precarious.

The example of one cross-region widow, Meena Devi, from Bahu Jamalpur village in the Rohtak district, is illustrative. With the death of her husband, Raj, in a road accident in nearby Rohtak, Raj's brothers had wanted her to vacate the house where she was living with her two small sons, ages five and seven. The escalation in land prices in this village, as a result of it becoming a part of the NCR of Delhi, had made the 135-square-meters plot of land valuable enough for other family members to use threats of kidnapping and of killing of her two sons to seize her marriage certificate from Assam and to forcibly evict her. In Meena's case, that outcome was avoided only because of the intervention of an elderly female neighbor, Vidya Devi, who lived directly across from Meena's house. She met me in Meena's reacquired home, where Meena introduced her as her "village mother." On my asking Vidya Devi why she had singularly taken the trouble to lobby the elected village council and the council chief (*gram pradhan*) and face up to Meena Devi's conjugal family members, she disclosed, "I was also widowed thirty years ago. I know what it feels like. This woman was widowed and had no money at all. Her in-laws harassed her constantly. I personally went and demanded that her brother-in-law give all papers [marriage certificate and property registration papers] to me. I also followed it up with the village council chief (*panchayat pradhan*)."

It was Vidya Devi's personal experience of widowhood and attendant economic discrimination that made her Meena Devi's ally. The violation of inheritance rights for such widows and their children appears to be large-scale enough to have led the Alwar-based NGO Matsya Mewat Shiksha Evam Vikas Sansthan to work to ensure that women's inheritance claims regarding their deceased husbands' land and other productive assets are upheld. In particular, the advocacy work of Maulana Mohammad Hanif, a locally respected Meo religious leader, has resulted in the compulsory registration of the *nikahnama*, which, he says, "can be shown in the courts as proof if the property dispute is not resolved at the community level. It helps the women fight for their share in the inheritance." What needs to be emphasized here is that the normalization and legitimization of physical violence and other methods of coercion have a spillover effect on *all* women, whereby this behavior gets deployed against them with greater ease.

Gaining Dignity through Resistance and Refusal

Despite the compromised bargaining ability and the relative lack of fallback options that cross-region brides have to contend with in their conjugal families, they do not totally embody an abject victim persona. They push back against deceptions and curtailments imposed on their freedom of movement to secure small reprieves. Nor do they appear to docilely accept the exploitative extraction of reproductive and productive labor from them. Their acts of resistance and refusal, including the potential for refusal, work in tandem as the brides seek to reconfigure their place within the family setup, in the caste hierarchy, and in intimate relationships. This refusal to be conveniently pegged in dominant narratives of their victimhood and exploitability allows the brides some measure of reclaimed self-dignity.

I must admit that, in the instances of the brides' expressions of rebellious subjectivity, it is analytically difficult to differentiate between resistance and refusal because of the blurring of tactics that involve and integrate rejection and opposition. This dilemma is summed up by Prasse-Freeman, who states that "many micropolitical encounters that appear to evince elements of 'refusal' seem inextricably linked with 'resistance,' even to the point of being dialectically related, as ostensibly refusing subjects must seek out engagements with authorities, must conjure into being publics that will observe their performances of refusal" (2020, 3). Although the concept of everyday resistance has come under flak for its theoretical thinness on the subjectivity of individuals and its overemphasis on domination of the state (Ortner 1995), it is still a useful concept to employ when examining noncooperation and culturally specific measures of subordinate groups. In particular, its reclassification by Lilja and Vinthagen as "dispersed resistance," which is individualized, scattered across everyday subtle acts and loud overt acts, and productive in its impact seems more in line with current theorizations on refusal by Simpson (2016) and McGranahan (2016). Borrowing from Foucault's disciplinary power and biopower, Lilja and Vinthagen regard "resistance as a response to power from below—a practice that might challenge, negotiate, and undermine power" (2018, 215). This productive resistance seeks to destabilize disciplinary institutions that constrain subjectivities and control bodies and desires (Lilja and Vinthagen 2018, 211–212).

Here I turn to examine how cross-region brides often resort to random and dispersed forms of resistance that are "*integrated into social life* and a part of normality" (Vinthagen and Johansson 2013, 3; emphasis original), in order to avoid disciplining mechanisms. The enactment of such rebellions is also undertaken by local women during the performance of routine household activities. Unlike Gramscian counterhegemonic rebellions that seek to dismantle dominant hegemonies, everyday acts of resistance "stop short of outright defiance, and are more ordinary, indirect strategies of opposition, that often exist under the radar of the dominant group" (Kastrinou-Theodoropoulou 2009, 3). These strategies are used by the subalterns against their superordinates in circumstances wherein violence is used as a retaliatory or disciplining mechanism. The subalterns engage in these everyday acts of resistance without directly challenging or confronting the dominant ideology or powers; instead, their acts occur within the functioning of daily life, do not require coordination or planning, and are often undertaken individually. Thus, they escape detection by the elites against whom the resistances are waged.

Not all cross-region brides undertake such measures, but the very fact that a significant proportion (n=45), or 39 percent, of interviewed brides brought up such strategies during the interview stage merits serious scholarly attention to their conscious or unconscious intentions to contest and reshape gender relations and power dynamics within the household. The brides follow the "rules of the game," whether by doing their household chores or working in the fields, but it is within the nuances of everyday life that their resistances and refusals are articulated. Very much like the peasants in Scott's study (1990) who chose to undertake everyday acts of resistance, the brides adopt "under-the-radar activities" to avoid violent reprisals for their acts of subordination in the form of verbal or physical abuse from their mother-in-law or husband. Significantly, for the cross-region brides, the female relatives of their husbands and the local women belonging to the same caste as the conjugal families constitute the immediate and visible dominant group responsible for their oppression; it is against this group that their "everyday acts of resistance" are enacted.

The irony of their resistance lies in the fact that both categories of women—whether subordinate or dominant—are members of the larger subordinate group of "women" within the hegemonic patriarchal ideology. As Amoore states, "subaltern identities are embedded in complex overlapping social networks in which individuals simultaneously assume positions of domination and subordination" (2005, 23). This underscores the need to recognize that power hierarchies existing within subordinate groups can be quite fluid and context-specific. The very women who appear to be in dominant positions vis-à-vis cross-region brides might also be engaging in their own everyday acts of resistance, albeit against other groups of women or men that they perceive as dominant and oppressive. This contradiction is evident in intra-gender relations, wherein mothers-in-law exercise power and control over incoming daughters-in-law, yet both are subordinated by patriarchal ideology and expected to conform to its proscribed gender roles. Additionally, while other women higher up in the family power hierarchy, like the *jethanis*, might, in actuality, chafe against patriarchal controls and restraints, they simultaneously impose similar constraints on all incoming brides. To make matters more complex, in the case of caste ideology, an alliance is created between the dominant and subordinate groups belonging to a particular caste group—either between men and women or between various ranks of women, within both the household and the larger community.

Dispersed acts of the brides' resistance range from taking longer than usual to complete jobs assigned to them to spending more time fussing over children to pretending to fall sick. The women emphasized that the success of their covert resistance lies in having it remain undetected. For instance, Bundo, an Adivasi bride from Maharashtra who faced constant verbal and physical abuse at the hands of her husband and in-laws, chose to strategically feign tiredness. Her rationale was, "If they abuse me all the time, why should I work for them? I will not get up and do chores for them." At other times, the women said they cite unfamiliarity with physically arduous chores as a tactic to avoid or delay doing them (n=13). For instance, cattle rearing, because of the very nature of the work involved, is extremely taxing on women's labor and time. Some claim a fear of handling cattle or refuse to handle dung "because it is dirty and smelly," using these as ploys to reduce this portion of their workload (n=9). In instances where families do not have the option of relying on other women's labor in the household, given that cattle rearing is done almost entirely by women, they are forced to either sell off all the cattle or reduce the number to just one, kept for meeting the family's daily dairy needs. This particular resistance is significant, as rural families often derive a part of their household income from the sale of milk to the dairy industry, and so such a strategy bears direct financial repercussions on the family's, including the resisting bride's, economic well-being.

Unlike dispersed resistance, the power of refusal as a conceptual category lies in its hope for change and transformation. To clarify, resistance is defined as "intentional and hence conscious acts of defiance or opposition" (Seymour 2006, 305), whereas refusal is conceptualized as hopeful, willful (McGranahan 2016, 323), and as a "revenge of consent" (Simpson 2016, 330). Refusal "marks the point of a limit being reached: *we refuse to continue on this way*" (McGranahan 2016,

320; emphasis original). Utilizing these two frames of reference conjunctly allows for a richer and more nuanced understanding of the tactics employed by migrant brides to regain control over their bodies and labor, and their efforts to "avenge a prior of injustice" (Simpson 2016, 330) in order to reclaim their respect and dignity.

The subjectivity of the brides, whether local or cross-region, is expressed in two ways: the first consists of undertaking refusals against the perceived excessive demands for work made by the conjugal families, at home or in farming and animal husbandry, controls and regulations over their movements, or representational strategies that denigrate their caste or ethnic background. The second method involves disguising dispersed resistances within their everyday routine to escape detection and subsequent reprisals.

The local brides consciously and willfully defy demands made on them by their husbands and in-laws. As discussed earlier, the generative potential of refusal, through direct rejection of disciplining measures, allows them to renegotiate patriarchal bargains in their favor. They have the advantage of familial policing and support mechanisms to back them up. The payment of huge sums of dowry by the women's families also emboldens them, unlike earlier times, to come to their daughter's defense more often than before. Further, with women's labor being central to both the rural agrarian economy and the household, local women can use the threat of returning to their natal home (*maika*) to strike advantageous bargains. Their absence makes the smooth functioning of the household economy come to a standstill, particularly if there are no other women in the family to take on their workload. In other instances, it dumps an additional workload onto other female members already overburdened with their chores. According to a focus group of Ahir women from Banswa village in the Rewari district, "this refusal puts pressure on the conjugal families to conciliate the women quickly—despite making threats like 'we will get an outsider bride to replace you,'" meant to coerce the daughters-in-law into weaker bargaining positions. The Ahir women I spoke to were older, and many of them had daughters-in-law. Basking in the mild autumn sunlight that cast a rich glow to the mud and cow-dung plastered wall of a house behind them, they laughingly stated, "We have used these tactics in our time. But not as much as times were different then. . . . *Bahus* these days know how to push us into a corner. We have to compromise or else the household will not function smoothly (*ghar ki rail nahin chalegi*)."

This grammar of acute awareness about the productive role of refusal thus allows local brides to (re)shape hierarchical relationships in their favor. To illustrate, oftentimes, the terms for truce with the local brides include placatory gifts (*negs*), a reduced workload, better treatment by in-laws, or setting up a separate household for the couple. In contrast, the migrant brides, unable to use the threat of their parents coming to the rescue and burdened with truncated patriarchal bargains, recognize that undertaking tactics of overt rebellion or noncompliance can invite disciplining mechanisms, which range from physical violence to verbal abuse to denial of their freedom of movement and association. Such disciplining mechanisms against perceived insubordination are not limited to cross-region brides, but extend to the local women as well; the only difference is that the intensity and scale of the violence is far more in case of the former. Notwithstanding this, a few cross-region brides (n = 17) reported employing threats similar to those of the local women—such as, "If you make me work hard, I will leave you and go back home"—to leverage better deals for themselves within the household. This threat is similar to the ones that Vietnamese and Chosonjok brides employ when threatening to return to their native countries, to negotiate better deals with their Taiwanese or South Korean husbands (Freeman 2011; Wang 2007). In their case, the women's subjectivity is also based on the knowledge that the conjugal family stands to lose a lot from their return home, including "the money the husband paid to the commercial agency, the face lost in the neighborhood, and the loss of a good domestic helper" (Wang 2007, 720).

Brides also try persuading their husbands to set up separate households, as that allows them, to some extent, to get away from intimate acts of caste prejudice, ethnocentrism, and continual demands on their labor. This persuasion stems from their refusal to continue with this intolerance and refusal to accept its normalizing tendency. Sabana Bano, a Muslim woman from the Samastipur region of Bihar, married to a Meo *maulvi*, Deen Mohammad, from Ghasaulipur village in the Nuh district, was a case in point. She spoke about her difficult life in Nuh and the tough adjustment that she, as a more educated woman, had to make with her conjugal family members, who were all uneducated (*gawar*). She had wanted to pursue higher education, but they were resistant of her stepping out because of their strict observance of the veil, or *purdah*. Deen Mohammad decided to set up a separate household so that Sabana could live in peace, and this, according to her, was "something that the family and the community are not happy about." In another instance, Bishakha's refusal against the drudgery of ever-increasing household chores made her say "enough is enough" to her husband Satbir. This willful act allowed her to regain a modicum of control over her life, as Satbir negotiated with his family to allow him build a room on top of the single-story family house. When I met Bishakha, she mentioned that she was "separated" from the family—a term implying a severing of the gendered obligations of labor and responsibilities that are part and parcel of the patriarchal bargain that older women in a patrivirilocal household make over junior female members. Cross-region brides might succeed in this regard, but only in cases where the husband is more sensitive to his wife's predicament, has a modicum of economic independence, has already received his share of the paternal land, or is totally dependent on his wife because of old age or infirmity. Nonetheless, the articulation of willful and deliberate rejection, exhibited in the women's desire to move away, in itself constitutes a political act, as it proclaims loudly, "Your power has no authority over me" (Bhungalia 2020, 389).

A similar political act of refusal is evidenced in women's deliberate choice to not associate with kin members and villagers who other them. Chandana from Dhani Raghowas, a Dalit woman from Odisha who had experienced food-linked caste discrimination at the hands of her husband's caste equals, had decided not to fraternize with those who treated her differentially. In doing so, her stance of refusal dared the "enactment of inequity" (McGranahan 2016, 323), while simultaneously challenging hierarchical relationships. Her refusal allowed her to reclaim her self-dignity as now *she chose* who to interact with, and she made sure it was on her terms. The small group of Dalit cross-region brides in Dhani Raghowas, mobilized by Chandana's action, also opted to socialize among themselves, thus refusing their tormentors the opportunity to make fun of their accent, mock their dark skin, or remind them of their low-caste background. For their part, Manjuli and other cross-region brides from Rundh Murkhedi village, such as Binta, Mamoni, and Dharani, would gather after work in the afternoons at each other's places. Sitting on charpoys, they would converse and laugh in Odiya, the language of their region, and in doing so exclude local women from understanding what they said, even though they knew the reprisals that could potentially follow such acts. Bhungalia, in a study of laughter and power, contends that laughter is "a refusal to recognize the authoritative figure itself" (2019, 388). This collective gathering of cross-region brides, with their laughter and their retaining their mother tongue, disavowed the forcible assimilation that conjugal families and communities sought to exercise over them.

The women also often deliberately choose to shun the company of female conjugal relatives or local women, by "voluntarily" and "willfully" opting for the isolation of their rooms. Bishakha, a bride from West Bengal, taunted for her ethnicity and caste by village women, defended her self-imposed isolation: "I do not speak to any village woman. They just make fun of me. . . . It's better that I stay indoors." By climbing the metal stairs that led to her room located on the top floor of the joint family house, she chose to cut herself off from everyone. In doing so, she willfully refused to mingle with village women, and also refused to continue giving the women opportunities to torment her.

Other brides opt to undermine unequal relations of power by regulating their behavior. For instance, instead of taking part in the collective activities of getting firewood, fodder, or water, they opt to do these separately or at different times of day. As Namita, a bride from Tripura who lived in the same village,

Charwali Khas, as Bishakha, said, "The village water tap is a distance from here. I go there only after all others have [gotten their] water. . . . I do not speak to anyone." Similarly, Nurnesa stated that she and her younger sister-in-law, Khadija, would "go to the hillock behind the village (*pahad*) for collecting firewood only when the village women have returned. There is no point in engaging with them as they will only think of making fun of us."

Such voluntary acts shrink both the public and private spaces available to cross-region brides in their conjugal homes and communities. Yet, these acts allow individual brides to reclaim agency. It must be noted that seclusion or self-imposed isolation is an extreme form of coping strategy that negatively impacts the brides and takes a toll on their mental and physical health. During the course of interviews, over 10 percent of the women reported feeling depressed (n=17). It is worrying indeed that of the 116 brides interviewed, 5 brides stated that they often harbored suicidal thoughts, and two had attempted to kill themselves.

Here, the widespread cell phone networks and low cost of cell phone calls have come in handy for cross-region brides. Helping them alleviate some of their cultural isolation and loneliness, their cell phones are tools to bridge the vast distance between themselves and their natal communities. Most brides such as Kaushalya admitted that they chose to gloss over the details of their day-to-day reality so as to "not make them [the parents] worry and cry about our fate. They will only feel sad if we tell them about our wretched existence here." However, they also stated that, "hearing Ma's voice is enough for us."

Challenging Negative Representations

The women also openly resist and challenge stereotypical tropes of their families, caste groups, and ethnicities. In part, their overt challenges occur because they experience, firsthand, the impact of these discursive imageries on their everyday life and their status within the families and villages. As mentioned earlier, barbs such as "sold" (*bech diya*) and "bought" (*kharidan*) are frequently employed by conjugal family members and villagers in describing the brides and in eroding their agency. Brides such as Sabana Bano acknowledged that such terms and epithets "cut them deeply like a knife." They resist being labeled as "bought," as evident from Purnima, a cross-region bride married in Khaprauli village in the Rohtak district, asserting that, "our parents married us off through the proper customs and rites of our region."

Wedding albums and marriage photos are often employed as evidence by the brides to demonstrate the legitimacy and genuineness of their marriages, to silence their detractors who call them bought, and to reinstate their position as "married" women. Oftentimes, in a number of villages, brides would insist that I see their *shaadi ki photo* (wedding albums). They would then proceed to take out the albums from inside large tin trunks that usually stored valuables such as sarees and woolen clothes. Kusum, a bride from Jharkhand, whose mother-in-law had assumed that Kusum was "bought," stated that she had "started showing it [the wedding album] to my detractors in the village here. They eventually came around to accept that I was not a 'bought bride.'"

Equally, calling the brides low caste (*neech jaat*), or simply referring to them as Churhan or Chamaran, elicits sharp retorts from the brides about the duplicitous attitude of the conjugal families toward caste, such as, "At the time of marriage, where did concerns about marrying into the same caste vanish? All you wanted was a wife"; or, "At that time, you pleaded with my father to agree to the alliance. You knew we were low caste." Sushmita, a Dalit bride married to Hemant, a Brahmin man from the Rohtak district of Haryana, had to face a continuous barrage of caste slurs from her elder sister-in-law (*jethani*) and kin members. The family lived in the Brahmin-predominant section of their village, Dhaipur, and so there was no escaping caste discrimination for her. None of the neighbors, all Brahmins, would invite her for casual visits either. She also faced discrimination within the household, with taboos on food preparation and handling imposed on her by the immediate family. Refusing to continue living this caste-discriminatory existence, she defied it by threatening to run away and leave Hemant, her husband, with the humiliating label of "cuckolded husband." This refusal of hers generated into the two living separate from the in-laws, a result that brought her some relief from continual caste othering. Though she still faced caste slurs from her female relatives and neighbors, now she had a better riposte: "They call me Churhan or Chamaran. I retort back, 'Big deal.' Now that I rule this house, I will, instead, be called the 'Queen' of my husband's heart."

Negotiating Intimacy

It is perhaps unsurprising that only a handful of brides openly discussed how they negotiated intimacy with their husband and used it to strike advantageous bargains for themselves. Though the numbers were few (n=5), the very fact that these women voluntarily brought it up during discussions on resistance strategies merits discussion here. Sahin Bibi, a thirty-year-old Muslim woman from West Bengal married to Kallan, a Meo man in the Alwar district, stated,

> My husband cannot sexually satisfy any woman. He gets finished up before he enters me (*andar aane se pahle hi khatam ho jaata hai*). When-

ever he wants me to behave like a "proper" wife and do his bidding, I taunt him about it. I do not shy from telling my mother-in-law how her son cannot satisfy either me or any other woman. I tell this all in a loud voice so that the neighbors can also listen. This is so in case he decides to give me *talaq*.[10] I just want to make sure that he can never get another wife. There are times I get beaten up for this, but I have the satisfaction of hurting his manhood (*mardangi*).

Sahin Bibi's interview is telling on several counts. She used her intimate knowledge of her husband's problem of premature ejaculation as a bargaining tool. Her awareness of her marital precarity, caused by the ease with which Muslim men can divorce their wives, made her publicly humiliate his sexual prowess, closely linked to assertions of masculinity. Such a sharp affront to Kallan's masculinity also ran the danger of Sahin Bibi facing physical violence from him, a real and present danger given that he had once fractured the bones in her right lower forearm. Kallan and his family had not taken her to the hospital for an X-ray. Instead, she had to just bandage it with a *dupatta*, bear the pain, and pray to Allah that it healed fast. "It still hurts when I knead the dough. But I am not going to admit it," she said.

In all five cases where the brides brought up the subject, the inability of the men to successfully perform "masculinity" through male dominance in sexual relations was seized by their wives to push the boundaries of their own subordinate status. This allowed them to negotiate better deals with their husbands, using sex as a bartering tool. Their consciousness of the emasculatory vulnerability of the men vis-à-vis their lack of sexual prowess, its linkage to masculine virility, and the shame associated with the failure of manhood displays the women's sophisticated and nuanced understanding of how socially constructed roles of hypervirile maleness psychologically frustrate men. This subjectivity tends to get ignored in the haste, especially of anti-trafficking NGOs and the media, to project a hegemonic image of cross-region brides as mute victims. Though this sample size is too small to arrive at any conclusion in this regard, these voices of embodied autonomy offer counternarratives to the monolithic representation of cross-region brides as "sexual slaves" (Rahman 2009).

Marriage Mediation: Pushback against Assimilation

Arranging marriages for other women from the brides' natal kin groups and villages with men from their conjugal communities, and linking up with other cross-region brides from their natal regions, emerges as strategy, as examined in chapter 4. Through these actions, the women can push against the gradual shrinkage of the private and public spaces available to them to carve out new nonhostile spaces. This strategy also allows them to create the informal support and policing mechanism that they lack in the conjugal communities. Such matchmaking, deliberate in some cases, is in large part prompted by wariness on the part of the brides toward local women. This was evident in my interview with Geetu, a Dalit cross-region bride from Mandaherhi village in the Rohtak district, who said, "I fear that if I share my sorrows or worries with my neighbors, they might report back to my mother-in-law and to my husband. He might then beat me up in anger. That's the main reason why I don't take anyone into confidence here." As discussed in chapter 4, mediating the marriages of their blood sisters or first cousins into the same conjugal family, or into another family in the same village, also subtly shifts the bargaining power in the women's favor. The patriarchal negotiations and resistance and refusal strategies of the two daughters-in-law can now occur in unison.

Community building between women from the same natal region through marriage not only gives them strength in numbers, but their shared cultural heritage also reduces the degree of cultural isolation they feel on an everyday basis. Manasi, a bride from Odisha who now mediated marriages for men in Rewari, said that she started by informally arranging one for her elder brother-in-law, whose wife had died a few years prior. As she prepared tea for us, she continued, "Having a woman from my region as my *jethani* here allows us to speak in our language and reminiscence about home. Whenever we get nostalgic, we cook *pakhal baath aar bhaja* (fermented rice and fried vegetables) and sit on the roof and eat it together. [Village] women laugh at us but we do not care." Scholars have discussed how food is at the center of processes of negotiation of meanings, memories, and identities (Hage 2010). "Nostalgic food" is often linked to memories and is used as a symbolic resource to maintain cultural identities and re-create "home" in new environments (Hage 2010).

Friendship with Local Women

For the most part, the intense monitoring and surveillance of the brides and fears about being "reported back" to their in-laws or husbands restrict the women's opportunities to forge friendships with local women. Despite this, the brides try to snatch spaces for conversations with the local women during the performance of mundane household activities. Kaushalya, the bride from Maharashtra, mentioned, "What we do not do is go to their homes, sit there, and chat at length.

Our conversations are limited to what we can talk about standing with water pots on our heads." Other innocent activities, such as getting clothes tailored by woman neighbors, also provide an opportunity to create alliances, as in the case of Rajbala, a local woman who ran a tailoring business out of her home. She lived almost directly across from a cross-region bride, Manjuli. Rajbala had become friends with Manjuli, the bride of Bengali origin from Odisha, "from the very first day she came to our village. When I went to meet her, she started crying. Manjuli was lonely and did not have any inkling about life here." According to Rajbala, Manjuli was in a good marriage as her husband, Raju, was a simple-hearted man. But the same could not be said about other brides she encountered during the course of her tailoring business: "They often come alone. It is then that I ask them about how they are treated by the mothers-in-law and other relatives. At all other times, they are constantly looking over their shoulders to see if someone is watching them." A focus group of Jat women from Mandaherhi village in the Rohtak district similarly stated that going to the terrace while doing household chores allowed them a chance to ask about the women's well-being, as well as offer solace and, sometimes, a willingness to let the women use their own cell phones to call parents back home.

Some cross-region brides manage to create friendships that bypass surveillance from conjugal families, as evident from an interview with Sundari, a Bengali bride. Sundari's house stood out from the rest in the village lane just because it was lushly covered with *pui shak* or Malabar spinach, an edible leafy green creeper highly valued in Bengali cuisine but totally alien to Haryanvi cooking, which she had managed to grow there. Sundari's husband, Manohar, being landless, had migrated from his village in the Rohtak district to Surat, an industrial hub in the western state of Gujarat to work in a textile factory there. Sundari talked about what it was like staying alone in a hostile home environment: "I have one woman, a local, in this village as my confidante and friend. . . . She advises me on how to negotiate the customs here and deal with any difficult situation that I find myself in vis-à-vis my in-laws or other women in this family. But I am careful not to let my family here know about this friendship. She would be placed in a difficult position then."

Such overtures of friendship are not one-sided. The local women, despite their caste and ethnic prejudices and the hawk-like monitoring of the brides by the conjugal families, also try to make connections with the brides. In the process, some become their allies, as happened in the case of Manjuli and Rajbala. Manjuli affirmed that Rajbala was "like my elder sister. She was the first one who asked me if I had eaten anything, if I was thirsty. Others had not bothered with caring about this. I just leaned on her shoulder and cried and cried." Rajbala, who had walked over to Manjuli's house, asked me to take a keepsake photo of the twosome, one where both posed hugging each other. She said, "Now, we are inseparable and interact all the time. We discuss intimate matters with each other too—I can trust her. I finish my household chores and come over to her place. If she doesn't know something, I tell her how to go about it. I have never thought of her as an outsider. Whenever I interact with her, I find that there is a unique closeness and bonding. I speak to her just like I would to my sister."

Such friendships, while rare, rupture linear narratives of local women as uncaring and unsympathetic about the complex predicament that cross-region brides face. Oftentimes, acts of reaching out are underscored by a sentiment of pity (*daya*) toward the cross-region brides, who, as Birjo Devi, from Banswa village in the Rewari district, said, "have no one of their family to support them. So, we try to ensure that the unfortunate woman (*bechari*) does not suffer." Such measures, whether driven by pity or a desire for friendship, go a long way in destabilizing the negative impressions of the local women as the brides' oppressors. These friendships provide a more nuanced look at the way intra-gender relations are negotiated within the overarching oppressive ideologies of patriarchy and caste.

CONCLUSION

What Lies Ahead: Continued Dispossession or Reclaiming Rights?

As I end this book, in which I have sought to describe the lived reality of women in cross-region matrimonies in rural North India, which emerged on the North Indian marriage-scape in the mid- to late 1990s, I am reminded of the words spoken by Mehrunissa from Razzakpur village in the Nuh district: that poverty is a powerful tormenting force that shapes people's lives beyond their control. In my research and in this book, I have taken these women's poverty as the commencement of my analysis and sought to understand why it is that they cannot get married locally in their own regions anymore. Why is it that some regions of India have become the marriage destination for rural North Indian men who are rejected as marriage material in their own marriage markets? What is the everyday life for these migrating brides in their culturally alien conjugal homes, located across the vast breadth of India?

As the preceding pages have revealed, these matrimonies, by contravening firmly entrenched marriage rules of caste endogamy and sameness of religious identity, are a clear break from the marriage migration trajectories that women customarily continue to take within India. There appear to be far deeper causes than the commonly understood push factors of poverty and abundance of women in some parts of India and the pull factor of female deficit in North India that precipitate such alliances. Placing this analysis within the contemporary moment of capitalist accumulation in the region, one that began in the early 1990s when India willingly adopted neoliberal reforms, has facilitated a deeper insight about both the motives leading to the rise in these marriages and the lived experiences of the migrant brides.

Jayati Ghosh, a leading Indian feminist political economist, argues that the "use of patriarchal social relations . . . becomes fundamental to the accumulation process itself, which actually *requires* the continuing impoverishment of certain sections for its success" (2018, 28; emphasis original). Capital not only "exacerbates . . . patriarchal relations of rule" (Mohanty 2003, 231), it also intensifies gender disparities and unequal gender relations. The neoliberal class project is understood to reinforce social inequalities through the intensification of racist and caste ideologies (Mohanty 2003, 231). In India, the growth in neoliberal policies witnessed the ascendancy of Hindu supremacist ideology to the political center stage. This increased the marginalization of Dalits and Muslims, two historically othered communities. The economic basis of women's subordination (Mies 1998) cautions us to be attendant to how capitalism, to further its accumulative process, latches on to preexisting oppressive ideologies and modifies them to assist its acquisitive nature. In the instance of India, ideologies such as patriarchy, caste, ethnocentrism, and religious fundamentalism *facilitate* further capitalist accumulation by legitimizing access to and control of gendered laboring low-caste bodies.

Borrowing from David Harvey's conceptualization of accumulation by dispossession (2005) and extending it to the sharper constriction of matrimonial choices available locally to women from marginalized groups has allowed me to undertake a sharper and more pointed critique of the neoliberal moment in India and the unique gendered violence it has wreaked and continues to wreak on India's poor women and their intimate lives. As revealed in the preceding chapters, the spread of neoliberal ideology and the accumulative process has drastically reshaped social relations into those governed by a capitalist logic. It has normalized a marketized mindset that weighs everyone on a monetized scale. The transformation of social relations into those governed by capitalist logic has hyper-commodified women's bodies. Harvey (2005) notes that the transformation of the welfare state to a market-driven one converts low-class women into disposable workers who have no option but to resort to flexible, casual, informal, or risky labor practices to survive.

This logic of disposability and zero-sum choices is similarly evident in the instance of marriage-making for the low-class Dalit and Muslim women who live in India's development peripheries. The combination of commodity fetishism, capitalist social relations, and the use of dowry as capital has caused a dispossession of marriage choice for some women from these groups more than others. As I have shown in chapters 3 and 4, a number of factors such as female-headed households, lack of household assets, colorism, and birth order shape marriage outcomes for poor women. Instead of blaming the foreclosure of local marriage options on the greed of local men, we need to critique how ideologies such as patriarchy, caste, religious fundamentalism, and neoliberal capitalism create coercion for poor women and dispossess them of marriage options. The consequent "voluntary" decision to marry North Indian men—ones who have been rejected locally in their own marriage markets—makes the women embark on a journey, both literal and metaphorical, that renders them second-class citizens within conjugal communities. It also subjects them to varying degrees of oppressive disciplinary controls that resemble imprisonment.

Although the deficit of women of marriageable age in the two North Indian states of Haryana and Rajasthan is certainly a contributory factor for such matrimonies, the marriage squeeze is not equally felt by all men in Haryana and Rajasthan. Instead, as shown in chapter 3, it is largely experienced by the landless and marginal landowning men belonging to the lower classes of men from certain caste groups and religious communities, such as the dominant-peasant Hindu caste groups and the Meo Muslims. Significantly, the rise in cross-region marriages has occurred parallel to the agrarian distress that holds the region's rural areas in a vise grip. As detailed in chapters 2 and 3, the rural poor seek to cushion the impact of the neoliberal reprovisioning by extracting more labor from female family members on family farms or having them work as agricultural wage laborers. The continual replenishment of unpaid family female labor occurs through marriage. As a patriarchal social institution, marriage not only legitimizes the transfer of this labor from one household to another but also disguises its tradability under the garb of a rite of passage that most women in India, under patriarchy, are expected to go through.

For men rejected in their local marriage markets, the unavailability of wives translates into a direct loss of unpaid labor and income. Having exhausted all options locally, they turn to the next best option: travel across India, transgress customary marriage norms, and obtain brides from families that are in greater economic distress and that lack their own local marriage options. Such marriage strategies also echo the capitalist process of securing labor, evident through many men's comments that traveling across the breadth of India to its development peripheries allows them to obtain *kaamkaaji aurat* (able workhorses). Through these marriages, patriarchy neatly intersects with systemic oppressions to *facilitate* uninterrupted capitalist accumulation and stem agrarian unrest. The women's internalization of the hegemonic patriarchal ideology reduces the need for "overt" violence and coercion—otherwise central in accumulation by dispossession—and poor women of marriageable age "voluntarily" agree to these matrimonies and to the transference of their labor, via marriage, to North Indian families. The migrant brides pick up the tab of neoliberal reforms and cushion the destructive

impact of agrarian distress among impoverished rural communities in North India as their "free" family labor gets harnessed for social reproduction.

Chain migrations are a causal factor, but not all regions of India emerge as
bride-seeking "go-to regions of choice" for North Indian males. By embedding
the analysis in the material and structural bases of gendered oppressions, it becomes possible to evince a common arc from the two natal states of Odisha and
West Bengal. In these regions, the state-led acquisitive process of big capital has
led to large-scale evictions, dispossessions, and dislocations of people from their
land, resources, and livelihoods. The resulting rise in poverty, indebtedness, unemployment, female-headed households, and distress-led migration has heightened inequalities along caste, gender, and religious lines. Here again, I am
reminded of Madhusudhan, a father of a cross-region bride from Cooch Behar,
whose anguished words eloquently sum up the coercive nature of neoliberal matrimonial dispossession: "Do you think parents like to marry off their daughters
in a foreign land (*bidesh*)? No parent wants that. It is poverty that has *forced* me
to marry her off there."

A Tangled and Muddied Canvas of Matrimonial Motives

Contrary to the dominant anti-trafficking discourse of widespread bridal slavery and bride trafficking, trafficking constitutes only a small percentage of cross-
region marriages. The small numbers do not, in any way, condone the horrific
abuse and exploitation that trafficked women suffer at both the hands of those
who have trafficked them and those who benefit from their commoditization.
However, my research has shown that most marriages occur with the consent
of the women's families, with culturally specific marriage customs legitimizing
the unions. Yet our understanding is muddied even in these marriages because
marriage facilitators and commission-based brokers undertake deliberate cov-
erups and deceptions about the men and their socioeconomic realities. With this
knowledge, should we not consider the consent of the women and their families
as one underlined with deceit? Additionally, there is no denying that significant
numbers of cross-region brides, whether trafficked or not, face a highly regulated and circumscribed freedom of movement that makes them experience their
lived reality as "inmates of prisons" (*jailkhana*). However, as detailed in chapter 3, the "all brides as trafficked" discourse "is not the only way to tell and understand the story. Moreover, if it is read as *the* story, it obscures significant
variations among and between women and through time" (Constable 2006, 3;
emphasis original).

In its failure to recognize that even trafficked women might wrest some space in which to challenge or resist their exploitation, the bridal-slave narrative flattens the diverse trajectories of marriage migration into a singular reductive storyline of mute victimhood. It also erases the complex counternarratives of women who actively choose to continue in such marriages despite avenues of escape or repatriation. This singular emphasis on trauma narratives "suggests overall that women are victims whether they know it or not, and it obscures some of the ways they express resistance, exert influence and create change. It thus makes it difficult to imagine any *good* migration" (Constable 2006, 4; emphasis original).

In this book, I have urged a more productive frame of analysis that interrogates the intersections of ideologies such as patriarchy, caste, colorism, and ethnicity in shaping life outcomes for poor women. The embeddedness of patriarchal ideology and the low worth given to wives conveniently fuses with a neoliberal culture of marketized social relations to allow men and their families to normalize the commodification of all brides—not just cross-region brides. Arguably, the "internaliz[ation of] cannibalistic as well as predatory and fraudulent practises" (Harvey 2005, 148) allows marriage agents and traffickers to capitalize on the situation. The "redistribution through criminal violence" as "one of the few serious options for the poor" (Harvey 2007, 48) transforms some cross-region brides or their husbands into agents or traffickers.

Instead of problematically portraying women's parents as uncaring and as deliberately allowing their daughters to be trafficked, the Indian state should be recognized as an abettor to both bridal trafficking and so-called voluntary marriage migration—either of which consigns the subsequent migrant brides to a restricted existence and exposes them to violence, both physical and psychosocial, in their new homes and communities. By continuing to treat certain regions of India as its development peripheries, by sustaining structural discriminations against marginalized communities, and by supporting the neoliberal market ethos, the Indian state *enables and is a party to* low-class women's commodification, their dispossession of matrimonial options locally, and their consequent trafficking, exploitation, and abuse as migrant brides in rural North India. Ironically, the government's strong-arm carceral policy approaches and "rescue and repatriation" intervention measures, propelled in large part by pressure from the anti-trafficking lobby, allows the state to demonstrate its proactiveness in dealing with the so-called large-scale commodification of women. This then lets the Indian state off the hook without holding it accountable for its active role in the transformation of its citizens into commodities and second-class citizens.

As I showed in chapters 3 and 4, oftentimes, most women and their parents do regard these marriages as strategic hypergamous choices that constitute a conscious economic move up from their current poverty-stricken position. Compromised by the lack of productive assets and the lesser educational attainments that act as barriers to their economic independence, and hegemonized into believing that adult women *have* to get married, many women voluntarily migrate for marriage or harbor an awareness that they might potentially be trafficked in the future. Lamentably, in the Indian context, what is witnessed next is the unfolding of the neoliberal pathology of victim blaming (Stringer 2014), one that also runs the danger of embedding class bias by equating poor women's consensual and strategic marriage migration with trafficking.

The financialization of social relations, evidenced by the men paying marriage mediators a brokerage or commission fee to set up cross-region matrimonies, creates a problematic perception of these brides as commodities that can then be disciplined by their husbands and in-laws and literally put to use for the greater and efficient extraction of their labor. Such women's circumscribed freedom should, rightfully, be condemned as a gross violation of human and gender rights. In combination, using disciplining techniques and viewing daughters-in-law as dispensable commodities are strategically employed against "recalcitrant" local brides who seek to resist and push back against excessive work demands through threats like, "we will easily get a 'Biharan' by paying an 'agent' money." In this sense, the emergence of cross-region matrimonies has, overall, eroded *all* women's bargaining ability and reshaped, for the worse, inter- and intra-gender relations of power within conjugal families.

Lived Reality of Internal Othering

"Bahu Mol Ki" or "A Bought Bride," a Haryanvi song and video available on YouTube,[1] opens with two men hailing a van packed with villagers on a rural road. Upon the driver asking the duo to attend a "program" of music in a nearby village, the older man replies that they are headed to Bihar to source a bride for his son. From this opening scene, the five-minute-long song goes on to unfold, in detail, the lamentable transformation of Haryana's rural landscape as Bihari brides and their kin overrun the region. Striking a cautionary note to aspiring Haryanvi grooms, the singer reminds them of the yawning cultural difference that will make their life miserable if they opt to marry a Bihari woman. The singer, Janu Rakhi, uses caricatures of Bihari men walking down a village street wearing village attire, spitting betel-leaf juice on village streets, or wolfing down platefuls of rice with bare hands to underline his point. This song has had 2.76 million views since it was uploaded on YouTube in November 2019. "Bahu Mol Ki" appears to be part of a new genre of folk songs that revolves around the bride shortage in Haryana. These songs might be new, but their theme of ethnocentrism stems in large part from their unashamed depiction of stereotypes that locals have about Biharis, who are positioned civilizationally below the locals.

As mentioned in chapter 5, the fiction of ethnic collectivity and cultural difference is used to transform "minorities into deviants from the 'normal' and exclude them from important power resources" (Yuval-Davis 1997, 11). Belonging to a particular collectivity, constructed through social location and identification, also often demands the "internal other" shed or deny their own cultural or ethnic identity in order to be considered for inclusion. Fashioning and circulating a dichotomy of "us" versus "them" both creates and justifies a series of exclusionary regimes for these "othered" brides. Such regimes do not give them a moment's respite from the multiple and overlapping prejudices and discriminatory behavior they experience, as poisonous tentacles also extend within the private domain of the brides' own homes, where their husbands and extended family members also treat them differentially. The brides live their married lives with a clear realization that although their bodies are "needed" by the conjugal families for the labor they offer, as individuals in their own right, they are unwanted.

Ethnoracist ideology also provides the conjugal families and communities with justifications for the supposed filtering out or cleansing of undesirable cultural characteristics, a program that involves forcibly making the brides shed their cultural markers, including language and customs, and ensuring their conformity to the local customs and language. This form of assimilation is not benign. Instead, it is a deliberate and violent act of cultural erasing, one that makes no accommodation to respecting the women's cultural heritage.

Further, as proven throughout the book, the role of caste in the persistence of material inequalities for low castes while dominant caste groups continue to experience success in holding on to power and privilege adds further layers of oppression and exploitation. Engaging with a politics of difference to examine "social relations that convert difference into oppression" (Rege 1998, WS 40) is necessary to reposition cross-region matrimonies within the contemporary milieu of India, one that is riven by caste polarization and religious fundamentalism. It also provides a fresh architecture to reveal the subordinate location of low-caste cross-region brides in local caste hierarchies.

The fabrications of higher-caste identity among the migrant brides within the dominant-peasant caste groups are largely concocted to ensure that the edifice of local oppressive caste hierarchies remains intact through severe restrictions on local intercaste alliances. However, neither the families nor the conjugal kin groups and communities accept these women as caste equals. An overwhelming majority of these "intercaste" cross-region marriages, instead of promoting caste "integration," heighten the caste-based repression against these brides.

Since such marriages can be interpreted as political acts that threaten to destabilize caste hierarchies and attendant privileges, caste violence constitutes a ped-
agogical tool used to instruct migrant Dalit brides in how to avoid overstepping
caste boundaries. Additionally, class tensions within hierarchies of men are apparently neutralized by the local communities as well as the conservative and
ultra-patriarchal caste councils or *khap panchayats* turning a blind eye to the
open caste infractions contained in these alliances by saying, "at least the man's
household is functioning."

Challenges Ahead

The varied instances of cross-region brides' subjectivity as they try to negotiate
equations of power to their benefit, a topic discussed in chapters 5 and 6, limited
as they are, run counter to and contest hegemonic representational tropes of rural women as docile bodies. They push the boundaries defining religious, caste,
and ethnic identities as well as women's rank and status within the repressive
patriarchal ideology. They also demonstrate that defiance, refusal, and resistance
may not take conventional forms; instead, agency and rebellion can be exhibited by feigning compliance and passivity to avoid everyday acts of intimidation
and violence.

Nevertheless, the women, while displaying an awareness of their oppression
and subordination at an individual level, enact their resistances without a clear
consciousness of the hegemonic ideological constraints that provide legitimacy
for their oppression and subordination. In this sense, they exhibit Gramscian
"contradictory consciousness" (Gramsci 1971, 76); their rebellions, or challenges,
as they occur at an individual level, are not waged to overturn or dismantle the
dominant ideologies of caste, religion, or patriarchy through collective action.
To illustrate, the brides recognize the contradictions inherent in their role as
daughters-in-law within the patriarchal ideology—in which the simple fact of
being married justifies the extraction of their unpaid labor. Yet, they do not undertake actions to resist the control of patriarchal ideology. Additionally, while
the women might display critical insights about why they are subordinated and
othered, they still operate within the dominant paradigms by seeking legitimacy
for themselves within these constructs.

Despite such narratives of resistance and refusal, until now, compared to local
brides, an overwhelming number of cross-region brides suffer inequality, discrimination, and a higher incidence of gender subordination and gender violence. Although pragmatism guides the uneasy acceptance of cross-region brides in their
new homes and communities, it appears that their offspring are not extended this

instrumentalist generosity. In one stanza from the above-mentioned folk song "Bahu Mol Ki," the singer, Janu Rakhi, continues to list more grim consequences in store for Haryanvi men if they continue marrying Bihari women. An old man, seen earlier in the video as the father of the groom who married a Biharan, goes up to a group of small boys playing marbles. He pulls one boy up and looks at his face ruefully and then walks away, apparently rejecting his dark-skinned, part-Bihari grandson, while the singer laments, "dark-dark children will be born, no more will we recognize our own grandchildren" (*kale kale baalak hovengey, pahchane nahin jaavengey*).

The intergenerational transmission of othering of the children born of cross-region unions is an emerging contentious matter. Not considered "pure" enough, their "diluted" identity relegates them to second-class status within paternal communities and greatly affects their psychological well-being. So far, most of these children are quite young. However, as they reach adulthood, their political struggle as inheritors of parental resources will create huge tensions and fractures within rural North India, as they will seek to challenge ideologies that, up to now, have denied them their due rights.

Further, given that female deficit is a real problem in Haryana and Rajasthan, and given that families will most likely continue to seek brides from elsewhere, the criminalization strategy runs the risk of pushing such alliances underground. The fear of prosecutions may force families to adopt strategies to make their brides "invisible," and, if so, this will most likely be accomplished through the stricter regulation of their mobility and increased confinement at home. This would render the brides more vulnerable to gender-based violence and consequently prevent them from seeking timely interventions against their abuse. Criminalizing cross-region marriages also confers the tag of "illegality" to such alliances. These marriages then run the risk of being declared "void," with long-term legal consequences for the rights of the brides and the children born from such unions.

A range of imaginative and coordinated policy actions and grassroots initiatives are necessary to address this crisis. The reverberations from the surplus of unmarried males will continue to lead to an increased movement of women around the country for marriage. This intense marriage squeeze in India might potentially reshape historically hierarchically oppressive relations centered on caste, religion, and ethnicity. Thus far, the dominance of the "victim-trafficker" discourse has led the Indian government to adopt policing and law enforcement measures as *the* solution to these so-called coerced marriages. Various government schemes that include a number of measures like education-based savings schemes, such as Beti Bachao, Beti Padhao, translated roughly as "Save the Daughter, Educate the Daughters," which was launched by the government of

India in 2015, are welcome in their intent. However, what is needed is a commitment to tackle the bull by its horns, as they say, by discussing the embeddedness of the regressive patriarchal mindset that treats the girl child, and by extension, the adult female, as a dispensable commodity. Ensuring that women have access to productive resources and are able to protect their inheritance rights are steps that the Indian state should work toward. The failure to do so will "result in political agendas and public policies that fail to be adequately responsive to the interests of women from . . . marginalized groups" (Narayan 1997, 44).

I hope that this work can contribute in some modest measure to wider conversations and to improvements in practices and policies that can support the women, men, and children whose lives are so deeply affected by cross-region marriages in India today. To date, the evidence shows that the male marriage squeeze has only accentuated the fault lines of caste and ethnicity, which has led to a worsening of gender status and rights for the migrating brides in particular, and for all women in general. There is a great need to acknowledge the "differences" of caste, class, ethnicity, religion, location, and even color that exist within the constructed category of cross-region bride, and how these significantly alter the women's status and lived experience in their conjugal homes and communities. Such a focus might help future scholarship analytically recognize the messiness and contradictions that characterize the position of the migrant brides. Relatedly, it might illuminate a more complex view to gain a nuanced understanding about these marriages and the rights and status of cross-region brides. This can contribute to shaping future strategies for engagement in gender rights and gender justice for women in India.

As feminists and activists, our goal should be to tackle, as Simpson writes, "how to change a story that is always being told" (2014, 177). Only by looking at the circumstances and life trajectories of marginalized women in this way can we truly understand their experiences and acquire insight about the novel articulations of the gendered nature of neoliberal capitalist dispossession. In doing so, we can be attentive to the specific needs and demands of brides who, despite all odds, choose to continue in their cross-region matrimonies and to—within those marriages—defy and refuse their abject victimhood. Because of their generative nature, refusals are hopeful as they imagine a different possibility. In that regard, the brides' refusals, stemming from their compromised existence and constrained choices, are not just "the revenge of the consent" (McGranahan 2016, 323). These refusals are their revenge *against* the forcible consent that neoliberal accumulation extracts from them by having them accede to marriage migration. Such refusals are far more transgressive, are political, and are aimed at dislocating existing social hierarchies and inequities. The brides' small acts of refusal, directed at reclaiming dignity and asserting their rights, loudly proclaim their agency. In the words of Bundo, an Adivasi bride from Maharashtra:

> Now, this is both my home and the place of existence. No one can dislodge me.
> *Yaahi ab mera ghar hai, sab kuch hai. Dati rahoongi.*

LIST OF INTERVIEWEES DIRECTLY QUOTED

ROHTAK DISTRICT, HARYANA

Khurdpur (9 April 2011)

Veena—cross-region bride
Devesh—husband of a cross-region bride, Veena
Neetu—cross-region bride
Geeta—cross-region bride
Santosh*—fieldworker
Sandeep*—fieldworker
Pradeep—taxi driver

Bamanpur (7 October 2011)

Focus group village women

Mandaherhi (7, 8, and 9 October 2011)

Geetu—cross-region bride
Kaushalya—cross-region bride
Pavan—husband of a cross-region bride, Kaushalya
Madhu Bala—Jat village woman
Sube Singh—Jat village man
Dhoop Singh—father-in-law
Nutan—cross-region bride
Focus group Jat women

Rundh Murkhedi (9 and 10 October 2011)

Manjuli—cross-region bride
Raju—husband of a cross-region bride, Manjuli
Mamoni—cross-region bride
Karam Beer—husband of a cross-region bride, Dharani
Dharani—cross-region bride
Satbeer—unmarried male
Binta—cross-region bride
Rajbala—neighbor and friend of Manjuli
Focus group village women

Charwali Khas (11 October 2011)

Namita—cross-region bride
Bishakha—cross-region bride

Khaprauli (12 October 2011)

Anju Devi—husband's sister (*nanad*)
Purnima—cross-region bride

Nagla Kasauda (12 and 13 October 2011)

Focus group young men (mixed caste)
Focus group Jat men
Focus group mixed-caste men

Palagarh (13 October 2011)

Pushpa—Jat village woman

Ghani Palthana (14 October 2011)

Focus group mixed-caste women
Focus group Bihari male migrant agricultural workers

Uncha Tendroli (23 September 2014)

Mukesh Devi—mother-in-law
Chaitali—cross-region bride / bride mediator
Ajay—husband of a cross-region bride, Chaitali / husband mediator
Sukh Chain—husband of a cross-region bride, Babki
Sampa—cross-region bride
Sree Chand—husband of a cross-region bride, Sampa / former
  husband mediator

Nila—cross-region bride
Kakoli—cross-region bride

Asrapur (24 September 2014)

Sundari—cross-region bride

Dhaipur (25 September 2014)

Bundo—cross-region bride
Mukesh—husband of a cross-region bride, Asha
Sushmita—cross-region bride

Bahu Jamalpur (25 September 2014)

Meena Devi—cross-region bride
Vidya Devi—village woman

JIND DISTRICT, HARYANA

Vinodha Kalan* (21 July 2012)

Nafe Singh Nain, President of Sarv Jat Khap Maha Panchayat (Supreme Council of Jat Caste Groups)*

HISAR DISTRICT, HARYANA

Narnaund Town* (21 July 2012)

Phool Singh Petwar, member of Petwar Tapa, Satrol Khap Panchayat*
Satbir Singh—Sarpanch, Petwar village*

SONIPAT DISTRICT, HARYANA

Sisana* (21 July 2012)

Focus group Dahiya Khap Panchayat*

Sisana* (24 July 2014)

Meher Singh Dahiya, Secretary, Dahiya Khap Panchayat*

Chota Rampur (24 September 2014)

Aparna—cross-region bride / bride mediator
Ram Bhajan—husband of a cross-region bride, Aparna / husband mediator
Deepika—aspiring cross-region bride

REWARI DISTRICT, HARYANA

Banswa (31 October 2011)

> Achala—cross-region bride
> Narangi Devi—mother-in-law of a cross-region bride, Achala
> Focus group Ahir women

Tehrapur (1 November 2011)

> Krishna Devi—mother-in-law of a cross-region bride, Sharbana
> Sharbana—cross-region bride
> Kusum—cross-region bride

Garhi Hakimpur (1 November 2011)

> Shamsher Yadav—village man
> Balwant Devi—village woman

Dhanauti (1 November 2011)

> Damini—cross-region bride / bride mediator
> Biju and Sondhya—parents of a cross-region bride

Dhani Raghowas (2 November 2011)

> Chandana—cross-region bride
> Chet Ram—husband of a cross-region bride, Chandana
> Jhimpi—cross-region bride (also Chandana's niece and Janaki's daughter)
> Kanaklata—cross-region bride
> Nirmal Devi—Yadav village woman
> Rajlata—Yadav village woman
> Shakuntala—Yadav village woman
> Focus group Yadav women
> Focus group cross-region brides
> Bimla Devi, president, Shakti Parishad*

Charakpur (3 November 2011)

> Focus group Dalit village women

Murwara Khurd (12 November 2011)

> Manasi—cross-region bride / mediator
> Bhuru Lal—husband of a cross-region bride, Manasi / mediator

NUH DISTRICT, HARYANA

Meerpur

Dr Abdul Aziz*—15 April 2011 and 31 August 2014
Amjad (Nooru's eldest brother-in-law)—30 August 2014
Focus group Meo men—30 August 2014
Mamtaaj—cross-region bride—31 August 2014
Nooru—cross-region bride—21 September 2014
Mobin—Nooru's eldest brother-in-law (*jeth*)—21 September 2014
Saripan—mother-in-law of a cross-region bride, Nooru—21
    September 2014
Mammal—Nooru's father—21 September 2014
Focus group Meo men—21 September 2014

Sheikh Ismailpur (28 August 2014)

Tahira—trafficked cross-region bride
Mubarik—husband of a trafficked cross-region bride, Tahira
Akhtari Bano—cross-region bride

Ghasaulipura (29 August 2014)

Parbeen Bano—cross-region bride
Tahir—husband of a cross-region bride, Parbeen Bano
Sabana Bano—cross-region bride

Sheikhpura village (29 August 2014)

Focus group Meo women
Subhani—village woman
Focus group Meo men and women

Rawalpura (30 August 2014)

Sharifa Bano—mother-in-law of a cross-region bride, Saira
Rabiya—cross-region bride

Razzakpur (31 August 2014)

Mubina Bano—cross-region bride
Mehrunissa—cross-region bride
Nagma—cross-region bride

ALWAR DISTRICT, RAJASTHAN

Alwar City*

Virendra Vidrohi, secretary, NGO Matsya Mewat Evam Sikshan Vikas
  Kendra*—23 October 2011; 19 December 2011; and 26 July 2012
Maulana Mohammad Hanif*—19 December 2011

Mian Ka Vas (16 December 2011)

Piroji—mother-in-law of a cross-region bride, Karima
Sitara—cross-region bride
Mohar Mohammad—husband of Sitara

Nindoli (16 December 2011)

Nurnesa—cross-region bride
Khadija—cross-region bride
Subhan Khan—husband of a cross-region bride, Nurnesa

Rasoolpur (16 December 2011)

Imrana—trafficked cross-region bride

Undhra Jaleera (17 December 2011)

Ashrafi—mother-in-law of a cross-region bride

Bardhakhui (18 December 2011)

Saroj Bala—cross-region bride
Hukum Chand—husband of a cross-region bride, Saroj Bala

Khusropur (24 July 2012)

Sitabi—cross-region bride
Miskina—cross-region bride

Khadrauli (25 July 2012)

Farjana—trafficked cross-region bride
Majeda Bibi—cross-region bride
Uahin Bibi   cross-region bride

JHUNJHUNU DISTRICT, RAJASTHAN

Jhunjhunu City*

Rajan Chowdhary, secretary, Shikshit Rojgar Kendra Prabandhak
  Samiti*—1 October 2011 and 26 July 2012

Jogaram Jhangid, collector, Jhunjhunu District*—26 July 2012

O. P. Kataria, additional superintendent police (S.P.), Jhunjhunu District*—26 July 2012

Ramsar (1 and 2 October 2011; 13, 14, and 15 November 2011; 15 December 2011; 26 and 27 July 2012)

Pradeep—brother of a husband, Bijai—1 October 2011; 13 and 15 November 2011; 15 December 2011; 26 and 27 July 2012

Phoola Devi—mother-in-law (Pradeep and Bijai's mother)—2 October 2011; 13 and 15 November, 15 December, and 27 July 2012

Bijai—prospective groom—2 October 2011

Sumer Singh—father-in-law of a cross-region bride—27 July 2012

Focus group village men—27 July 2012

Rajjo—Pradeep's wife—2 October 2011; 15 November 2011; 27 July 2012

Hindroli

Kamlesh—sister of Bijai and Pradeep—3 October 2011; 16 November 2011; 15 December 2011; 27 July 2012

Pradeep—brother of Kamlesh and Bijai—16 November 2011

Jatianawas (13 November 2011)

Relu Ram—father-in-law of a cross-region bride

Banherapur (14 November 2011)

Meena Devi—village woman

Kesariyagarh (15 November 2011)

Satinder—marriage agent

Chak Peepalraha (17 November 2011)

Vahida Bano—cross-region bride

Marunima (Mumtaaj)—cross-region bride

Rehana—mother-in-law of a cross-region bride

BALESHWAR DISTRICT, ODISHA

Nimaipur (27 November 2011)

Bijoy—brother of a cross-region bride

Puspalata—mother of cross-region brides (also mother of Bijoy)

Hari—brother of a cross-region bride, Sarmila

Prabha Devi—mother of cross-region bride, Sarmila (also mother of Hari)
Vinod—Sarmila's husband
Binata Devi—mother of a trafficked cross-region bride, Jharana
Jagadish—brother of Binata Devi and uncle of trafficked cross-region bride, Jharana

Tentuliapal (28 November 2011)

Jasoda Das and Bhagirath Das—parents of a cross-region bride
Mohua—returnee cross-region bride

Iswardhuli (29 November 2011)

Ganga Chand Das—brother of a cross-region bride
Chabirani—mother of a cross-region bride

Gaganpada (30 December 2011)

Bishnu Parda—brother of a cross-region bride

Anantapada (30 November 2011)

Parimal—brother of a cross-region bride

Palasa Gandia (1 December 2011)

Janaki—mother of a bride, Jhimpi (also sister of Chandana, a cross-region bride)

Kusumpada (1 and 2 December 2011)

Subhash Bhanja—brother of a cross-region bride
Sukanti—mother of a cross-region bride, Bullu
Bullu—cross-region bride
Ajay Das—brother of a cross-region bride

COOCH BEHAR DISTRICT, WEST BENGAL
Cooch Behar City*

Shankar Dutta Gupta, journalist, district correspondent of the regional newspapers *Uttarbanga Sambad* and *Dainik Jagron**—
17 September 2014

Purbi Jodaipur (14 October 2014)

Biplab Das—father of a cross-region bride, Aparna / locator
Sukanto Das—brother of a cross-region bride
Usha Rani—mother of a cross-region bride

Shailabari (14 October 2014)

    Shunjit Das—father of a cross-region bride

Dakhin Nuapur (15 October 2014)

    Imtiaz—father of a cross-region bride
    Ahmeduddin—father of a cross-region bride
    Nijammudin—father of a cross-region bride

Mohuagacherpur (15 October 2014)

    Bhajendra Das—brother of a cross-region bride

Dinpur (16 October 2014)

    Lakshmi Rani—mother of a trafficked cross-region bride
    Shabban—brother of a cross-region bride

NEW DELHI

Shafiqur Rahman*—28 July 2012
Ravi Kant*—4 August 2012

Note: All names of people, cities, towns, and villages marked with * are real, whereas the rest are pseudonyms.

Glossary

Adivasi: Literally translates as the "original people." Also called the tribal people of India. See also Scheduled Tribes.

Ahir: Peasant-pastoral caste ritually located in the Shudra varna with Other Backward Class (OBC) status in Haryana and Rajasthan.

bahu: Daughter-in-law.

Bangal: Colloquial term for the province of West Bengal.

Bangalan (Bengalan): A woman hailing from the province of West Bengal.

bejaat: Literally translates as "casteless." Usually denotes people whose ranking in the caste hierarchy is suspect.

bichola: Go-between or mediator. Also called *bicholi* (feminine).

bigha: Unit of land measurement. Four bighas equal roughly one acre of land.

Bihari (Biharan): People from the province of Bihar. Biharan refers to the women from Bihar.

block: An administrative unit of a district consisting of a cluster of villages. Also called *tehsil.*

Child Sex Ratio (CSR): Ratio of the female population to 1,000 males.

Dalit: A politically aware self-identifying term, translated as crushed or broken in Hindi, used by groups considered untouchables.

district: Each state is divided into several administrative divisions called districts or *zilas.* See also block.

dominant-peasant caste: Caste group that owns the majority of land in any particular region.

dooj baar: Moniker for remarriage.

endogamy: Marriage within the same caste group.

exogamy: Marriage outside one's subcaste group or patrilineal clans (*gotra*). Rules of exogamy prohibit matrimony within the father's, the mother's and the paternal grandmother's *gotra.* Village exogamy involves the practice of marriage outside one's own village. See also *got.*

got (gotra): Exogamous patrilineal clans that are a part of a particular subcaste group or *jati.*

Hindutva: A chauvinistic, right-wing Hindu majoritarian nationalist ideology advocating formation of a Hindu nation.

Jamaat: Religious congregation of people or religious tours. Also refers to the Tablighi Jama'at.

Jat: Subcaste within the Shudra varna.

jati: A closed social subcaste group within a varna. *Jati* is usually territorially bound, endogamous, and consists of several exogamous patrilineal clans called *gots* or *gotras*.

jeth: Husband's elder brother.

jethani: Husband's elder brother's wife.

khap: A cluster of villages united by caste and geography. Also formed by the same *gotra* or clan families from several neighboring villages.

khap panchayat (**khaps**): Non-elected nonjudicial clan or gotra caste councils. These all-male *khaps* are prevalent in the North Indian regions of Haryana, Western Uttar Pradesh, and parts of Rajasthan.

killa (kille): Unit of land measurement. One killa is roughly equal to one acre of land.

nanad: Husband's sister.

neech jat (neech zat): Low caste or "untouchable" caste. Among the Muslims, it refers to groups of Muslims that converted from Hinduism to Islam.

nikahnama: Islamic marriage certificate. Also, a prenuptial agreement between the groom and the bride.

NSS National Sample Survey (NSSO): National Sample Survey Office of India (NSSO) that conducts socioeconomic surveys on themes like consumer expenditure, employment-unemployment, social expenditure on health and education, and land and livestock holding, and debt and investment.

Other Backward Classes (OBC): An administrative category of the Indian state for caste groups that are considered economically, educationally, and socially depressed.

panchayat (*Gram Panchayat*): Elected council that functions as a local self-governance unit at the village level.

paro: A term for non-Meo women married to Meo men derived from the Hindi words *us paar* or *paar ka*, meaning the "other side."

reservations: Affirmative policies taken by the Indian state for socioeconomically marginalized groups.

Scheduled Caste (SC): An official Indian term for a group of caste groups considered outside the fourfold varna division in the caste system and eligible for affirmative policies.

Scheduled Tribe (ST): Scheduled Tribe or ST is an officially recognized term within India to refer to its autochthonous communities.

Shudra: Fourth varna within the Brahmanical caste hierarchy consisting of peasant proprietary and artisan classes, with tremendous socioeconomic variations amongst its constituent subcastes. See also Dalit and Untouchable.

Tablighi Jama'at (TJ): Sunni Islamic revival movement, Tabligh, or "call to faith."

untouchables: See Dalits

Yadav: An umbrella caste term for a number of cattle herder and cowherd castes.

Notes

PREFACE

1. Unless specified otherwise, all names for individuals and villages used in this book are pseudonyms.

2. Santosh and Sandeep are the real names of research assistants who worked with me during this study. Dalit is a politically aware, self-identifying term, translated as crushed or broken in Hindi, used by groups considered to be "untouchables."

INTRODUCTION

1. "Get Me a Bride, Take My Vote: Haryana Bachelors Tell Candidates," Rediff.com, 9 April 2014, http://www.rediff.com/news/report/ls-election-get-me-a-bride-take-my -vote-haryana-bachelors-tell-candidates/20140409.htm.

2. Press Trust of India (PTI), "BJP leader O.P. Dhankar Promises Brides from Bihar for Haryana's Youth," *Economic Times*, 6 July 2014, http://articles.economictimes .indiatimes.com/2014-07-06/news/51108003_1_brides-haryana-youths-sushil-modi.

3. The Meo self-identify as a distinct sociocultural ethnic community and, despite their Muslim religion, trace their lineage to the Hindu Rajputs in North India. They are considered both a caste group and a distinct religious faith within Islam because of this dual identity. They have historically inhabited a geographically contiguous space called Mewat, or the "land of the Meo," understood more as a cultural space than an administrative unit, that traverses from southern Haryana, through part of northeast Rajasthan, to Western Uttar Pradesh. However, it is in the district of Nuh, Haryana, that the Meo constitute an overwhelming majority, with another significant pocket localized in a few administrative blocks, or *tehsils*, in the Alwar district in Rajasthan.

4. Adivasis is a term used for a group of ethnic and tribal groups considered India's autochthonous population. The Constitution of India recognizes them as "Scheduled Tribes," with the "Scheduled" here referring to a schedule that lists tribes that enjoy special status.

5. S. Rukmini, "Just 5% of Indian Marriages Are Inter-Caste: Survey," *The Hindu*, 13 November 2014, http://www.thehindu.com/data/just-5-per-cent-of-indian-marriages-are -intercaste/article6591502.ece.

6. Elena del Estal, "'I Was Bought for 50,00 Rupees': India's Trafficked Brides—In Pictures," *The Guardian*, 7 March 2018, https://www.theguardian.com/global-development /2018/mar/07/india-girls-women-trafficked-brides-sexual-domestic-slavery; Sindhuja Parthasarathy, "Haryana's Slave Brides: For Trafficked Women, A Life Lived on the Margins," *Firstpost*, 10 September 2018, https://www.firstpost.com/long-reads/haryanas -slave-brides-for-trafficked-women-a-life-lived-on-the-margins-5142721.html.

7. Neeraj Chauhan, "Well-Oiled Network Gets 50000 Bangladeshi Girls Trafficked into India Every Year," *Times News Network*, 18 January 2018, https://timesofindia .indiatimes.com/india/well-oiled-network-gets-50000-bangladeshi-girls-trafficked -into-india-every-year/articleshow/62436540.cms.

8. This might change with one section of the Hindu Right launching a scheme, in late 2019, for the marriage of Indian men to Nepali women as a natural continuum to the mythology of the Hindu god king Ram's marriage to Sita, the princess of Janakpur, a

border district of Nepal. See Rohan Dua, "Ram Janaki Baraat: Nepal Brides for 108 Men from UP, MP, Bihar," *Times News Network*, 19 November 2019, https://timesofindia .indiatimes.com/city/lucknow/ram-janki-baraat-nepal-brides-for-108-from-india /articleshow/72118177.cms.

9. Vishal Joshi, "Dalit Locality Attacked, Water Supply Cut after Inter-caste Marriage in Haryana," *Hindustan Times*, 15 April 2013, http://www.hindustantimes.com/india /dalit-locality-attacked-water-supply-cut-after-inter-caste-marriage-in-haryana/story -MFjl6c9WiHan6JoqU8fW2O.html.

10. A *khap* is a cluster of villages united by caste and geography. *Khaps* are formed by the same *gotra*, or clan families from several neighboring villages. These are nonelected, nonjudicial clan or *gotra* councils that are solely governed by men from the same *gotra*. *Khap panchayats* are prevalent in Haryana, Western Uttar Pradesh, and parts of Rajasthan. *Khap panchayats* of the dominant castes regulate social behavior within the caste and the village and between caste groups, through the use of decrees of social boycott and other forms of exclusionary punishment. All caste groups, including the Dalits, have to toe the line of a particular dominant caste *khap* in their region, with no choice in the matter. *Khap panchayats* have adopted a gender-regressive stance through edicts that sanction so-called honor killings of women who defy caste rules on marriage, and through sanctions on wearing Western attire and using cellphones.

11. The National Capital Region of Delhi, or NCR for short, refers to a circle of urban area around the Union Territory of Delhi that is drawn from the neighboring states of Haryana, Uttar Pradesh, and Rajasthan.

1. A SOCIETY IN FLUX

1. Vishnu Padmanabhan, "The Land Challenge Underlying India's Farm Crisis," *Live Mint*, 15 October 2018, https://www.livemint.com/Politics/SOG43o5ypqO13j0QflaawM /The-land-challenge-underlying-Indias-farm-crisis.html.

2. P. Sainath, "Farmers Suicides Rates Soar above the Rest," *The Hindu*, 18 May 2013, https://www.thehindu.com/opinion/columns/sainath/farmers-suicide-rates-soar -above-the-rest/article4725101.ece.

3. "Income Inequality Gets Worse; India's Top 1% Bag 73% of the Country's Wealth, Says Oxfam," *Businesstoday.in*, 30 January 2019, https://www.businesstoday.in/current /economy-politics/oxfam-india-wealth-report-income-inequality-richests-poor/story /268541.html.

4. Prachi Salve, "India's SEZ Failures a Cautionary Tale for Land Acquisition Bill," *Business Standard*, 20 May 2015, http://www.business-standard.com/article/specials /india-s-sez-failures-a-cautionary-tale-for-land-acquisition-move-115052000399_1 .html.

5. Times News Network (TNN), "Government to Set Up Japanese Township in Rohtak," *Times of India*, 11 November 2010, http://timesofindia.indiatimes.com/city/gurgaon/Govern ment-to-set-up-Japanese-township-in-Rohtak/articleshow/6904396.cms.

6. See Anup Roy, "High on Real Estate Boom, Sampla Farmers Couldn't Care Less," *Live Mint*, 20 June 2008, https://www.livemint.com/Politics/5PiCc9aTpvbKoHjhCk0UeN /High-on-real-estate-boom-Sampla-farmers-couldn8217t-care.html.

7. Christophe Jaffrelot and A. Kalaiyasaran. "Jats in Wonderlessland: Crisis of Haryana's Dominant Castes Mirrors India's Challenge: Lack of Good Jobs," *Indian Express*, 10 March 2017, https://indianexpress.com/article/opinion/columns/jats-in-wonderlessland -quote-stir-jat-agitation-obc-status-haryana-employment-4562573/.

8. A new housing program called the Indira Awaas Yojana (renamed Pradhan Mantri Gramin Awaas Yojana in 2015) now provides cash to the rural poor for building concrete dwellings.

9. Shankar Dutta Gupta, journalist and district correspondent for the regional news-papers *Uttarbanga Sambad* and *Dainik Jagron*, 17 September 2014, Cooch Behar, West Bengal.

10. M. Rajshekhar, "Why Lakhs of People Leave Odisha to Work in Distant Unsafe Brick-Kilns," *Scroll.in*, 9 September 2015, http://scroll.in/article/747416/why-lakhs-of-people-leave-odisha-to-work-in-distant-unsafe-brick-kilns.

11. See the entire journal issue of *Labour File* 9, no. 1–2 (2014), for several articles de-tailing the distress and seasonal migration experienced by brick kiln workers, http://www.labourfile.com/issue.php?id=35.

12. The men are paid Rs 200–300 per day for a period of five to six months. The work is steady and continuous, unlike the erratic nature of employment and low wages locally. See Sreelatha Menon, "Kerala, a 'Dubai' for Bengali Migrants," *Business Standard*, 20 Janu-ary 2013, https://www.business-standard.com/article/economy-policy/kerala-a-dubai-for-bengali-migrants-111072700087_1.html.

13. Neeta Lal, "Poor Bear the Brunt of Corruption in India's Food Distribution Sys-tem," *Inter Press Service News Agency*, 1 July 2015, www.ipsnews.net/2015/07/poor-bear-the-brunt-of-corruption-in-indias-food-distribution-system/.

14. Pradeep Baisakh, "MGNREGA Performs Poorly in Poverty-Stricken Orissa," *In-dia Water Portal*, 9 January 2011, https://www.indiawaterportal.org/news/mgnrega-performs-poorly-poverty-stricken-orissa-infochange-india.

15. N. D. Shiva Kumar, "Unemployment Rate Increases in India," *Times of India*, 23 June 2013, http://timesofindia.indiatimes.com/india/Unemployment-rate-increases-in-India/articleshow/20730480.cms.

16. According to the Tea Board of India, anyone growing tea on fewer than 25 acres of land is a small tea grower. See Centre for Education and Communication, "Small Tea Growers," https://www.cec-india.org/small-tea-growers.php.

17. Special correspondent, "Small Tea Production Goes Up," *The Telegraph*, 14 Feb-ruary 2017, https://www.telegraphindia.com/west-bengal/small-tea-production-goes-up/cid/1525783.

18. Mamtaaj was referring to the riots that occurred in the Goalpara district of As-sam after the demolition of the Babri Mosque in 1992.

19. *Paro* is a term used for any non-Meo woman married to a Meo man. Nowadays, it is used as an exclusionary and abusive term of reference, particularly for the cross-region brides. Interestingly, it is defiantly appropriated by the migrant brides when re-ferring to themselves.

20. Hindutva, literally translating into Hinduness, denotes a chauvinistic, right-wing, Hindu majoritarian nationalist ideology advocating for the formation of a Hindu nation. It was coined by V. D. Savarkar, the founder of the Hindu supremacist group Rashtriya Swayamsevak Sangh, or the National Volunteer Corp, in his 1923 book, *Who Is a Hindu?* (Bombay: Veer Savarkar Sadan).

21. Since the Partition of India in 1947, the appeal of the Hindu Right has been con-fined to the Hindu upper castes, and the lower- and middle-class sections of the urban population in the Hindi-speaking belt of North India.

22. Hindutva, as a chauvinistic Hindu nationalist rhetoric with no space for reli-gious minorities or social dissent, has sought to unite all Hindus around a perceived historical wrong of the razing of a temple that supposedly marked the birth site of the Hindu god Ram in the fifteenth century, by the Mughal ruler Babar, and the construc-tion of a mosque, Babri Mosque, on the site of the demolished temple (Rajagopal 2001, 191–192).

23. The Bharatiya Janata Party (BJP), or the Indian People's Party, is a right-wing Hindu nationalist party with a fascist Hindutva ideology as its core principle. Vehemently

anti-Muslim, it openly advocates the establishment of a Hindu nation and the conversion of Muslims into Hindus. The BJP has a decidedly upper caste, or *savarna*, character.

24. Babri Masjid, a mosque in the town of Ayodhya in the North Indian state of Uttar Pradesh, was built in 1528–1529 by a Muslim courtier during the rule of the Mughal ruler Babur. A section of Hindus claimed that it was built over a structure commemorating the birthplace of the god king Ram. The dispute, known popularly as the Ayodhya controversy, was used by Hindu fundamentalist groups to galvanize militant Hindus to demolish the mosque.

25. Read Neyaz Farooquee's *An Ordinary Man's Guide to Radicalism* (2018) and Nazia Ekrum's *Mothering a Muslim: The Dark Secret in Our Schools and Playgrounds* (2017) for intimate accounts of Indian Muslims about their ghettoization, internal othering, and second-class-citizen status in India.

26. In North India, Dalit politics emerged center stage, with the Bahujan Samaj Party, a political party formed in 1984, advocating the Dalit cause and acquiring a sizable chunk of Dalit votes (Jaffrelot 2011, 501–502) to form a coalition government at the state level in Uttar Pradesh in 1993. Its Dalit vote-bank allowed it to expand its electoral fortunes in subsequent elections and extend state funds and programs for their socioeconomic development.

27. The Untouchability (Offenses) Act of 1955 barred caste-based exclusion, discrimination, and segregation by making each a punishable act.

28. Deepender Deswal, "Dalits Flee Haryana Village after Upper Caste Attacks," *Times of India*, 15 April 2013, http://timesofindia.indiatimes.com/india/Dalits-flee-Haryana -village-after-upper-caste-attacks/articleshow/19571623.cms.

29. Vishal Joshi, "Dalit Locality Attached, Water Supply Cut after Inter-caste Marriage in Haryana," *Hindustan Times*, 15 April 2013, https://www.hindustantimes.com /india/dalit-locality-attacked-water-supply-cut-after-inter-caste-marriage-in-haryana /story-MFjl6c9WiHan6JoqU8fW2O.html; Deepender Deswal, "Inter-caste Marriages Taking Toll in Jatland," *Times of India*, 20 April 2013, http://timesofindia.indiatimes.com /india/Inter-caste-marriages-taking-toll-in-Jatland/articleshow/19642268.cms.

30. Chander Suta Dogra, "Women's Right to Inheritance Still a Struggle," *The Hindu*, 22 October 2013, http://www.thehindu.com/todays-paper/womens-right-to-inheritance -still-a-struggle/article5259283.ece.

31. See pages 61–81 of Ranjana Padhi's (2012) book, *Those Who Did Not Die*, for an excellent summing up of the impact of the agrarian crisis on the expectations of dowry, the indebtedness of dowry providers in Punjab, and farmer suicides there.

32. *Jahez* is an Urdu word for "dowry."

33. C. R. Jaychandran, "India Terminated 10 Mn Daughters," *Hindustan Times*, 9 January 2006, https://www.hindustantimes.com/india/india-terminated-10-mn-daughters /story-KeUZZpTIojP4GotY23JphI.html.

2. SOME MEN ARE MORE INELIGIBLE THAN OTHERS

1. Part of this chapter was published as "Caste and Cross-Region Marriages in Haryana, India: Experience of Dalit Cross-Region Brides in Jat Households," in *Modern Asian Studies* 52 (2): 492–531.

2. Sabina Dewan, "Only 4.75 Million Join Workforce Annually in India, Not 12 Million as Claimed," *New Indian Express*, 22 May 2018, http://www.newindianexpress.com /nation/2018/may/22/only-475-million-join-workforce-annually-in-india-not-12 -million-as-claimed-1817846.html.

3. Surya Sarathi Ray, "Unemployment Rate Highest in Five Years in 2015–16: Government Data," *Financial Express*, 29 September 2016, https://www.financialexpress.com /economy/unemployment-rate-highest-in-five-years-in-2015-16-government-data /396504/.

4. *Tapa* is a unit of *khap panchayat* that comprises a specific number of villages. Several *tapas* come together to constitute one *khap*. In the case of Satrol Khap, Petwar Tapa controls a cluster of twelve villages in the Hisar district of Haryana.

5. In Haryana, one acre of land is equal to four *bigha* of land.

6. The Thakur caste belongs to the second category of Kshtriyas in the Brahmanical caste hierarchy.

7. Churhi alludes to a female of the Churha caste group, ranked as "untouchable" within the Brahmanical caste hierarchy. Their traditional occupation was sweeping and removing waste, hence the "dirty" or "polluting" stigma associated with these groups.

8. Sukhbir Siwach, "Backward Mewat Tops in Girl Child Numbers," *Times of India*, 6 April 2011, http://timesofindia.indiatimes.com/india/Backward-Mewat-tops-in-girl-child-numbers/articleshow/7880427.cms.

9. Chitleen K. Sethi, "Low Literacy Translates into High Child Sex Ratio in Haryana, Shows Census," *Indian Express*, 6 April 2011, http://archive.indianexpress.com/news/low-literacy-translates-into-high-child-sex-ratio-in-haryana-shows-census/772378/0.

10. "Discrimination against Mewati Farmers in Land Acquisition by Haryana Government," *New Delhi Samachar*, 25 March 2012, http://sagarnewstime.blogspot.com/2012/03/discrimination-against-mewati-famers.html.

11. Ashwini Deshpande's (2013) book, *Affirmative Action in India*, looks at examples of studies done on the hiring practices of private companies by using fictitious Muslim and Dalit names.

12. Meoni is a colloquial term for a Meo woman.

3. THE LAMENT OF THE POOR

1. Muh Dikhai, literally translating as "revealing face," is a post-wedding ritual meant to introduce the bride to women of her husband's extended family and the community. The bride is offered a token gift, either of money or clothes, by the women who participate in the ritual.

2. Press Trust of India, "2017 Brought Multi-Crore Investment Proposals to Jharkhand," *Economic Times*, 30 December 2017, https://economictimes.indiatimes.com/news/politics-and-nation/2017-brought-multi-crore-investment-proposals-to-jharkhand/articleshow/62305228.cms.

3. Saurabh Gupta, "Protests in Jharkhand after 4 Die in Police Firing over Land Acquisition," *NDTV*, 5 October 2016, https://www.ndtv.com/india-news/protests-in-jharkhand-after-4-die-in-police-firing-over-land-acquisition-1470305.

4. BS Reporter, "MoU Signed Players Invest Rs 2.15 Lakh Cr in Odisha," *Business Standard*, 1 December 2014, http://www.business-standard.com/article/economy-policy/mou-signed-players-invest-rs-2-15-lakh-cr-in-odisha-114120100832_1.html.

5. The betel leaf plant is a vine belonging to the pepper family and is consumed mostly in Asia as *pan*, a mixture of betel leaf, areca nut, and lime. Middlemen and traders in Mumbai, who buy all the leaves, decide on the price of the betel leaf.

6. On this, see Mohanty 1990 (351–352).

7. The Left Front, which came to power in 1977, comprised the Communist Party of India (Marxist), the Forward Bloc, the Revolutionary Socialist Party, the Marxist Forward Bloc, the Revolutionary Communist Party of India, and the Biplabi Bangla Congress. In later years, the Communist Party of India informally joined the Front.

8. The mass uprisings of rural people in Singur in 2006 and Nandigram in 2007 against the government's hasty acquisition of land for big capital led to the unleashing of state terror on the protestors, including police shootings, beatings, and sexual violence against women protestors. See People's Tribunal on Nandigram, "Nandigram Violence a

'State Sponsored Massacre,'" *Countercurrents*, 9 August 2007, http://www.countercurrents .org/tribunal090807.htm.

9. The *kadamba*, or bur-flower tree, scientifically known as *Neolamarckia cadamba*, is a native of South and Southeast Asia. Eating its fruit is seen by the locals in Cooch Behar as a last resort of the destitute and extremely poor.

10. The murder or suicide of a married woman based on a dispute over the dowry.

11. Sanjeev Kumar Patro, "Crimes against Women: Odisha among Top 10," *The Pioneer*, 5 July 2015, https://www.dailypioneer.com/2015/state-editions/crimes-against -women-odisha-among-top-10.html.

12. According to the Prime Minister's High-Level Committee's Report 2006, known as the *Sachar Committee Report*, considered a landmark report for bringing to the fore the multidimensional impact of systemic discrimination against Indian Muslims, over 31 percent of Muslims live below the poverty line.

13. Christophe Jaffrelot, "The Myth of Appeasement," *Indian Express*, 20 April 2018, http://indianexpress.com/article/opinion/columns/muslims-socio-economic -development-5144318/.

14. Esha Roy, "Almost 80% of Rural Muslims in West Bengal Are Borderline Poor: Report," *Indian Express*, 15 February 2016, http://indianexpress.com/article/cities /kolkata/80-rural-muslims-near-poverty-report/.

15. Madhuparna Das, "Muslims a Poor Lot in West Bengal: Amartya Sen's Report," *Economic Times*, 2 March 2016, https://economictimes.indiatimes.com/news/politics -and-nation/muslims-a-poor-lot-in-west-bengal-amartya-sens-report/articleshow /51217184.cms?from=mdr; Palash Ghosh, "Surprise, Surprise: Muslims Are India's Poorest and Worst Educated Religious Group," *International Business Times*, 21 August 2013, https://www.ibtimes.com/surprise-surprise-muslims-are-indias-poorest-worst-educated -religious-group-1392849.

16. Subir Bhaumik, "What Lies behind Assam Violence," *BBC News*, 26 July 2012, http://www.bbc.com/news/world-asia-india-18993905.

17. The rape of women is used as a tool of warfare, to subjugate and/or ethnically cleanse an entire community. See Koo 2002.

18. The Muslim bride was referring to the Hindu-Muslim riots of 1989 that took place in Bhagalpur in the state of Bihar. The riots occurred primarily as a consequence of the mobilization of the Hindu supremacists against the Muslims there. The riots lasted over a period of two months and engulfed nearly 250 villages surrounding the town of Bhagalpur. More than nine hundred Muslims were killed and approximately fifty thousand were displaced.

19. Margaret Hunter uses statistical data and qualitative interviews with women with varying shades of skin tone among the African American and Mexican American communities to prove that skin tone works as "capital": it enables women with lighter skin within these racialized/ethnic groups to get better jobs, a higher level of education, and even spouses with higher incomes and educations. See Hunter 2007 for more.

20. Lydia Durairaj, "The Indian Whitening Cream Market Is Expanding at a Rate of 18% a Year," *Weekend Leader*, 27 July 2012, http://www.theweekendleader.com/Causes /1249/scare-and-sell.html.

21. Ronald Hall and Neha Mishra, "Tall, Fair, and Debonair: The Ideal Indian Man, According to Beauty Products and Bollywood," *Quartz India*, 29 March 2018, https://qz .com/india/1240384/indian-men-buy-skin-whitening-creams-to-achieve-bollywoods -beauty-ideal/.

22. See advertisements by Fair and Lovely, a leading skin-whitening cosmetic brand in India.

23. This appears to be changing, as new studies show a decline in CSR in West Bengal. See Subhro Niyogi, "At 911 girls to 1,000 boys, West Bengal Birth Sex Ratio Turns Dismal," *Times of India*, 29 January 2019, https://timesofindia.indiatimes.com/city/kolkata /at-911-girls-to-1000-boys-state-birth-sex-ratio-turns-dismal/articleshow/67732392.cms.

4. TRAFFICKED? OR MARRIED? WHEREIN LIES THE TRUTH?

1. Since 2009, a centrally administered social assistance program has provided a small monthly widow's pension. Lack of knowledge, in the initial phase, prevented many people such as Binata Devi from benefiting from it.

2. See the websites of Empower People (http://www.empowerpeople.org.in/) and Shakti Vahini (https://shaktivahini.org/), two prominent Indian anti-trafficking NGOs.

3. "India's Slave Brides," *Al Jazeera*, 10 November 2016, https://www.aljazeera.com /programmes/101east/2016/11/india-slave-brides-161108114930893.html; "The Story of India's Slave Brides," *BBC News*, 25 November 2014, http://www.bbc.com/news/world-asia -india-30189014; Elena del Estal, "'I Was Bought for 50,000 Rupees': India's Trafficked Brides—In Pictures," *The Guardian*, 7 March 2018, https://www.theguardian.com/global -development/2018/mar/07/india-girls-women-trafficked-brides-sexual-domestic-slavery.

4. As an example, see "Bridal Slaves," *Al Jazeera*, 15 November 2011, http://www .aljazeera.com/programmes/slaverya21stcenturyevil/2011/10/2011101013102368710.html.

5. Md. Ali, "Empower People: Rescuing Girls from Bride Trafficking," *Global Human Trafficking Watch,* 27 February 2011, http://globantihumantraffickwatch.blogspot.com /2011/03/empower-people-rescuing-girls-from.html.

6. Stockholm Syndrome is a psychological response in which hostages and kidnapped people, especially women, develop affection and/or empathy with their captors and thus deny their captive status.

7. Similarly, Vietnamese bride brokers also cultivate a "good wife" persona to attract potential Malaysian male customers. See Chee, Yeoh, and Vu 2012.

8. A number of brides used the terms *naseeb, taqdeer,* or *kismet* to allude to their belief in fate or destiny. The belief that their lives as brides in distant lands was a predestined or preordained outcome allowed them to make peace with their existence.

9. Paycheck.in., "Minimum Wage in Haryana w.e.f. July 1, 2016," https://paycheck.in /salary/minimumwages/haryana/minimum-wage-in-haryana-w-e-f-july-1-2016.

10. Paycheck.in., "Minimum Wage in Rajasthan W.E.F. April 1, 2016 to September 30, 2016," https://paycheck.in/salary/minimumwages/rajasthan/minimum-wage-in-rajasthan -w-e-f-april-1-2016-to-september-30-2016.

11. Muslim men in India can have four wives.

12. India has numerous laws pertaining to trafficking, such as the Immoral Traffic Prevention Act (1956, amended in 1986), and provisions on trafficking in the Indian Penal Code, (IPC) such as Sections 30 and 370a (criminalizing trafficking and use of services of a trafficked person); Section 371 (slavery); Sections 365 and 367 (kidnapping or abduction); Sections 366A, 366B, 372 and 373 (procuring, buying and selling minors for prostitution); and Section 374 (unlawful compulsory labor).

13. Himanshu Pabreja and Ankit Sharama, "The Indian Anti-Trafficking Bill, 2018: A Misguided Attempt to Resolve the Human Trafficking Crisis in India," *Oxford Human Rights Hub: A Global Perspective on Human Rights,* 15 January 2019, https://ohrh.law.ox .ac.uk/the-indian-anti-trafficking-bill-2018-a-misguided-attempt-to-resolve-the -human-trafficking-crisis-in-india/.

14. Marriage scamsters appear to operate more in Rajasthan than in Haryana. Female gang members, posing as brides, get married to the men and, after a few days, decamp with the jewelry and money gifted to the newlyweds. For more, read a number of online

accounts, such as "2 Days after Wedding, Bride Ran Away with Gold, Cash. She Was in a Gang," *NDTV*, 9 May 2018, https://www.ndtv.com/jaipur-news/woman-who-faked-wed dings-to-steal-gold-cash-arrested-in-rajasthan-1849226.

15. Rajan Chowdhary, secretary, Shikshit Rojgar Kendra Prabandhak Samiti, 1 October 2011, Jhunjhunu, Rajasthan; Jogaram Jhangid, Collector, 26 July 2012, Jhunjhunu District, Rajasthan; O. P. Kataria, additional superintendent of police (S.P.), 26 July 2012, Jhunjhunu, Rajasthan.

16. According to interviews with local NGOs, cross-region marriages emerged on the Rajasthan marriage-scape only from the mid- to late 2000s. Virendra Vidrohi, secretary, Matsya Mewat Evam Sikshan Vikas Kendra, Alwar, Rajasthan; Rajan Chowdhary, secretary, Shikshit Rojgar Kendra Prabandhak Samiti, Jhunjhunu, Rajasthan.

17. Aadhar is a unique identification number given to every citizen of India that serves as proof of identity and address for the Aadhar holder.

18. In August 2013, the registration of marriages became compulsory in India for all religions. See "Marriage Registration to Become Mandatory," *Times of India*, 14 August 2013, http://timesofindia.indiatimes.com/india/Marriage-registration-to-become -mandatory/articleshow/21814554.cms.

19. A fixed deposit is a lump-sum financial instrument offered by banks that carries a high rate of interest for a locked-in period of time (known in the United States as a CD, or certificate of deposit).

20. Scholars working on intra-Asia cross-border marriages similarly note the barriers in reintegration that returnee brides face on account of their "loss of face" and lack of resources and skill sets, barring them from economic independence. For more, see Duong, Bélanger, and Hong 2007 and Freeman 2011.

21. The children are usually left in the care of their maternal grandparents, thus raising questions about their neglect, abuse, and/or trauma from abandonment.

5. THE STAIN OF THE INTERNAL OTHER

1. See Chowdhry 2009, *Gender Discrimination in Land Ownership*, for case studies from across India.

2. Anupma Mehta, "Gender Gap in Land Ownership: Legislation and Gender-Based Agri Land Allotment Would Help," *Business Standard*, 17 April 2018, https://www.ncaer .org/news_details.php?nID=252&nID=252.

3. Shakti Parishad is a grassroots feminist organization working in select rural areas of Rewari. Comprising village women entirely, it runs legal camps and provides legal aid to their peers.

4. Alison Saldanha and Chaitanya Mallapur, "Over Decade, Crime Rate against Dalits Up 25%, Cases Pending Investigation Up 99%," *IndiaSpend*, 4 April 2018, https://www .indiaspend.com/over-a-decade-crime-rate-against-dalits-rose-by-746-746/; Express Web Desk, "Bihar Has Highest Rate of Crime against SC/STs, Bengal Lowest: NCRB Data," *Indian Express*, 14 April 2018, https://indianexpress.com/article/india/crimes -against-sc-sts-140-higher-than-that-of-general-public-in-gujarat-data-5136267/.

5. Parts of this chapter were published as "Caste and Cross-Region Marriages in Haryana, India: Experience of Dalit Cross-Region Brides in Jat Households," in *Modern Asian Studies* 52 (2): 492–531; "An Unwanted Weed: Children of Cross-Region Unions Confront Intergenerational Stigma of Caste, Ethnicity and Religion," in *Journal of Intercultural Studies* 39 (4): 382–398; and "Colorism as Marriage Capital: Cross-Region Marriage Migration in India and Dark-Skinned Migrant Brides," in *Gender & Society* 35 (1): 85–109.

6. Deepa Tak and Tina Aranha, "Cast(e)ing Food: Interrogating Popular Media," *Sahapedia*, 10 December 2015, http://www.sahapedia.org/casteing-food-interrogating-popu lar-media.

7. Pushpesh Pant, "There's No Meat to the Vegetarianism Myth," *Outlook*, 19 October 2015, http://www.outlookindia.com/magazine/story/theres-no-meat-to-the-vegeta rianism-myth/295546.

8. Amrit Dhillon, "In India, Caste System Ensures You Are What You Eat," *Post Magazine*, 27 July 2014, http://www.scmp.com/magazines/post-magazine/article/1558061 /you-are-what-you-eat.

9. Churhi and Chamaran are terms for women from the Churha or Chamar caste groups, considered as untouchables by the caste Hindus.

10. Sanjay K. Singh, "Calling an SC 'Chamar' Offensive, Punishable, Says Apex Court," *Economic Times*, 20 August 2008, https://economictimes.indiatimes.com/news/politics -and-nation/calling-an-sc-chamar-offensive-punishable-says-apex-court/articleshow /3382559.cms.

11. Seema Chishti, "Biggest Caste Survey: One in Four Indians Admit to Practising Untouchability," *Indian Express*, 29 November 2014, http://indianexpress.com/article /india/india-others/one-in-four-indians-admit-to-practising-untouchability-biggest -caste-survey/.

12. Priyali Prakash, "'Didn't Want Victims to Be Statistics': Film on Lynchings in India Wants to Start a Conversation," *Scroll.in*, 5 March 2019, https://scroll.in/reel/915090 /didnt-want-victims-to-be-statistics-film-on-lynchings-in-india-wants-to-start-a -conversation.

13. Kiran Mirchandani (2012) has used this term to refer to a process through which Indian call-center workers have to mimic their Western customers and shed their native accents and ways of speaking English.

14. The call-center workers often face racialized violence during phone calls with Western customers. For more, see pages 101–118 in Kiran Mirchandani 2012.

15. Nivedita Rao, "Who Is Paying for India's Healthcare?" *The Wire*, 14 April 2018, https://thewire.in/health/who-is-paying-for-indias-healthcare.

16. Mitra Phukan, Munish Tamang, and Manjit Baruah, "Northeast India: The Internal Other?" *Lila Interactions*, 17 February 2014, http://www.lilainteractions.in/2014-2-6 -mitra-phukan-munish-tamang-manjeeet-baruah-northeast-india-the-internal-other/.

17. Yenthom Jilangama, "Let's Stop Pretending There's No Racism in India," *The Hindu*, 29 May 2012, http://www.thehindu.com/opinion/op-ed/lets-stop-pretending -theres-no-racism-in-india/article3466554.ece.

18. Pranav Chaudhary, "Maximum People from Bihar Migrate to Delhi," *Times of India*, 28 March 2016, https://timesofindia.indiatimes.com/city/patna/Maximum-people -from-Bihar-migrate-to-Delhi/articleshow/51590085.cms.

19. During the early phase of British colonial rule in India, the Bengal Presidency included Bangladesh and the current-day Indian states of Bihar, West Bengal, Assam, Tripura, Odisha, and Meghalaya within it.

20. For more, see Bipan Chandra 1999.

21. A number of Hindi films released in the 2000s, such as *Apharan* (2005), *Gangajal* (2003), and *Gangs of Wasseypur* (2012) have helped reinforce the homogenized falsehood of pathologically diabolical and villainous Biharis.

22. Ayesha Arvind and Heena Kausar, "Racist Attacks on the Rise: Frightened North-East Migrants Ponder Return to Home States as Delhi Violence Worsens," *Daily Mail*, 11 February 2014, http://www.dailymail.co.uk/indiahome/indianews/article-2557122 /Racist-attacks-rise-Frightened-North-East-migrants-ponder-return-home-states -Delhi-violence-worsens.html.

23. Food has been a source of exclusion and stereotyping in other cultures as well and is encircled with variables of race, gender, class, and power. For more, see Psyche Williams-Forson 2013.

24. See, for example, Richard Kamei, "India's Racial Hatred Kills Nido Taniam in Delhi," *Countercurrents*, 2 February 2014, http://www.countercurrents.org/kamei020214 .htm.

25. Sushmita Dutta, "BJP Leader O. P. Dhankar Stokes Controversy, Promises 'Bihari Wives for Haryana Men,'" *Zee News*, 7 July 2014, http://zeenews.india.com/news/nation /bjp-leader-op-dhankar-stokes-controversy-promises-bihari-wives-for-haryana-men _945483.html.

26. O. P. Dhankar was elected as a legislator to the Haryana Assembly in 2014 and became a cabinet minister in the BJP majority government.

27. Jyoti Gupta, "Understanding Colorism: An Interview with Dr. Radhika Parameswaran," 3 August 2014, http://jyotigupta.org/understanding-colorism-an-inter view-with-dr-radhika-parameswaran/.

6. DOCILE BRIDES, EFFICIENT WORKERS

1. George Souvlis, "Feminism and the Refusal of Work: An Interview with Kathi Weeks," *Krutyka Polityczna & European Alternatives*, 28 August 2017, http://politicalcritique.org /world/2017/souvlis-weeks-feminism-marxism-work-interview/.

2. *Bhaat*, also called *bhaat nuana*, is a pre-wedding ceremony in which the groom's or bride's maternal uncles are invited by their sister for a meal of rice or *bhaat*. They come bearing gifts for the entire family.

3. *Chuchak* is another life-cycle ceremony performed by the maternal side of the family. This occurs one month after the birth of a child.

4. *Tola* is used as a measure for gold and silver in India. One *tola* equals 11.33 grams.

5. Critical masculinity studies in India are based on South Asian men's experiences within the intersection of caste ideology, the colonial encounter, religious fundamental-ism (in particular, chauvinistic Hindutva or right-wing Hindu ideology), and local forms of patriarchy. For more, see Chopra, Osella, and Osella (2004) and Chowdhry (2019).

6. The district of Nuh, after becoming a part of the NCR of Delhi, has seen an up-ward climb in land rates. For more, read Chander Suta Dogra, "The Sunday Story: Hary-ana's Out-lawed Daughters," *Indian Express*, 15 February 2015, http://indianexpress .com/article/india/india-others/the-sunday-story-haryanas-out-lawed-daughters/.

7. The prevailing local custom here denies daughters' equal inheritance to paternal property, despite legislation affirming equal inheritance rights for daughters. Women also weigh their long-term fallback options and calculatingly choose to gift away their share to their brother/s in exchange for the latter maintaining relations with them after mar-riage. For more, read Chowdhry 2012.

8. Suta Dogra, "The Sunday Story."

9. Sukhbir Siwach, "Rewari Farmers Oppose Land Acquisition Citing Less Compen-sation," *Times of India*, 11 December 2014, http://timesofindia.indiatimes.com/city /chandigarh/Rewari-farmers-oppose-land-acquisition-citing-less-compensation /articleshow/45466757.cms.

10. Prior to 2019, a Muslim man could divorce his wife by simply saying *talaq* (divorce) three times to her. Such instantaneous annulment of marriage is no longer possible.

CONCLUSION

1. Chahat Music, "Bahu Mol Ki," YouTube, 12 November 2019, https://www.youtube .com/watch?v=GJOzrChMDx0.

References

Agarwal, Bina. 1994. *A Field of One's Own: Gender and Land Rights in South Asia.* Cambridge, UK: Cambridge University Press.

——. 1997. "'Bargaining' and Gender Relations: Within and Beyond the Household." *Feminist Economics* 3 (1): 1–51.

——. 2012. "Food Security, Productivity, and Gender Inequality." Working Paper No. 320. Bangalore: Institute of Economic Growth (IEG). http://www.binaagarwal.com /downloads/apapers/Food%20security,%20productivity,%20gender%20inequality .pdf.

Aggarwal, Partap Chand. 1971. *Caste, Religion and Power: An Indian Case Study.* New Delhi: Shri Ram Centre for Industrial Relations and Human Resources.

Ahlawat, Neerja. 2009. "Missing Brides in Rural Haryana: A Study of Adverse Sex Ratio, Poverty and Addiction." *Social Change* 39, no. 1 (March): 46–63.

——. 2016. "The Dark Side of the Marriage Squeeze: Violence against Cross-Region Brides in Haryana." In *Too Many Men Too Few Women: Social Consequences of Gender Imbalance in India and China*, edited by Ravinder Kaur, 197–219. New Delhi: Orient BlackSwan.

Ahuja, Amit, and Susan L. Ostermann. 2016. "Crossing Caste Boundaries in the Modern Indian Marriage Market." *Studies in Comparative International Development* 51 (3): 365–387.

Aiyar, Swaminathan S. 2015. "Capitalism's Assault on the Indian Caste System." *Policy Analysis* 776 (July 21). Accessed 3 March 2016. http://www.cato.org/publications /policy-analysis/capitalisms-assault-on-the-indian-caste-system.

All India Democratic Women's Association (AIDWA). 2003. *Expanding Dimensions of Dowry.* New Delhi: AIDWA.

Amoore, Louise. 2005. *The Global Resistance Reader.* London: Taylor & Francis.

Ansari, Mahmood. 2001. "Migration from the Rural Region: A Study from Bihar in India." *Journal of Assam University* 6 (1). http://www.academia.edu/4679123 /Migration_from_the_Rural_Region_A_Study_from_Bihar_in_India.

Anti-slavery International. 2017. "Slavery in India's Brick Kilns & the Payment System: Way Forward in the Fight for Fair Wages, Decent Work and Eradication of Slavery." Anti-Slavery International and Volunteers for Social Justice. https://www .antislavery.org/wp-content/uploads/2017/09/Slavery-In-Indias-Brick-Kilns-The -Payment-System.pdf.

Aranda, Elizabeth M., and Guillermo Rebollo-Gil. 2004. "Ethnoracism and the 'Sandwiched' Minorities." *American Behavioral Scientist* 47 (7): 910–927.

Ayyar, Varsha, and Lalit Khandare. 2013. "Mapping Color and Caste Discrimination in Indian Society." In *The Melanin Millennium: Skin Color as 21st Century International Discourse*, edited by R. E. Hall, 71–95. New York: Springer.

Babu, Gopalan Reethesh, and Bontha Verraju Babu. 2011. "Dowry Deaths: A Neglected Public Health Issue in India." *International Health* 3 (1): 35–43.

Badruddoja, Roksana. 2005. "Color, Beauty, and Marriage: The Ivory Skin Model." *South Asian Graduate Research Journal (SAGAR)* 15:43–79.

Bakker, Isabella. 2007. "Social Reproduction and the Constitution of a Gendered Political Economy." *New Political Economy* 12 (4): 541–556.

Balagopal, Kandall. 1987. "Review: An Ideology for the Provincial Propertied Class." *Economic and Political Weekly* 22 (36/37): 1544–1546.

Ballard, Roger. 1990. "Migration and Kinship." In *South Asians Overseas: Contexts and Communities*, edited by C. Clarke, S. Vertovek, and C. Peach, 219–249. Cambridge, UK: Cambridge University Press.

Bannerji, Himani. 2016. "Patriarchy in the Era of Neoliberalism: The Case of India." *Social Scientist* 44 (3/4): 3–27.

Basole, Amit. 2010. "Agrarian Change in North India: Evidence from Haryana and Uttar Pradesh." *Sanhati*. http://sanhati.com/excerpted/2750/#sthash.eJJkpLxI.dpuf.

Basu, Amrita. 1996. "Mass Mobilization or Elite Conspiracy? The Puzzle of Hindu Nationalism." In *Contesting the Nation: Religion, Community, and the Politics of Democracy in India*, edited by David Ludden, 55–80. Philadelphia: University of Pennsylvania Press.

Basu, Srimati. 2005. *Dowry & Inheritance*. New Delhi: Kali for Women.

Basu, Tapan, Pradip Datta, Sumit Sarkar, Tanika Sarkar, and Sambuddha Sen. 1993. *Khakhi Shorts Saffron Flags: A Critique of the Hindu Right*. Tracts for the Times, Book 1. New Delhi: Orient Longman.

Behrman, Julia, Ruth Meinzen-Dick, and Agnes Quisumbing. 2012. "The Gender Implications of Large-Scale Land Deals." *Journal of Peasant Studies* 39 (1): 49–79.

Bhaduri, Amit. 2008. "Predatory Growth." *Economic & Political Weekly* 43 (16): 10–14.

Bhalla, Sheila. 1999. "Liberalisation, Rural Labour Markets and the Mobilisation of Farm Workers: The Haryana Story in an All-India Context." *Journal of Peasant Studies* 26 (2/3): 25–70.

Bhatty, Zarina. 1996. "Social Stratification among Muslims in India." In *Caste: Its Twentieth Century Avatar*, edited by M. N. Srinivas, 244–261. New Delhi: Viking.

Bhungalia, Lisa. 2020. "Laughing at Power: Humor, Transgression, and the Politics of Refusal in Palestine." *Environment and Planning C: Politics and Space* 38 (3): 387–404.

Bird, Sharon R. 1996. "Welcome to the Men's Club: Homosociality and the Maintenance of Hegemonic Masculinity." *Gender & Society* 10 (2): 120–132.

Blanchett, Thérèse. 2003. *Bangladeshi Girls Sold as Wives in North India*. Report. Dhaka: Drishti Research Centre. http://www.empowerpeople.org.in/uploads/3/7/2/4/3724 202/bangladeshi_girls_sold_as_wives_in_north_india.-blanchet_2003.pdf.

Bloch, Francis, and Vijayendra Rao. 2002. "Terror as a Bargaining Instrument: A Case Study of Dowry Violence in Rural India." *American Economic Review* 92 (4): 1029–1043.

Brunovskis, Anette, and Rebecca Surtees. 2010. "Untold Stories: Biases and Selection Effects in Research with Victims of Trafficking for Sexual Exploitation: Untold Stories: Research on Sex Trafficking." *International Migration* 48 (4): 1–37.

Chacko, Priya. 2012. *Indian Foreign Policy: The Politics of Postcolonial Identity from 1947 to 2004*. New York: Routledge.

Chakravarti, Uma. 2003. *Gendering Caste: Through a Feminist Lens*. Calcutta: Stree.

——. 2004. "Conceptualising Brahmanical Patriarchy in Early India: Gender, Caste, Class and State." In *Class, Caste, Gender, Readings on Indian Government and Politics*, edited by Manorajan Mohanty, 271–295. Delhi: Oxford University Press.

Chand, Ramesh, P. A. Lakshmi Prasanna, and Aruna Singh. 2011. "Farm Size and Productivity: Understanding the Strengths of Smallholders and Improving Their Livelihoods." *Economic and Political Weekly* 46 (26/27): 5–11.

Chandra, Bipan. 1999. "Stages of Colonialism and the Colonial State." In *Essays on Colonialism*, 58–78. Delhi: Orient Longman.

Chandrasekhar, C. P., and Jayati Ghosh. 2002. *The Market That Failed: A Decade of Neoliberal Economic Reforms in India*. Delhi: Leftword Books.

Chao, Antonia. 2004. "The Modern State, Citizenship, and the Intimate Life: A Case Study of Taiwan's Glorious Citizens and Their Mainland Wives." *Taiwanese Sociology* 8 (December): 1–41.

Charsley, Katharine. 2013. *Transnational Pakistani Connections: Marrying "Back Home."* New York: Oxford University Press.

Charsley, Katharine, and Evelyn Ersanilli. 2019. "The 'Mangetar Trap'? Work, Family and Pakistani Migrant Husbands." *NORMA* 14 (2): 128–145.

Chaudhry, Shruti. 2018. "'Now It Is Difficult to Get Married': Contextualising Cross-Regional Marriage and Bachelorhood in a North Indian Village." In *Scarce Women and Surplus Men in China and India: Macro Demographics versus Local Dynamics*, edited by Sharada Srinivasan and Shuzhuo Li, 85–104. Cham: Springer.

Chaudhry, Shruti, and Tanisha D. Mohan. 2011. "Of Marriage and Migration: Bengali and Bihari Brides in a U.P. Village." *Indian Journal of Gender Studies* 18 (3): 311–340.

Chauhan, Abha. 2003. "Kinship Principles and the Pattern of Marriage Alliance: The Meos of Mewat." *Sociological Bulletin* 52 (1): 71–90.

——. 2004. "Custom, Religion and Social Change among the Meos of Mewat." In *Emerging Social Science Concerns: Festschrift in Honour of Professor Yogesh Atal*, edited by Surendra K. Gupta and Yogesh Atal, 362–374. New Delhi: Concept Publishing.

——. 2005. "Village Exogamy and Kinship Rules of the Meo of North India: A Gender Perspective." *Eastern Anthropologist* 58 (3/4): 538–553.

Chee, Heng Leng, Brenda S. A. Yeoh, and Thi Kieu Dung Vu. 2012. "From Client to Matchmakers: Social Capital in the Making of Commercial Matchmaking Agents in Malaysia." *Pacific Affairs* 85, no. 1 (March): 91–115.

Cheng, Isabelle. 2013. "Making Foreign Women the Mother of Our Nation: The Exclusion and Assimilation of Immigrant Women in Taiwan." *Asian Ethnicity* 14 (2): 157–179.

Chhikara, Kuldip S., and Anand S. Kodan. 2013. "Farmers' Indebtedness in Haryana: A Study." *Journal of Rural Development* 32 (4): 347–365.

Chisti, Anees. 2007. "Sachar Committee Report: A Review." *Seminar* 45, no. 1 (April). http://www.mainstreamweekly.net/article95.html.

Chopra, Radhika, Caroline Osella, and Filippo Osella, eds. 2004. *South Asian Masculinities: Context of Change, Sites of Continuity*. Delhi: Kali for Women.

Chowdhry, Prem. 2005. "Crisis of Masculinity in Haryana: The Unmarried, the Unemployed and the Aged." *Economic and Political Weekly* 40 (49): 5189–5198.

——. 2007. *Contentious Marriages, Eloping Couples: Gender, Caste, and Patriarchy in Northern India*. New Delhi: Oxford University Press.

——, ed. 2009. *Gender Discrimination in Land Ownership*. Delhi: Sage Publications.

——. 2011. *Political Economy of Production and Reproduction: Caste, Custom, and Community in North India*. New Delhi: Oxford University Press.

——. 2012. *Reduction of Violence against Women: Property Ownership and Economic Independence in India*. Report. UN Women. http://www2.unwomen.org/-/media/field%20office%20eseasia/docs/publications/2015/southasia/reportstudies/06_economic%20empowerment/violence-propertyrights2%20pdf.ashx?v=1&d=20141202T120141.

——. 2019. *Gender, Power and Identity: Essays on Masculinities in Rural North India*. New Delhi: Orient BlackSwan.

Chuang, Janie A. 2010. "Rescuing Trafficking from Ideological Capture: Prostitution Reform and Anti-trafficking." *University of Pennsylvania Law Review* 158:1656–1728.

Cilliers, Paul. 1998. *Complexity and Postmodernism: Understanding Complex Systems.* London: Routledge.

Constable, Nicole. 2005a. "Introduction: Cross-Border Marriages, Gendered Mobility and Global Hypergamy." In *Cross-Border Marriages: Gender and Mobility in Transnational Asia*, 1–16. Philadelphia: University of Pennsylvania Press.

———. 2005b. "A Tale of Two Marriages: International Matchmaking and Gendered Mobility." In *Cross-Border Marriages: Gender and Mobility in Transnational Asia*, 166–186. Philadelphia: University of Pennsylvania Press.

———. 2006. "Brides, Maids, and Prostitutes: Reflections on the Study of 'Trafficked' Women." *Portal: Journal of Multidisciplinary International Studies* 3, no. 2 (July): 1–15.

Darling, Malcolm. [1925] 1977. *The Punjab Peasant in Prosperity and Debt.* New Delhi: Manohar Books.

Das, N. 2006. "Cultural Diversity, Religious Syncretism and People of India: An Anthropological Interpretation." *Bangladesh Sociology.* https://www.bangladeshsoci ology.org/BEJS%203.2%20Das.pdf.

Das, Upasak. 2015. "Can the Rural Employment Guarantee Scheme Reduce Rural Out-Migration: Evidence from West Bengal, India." *Journal of Development Studies* 51, no. 6 (June): 621–641.

Das Gupta, Monica, Jiang Zhenghua, Li Bohua, Xie Zhenming, Chung Woojin, and Bae Hwa-Ok. 2003. "Why Is Son Preference So Persistent in East and South Asia? A Cross-Country Study of China, India and the Republic of Korea." *Journal of Development Studies* 40 (2): 153–187.

D'Costa, Anthony P., and Achin Chakraborty. 2017. *The Land Question in India: State, Dispossession, and Capitalist Transition.* New Delhi: Oxford University Press.

Deaton, Andre, and Jean Dreze. 2002. "Poverty and Inequality in India: A Reexamination." *Economic and Political Weekly* 37 (36): 3729–3748.

Deshingkar, Priya, and Shaheen Akter. 2009. *Migration and Human Development in India.* United Nations Development Programme Human Development Reports Research Paper 2009/13 (April). http://hdr.undp.org/sites/default/files/hdrp_2009_13.pdf.

Deshingkar, Priya, Sushil Kumar, Harendra Kumar Chobey, and Dhananjay Kumar. 2006. *The Role of Migration and Remittances in Promoting Livelihoods in Bihar.* London: Overseas Development Institute. https://www.odi.org/sites/odi.org.uk/files /odi-assets/publications-opinion-files/2354.pdf.

Deshpande, Ashwini. 2011. *The Grammar of Caste.* New Delhi: Oxford University Press.

———. 2013. *Affirmative Action in India.* Delhi: Oxford University Press.

Doezema, Jo. 2010. *Sex Slaves and Discourse Masters: The Construction of Trafficking.* London: Zed Books.

Dube, Leela. 1996. "Caste and Women." In *Caste: Its Twentieth Century Avatar*, edited by M.N. Srinivas, 1–27. New Delhi: Penguin.

Duong, Le Bach, Danièle Bélanger, and Khuat Thu Hong. 2007. "Transnational Migration, Marriage and Trafficking at the China-Vietnam Border." In *Watering the Neighbour's Garden: The Growing Demographic Female Deficit in Asia*, edited by Isabelle Attané and Christophe Z. Guilmoto, 393–425. Paris: Committee for International Cooperation in National Research in Demography.

Ekrum, Nazia. 2017. *Mothering a Muslim: The Dark Secret in Our Schools and Playgrounds.* New Delhi: Juggernaut Books.

Faier, Lieba. 2009. *Intimate Encounters: Filipina Women and the Remaking of Rural Japan.* Berkeley: University of California Press.

Farooquee, Neyaz. 2018. *An Ordinary Man's Guide to Radicalism: Growing Up Muslim in India*. Chennai: Westland Publications.

Feingold, David A. 2005. "Human Trafficking." *Foreign Policy* (Sept/Oct): 26–32.

Freeman, Caren. 2011. *Making and Faking Kinship: Marriage and Labour Migration between China and South Korea*. Cornell: Cornell University Press.

Fulford, Scott. 2013. "The Puzzle of Marriage Migration in India." Working Paper no. 820. Boston College Working Papers in Economics. http://fmwww.bc.edu/EC-P/wp820.pdf.

Garikipati, Supriya, and Stephan Pfaffenzeller. 2012. "The Gendered Burden of Liberalisation: The Impact of India's Economic Reforms on its Female Agricultural Labour." *Journal of International Development* 24 (7): 841–864.

Ghosh, Biswajit. 2010a. "Context and Issues of Gender Discourse Today: The Case of West Bengal." In *Women in India: Motherhood and Multiple Identities*, edited by Swapan Kumar Pramanick and Samita Manna, 41–71. New Delhi: Serial Publications.

——. 2010b. "Persistence of the Practise of Dowry in Rural West Bengal." *Journal of Social Work & Social Development* 1, no. 1 (June): 1–17.

Ghosh, Jayati. 2015. "Growth, Industrialisation and Inequality in India." *Journal of the Asia Pacific Economy* 20 (1): 42–56.

——. 2018. "Gendered Labour Markets and Capitalist Accumulation." *Japanese Political Economy* 44 (1/4): 25–41.

Gopalakrishnan, Shankar. 2006. "Defining, Constructing and Policing a 'New India': Relationship between Neoliberalism and Hindutva." *Economic and Political Weekly* 41 (26): 2803–2813.

Gramsci, Antonio. 1971. *Selections from the Prison Notebooks*. Translated and edited by Quintin Hoare and Geoffrey Nowell Smith. New York: International Publishers.

Grover, Shalini. 2009. *Marriage, Love, Caste, and Kinship Support: Lived Experiences of the Urban Poor in India*. New Delhi: Sage Publications.

Guilmoto, Christophe Z. 2012. "Skewed Sex Ratios at Birth and Future Marriage Squeeze in China and India, 2005–2100." *Demography* 49:77–100.

Gupta, Jayati. 1997. "Voices Break the Silence." In *A Just Right: Women's Ownership of Natural Resources and Livelihood Security*, edited by Nitya Rao and Luise Rurup, 135–169. New Delhi: Friedrich Ebert Stiftung.

Guru, Gopal. 1995. "Dalit Women Talk Differently." *Economic and Political Weekly* 30 (41/42): 2548–2550.

Hage, Ghassan. 2010. "Migration, Food, Memory, and Home-Building." In *Memory: Histories, Theories, Debates*, edited by Susannah Radstone and Bill Schwarz, 416–427. New York: Fordham University Press.

Haque, Tajamul. nd. "Impact of Land Leasing Restrictions on Agricultural Efficiency and Equity in India." http://www.landandpoverty.com/agenda/pdfs/paper/haque_full_paper.pdf.

Harman, Chris. 2004. "India after the Election: A Rough Guide." *International Socialism* 103 (Summer): 49–94.

Hartsock, Nancy. 2006. "Globalization and Primitive Accumulation: The Contributions of David's Dialectical Marxism." In *David Harvey: A Critical Reader*, edited by Noel Castree and David Gregory, 167–190. Malden: Blackwell.

Harvey, David. 1992. "Postmodern Morality Plays." *Antipode* 24 (4): 300–326.

——. 1996. *Justice, Nature, and the Geography of Difference*. Cambridge, MA: Blackwell Publishers.

——. 2003. *The New Imperialism*. New Delhi: Oxford University Press.

——. 2005. *Brief History of Neoliberalism*. Oxford: Oxford University Press.

——. 2020. "Culture and War." *Anti-Capitalist Chronicles*, 16 January 2020. https://anticapitalistchronicles.libsyn.com/culture-and-war.

Hsia, Hsiao-Chuan. 2004. "Internationalization of Capital and the Trade in Asian Women: The Case of 'Foreign Brides' in Taiwan." In *Women and Globalization*, edited by Delia D. Aguilar and Anne E. Lacsamana, 181–229. Amherst: Humanity Books.

——. 2008. "Beyond Victimization: The Empowerment of 'Foreign Brides' in Resisting Capitalist Globalization." *China Journal of Social Work* 1 (2): 130–148.

Hulme, Peter. 1986. *Colonial Encounters: Europe and the Native Caribbean 1492–1797*. London: Methuen.

Human Rights Watch. 2013. "Take Action to Improve Condition of Dalit Women: Women and Girls Facing Caste Discrimination Need Special Protection." Human Rights Watch. June 7. https://www.hrw.org/news/2013/06/07/take-action-improve-conditions-dalit-women.

——. 2014. *They Say We're Dirty: Denying an Education to India's Marginalised*. Human Rights Watch. https://www.hrw.org/sites/default/files/reports/india0414_ForUpload_1.pdf.——. 2007. "The Persistent Problem of Colorism: Skin Tone, Status and Inequality." *Social Compass* 1 (1): 237–254.

Hwang, Min-Chul. 2015. "Exploring Marriage Migrants' Citizenship Acquisition in South Korea." *Asian and Pacific Migration Journal* 24 (3): 376–402.

IIPS (International Institute for Population Sciences) and Macro International. 2007. *National Family Health Survey (NFHS-3), 2005–06: India: Volume I*. Mumbai: IIPS. https://dhsprogram.com/pubs/pdf/FRIND3/FRIND3-Vol1AndVol2.pdf.

Irudayam, Aloysius S. J., Jayshree P. Mangubhai, and Joel G. Lee. 2014. *Dalit Women Speak Out: Caste, Class and Gender Violence in India*. New Delhi: Zubaan Books.

Jaffrelot, Christophe. 2011. *Religion, Caste and Politics in India*. New York: Columbia University Press.

Jaiswal, Suvira. 2000. *Caste: Origin, Function and Dimensions of Change*. New Delhi: Manohar Publishers.

Jamous, Raymond. 2003. *Kinship and Rituals among the Meo of Northern India: Locating Sibling Relationship*. New Delhi: Oxford University Press.

Jeffery, Patricia. 2014. "Supply-and-Demand Demographics: Dowry, Daughter Aversion and Marriage Markets in Contemporary North India." *Contemporary South Asia* 22 (2): 171–188.

Jeffery, Patricia, and Roger Jeffery. 1996. *Don't Marry Me to a Plowman! Women's Everyday Lives in Rural North India*. Boulder: Westview Press.

Jegathesan, Mythri. 2019. *Tea and Solidarity: Tamil Women & Work in Postwar Sri Lanka*. Seattle: University of Washington Press.

Jeyaseela, Stephen S. 2006. *Literature, Caste and Society: The Masks and Veils*. Delhi: Kalpaz Publishers.

Jha, Prabhat, Maya A. Kesler, Rajesh Kumar, Faujdar Ram, Usha Ram, Lukasz Aleksandrowicz, Diego G. Bassani, Shailaja Chandra, and Jayant K. Banthia. 2011. "Trends in Selective Abortions of Girls in India: Analysis of Nationally Representative Birth Histories from 1990 to 2005 and Census Data from 1991 to 2011." *The Lancet* 377 (9781): 1921–1928.

Jodhka, Surinder. 1999. "Haryana: Change of Government and Beyond." *Economic and Political Weekly* 34 (32): 2217–2218.

——. 2015. *Caste in Contemporary India*. New Delhi: Routledge.

——. 2016. "Ascriptive Hierarchies: Caste and Its Reproduction in Contemporary India." *Current Sociology* 64 (2): 228–243.

John, Mary, Ravinder Kaur, Rajni Palriwala, and Saraswati Raju. 2009. "Dispensing with Daughters: Technology, Society, Economy in North India." *Economic and Political Weekly* 44 (15): 16–19.

Kamat, Anant Raoji. 1979. "The Emerging Situation: A Socio-Structural Analysis." *Economic and Political Weekly* 14 (7/8) (Annual Number: Class and Caste in India): 349–354.

Kandiyoti, Deniz. 1988. "Bargaining with Patriarchy." *Gender & Society* 2 (3): 274–290.

Kapadia, Karen. 2002. "Politics of Identity: Social Inequalities and Economic Growth." In *The Violence of Development: The Political Economy of Gender*, 1–40. New York: Zed Books.

Kastrinou-Theodoropoulou, Maria. 2009. "Editorial Note: Political Anthropology and the Fabrics of Resistance." *Durham Anthropology Journal* 16 (2): 3–7.

Kaur, Ravinder. 2004. "Across Region Marriages: Poverty, Female Migration and the Sex Ratio." *Economic and Political Weekly* 39 (25): 2595–2603.

——. 2008. "Missing Women and Brides from Faraway: Social Consequences of the Skewed Sex Ratio in India." In *AAS (Austrian Academy of Sciences) Working Papers in Social Anthropology*, edited by Andre Gingrich and Helmut Lukas, 1–13. Accessed 9 September 2011. http://hw.oeaw.ac.at/0xc1aa500d_0x001a819c.

——. 2012. "Marriage and Migration Citizenship and Marital Experience in Cross-Border Marriages Between Uttar Pradesh, West Bengal and Bangladesh." *Economic and Political Weekly* 47 (43): 78–89.

——. 2016. *Too Many Men Too Few Women: Social Consequences of Gender Imbalance in India and China*. New Delhi: Orient BlackSwan.

Kennedy, Loraine. 2019. "The Politics of Land Acquisition in Haryana: Managing Dominant Caste Interests in the Name of Development." *Journal of Contemporary Asia* 50 (5): 743–760.

Koo, Katrina L. 2002. "Confronting a Disciplinary Blindness: Women, War and Rape in the International Politics of Security." *Australian Journal of Political Science* 37 (3): 525–536.

Kosambi, Damodar D. 1997. *The Culture and Civilization of Ancient India in Historical Outline*. Delhi: Vikas Publishing House.

Krishnaraj, Maithreyi. 2006. "Food Security, Agrarian Crisis and Rural Livelihoods: Implications for Women." *Economic and Political Weekly* 41 (52): 5376–5388.

Kukreja, Reena. 2017. "Caste and Cross-Region Marriages in Haryana, India: Experience of Dalit Cross-Region Brides in Jat Households." *Modern Asian Studies* 52 (2): 492–531.

——. 2018. "An Unwanted Weed: Children of Cross-Region Unions Confront Intergenerational Stigma of Caste, Ethnicity and Religion." *Journal of Intercultural Studies* 39 (4): 382–398.

——. 2021. "Colorism as Marriage Capital: Cross-Region Marriage Migration in India and Dark-Skinned Migrant Brides." *Gender & Society* 35 (1): 85–109.

Kumari, Ranjana. 1989. *Brides Are Not for Burning: Dowry Victims in India*. Delhi: Radiant Publishers.

Lee, Yean-Ju, Dong-Hoon Seol, and Sung-Nam Cho. 2006. "International Marriages in South Korea: The Significance of Nationality and Ethnicity." *Journal of Population Research* 23 (2): 165–182.

Levein, Michael. 2012. "The Land Question: Special Economic Zones and the Political Economy of Dispossession in India." *Journal of Peasant Studies* 39 (3/4): 933–969.

——. 2017. "Gender and Land Dispossession: A Comparative Analysis." *Journal of Peasant Studies* 44 (6): 1111–1134.

——. 2018. *Dispossession without Development: Land Grabs in Neoliberal India*. New York: Oxford University Press.

Li, Tania. 2014. *Land's End: Capitalist Relations on an Indigenous Frontier*. Durham: Duke University Press.

Lilja, Mona, and Stellan Vinthagen. 2018. "Dispersed Resistance: Unpacking the Spectrum and Properties of Glaring and Everyday Resistance." *Journal of Political Power* 11 (2): 211–229.

Mahler, Sarah J., and Patricia R. Pessar. 2001. "Gendered Geographies of Power: Analysing Gender across Transnational Spaces." *Identities* 7 (4): 441–449.

Majumdar, Arup. 2014. "Impact of Land Acquisition on Women: An Anthropological Case Study on Gokulpur, Paschim Medinipur (India)." *International Journal of Interdisciplinary and Multidisciplinary Studies (IJIMS)* 1 (4): 26–34.

Marx, Karl. 2011. *Capital Volume One: A Critique of Political Economy*, edited by Friedrich Engels. Mineola: Dover Publications.

Mathew, Tayler J. 2013. "The Relationship between Skin Complexion and Social Outcomes: How Colorism Affects the Lives of African American Women." Ph. D. diss., Clark-Atlanta University, Atlanta, Georgia.

Maunaguru, Sidharthan. 2019. *Marrying for a Future: Transnational Sri Lankan Tamil Marriages in the Shadow of War*. Seattle: University of Washington Press.

Mayaram, Shail. 2003. *Against History, Against State: Counterperspectives from the Margins*. New York: Columbia University Press.

McGranahan, Carol. 2016. "Theorizing Refusal: An Introduction." *Cultural Anthropology* 31 (3): 319–325.

Mehta, Deepak. 2014. "Violence and Masculinity." *Exploring South Asian Masculinities Online Seminar*. http://www.menengagedilli2014.net/uploads/2/4/5/3/24534141 /exploring-south-asian-masculinities-online-seminar.pdf.

Mies, Maria. 1998. *Patriarchy and Accumulation on a World Scale: Women in the International Division of Labour*. London: Zed Books.

Mirchandani, Kiran. 2012. *Phone Clones: Authenticity Work in the Transnational Economy*. Cornell: Cornell University Press.

Mishra, Kartik. 2019. "Accumulation by Dispossession and Electoral Democracies: An Analysis of Land Acquisition for Special Economic Zones in India." *UMass Amherst Economics Working Papers*. https://scholarworks.umass.edu/cgi/viewcontent .cgi?article=1276&context=econ_workingpaper.

Mishra, Neha. 2015. "India and Colorism: The Finer Nuances." *Washington University Global Studies Law Review* 14 (4) (Global Perspectives on Colorism, Symposium Edition): 725–750. http://openscholarship.wustl.edu/law_globalstudies/vol14 /iss4/14/.

Mishra, Paro. 2013. "Sex Ratios, Cross-Region Marriages and the Challenge to Caste Endogamy in Haryana." *Economic and Political Weekly* 48 (35): 70–78.

——. 2016. "Imbalanced Sex-Ratio and Cross-region Marriage: The Challenge of Transcending Caste Boundaries." In *Too Many Men Too Few Women: Social Consequences of Gender Imbalance in India and China*, edited by Ravinder Kaur, 220–245. New Delhi: Orient BlackSwan.

Mody, Pervez. 2008. *The Intimate State: Love-Making and the Law in Delhi*. New Delhi: Routledge.

Mohanty, Chandra T. 2003. *Feminism without Borders: Decolonizing Theory, Practising Solidarity*. Durham: Duke University Press.

Mohanty, Manoranjan. 1990. "Class, Caste and Dominance in Backward State: Orissa." In *Dominance and State Power in Modern India*, edited by Francine Frankel and M.S.A. Rao, 351–352. Delhi: Oxford University Press.

Mondal, Bidisha, Jayati Ghosh, Shiney Chakraborty, and Sona Mitra. 2018. "Women Workers in India: Labour Force Trends, Occupational Diversification and Wage Gaps." State of Working India Background Paper—03. Azim Premji University. https://cse.azimpremjiuniversity.edu.in/wp-content/uploads/2019/01/SWI_2018 _Background_Paper_Mondal.pdf.

Mukherjee, Sonali. 2015. "Structural Basis of Gender Violence in Cross-Regional Marriages: Tales from Haryana, India." In *Violence and Crime in the Family: Patterns, Causes, and Consequences (Contemporary Perspectives in Family Research, Volume 9)*, edited by Sheila Royo Maxwell and Samson Lee Blair, 73–97. Emerald Group Publishing. doi:http://dx.doi.org/10.1108/S1530-353520150000009004.

Nakamatsu, Tomoko. 2005. "Faces of Asian Brides: Gender, Race, and Class in the Representations of Immigrant Women in Japan." *Women's Studies International Forum* 28:405–417.

Nanda, Priya, Gautam Abhishek, Ravi Verma, Arushi Khanna, Nizamuddin Khan, Dhanashri Brahme, Shobhana Boyle, and Sanjay Kumar. 2014. *Study on Masculinity, Intimate Partner Violence and Son Preference in India*. New Delhi: International Center for Research on Women.

Narayan, Uma. 1997. *Dislocating Cultures: Identities, Traditions, and Third World Feminism*. London: Routledge.

Navsarjan Trust, FEDO, and the International Dalit Solidarity Network. 2013. "The Situation of Dalit Rural Women." Submission to Discussion on CEDAW General Comment on rural women—Article 14. (September). http://www.ohchr.org/Documents /HRBodies/CEDAW/RuralWomen/FEDONavsarjanTrustIDS.pdf.

Navsarjan Trust, and Robert F. Kennedy Robert Center for Justice & Human Rights. 2011. *Understanding Untouchability: A Comprehensive Study of Practises and Conditions in 1589 Villages*. http://navsarjan.org/Documents/Untouchability_Report_FINAL _Complete.pdf.

Navsarjan Trust, The All India Dalit Mahila Adhikar Manch (AIDMAM), and The International Dalit Solidarity Network (IDSN). 2014. *Alternative Report to the UN Committee on the Elimination of All Forms of Discrimination Against Women (CEDAW) for the Examination of the 4th and 5th Periodic Reports of India at the 58th CEDAW Session in July 2014: Multiple Discrimination Against Dalit Women*. June. CEDAW India. http://tbinternet.ohchr.org/Treaties/CEDAW/Shared%20Doc uments/Ind/INT_CEDAW_NGO_Ind_17408_E.pdf.

Nyugen, Xoan, and Xuyen Tran. 2010. "Vietnamese-Taiwanese Marriages." In *Asian Cross-Border Marriage Migration: Demographic Patterns and Social Issues*, edited by Wen-Shan Yang and Melody Chia-Wen Lu, 157–178. Amsterdam: Amsterdam University Press.

Olsen, Wendy. 2004. "Triangulation in Social Research: Qualitative and Quantitative Methods Can Really Be Mixed." Accessed 16 March 2012. http://research.apc.org /images/5/54/Triangulation.pdf.

Oommen, Tharailath. K. 2002. "Race, Religion, and Caste: Anthropological and Sociological Perspectives." *Comparative Sociology* 1 (2): 115–126.

Ortner, Sherry B. 1995. "Resistance and the Problem of Ethnographic Refusal." *Comparative Studies in Society and History* 37 (1): 173–193.

Osella, Caroline, and Filippo Osella. 2006. *Men and Masculinity in South India*. Delhi: Anthem Press.

Padhi, Ranjana. 2012. *Those Who Did Not Die*. New Delhi: Sage Publications.

Palriwala, Rajni. 2009. "The Spider's Web: Seeing Dowry, Fighting Dowry." In *Dowry: Bridging the Gap between Theory and Practice*, edited by Tamsin Bradley, Emma Tomalin, and Mangala Subramaniam, 144–176. New Delhi: Women Unlimited.

Palriwala, Rajni, and Patricia Uberoi. 2008. "Exploring the Links: Gender Issues in Marriage and Migration." In *Marriage, Migration and Gender,* edited by Patricia Uberoi and Rajni Palriwala, 23–62. New Delhi: Sage Publications.

Pandey, Gyanendra. 2001. *Remembering Partition: Violence, Nationalism, and History in India.* Cambridge, UK: Cambridge University Press.

Pandey, Kamal Kumar, and Rishi Kant. 2003. *Female Foeticide, Coerced Marriage and Bonded Labour in Haryana and Punjab.* Faridabad: Shakti Vahini.

Parameswaran, Radhika, and Kavitha Cardoza. 2009. "Melanin on the Margins: Advertising and the Cultural Politics of Fair/Light/White Beauty in India." *Journalism & Communication* Monographs 11 (3): 213–274.

Pattnaik, Itishree, and Kuntala Lahiri-Dutt. 2020. "What Determines Women's Agricultural Participation? A Comparative Study of Landholding Households in Rural India." *Journal of Rural Studies* 76:25–39.

Pattnaik, Itishree, Kuntala Lahiri-Dutt, Stewart Lockie, and Bill Pritchard. 2018. "The Feminization of Agriculture or the Feminization of Agrarian Distress? Tracking the Trajectory of Women in Agriculture in India." *Journal of the Asia Pacific Economy* 23 (1): 138–155

Percot, Marie. 2012. "Transnational Masculinity: Indian Nurses' Husbands in Ireland." *e-Migrinter* 8:74–86.

Pessar, Patricia R., and Sarah J. Mahler. 2003. "Transnational Migration: Bringing Gender In." *International Migration Review* 37 (3): 812–846.

Piper, Nicola, and Mina Roces. 2003. "Introduction: Marriage and Migration in an Age of Globalization." In *Wife or Worker? Asian Women and Migration,* edited by Nicola Piper and Mina Roces, 1–22. Boulder: Rowman and Littlefield.

Prashad, Vijay. 2000. *Untouchable Freedom: A Social History of a Dalit Community.* New Delhi: Oxford University Press.

Prasse-Freeman, Elliott. 2020. "Resistance/Refusal: Politics of Manoeuvre under Diffuse Regimes of Governmentality." *Anthropological Theory.* https://doi.org/10.1177/1463499620940218.

Punam. 2015. "Effects of Land Acquisition Policy on Farmers in Haryana." *International Journal of Advanced Research in Management and Social Sciences* 4 (1): 105–114. http://www.garph.co.uk/IJARMSS/Jan2015/11.pdf.

Pushpendra. 2002. "Dalit Assertion through Electoral Politics." In *Caste and Democratic Politics in India,* edited by Ghanshyam Shah, 356–384. Delhi: Permanent Black.

Radhakrishna, Rokkam, and S. Chandrasekhar. 2008. "Overview: Growth: Achievements and Distress." In *India Development Report 2008,* edited by Rokkam Radhakrishna, 1–20. Delhi: Oxford University Press.

Rahman, Shafiqur. 2009. *Paro: Mewat Mein Kharidi Hui Ek Aurat.* Delhi: Jagori (Hindi).

Rajagopal, Arvind. 2001. *Politics after Television: Hindu Nationalism and the Reshaping of the Public in India.* Cambridge, UK: Cambridge University Press.

Rao, Anupama. 2003. "Introduction." In *Gender and Caste: Contemporary Issues in Indian Feminism,* 1–47. New Delhi. Kali for Women.

——. 2009. *The Caste Question: Dalits and the Politics of Modern India.* Berkeley: University of California Press.

Rawal, Vikas. 2013–2014. "Changes in the Distribution of Operational Landholdings in Rural India." *Review of Agrarian Studies* 3 (2) (July–January). http://ras.org.in/changes_in_the_distribution_of_operational_landholdings_in_rural_india.

Reddy, Narasimha D., and Srijit Mishra. 2009. "Agriculture in the Reforms Regime." In *Agrarian Crisis in India,* edited by D. Narasimha Reddy and Srijit Mishra, 3–44. New Delhi: Oxford University Press.

Rege, Sharmila. 1995. "Caste and Gender: The Violence against Women in India." In *Dalit Women in India: Issues & Perspectives*, edited by Prahlad Ganganand Jogdand, 18–36. New Delhi: Gyan Publishing House.

——. 1998. "Dalit Women Talk Differently: A Critique of Difference and towards a Dalit Feminist Standpoint Position." *Economic and Political Weekly* 33 (44): WS 39–46.

——. 2006. *Writing Caste/Writing Gender: Narrating Dalit Women's Testimonios*. New Delhi: Zubaan.

——. 2013. *Against the Madness of Manu: B.R. Ambedkar's Writings on Brahmanical Patriarchy*. New Delhi: Navayana Publications.

Reinharz, Shulamit. 1992. *Feminist Methods in Social Research*. New York: Oxford University Press.

Research Unit in Political Economy. 2005. "Budget 2005–06: Seeing Through the Propaganda." *Aspects of India's Economy* 39/40 (June). http://rupe-india.org/39/propaganda.html.

Rohwerder, Brigitte. 2018. *Disability Stigma in Developing Countries*. Brighton, UK: Institute of Development Studies.

Rondilla, Joanne L. 2009. "Filipinos and the Color Complex: Ideal Asian Beauty." In *Shades of Difference: Why Skin Color Matters*, edited by Evelyn Nakano Glenn, 63–80. Stanford: Stanford University Press.

Rondilla, Joanne L., and Paul Spickard. 2007. *Is Lighter Better? Skin-Tone Discrimination among Asian Americans*. Lanham: Rowman & Littlefield.

Rosenzweig, Mark R., and Oded Stark. 1989. "Consumption Smoothing, Migration, and Marriage: Evidence from Rural India." *Journal of Political Economy* 97 (4): 905–926.

Roy, Durgadas, and Manab Sen. 2011. *Final Report on "Poverty, Hunger and Public Action": An Empirical Study of On-going Decentralisation Initiatives in West Bengal, February 2010–November 2010*. Loka Kalyan Parishad, with assistance from the Planning Commission, Government of India. http://planningcommission.nic.in/reports/sereport/ser/ser_hung2802.pdf.

Sabharwal, Nidhi Sadana, and Wandana Sonalkar. 2015. "Dalit Women in India: At the Crossroads of Gender, Caste, and Class." *Global Justice: Theory Practise Rhetoric* 8 (1): 44–73.

Sabur, Seuty. 2014. "Marital Mobility in the Bangladeshi Middle Class: Matchmaking Strategies and Transnational Networks." *South Asia: Journal of South Asian Studies* 37 (4): 586–604.

Saha, Suranjit Kumar. 1986. "Historical Premises of India's Tribal Problem." *Journal of Contemporary Asia* 16 (3): 274–319.

Sanghera, Jyoti. 2005. "Unpacking the Trafficking Discourse." In *Trafficking and Prostitution Reconsidered: New Perspectives on Migration, Sex Work and Human Rights*, edited by Kamala Kempado, Jyoti Sanghera, and Bandana Pattanaik, 3–24. London: Paradigm.

Sapkal, Rahul S., and Nilambar Chhetri. 2019. "Precarious Work, Globalization and Informalization of Workforce: Empirical Evidence from India." In *Globalization, Labour Market Institutions, Processes and Policies in India*, edited by K. Shyam Sundar, 143–164. Singapore: Palgrave Macmillan.

Sarker, Kanchan. 2009. "Economic Growth and Social Inequality: Does the Trickle Down Effect Really Take Place?" *New Proposals: Journal of Marxism and Interdisciplinary Inquiry* 3 (1): 42–60.

Savarkar, Vinayak Damodar. 1923. *Essentials of Hindutva: Who Is a Hindu?* Bombay: Veer Savarkar Sadan.

Scott, James C. 1990. *Domination and the Arts of Resistance: Hidden Transcripts*. New Haven: Yale University Press.

Sen, Amartya. 1990. "More Than 100 Million Women Are Missing." *New York Review of Books*, 20 December. http://www.nybooks.com/articles/1990/12/20/more-than -100-million-women-are-missing/.

Sen, Kunal, and Kusum Das. 2014. "Where Have All the Workers Gone? The Puzzle of Declining Labour Intensity in Organised Indian Manufacturing." Development Economics and Public Policy Working Paper Series WP No. 35 / 2014. Institute for Development Policy and Management, University of Manchester.

Sethi, Raj Mohini. 2009. "Gendered Spaces: Agrarian Economy of Haryana." In *Gender Discrimination in Land Ownership*, edited by Prem Chowdhry, 41–58. Delhi: Sage Publications.

Seymour, Susan. 2006. "Resistance." *Anthropological Theory* 6 (3): 303–321.

Shah, Ghanshyam, Harsh Mander, Sukhadeo Thorat, Satish Desphande, and Amita Baviskar. 2006. *Untouchability in Rural India*. New Delhi: Sage Publications.

Shamsh, Shamsuddin. 1983. *Meos of India: Their Customs and Laws*. New Delhi: Deep & Deep Publishing.

Shani, Ornit. 2011. "The Politics of Communalism and Caste." In *A Companion to the Anthropology of India*, edited by Isabelle Clark-Decès, 297–312. Malden: Wiley-Blackwell.

Sikand, Yoginder. 1995. "Meonis of Mewat." *Economic and Political Weekly* 30 (10): 490–492.

Simpson, Audra. 2014. *Mohawk Interruptus: Political Life across the Borders of Settler States*. Durham: Duke University Press.

——. 2016. "Consent's Revenge." *Cultural Anthropology* 31 (3): 326–333.

Srinivas, M. N. 1952. *Religion and Society amongst the Coorgs of South India*. Oxford: Clarendon Press.

Srinivasan, Sharada, and Shuzhuo Li. 2018. *Scarce Women and Surplus Men in China and India: Macro Demographics versus Local Dynamics*. Cham, Switzerland: Springer International.

Srivastava, Nisha. 2011. "Feminisation of Agriculture: What Do Survey Data Tell Us?" *Journal of Rural Development* 30 (3): 341–359.

Srivastava, Nisha, and Ravi Srivastava. 2010. "Women, Work and Employment Outcomes in Rural India." *Economic and Political Weekly* 45 (28): 49–63.

Stringer, Rebecca. 2014. *Knowing Victims: Feminism, Agency and Victim Politics in Neo-liberal Times*. Sussex, UK: Routledge.

Suzuki, Nobue. 2005. "Tripartite Desires: Filipina-Japanese Marriages and Fantasies of Transnational Traversal." In *Cross-Border Marriages: Gender and Mobility in Transnational Asia*, edited by Nicole Constable, 124–144. Philadelphia: University of Pennsylvania Press.

Teltumbde, Anil. 2008. *Khairlanji: A Strange and Bitter Crop*. New Delhi: Navayana.

——. 2010. *The Persistence of Caste: The Khairlanji Murders & India's Hidden Apartheid*. London: Zed Books.

——. 2012. "Jatland: Rape Republic." *Countercurrents*. http://www.countercurrents.org /teltumbde051112.htm.

——. 2018. *Republic of Caste: Thinking Equality in the Time of Neoliberal Hindutva*. New Delhi: Navayana.

Thai, Hung Cam. 2008. *For Better or For Worse: Vietnamese International Marriages in the New Global Economy*. New Brunswick: Rutgers University Press.

Thorat, Amit. 2010. "Ethnicity, Caste and Religion: Implications for Poverty Outcomes." *Economic and Political Weekly* 45 (52): 47–53.

Thorat, Sukhadeo. 2002. "Oppression and Denial: Dalit Discrimination in the 1990s." *Economic and Political Weekly* 37 (6): 572–578.

Thorat, Sukhadeo, and Paul Attewell. 2007. "The Legacy of Social Exclusion: A Correspondence Study of Job Discrimination in India." *Economic and Political Weekly* 42 (41): 4141–4145.

Toyota, Mika. 2008. "Editorial Introduction: International Marriage, Rights and the State in East and Southeast Asia." *Citizenship Studies* 12 (1): 1–7.

Treitler, Vilna Bashi. 2013. *The Ethnic Project: Transforming Racial Fictions into Ethnic Factions.* Stanford: Stanford University Press.

Tseng, Hsun-Hui. 2015. "Gender and Power Dynamics in Transnational Marriage Brokerage: The Ban on Commercial Matchmaking in Taiwan Reconsidered." *Cross-Currents: East Asian History and Culture Review* 15:108–132. https://cross-currents.berkeley.edu/e-journal/issue-15/tseng.

Tseng, Yen-Fen. 2011. "Marriage Migration to East Asia: Current Issues and Propositions in Making Comparisons." In *Asian Cross-Border Marriage Migration: Demographic Patterns and Social Issues*, edited by Melody Lu and Wen-Shan Yang, 31–48. Amsterdam: Amsterdam University Press.

Uberoi, Patricia. 2006. *Freedom and Destiny: Gender, Family, and Popular Culture in India.* New Delhi: Oxford University Press.

UNICEF. 2014. "All Children in School by 2015: Global Initiative on Out-of-School Children South Asia Regional Study." UNICEF. 26 January. https://www.unicef.org/education/files/SouthAsia_OOSCI_Study__Executive_Summary_26Jan_14Final.pdf.

UNODC South Asia (United Nations Office on Drugs and Crime). 2013. *Current Status of Victim Service Providers and Criminal Justice Actors in India on Anti Human Trafficking: A Country Assessment 2013.* https://www.unodc.org/documents/south asia//reports/Human_Trafficking-10-05-13.pdf.

Vanaik, Achin. 2001. "The New Indian Right." *New Left Review* 11 (9): 43–67.

Van Liempt, Ilse. 2006. "Trafficking in Human Beings: Conceptual Dilemmas." In *Trafficking and Women's Rights*, edited by Christien L. van den Anker and Jeroen Doomernik, 27–43. New York: Palgrave Macmillan.

Vatuk, Sylvia. 2007. "Islamic Feminism in India: Indian Muslim Women Activists and the Reform of Muslim Personal Law." *Modern Asian Studies* 42 (2/3): 489–518.

Venkateshwarlu, Davuluri, and Lucia da Corta. 2001. "Transformations in Age and Gender of Unfree Workers on Hybrid Cottonseed Farms in Andhra Pradesh." *Journal of Peasant Studies* 28 (3): 1–36.

Verkuyten, Maykel, and Jochem Thijs. 2002. "Racist Victimization among Children in The Netherlands: The Effect of Ethnic Group and School." *Ethnic and Racial Studies* 25 (2): 310–331.

Vinthagen, Stellan, and Anna Johansson. 2013. "Everyday Resistance: Exploration of a Concept and Its Theories." *Resistance Studies Magazine* 1. http://rsmag.nfshost.com/wp-content/uploads/Vinthagen-Johansson-2013-Everyday-resistance-Concept-Theory.pdf.

Vishwanath, L. S. 2007. "Female Infanticide, Property and the Colonial State." In *Sex-Selective Abortion in India: Gender, Society and New Reproductive Technologies*, edited by Tulsi Patel, 269–285. New Delhi: Sage Publications.

Waheed, Abdul. 2009. "Dowry among Indian Muslims: Ideals and Practices." *Indian Journal of Gender Studies* 16 (1): 47–75.

Walker, Katharine Le Mons. 2008. "Neoliberalism on the Ground in Rural India: Predatory Growth, Agrarian Crisis, Internal Colonization, and the Intensification of Class Struggle." *Journal of Peasant Studies* 35 (4): 557–620.

Wang, Hong-zen. 2007. "Hidden Spaces of Resistance of the Subordinated: Case Studies from Vietnamese Female Migrant Partners in Taiwan." *International Migration Review* 41 (3): 706–727.

Wang, Hong-Zen, and Shu-Ming Chang. 2002. "The Commodification of International Marriages: Cross-Border Marriage Business in Taiwan and Viet Nam." *International Migration* 40 (6): 93–116.

Wang, Yi-han. 2010. "From 'Farming Daughters' to 'Virgin Brides': Representation of Vietnamese Immigrant Wives in Taiwan." *Gender, Technology and Development* 14 (2): 217–239.

Weitzer, Ronald. 2011. "Sex Trafficking and the Sex Industry: The Need for Evidence-Based Theory and Legislation." *Journal of Criminal Law and Criminology* 101 (4): 1337–1369.

——. 2014. "New Directions in Research on Human Trafficking." *ANNALS of the American Academy of Political and Social Science* 653 (1): 6–24.

Whitehead, Judith. 2016. "Intersectionality and Primary Accumulation: Caste and Gender in India under the Sign of Monopoly-Finance Capital in India." *Monthly Review*, November 2016. https://monthlyreview.org/2016/11/01/intersectionality-and-primary-accumulation/.

Williams, Lucy. 2010. *Global Marriage: Cross-Border Marriage Migration in Global Context*. London: Palgrave Macmillan.

Williams, Raymond. 1961. *The Long Revolution*. London: Chatto & Windus.

Williams-Forson, Psyche. 2013. "More Than Just the 'Big Piece of Chicken': The Power of Race, Class, and Food in American Consciousness." In *Food and Culture: A Reader*, 3rd ed., edited by Carole Counihan and Penny Van Esterik, 342–353. New York: Routledge.

WSS (Women against Sexual Violence and State Repression). 2014. *Speak! The Truth Is Still Alive: Land, Caste, and Sexual Violence against Dalit Girls and Women in Haryana*. Special Report. New Delhi: WSS. https://wssnet.files.wordpress.com/2014/07/wss-haryana-report-compiled.pdf.

Yuval-Davis, Nira. 1997. *Gender and Nation*. London: Sage Publications.

GOVERNMENT SOURCES

Census of India. 2011a. "Haryana District Census Handbook Mewat Series 07 Part XII-B." Haryana: Directorate of Census Operations, Government of India. http://www.censusindia.gov.in/2011census/dchb/0619_PART_B_DCHB_MEWAT.pdf.

——. 2011b. "Missing . . . Mapping the Adverse Child Sex Ratio in India Census 2011." Directorate of Census Operations, Government of India. http://www.censusindia.gov.in/2011census/missing.pdf.

——. 2011c. "Population Composition." Directorate of Census Operations, Government of India. http://www.censusindia.gov.in/vital_statistics/SRS_Report/9Chap%202%20-%202011.pdf.

——. 2011d. "West Bengal: District Census Handbook Koch Bihar Series 20, Part XII-B": West Bengal: Directorate of Census Operations, Government of India, 2011. http://www.censusindia.gov.in/2011census/dchb/1903_PART_B_DCHB_KOCH%20BIHAR.pdf.

Census Population. 2011. "Rajasthan Census Population Data 2011." http://www.census2011.co.in/census/state/rajasthan.html.

Centre for Studies in Social Sciences. nd. "Minority Concentration District Project Cooch Behar, West Bengal." Ministry of Minority Affairs, Government of India. http://www.icssr.org/coochbehar_mcd_report_final.pdf.

Delhi Development Authority (DDA). 2007. "Master Plan for Delhi—2021." February 7. Delhi Development Authority. http://dda.org.in/ddanew/pdf/Planning/reprint%20mpd2021.pdf.

Department of Agriculture. 2012. *Rajasthan Agricultural Competitiveness Project 2012: Social Assessment and Management Framework Report*. February. Government of Rajasthan. http://documents.worldbank.org/curated/en/963831468040752151/text/RP12280v20RP0P07856B0SAR0RI0P124614.txt.

Department of Agriculture, Cooperation & Farmers Welfare. 2020. *All India Report on Agriculture Census 2015–16*. Ministry of Agriculture & Farmers Welfare, Government of India. http://agcensus.nic.in/document/agcen1516/ac_1516_report_final-220221.pdf.

Department of Economic Analysis and Research. 2014. "Agricultural Land Holdings Pattern in India." *Nabard Rural Pulse* 1 (Jan–Feb). https://www.nabard.org/Publication/Rural_Pulse_final142014.pdf.

Government of Haryana. nd. *Comprehensive District Agriculture Plan (C-DAP) District Mewat, Haryana*. Agriculture Department. http://agriharyana.nic.in/RKVY/C-DAPs/C-DAP,%20Mewat.doc.

Government of India. n.d. "State of the Economy: An Analytical Overview and Outlook for Policy." *Economic Survey 2017–18: Volume I*. https://www.thehinducentre.com/multimedia/archive/03223/Economic_Survey_20_3223793a.pdf.

Government of India. 1980. *Report of the Backward Classes Commission (Mandal Commission Report)*. National Commission for Backward Classes, Government of India. http://www.ncbc.nic.in/Writereaddata/Mandal%20Commission%20Report%20of%20the%201st%20Part%20English635228715105764974.pdf.

Government of India. 2017. *Youth in India*. https://www.thehinducentre.com/multimedia/archive/03188/Youth_in_India-201_3188240a.pdf.

Government of Jharkhand. nd. "Eliminating Poverty: Creating Jobs and Strengthening Social Programs." http://niti.gov.in/writereaddata/files/Jharkhand%20presentation.pdf.

Government of Odisha. 2015. *Odisha Economic Survey 2014–2015: Rising Trend of Per Capita Income at Market Prices at Current Price of Odisha*. February. Planning and Coordination Department, Government of Odisha. http://www.indiaenvironmentportal.org.in/files/file/Odisha%20Economic_Survey_2014-15.pdf.

Ministry of Finance. 2018. "Annual Economic Survey 2017–2018 Vol I." Government of India. http://mofapp.nic.in:8080/economicsurvey/.

MSME-Development Institute. nd. *Brief Industrial Profile of Mewat: Micro, Small and Medium Enterprises*. Ministry of MSME, Government of India. http://www.msmedikarnal.gov.in/dps/mewat.pdf.

MSME-Development Institute, Jaipur. 2016. *Brief Industrial Profile of Alwar District 2015–2016*. Ministry of MSME, Government of India. http://dcmsme.gov.in/dips/2016-17/DIPR%20Alwar.pdf.

National Informatics Centre Cooch Behar. 2012. "Cooch Behar District Profile." Government of West Bengal. http://coochbehar.nic.in/htmfiles/distsummaryprofile.html.

NCRB (National Crimes Record Bureau). 2011. *Accidental Deaths and Suicides in India 2011*. National Crimes Record Bureau, Ministry of Home Affairs, Government of India. http://ncrb.nic.in/StatPublications/ADSI/ADSI2011/ADSIHome2011.htm.

NSSO (National Sample Survey Office). 2005. "Indebtedness of Farmer Households: Situation Assessment Survey of Farmers. NSS 59th Round. June–December 2003." May. National Sample Survey Organization, Ministry of Statistics and Implementation, Government of India.

——. 2014. *Key Indicators of Situation of Agricultural Households in India: NSS 70th Round January-December 2013*. December. Ministry of Statistics and Programme Implementation, Government of India. http://www.indiaenvironmentportal.org

.in/files/file/key%20indicators%20of%20agricultural%20households%20in%20
India.pdf.

Planning Commission, Government of India. 2006. *Rajasthan Development Report*. New
Delhi: Academic Publishers. http://planningcommission.nic.in/plans/stateplan/sdr
/sdr_rajasthan.pdf.

Prime Minister's High Level Committee. 2006. *Social, Economic and Educational Status
of the Muslim Community in India: A Report*. Cabinet Secretariat, Government
of India. http://mhrd.gov.in/sites/upload_files/mhrd/files/sachar_comm.pdf.

Rural Development Department, Haryana. nd. *No. of Rural BPL Households in the State
along with Definition of Rural Poverty*. Government of Haryana. http://www
.haryanarural.gov.in/bplnote.pdf.

Sehgal Foundation. 2015. *Identifying Backwardness of Mewat Region in Haryana: A Block
Level Analysis*. Study sponsored by Research Division, NITI Aayog, Government
of India. https://dokumen.tips/documents/identifying-backwardness-of-mewat
-region-in-haryana.html.

Socio Economic Caste Census. 2011a. "Household Land Ownership Pattern (Rural)."
Department of Rural Development, Ministry of Rural Development, Government
of India. http://secc.gov.in/statewiseLandOwnershipReport?reportType=Land%20
Ownership.

——. 2011b. "West Bengal: Main Source of Household Income (Rural)." Ministry of Rural Development, Government of India. http://www.secc.gov.in/statewiseDistrict
LandOwnershipReport.

——. 2011c. "Odisha: Main Source of Household Income (Rural)." Ministry of Rural Development, Government of India. http://www.secc.gov.in/statewiseDistrictLand
OwnershipReport.

Index

abortions. *See* sex-selective abortions

accountability by marriage mediators, 150–51, 153. *See also* land acquisitions; marriage mediators

accumulation by dispossession theory, 4, 12–14, 16, 207, 228, 229. *See also* capital accumulation; coercive land appropriation; dispossession; land ownership

active submission as agency (concept), 122

Adivasi, 6, 16, 249, 251n4

adjustment of migrant brides, 5, 11, 79, 172, 179, 192–94, 219. *See also* assimilation; marriage migration

adla-badla, 63

affirmative reservation policy, 52, 159

agency, 129–30, 148–51. *See also* freedom of movement; refusal strategies; resistance strategies

aging, 77, 204–5

agrarian crisis: description of, 35–36, 207; dowry commercialization and, 55, 60–61; female labor and, 15, 17, 195; labor migration due to, 43–44; poverty due to, 75, 100, 212. *See also* agrarian reforms; feminization of agriculture; neoliberal economic reforms; New Economic Policy (NEP); suicide; women's labor

agrarian reforms, 34–37. *See also* agrarian crisis; feminization of agriculture

agricultural labor: by Dalits, 53; economic viability of, 33–34, 36, 64–66; by Jats and Yadavs, 38–39; of Meo Muslims, 87, 89; by women, 20–21, 33, 47–49. *See also* feminization of agriculture; land ownership; sharecropping farming; tenant farming

agricultural metaphors, 189

agro-industrial tea plantations, 21

Ahirs (caste), 6, 68, 79, 161, 190, 218, 249

alcoholism, 149

All India Dalit Women's Forum, 18

anti-trafficking activism, 122–23, 140. *See also* bride trafficking

anuloma, 81. *See also* intercaste marriage

army men, 134–35

arranged marriages, 115–20. *See also* marriage

assimilation: of caste, 4; linguistic, 11, 79, 127, 130, 136, 175–78, 194; resistance to, 223–24; through marriage, 5, 15, 174; violence of, 22, 169, 185, 233. *See also* adjustment of migrant brides; cultural assimilation; internal other; othering; resistance strategies

atta-batta, 63

author's positionality, xv, 158

avarna, 6

Avivahit Purush Sangathan (Unmarried Men's Collective), 1

Babri Masjid mosque and riots, 51, 107–8, 174, 253n18, 254n24. *See also* Indian Muslims

baharwalis, as term, 199, 200

Bahu Dilao, Vote Pao (Get me a bride, take my vote) political slogan, 1

Bahujan Samaj Party, 254n26

"Bahu Mol Ki" / "A Bought Bride" (song), 232–33, 235

Bangalan, xi, 195, 200, 249. *See also paro,* as term

Bangladesh, 10, 149, 150, 259n19

Bannerji, Himani, 17, 100

beauty as capital. *See* colorism

bejaat, 174, 249. *See also kaffir,* as term

Bengali language, 30, 175, 177–78. *See also* linguistic assimilation

betel-leaf farming and plantations, 46, 96, 98, 111

beyki hui, as term, 145

Bhaat, 197, 260n2

Bharatiya Janata Party (BJP), 51, 182–83, 253n23, 260n26. *See also* Hindu Right

bhatti, 43. *See also* brick kiln work

bhola, ix, 32, 73

bichola and *bicholia,* 126, 134, 139, 249. *See also* bride trafficking; marriage mediators

Bihari (Biharan): othering of, 179–84, 189; songs about brides, 232–33; as term, xi, 179, 249

birth order, 112–14. *See also* children

Lightning Source UK Ltd.
Milton Keynes UK
UKHW011950051022
409984UK00005B/589

9 781501 764134